DISPOSABLE PEOPLE?

DISPOSABLE PEOPLE?

THE PLIGHT OF REFUGEES

Judy A. Mayotte

ORBIS BOOKS

Maryknoll, New York 10545

The Catholic Foreign Mission Society of America (Maryknoll) recruits and trains people for overseas missionary service. Through Orbis Books, Maryknoll aims to foster the international dialogue that is essential to mission. The books published, however, reflect the opinions of their authors and are not meant to represent the official position of the society.

Library of Congress Cataloging-in-Publication Data

Mayotte, Judy A.
    Disposable people?: the plight of refugees / Judy A. Mayotte.
        p.   cm.
    Includes bibliographical references and index.
    ISBN 0-88344-839-4
    1. Refugees.   2. Refugees—Cambodia—Case studies.   3. Refugees—
Afghanistan—Case studies.   4. Refugees—Ethiopia—Eritrea—Case
studies.   I. Title
HV640.M38   1992
325'.21'0722—dc20   92-29489
                                                              CIP

They gave me roots and wings.
In memory of my parents, Beulah and Bill,
and
my husband, Jack.
In thanks to my siblings,
Moira Lee and Fred, Jane and Jim, and Dick.

Ndovu wawili wakipambana
ziumiazo ni nyasi

When two elephants fight,
it is the grass that gets hurt.
—African proverb

CONTENTS

FOREWORD

Mrs. Sadako Ogata
United Nations High Commissioner for Refugees

Eighteen million refugees is too large a number to comprehend in human terms. And so, very often, the women, men, and children who make up the world's refugee population are dealt with as abstractions. They are mouths to feed, bodies to shelter, unknown victims of persecution and violence. In this book, Judy Mayotte brings us face to face with refugees. Her accounts of people and communities who have suffered the fear and pain of displacement show both their strength and their vulnerability. The combination is instantly recognizable in human terms, and demonstrates how much we all have in common with refugees.

Many of the people who have lived so long in exile now have a real possibility of returning to their home countries. The paralysis of the Cold War, which prevented any resolution of the conflicts that forced them to flee, has ended. Those who return are attended by hopes and by grave uncertainties. Mayotte makes the point that this is not the time for these people to be abandoned by the international community. If their homecoming is to meet the standards of safety and dignity at which the United Nations High Commission for Refugees aims, the international community will have to mobilize resources to provide protection and assistance to the returnees until they can re-establish themselves at home. The cooperation of governments in their countries of asylum and their home countries is essential to the process, as is external support for political reconciliation and economic reconstruction.

The refugees who are the focus of this book—from Cambodia, Afghanistan, Sudan, and Eritrea—are returning to lands devastated by war, littered with mines, infested with disease, crowded with demobilized soldiers and internally displaced people. There is little infrastructure, few resources, few people with appropriate training for reconstruction. The threat of renewed fighting is ever-present. The "durable solution" represented by repatriation is fragile. To consolidate it, a peace process must continue in which freedom from want is seen to be an esential partner of freedom from war.

For many years, the countries discussed in this book consistently drew one form of international attention: external powers helped to fuel the conflicts that caused people to flee from their homes. The end of East-West confrontation enlarged the possibilities for resolution of long-standing conflicts. But it also carries the risk of more general turning away from the needs of people who now may hope to return, or may simply see no practical alternative to repatriation. Their needs are not only physical; protection of human rights is equally fundamental to their safety, dignity, and stability in their countries of origin.

The complex problems of refugees demonstrate that any durable new order in the world can only be defined by international cooperation and solidarity. It is an illusion to think that we can safely turn away from refugees once they have crossed back across a border. A vivid appreciation of the human costs of displacement, as presented in this book, reinforces the determination to act upon our moral and political obligations to help them rebuild their countries and their lives. This is not a one-way exchange. Judy Mayotte quotes a motto that hung in the women's sewing center in an Eritrean refugee camp in Sudan: "I am called a refugee. But I have made that into a ministry of peace."

ACKNOWLEDGMENTS

There are hundreds who contributed to this book, and to each I give my thanks. But it was the refugees—Afghans, Cambodians, Eritreans, and Sudanese—living in exile in Pakistan, Thailand, and Sudan who made it happen. Without their generous spirit in telling their stories, there would have been no book. Being among them was one of the most privileged times of my life.

I could not have reached the refugees without the help of others. The John D. and Catherine T. MacArthur Foundation believed in the project. Their generous funding enabled me to devote my time exclusively to researching and writing the book. My particular thanks goes to James Furman, former executive vice-president of the MacArthur Foundation. My thanks, too, go to the Refugee Policy Group for housing my funds, especially to Dennis Gallagher, Susan Forbes Martin, and Dejene Negash.

Government officials from each of the countries I visited facilitated my research. I would like to thank former Ambassador Vitthya Vejjajiva from Thailand to the United States and Mr. Jukr Boonlong; former Ambassador Jamsheed Marker from Pakistan to the United States; Mr. Hassan B. Abdelwahab, former Minister Plenipotentiary from Sudan to the United States; and Mr. Chum Bunrong, Press Director in the Cambodian Ministry of Foreign Affairs. Many in our own Bureau for Refugee Programs in the Department of State assisted me, especially Sheppie Abramowitz.

More than anyone else, perhaps, Robert DeVecchi, executive director of the International Rescue Committee, smoothed the way for my access to the refugees. In each country he asked his staff to take care of me. And they did. They gave not only their time, but gracious hospitality. I would particularly like to thank Susan and Tom Yates in Pakistan; Jim Anderson in Thailand; and Randy Martin and Abrahazion Woldai and Neelofer Niazi in Sudan.

UNHCR personnel in every country I visited did everything they could to help me, especially John McCallin in Washington, D.C., Raymond Hall in Geneva, and Michel Gabaudan in Pakistan.

In Bangkok Diane and Bill Dawkins opened their home to me. At Site 2 camp in Thailand the American Refugee Committee did the same and took me to the camp each day. I am grateful to Bob Medrala, ARC director in Thailand, for making that possible. Dr. Louis Braile, of ARC, and Susan Walker, director of Operation Handicap International in Thailand, provided me with so much inspiration and information. Doreen Blomstrand and the staff of the

Christian Missionary and Alliance (CAMA) housed me and gave me access to Site 8. I would also like to give special thanks to Andy Pendleton, senior camp officer for UNBRO in Site 2, and Mary Chaffee of the Joint Voluntary Agency in Bangkok.

On my first visit to Sudan, I arrived after midnight and did not know a word of Arabic. I was not certain how I would ask a taxi driver to take me to the Acropole Hotel. That was not necessary, for George Pagoulatos, one of the three brothers who own the hotel, sent a car for me. There is no hotel in the world quite like the Acropole, and it is because of the Pagoulatos family.

I will never know their names and I will never see them again, but I fell among some very special people one night when I was traveling between Khartoum and Port Sudan. Our bus broke down. Eight of us were not fortunate enough to crowd onto a second bus that stopped some time later to pick up the stranded passengers. Much later, a truck driver offered us a ride. The four men in our party jumped into the back of the truck; we three women and one child (myself the only foreigner) crowded into the cab. Around dawn when we arrived in Port Sudan, the woman with the child pulled my hand toward her and placed on my finger a tin ring with a small stone. I will treasure it always. One of the men took me to his home until I could get to the Comboni school later in the morning. The truck driver stopped in a village to borrow pillows for me and the women next to me to sit on (there was only the driver's seat in the cab). He refused any offer of pay at the end of the journey. The people of Sudan are like those I journeyed with that night. I would also like to thank Father Ed Brady, S.J., in Khartoum and Sister Margaret Donohue in Port Sudan, both with Jesuit Refugee Services, and Steve and Gemma Watson and Dr. James of Save the Children US in Showak.

In Pakistan, besides the IRC staff, there is no one who inspired me quite like Elizabeth Neuenschwander, an amazing Swiss woman, with Catholic Relief Services in Quetta, who has worked for more than thirty-five years in the far corners of the globe and walked with the poor. Thank you, Elizabeth, for so much.

I visited Cambodia before the peace accord. While there, I broke some bones. When I asked what I should pay for medical services, I was stunned when another doctor told me there was no charge but that the doctor who treated me would appreciate a letter of thanks. Many kept me going to finish my meetings, and I am grateful to them. But what was most special were evenings in my hotel room when some of the women who worked there would sit at the edge of my bed and teach me a few Khmer words.

In Eritrea, I could not have witnessed the end of thirty years of war and the euphoria of the birth of a nation without the help of Tsehai Habte Mariam in the EPLF office in Washington. She put me in touch with Askalu Menkerios in Asmara, and Askalu did all the rest.

Like the MacArthur Foundation, the people of Orbis Books believed in the project. Without them the book would not have come to completion. Thank you Robert Gormley and Robert Ellsberg, and all at Orbis. But thank you, especially, Sue Perry. You are an incredible editor. My thanks, too, go to Catherine Costello, a tireless production coordinator.

During the course of research and writing this book, my sisters Moira Lee and Jane dubbed me the "bag lady." They and the Maryknoll Sisters took me in. God love them.

ABBREVIATIONS

AIG	Afghan Interim Government
CGDK	Coalition Government of Democratic Kampuchea
Dergue	Name used for the Provisional Military Administrative Council, the ruling body in Ethiopia under Mengistu Haile Mariam, 1974-1991.
DPPU	Displaced Persons Protection Unit (Thailand)
DUP	Democratic Unionist Party (Sudan)
ELF	Eritrean Liberation Front
EPLF	Eritrean People's Liberation Front
EPRDF	Ethiopian People's Revolutionary Democratic Front
FUNCINPEC	National United Front for an Independent, Neutral, Peaceful, and Cooperative Cambodia
ICRC	International Committee of the Red Cross
IRC	International Rescue Committee
Khmer Rouge	The name of Democratic Kampuchea's guerilla group led by Pol Pot
Khmer	The people of Cambodia
KPNLF	Khmer People's National Liberation Front
NGO	Nongovernmental organization
NIF	National Islamic Front (Sudan)
PDPA	People's Democratic Party of Afghanistan
PGE	Provisional Government of Eritrea
RCC	Revolutionary Command Council, the ruling body in Sudan under Lieutenant-General Omar al-Bashir
Shari'a	Islamic Law
SNC	Supreme National Council, the transitional governing body in Cambodia
SPLA	Sudan People's Liberation Army
TPLF	Tigrayan People's Liberation Front (Ethiopia)
UN	United Nations
UNBRO	United Nations Border Relief Operation
UNDP	United Nations Development Program
UNHCR	United Nations High Commissioner for Refugees
UNICEF	United Nations International Children's Emergency Fund

UNOCO	United Nations Humanitarian and Economic Assistance Programmes relating to Afghanistan (Operation Salam)
UNTAC	United Nations Transitional Authority in Cambodia
USAID	United States Agency for International Development
WFP	World Food Program

In the text, I changed the names of the majority of the refugee men and womens. Many of them requested that I not use their names. In addition, some of the stories recounted are, in fact, combined stories of more than one person. In the bibliography, I did not list the more than two hundred interviews I made over the course of my research for *Disposable People?*

INTRODUCTION

As I write, it is the last week in May 1992, the Memorial Day weekend. I was struck by two front-page feature pictures in the Sunday and Monday editions of *The New York Times*. Both were of sunny beaches. New York had finally been blessed with a warm Saturday. Sunday's front-page photo showed people crowded together on Jones Beach, enjoying the day. Children built a sand castle while their father, close by in a lounge chair, read a book. Teens carrying boom boxes stepped over people, as a mother wearing a white-billed hat put suntan lotion on her daughter's face. Umbrellas dotted the landscape almost to the water in which swimmers cooled off.[1]

Monday's front-page lead photo pictured a cluster of Haitians on a coast guard cutter at Guantanamo Bay in Cuba. They were not seated or reading or listening to music or swimming or relaxing or smiling. They stood packed, body to body, looking over the boat's guard rail. Their faces were taut with anxiety, fear, and frustration. The accompanying story was written on another beach, this one in Kennebunkport, Maine. President Bush had made an executive decision to authorize the coast guard to interdict boatloads of Haitian asylum seekers fleeing military oppression and hunger, and return them directly to Haiti's beaches.[2]

While looking at the two photos, I recalled George Steiner's reflection on the Jewish people of the Holocaust. Steiner wrote:

> While Jews were being murdered in Treblinka, the overwhelming plurality of human beings, two miles away on Polish farms, 5,000 miles away in New York, were sleeping or eating or going to a film or making love or worrying about the dentist. This is where my imagination balks. The two orders of simultaneous experience are so different, so irreconcilable to any common norm of human values, their coexistence is so hideous a paradox—Treblinka is both because some men have built it, and almost all other men have let it be—that I puzzle over time. Are there as science fiction and Gnostic speculation imply, different species of time in the same world, "good time," and enveloping folds of inhuman time in which men fall into the slow hands of living damnation?[3]

Over the last three years I have been traveling between two time zones: "good time" and "inhuman time"—among refugees who have not seen their homelands for more than a decade. I was different from the refugees in that

I could leave the "inhuman time" and return to the "good time" at will. I could cross back over the River Styx.

On all the inhabitable continents, one can find refugees who have fled from more than fifty nations because of war and persecution. Some refugees I met had lived in exile from their homelands for more than thirty years, while others had arrived in a refugee camp only the day before. Millions became refugees during the decades of the seventies and eighties. Today thousands continue to seek safety from embattled areas and oppressive rulers.

In the end I chose to spend the greater part of three years among three groups of long-term refugees, most of whom have lived in exile more than a decade. They are the 370,000 Khmer who live in camps on the Thai-Cambodian border; the 3.5 million Afghans who live in mud refugee villages in Pakistan (as opposed to the other 2 million Afghans who fled to Iran); and some of the 500,000 Eritreans who, instead of living in protected camps of the United Nations High Commissioner for Refugees (UNHCR), opted to live illegally in Sudanese cities.

The people you will meet in this book serve as voices for Guatemalans in Mexico, Mozambicans in Malawi, Vietnamese in Hong Kong, Laotians in Thailand, Burmese in Bangladesh, Tibetans in Nepal and India, Tamils in India, Palestinians in Gaza, the West Bank, Lebanon, and Jordan, to mention only some of the other refugees around the world. They speak, too, for the more than 23 million internally displaced within their own countries—Sudanese, Afghans, Kurds, Mozambicans, Sri Lankans, Peruvians, Somalians, and all those who are caught up in new struggles breaking out in republics and nations that were once a part of the former Soviet Union or the Soviet bloc.

WHO IS A REFUGEE?

In the late 1970s and throughout the 1980s, millions of people set aside dreams and aspirations, escaped from their war-torn homelands, and crossed into lands not their own. Floods of refugees surged across borders in a single day, week, or month—Ethiopians, Cambodians, Vietnamese, and Mozambicans. Entire villages fled together. Most often, people left the world's poorest countries and received asylum in countries just as desperately poor.

We remember well the nightly news reports of the mainly war-induced Ethiopian famine of 1984. Men and women, old and young, their numbers legion, appeared on our television screens. Barefooted men, raggedly clothed, carried cloth-wrapped bundles on their heads. Each seemed to have a walking stick and a plastic water jug. Women and children mingled farther behind, their clothing torn and soiled. On their veiled heads, they carried woven baskets, water jugs, and clay cooking vessels. Children, too tired or too small to walk, rode in shawls tied around their mothers' backs. They stopped in barren, sandy, practically treeless areas. They clustered their few belongings close to them and gathered what wood they could find. The men poked sticks into the ground and hung thin cloths—poor shelter from the burning sun or cold desert nights.

We saw them tired, sick, hungry, frightened, and dying. They sat enervated, too weak to brush flies from their gaunt faces. We watched in horror as children with bone-tight skin and bloated bellies died in their mothers' emaciated arms. Others, too listless to cry, could not get milk from their mothers' dry breasts. Epidemics hit old and young alike in overcrowded, unsanitary, hastily established camps. We sent relief and watched until our eyes could take no more. We too were enervated. We moved on to other stories. Africa and famine and death faded from our minds.

More recently, in March 1991, following the Persian Gulf War, we watched nearly two million Kurdish people eluding the pursuit of Saddam Hussein's forces. Their departure from their homes was a hurried escape from probable extermination. We were numbed by the sixty-mile stretch of humanity we saw inching into the rugged, northern mountain terrain that divides Iraq from Turkey and Iran. Such columns were multiple. "It is as though all northern Iraq has gotten up and walked," one reporter commented.[4] Most were women, children, and the elderly. Some of the children were barefoot; all were inadequately clothed for such a journey. Mud—mud and relentless rain—pursued and stalled them as they pressed at Turkey's borders where most were turned back. Others were allowed to cross over into Iran.

Within the last year, boatloads of Albanians, Vietnamese, and Haitians have been summarily returned before being given the chance to apply for asylum in Italy, Hong Kong, and the United States. Some refugees have been turned away for obviously political reasons. Others, because a potential host country cannot carry or does not want the burden of a refugee population. An additional problem is that countries who grant asylum find it difficult to determine whether each fleeing person fits the legal definition of a refugee.

As stated by the 1951 United Nations Convention Relating to the Status of Refugees, any person is a refugee who,

> As a result of events occurring before January 1951 and owing to well-founded fear of being persecuted for reasons of race, religion or nationality, membership of a particular social group or political opinion, is outside the country of his nationality and is unable, or owing to such fear, is unwilling to avail himself of the protection of that country; or who, not having a nationality and being outside the country of his former habitual residence, is unable, or owing to such fear, is unwilling to return to it.[5]

According to this definition, no one could be considered a refugee if the event that precipitated flight occurred after 1951. This Convention was written to apply to Europeans displaced as a result of World War II. The U.N.'s subsequent 1967 Protocol adjusted the definition to include those who fled after 1951 and who came from countries outside of Europe. The 1951 Convention with its 1967 Protocol remains the *official definition* of a refugee, yet, in the strictest sense, most of today's refugees do not qualify.

Because of large numbers of Africans fleeing their homelands in the late 1950s and early 1960s as the result of civil wars, wars of liberation, or inter-African conflicts, members of the Organization of African Unity (OAU) broadened the definition of a refugee at a 1969 convention. Not only were those who had a "well-founded fear of persecution" included, but also any person who, "owing to external aggression, occupation, foreign domination or events seriously disturbing public order in either part or the whole of his country of origin or nationality, is compelled to leave his place of habitual residence in order to seek refuge in another place outside his country of origin or nationality."[6] Though the OAU directive is not the legal definition of a refugee, most of the nations that signed the 1951 Convention and/or the 1967 Protocol observe this broader definition of refugee status.

Under the official definition, individuals may not be able to prove—should they return to their homeland—that they would, in all probability, be "persecuted." But the vast majority of those who flee do not get into rickety boats and risk pirate attacks, or cross steep, snow-covered mountains, or willingly live under burlap, behind barbed-wire, or in 6 x 8-foot spaces stacked three high and twelve or more deep *unless* they are fleeing for their lives. And they *do* flee from bombardments, scorched-earth wars, calculated starvation, and oppressive rulers. At the very least, those who take such chances should be given the opportunity to plead their case in a fair, professional, and unhurried interview, or be given temporary haven until the tumult in their country subsides.

REFUGEE NEEDS IN EXILE

Most refugees who survive the first weeks and months of flight continue to languish in refugee camps. The vast majority of today's eighteen million refugees have lived at least five years in exile. Rooted only in their rootlessness, they have lived unnoticed ten, fifteen, forty years. In refugee camps miles from the main roads and in countries not generally on a tourist's agenda, refugees go from the "visible emergency of flight to the invisible emergency of stagnation."[7] "Nonbelonging" becomes a way of belonging.

These refugees are men and women whose freedom has been snatched from them. At one time their lives were rooted in the security of family, tradition, and homeland. The masses of people we see on our television screens, huddled, squatting, staring with vacuous eyes—they are farmers, doctors, engineers, highly educated, nonliterate, mothers, fathers, sons, daughters.

Shrapnel shattered their security in a million fragments and sent them fleeing, family members often separated from one another, everyone separated from home. They left behind things—important things that were the symbols of their traditions and the keepers of their memory.[8] They left cemeteries where they had buried their beloved dead—vessels of their history.

They left parks and lanes and that special fruit tree beside the house. They left their mosques, pagodas, churches, homes, pots and pans, and pictures. They will resurrect their songs and dances only when they return to their farms, villages, and towns.

Long, troubling years of exile follow abrupt, radical, violent, irrevocable change. When refugees cross frontiers, the continuum of their lives is interrupted. The old is no more; the new, not yet. They bring with them all that they are. They carry within themselves both peace and war, strength and fragility. They are forced to rethink and reshape their lives. Stagnated in the present, they continue to live with hopes for the future and hold on to dreams that do not include bombs, torture, killing, or flight.

Refugees are capable people who grasp for control over their lives as months of exile turn into years. Each has a past that can empower the present. Even in their rootlessness, refugees can creatively contribute to the composition of their futures. From the first moment a refugee crosses a border, he or she needs food and shelter—this is relief. But from this moment, each refugee needs much more—and this is development. *Relief* and *development* are worlds apart. Trauma needs relief, but living demands development. Relief leads to dependency; development is empowering and champions self-sufficiency.

For a moment, put yourself in the place of a refugee. What are the questions you would ask when you find yourself in a refugee camp in a strange land? How would you like to be seen? Would you want to be viewed as a pitifully helpless person, when the day before you were tilling a field or nursing sick patients or tending to your family? Would you ask questions like: Where will we live? What will we eat? Where will the children go to school? Will they forget their language, culture, and traditions? Will they be safe from shelling? Will they have access to medical help if they need it? Will I be able to work? If I am not able to do the work I did in my country, will I have the opportunity to learn a new skill? Can I plant a garden, or will there be nothing but concrete surrounding these barracks? What will I do in the years ahead? Will I ever be able to go home? How will our grandmother and others who could not flee be taken care of? Have they all died?

Providing the kind of help that enables a person to resume a semblance of normality while living in exile requires a great deal of money. But part of the problem here is "compassion fatigue." We are inundated with disasters in every corner of the globe, each clamoring for immediate and substantial attention and assistance. The 1991 cyclone in Bangladesh came on the heels of the plight of the Kurds. Today, while we try to shore up the new republics from the broken Soviet Union, we turn our heads away from the forty million lives at risk on the African continent from "Cairo to Capetown."[9] A drought more pernicious than the one in the 1980s is on the horizon. Lionel Rosenblatt notes, "In Malawi, many people have resorted to eating the bulbs or roots of water lilies for nourishment, as well as grass and leaves . . . Malawi hosts more than 1 million refugees . . . who will be at risk if the general population is not also adequately supplied."[10] And the larger donor nations are facing their own economic hardships (albeit of a different scale), turning inward to seek solutions for problems at home. Donations for humanitarian needs have taken a meteoric plunge. While there are double the number of refugees in the world in 1992 than there were a decade ago, donor contributions have not kept pace. Lionel Rosenblatt points out, "[I]n 1980, the United States contributed $25.00 per refugee in the world; today it spends $12.00."[11]

Over the past two or three years, because of cuts in assistance to refugees living in camps throughout the world, programs viewed as "luxuries," such as education, have been reduced or eliminated, and basics in food, shelter, and medicine significantly reduced. Budgetary curbs frustrate the UNHCR's ability to fulfill its mandate to provide international protection and permanent solutions for refugees. The UNHCR is not alone among U.N. organizations or nongovernmental organizations (NGOs) facing such constraints. For example, while U.N. peace-keeping forces are in greater demand today than they have ever been, the United Nations does not have funds to meet the needs. Member nations, the United States included, are $1.5 billion in arrears in both general U.N. funds and special peace-keeping funds.[12] Mark Sommer, a global security expert, points out:

> The world spends three times as much in a *day* preparing for war as it does in a *year* protecting the peace. The annual ratio is close to 1,000 to 1. For half the price of an aircraft carrier, the UN will patrol the peace for a year in Yugoslavia, Cambodia, El Salvador, and a dozen other hot spots that have themselves cost billions and have taken innumerable lives.[13]

Without leadership, international relief, and generous donations, more and more refugees will live out their lives on hold, unable to return to their homelands, yet unable to establish any footing in exile. Among those most affected by massive cuts are children. A generation of children has been born in camps in Pakistan, Thailand, Sudan, and a host of other countries. They know no other life. A young Cambodian refugee child, for example, has never seen a water buffalo or a rice paddy, though the child's family had previously made a living from cultivating rice.

Most refugee children have never known a life without war. Think of your own childhood. You went to school. You did not live in dread of the day planes would bombard your town or tanks would roll through your streets or your parents would be shot in front of you by soldiers. You played with abandon. You were not required to become an adult when you were only ten or eleven years old. Palestinians have seen two generations born without a homeland. The vast majority of refuge children have had no formal education, yet they will be the leaders of the next generation in their war-torn countries—stunted leaders, at best.

REFUGEES AS BY-PRODUCTS OF WAR

Refugees often flee their homes because of war. And people remain refugees because of wars fought too long. Most of these conflicts are not simply internal and isolated; they are not, in reality, merely between two opponents. Alignments today are almost without exception *international*. Foreign involvement, especially during the cold-war era, influenced the length of a conflict, and subsequently the nature of the refugee flow. As the East-West cold war grew hot on the soil of southern lands, tens of millions of civilians became refugees, were internally displaced, or died. The refugees, the fetid corpses, and the burned-out tanks and trucks we view in the newspapers or on television are "the rubbish of war,"[14] the residue of chaos, the "flotsam of power struggles—world, regional, national, and local."[15]

Refugees, the by-products of war, become disposable people—political pawns of leaders, their own as well as those who have a strategic interest in the conflict. In southern Sudan, for example, it seems that John Garang, leader of the Sudan People's Liberation Army (SPLA), devised an ingenious plan for feeding the young boys he was preparing to be his future soldiers. In one remote, inaccessible camp, as many as 10,000 boys lived on grain dropped from C-130 transport planes. Relief agencies thought the boys were orphans fleeing the war that encroached on their southern Sudanese villages. In fact, the boys had been led there as emaciated children with the purpose of feeding them and training them as soldiers in the future. Some as young as three years old were held for this purpose. The question was whether or not to continue feeding the boys, as not only the boys but also the military had access to the food. The International Committee of the Red Cross (ICRC) delegate for Africa answered unequivocally in the affirmative: "It is not a dilemma for us. Even if they are incorporated into the future SPLA, as far as we're concerned if you are under 15, you are an innocent victim."[16]

The Khmer people who fled to Thailand in 1979 were political pawns of a superpower proxy war. The camps in Thailand in which the Khmer civilian refugees lived were intended to be "temporary" safe havens where "humanitarian relief" could reach 350,000 Khmer civilians. The camps became long-term "civilian" holding centers that fed the "hidden border" military encampments and gave credibility to a government-in-exile in which the Khmer people had no voice. I know of no refugee population that has not been used to promote the objectives of the warring parties.

REFUGEES AND THE AFTERMATH OF WAR

Just as refugee or displaced-person flows are neither tidy or predictable, nor are the ends and aftermath of the wars that caused them to flee their homes. When I began to write *Disposable People?* there was seemingly no end in sight of the wars in Cambodia, Pakistan, Eritrea, or Sudan. Today, all but Sudan have declared peace, fragile and tenuous though that peace might be. In May 1991, Eritreans and Ethiopians overthrew the brutal seventeen-year reign of Mengistu Haile Mariam. On October 23, 1991, the four warring Cambodian parties signed a peace agreement. On April 27, 1992, ten days after the fall of President Najibullah and exactly fourteen years after a murderous coup brought war to Afghanistan, a hastily organized provisional government of *mujahideen* leaders in Peshawar, Pakistan, began its drive over the Khyber Pass to return to Kabul.

It's hard to believe that the cold war began half a century ago. When it began to thaw, strategic interests of the U.S. government and the government of the then U.S.S.R. changed dramatically. For fifty years they had "contained" each other on other people's soil. Warring client states became proxies of the two sides and received billions in military assistance and troops to fight wars that had begun on a small scale. The demise of the Soviet Union had the greatest impact on countries like Cambodia, Afghanistan, and Eritrea, where prolonged wars had been fought because—directly or indirectly—the superpowers had kept them going. Once troops of the superpowers pulled out and monetary assistance was no longer forthcoming, local governments and troops could not keep the fires of war burning. The pullout of the superpowers did not, however, make the original enemies friends or make way for solid political, economic, or social structures. To date, skirmishes are still being fought between the Khmer Rouge and the Phnom Penh government in Cambodia. *Mujahideen* factions in Afghanistan, drawing lines on ethnic and sectarian grounds, are still vying for power and fighting with high-tech weapons left by the United States and the former Soviet Union. Eritrea is the only one of the four countries at peace, but it lies in limbo: it is no longer a province of Ethiopia and at the same time it is not yet a sovereign nation.

The aftermath of the war in each of these countries is devastating. The infrastructure is in ruins; with no economic base, there is no way to rebuild unless each country receives massive infusions of support from donor nations. But changing strategic interests and domestic economic woes in donor countries offer little hope that sufficient money will be forthcoming, either for assistance in returning millions of refugees or in rehabilitating the land.

Walking away from the ruins of these nations is neither in our best interests strategically or economically in the long run, nor is it morally acceptable. Substantial assistance now will encourage the development of economically viable economies and self-sufficiency, as well as the cessation of residual internal strife.

Because of radical changes in Eastern Europe and the demise of the Soviet Union, much more money is being apportioned to that area of the world. The $24 billion assistance package for Russia, announced early in 1992, attests to this. But remember that the East-West conflict was fought mainly on the soil of other nations. As we give our assistance to the new Commonwealth of Independent States, we must also give significant assistance to nations like Cambodia, Afghanistan, Eritrea, and Ethiopia, whose destruction was due in part to the infusion of U.S. and Soviet military support. Millions of refugees are poised to return to their war-torn homelands, but their devastated homelands cannot accommodate them unless the global community lends support.

Consider the energy the Bush administration put into building a coalition force to eject Iraq from Kuwait. With a sense of utmost urgency and girded with strong political will, Secretary of State James Baker did not rest from his global sallies until an unprecedented force was in place in the Saudi desert along the Iraq and Kuwait borders. He met time and again with world leaders to convince them to join a coalition that would, he adjudged, liberate a nation overrun by a diabolical tyrant. He was indefatigable in raising funds in the billions of dollars for battle. Massive numbers of troops and armaments were gathered and dispersed with staggering speed.

With the same sort of political and moral will and with the same sort of aggressive campaign to obtain funds and partners in rebuilding, money could be found to restore decimated nations.

Similarly, at a time when more is expected of all the U.N. organizations and various NGOs, there is also a need for these organizations to streamline, to reevaluate their mandates, and to coordinate their efforts for the greater good of the people they assist. From the new Secretary General Boutros Boutros-Ghali, to the newly appointed Under Secretary General for Humanitarian Assistance, Ambassador Jan Eliasson, to the High Commissioner for Refugees, Mrs. Sadako Ogata, officials have pledged to make the United Nations a more positive and effective force in the world. It is up to the member nations, both through their actions and monetary pledges, to enable the now disjointed and cumbersome U.N. family of organizations to work more effectively and in greater harmony. The end of the cold war certainly opens the door of opportunity.

A Personal Note

As I walked among these people—the refugees and internally displaced—they took me into their homes and shared with me their hopes and dreams and aspirations for a safe and dignified return to their homelands. They *do* have hopes and dreams. They shared with me their meager food, their marriage and burial ceremonies, their laughter and tears. I witnessed countless acts of human kindness and generosity, and I encountered the consequences of their anger taken out on someone close to them. Once I was with them, I could no longer think in terms of masses and sheer numbers, nor could I distance myself from the magnitude of their suffering. What has happened to the world that *people* have become disposable?

Many people have asked me why I wrote on refugees rather than on some other group of people or some other topic. I suppose what emerges from inside of us and becomes a book or a show or a conversation has a lot to do with our own lives, past and present. From experiences of tumultuous change in my own life, I feel a twinge of what a refugee feels when the world comes tumbling down and life is forever different. And I know a little of what it is to be a survivor. As a woman, I can share in the lives of refugee women in a way no man can. And being a wanderer of sorts myself, I understand how refugees determine against all odds to grow where they are planted, to forever continue to compose their lives with laughter and with joy, even in the midst of pain, insecurity, and loss.

Not long ago, a friend asked me why, when I was trying so hard to get all the refugees home, did I not keep a permanent home for myself. After a long pause, all I could answer was that a permanent home would tie me down. There will always be more refugees who want and need to go home. Carel Sternberg, a wise and compassionate man who fled the Gestapo in 1938 and again in 1940, said simply: "The refugee condition, once experienced, does not wash off."

CAMBODIA

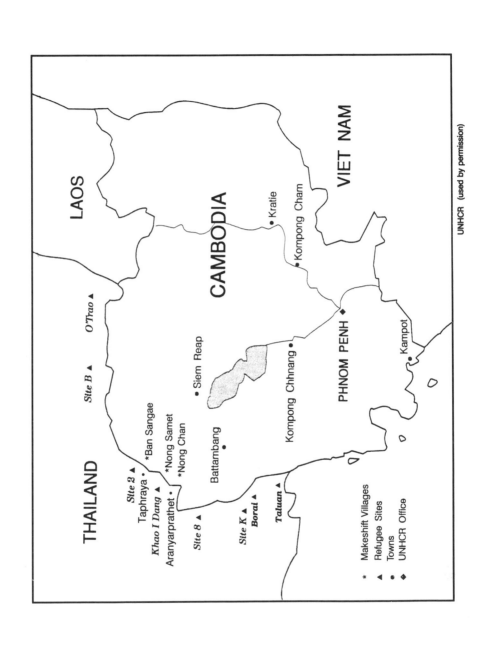

THAILAND

LAOS

CAMBODIA

VIET NAM

Site 3 ▲
Taphraya •
Khao I Dang ▲
Aranyarprathet •
*Ban Sangae
*Nong Samet
*Nong Chan

Site 8 ▲

Site B ▲

O'Trao ▲

• Siem Reap

Battambang
•

Kompong Chhnang •

Kratie •

Kompong Cham •

Site K ▲
Borai ▲
Taluan ▲

PHNOM PENH ◆

Kampot
•

* Makeshift Villages
▲ Refugee Sites
• Towns
◆ UNHCR Office

UNHCR (used by permission)

Doug Hulcher

Part of the tens of thousands of the Khmer refugees who fled to the Cambodian border in 1979.

1

FLIGHT CAMBODIA

When the forest burns, the flames are extinguished quickly
because the people worry about burning the forests.
But when my country burns with the smoke of war,
nobody puts out the fire.

—*Keng Sothol, refugee*
Thai-Cambodian border

Met Chhuon had been in flight for most of his short life. Born into a rice-farming family in a village in Cambodia's north central Siem Reap Province, Chhuon was only seven, almost eight, when his childhood ended in 1975. Though he was eager to continue his education in the village primary school, that was not to be. On April 17, 1975, Pol Pot, leader of Cambodia's communist Khmer Rouge, defeated the Cambodian government headed by Lon Nol and began his changes in the countryside and the cities. Chhuon would know all the horror of the Pol Pot regime. Today when Cambodians look back on their years under the Khmer Rouge, they preface their grim tales with, "In Pol Pot time . . ."

Chinese revolutionaries had advised Pol Pot, more Maoist than Mao himself, not to move too quickly or too radically. Scorning this advice, he began his sweeping changes the moment he victoriously entered Phnom Penh, Cambodia's graceful, capital city. Khieu Samphan, one of the Khmer Rouge leaders, boasted to Pol Pot not long after the Khmer Rouge took control of Cambodia: "We have fulfilled all the conditions to be one-hundred-percent Communist. We can surpass even our Chinese brothers. With one giant leap forward we can reach the goal of Communism, and not go through stages of socialism."[1]

Neither Chhuon nor his family nor the other villagers witnessed the pandemonium of the exodus from Phnom Penh and other Cambodian cities. He did not see citizens ordered from their homes, businesses, schools, and hospitals and forced to march to the countryside. But soon enough he would see the urban people spill into rural Cambodia, lost and confused and frightened at the nightmare of terror taking hold of their nation. All would be irrevocably transformed.

POL POT EMPTIES PHNOM PENH AND FORCES PEOPLE TO THE COUNTRYSIDE

Chhuon watched survivors pass on the road and others stop in his village. The first arrivals were those whose origins were linked to Chhuon's village, as the Khmer Rouge soldiers had ordered urban dwellers to return to the villages of their ancestors. Many sought out relatives. That was both a blessing and a danger for the new arrivals. The blessing was that relatives offered the "new people" shelter in their small grass homes until they could provide their own. The danger was the knowing. Throughout the country doctors, teachers, intellectuals, former soldiers in Lon Nol's army—all wanted to keep their identities secret from the Khmer Rouge. They were the people the Khmer Rouge categorized as enemies of their regime, and they feared that those who gave them shelter would reveal their identities to the Khmer Rouge. Pol Pot considered them threats to the total control he envisioned. They were candidates for extermination.

Chhuon's relatives from Phnom Penh were among those forced from the city. Just before the rainy season began in early May, Chhuon's uncle Soeun Sieth (his father's eldest brother), along with his wife, her parents, an aunt, and three of their children, arrived in the village. They had been some of the last to leave Phnom Penh, holding back in the vain hope that they would find the second son. Chhuon listened to their story.

Shelling just beyond the city's perimeter had increased daily during the week before April 17. When the uncle's family arose that Thursday morning, they knew the end of Cambodia's civil war was near. They optimistically thought only of the peace it would bring; they hoped for a return to a normal life. Soeun Sieth, a teacher in the upper school of a *lycee* on a quiet street not far from their home in the southern part of the city, went to work that morning. The two children in primary school stayed at home with their mother and grandparents; the two older children went to the *lycee* with their father. All agreed to meet at home if anything happened.

By midmorning the artillery shots were very loud. In fact, the Khmer Rouge had entered the city; soldiers were firing victory shots into the air. As the army's tanks and troops moved slowly down the wide boulevards, people waving white flags of surrender cheered them, more from a sense of relief than of identity and solidarity. They knew little of the Khmer Rouge who had kept themselves hidden in the Cambodian jungles for almost a decade. Simply put, the Khmer people were happy that the corrupt government of General Lon Nol had been toppled.

Others, who had strong reservations but who had not fled when Khmer Rouge victory seemed certain, were not on the streets that morning. They cowered in their homes. Still others seemed little concerned with the entry of the Khmer Rouge and went about their normal tasks. By nightfall, though, all had a premonition of the incomprehensible magnitude of the changes in store for them.

Tanks and soldiers fanned out from the city's center, around the extensive, well-kept parks, past the gilded Royal Palace, the delicate pagodas and rounded stupas, the Royal Library and the museum, and along the river's edge. By foot and by truck, the army veered from the main thoroughfares into the tree-lined side streets where quiet homes housed the city's families.

Victory march completed, the work of the revolution began. Young soldiers—some no older than twelve or thirteen—wearing bandoleers of cartridges, shot shells into the air and directed people to evacuate the city. With bull horns and sharp raps on doors, they ordered citizens from their houses, from offices, hospitals, and schools into the streets. Some were told they had half an hour to gather enough food and belongings for three days, after which they would return. Others were told to take nothing and leave immediately because they would be away from their homes no more than three or four hours. No one knew why the orders were given except what the soldiers told them: The Americans were going to bomb the city. After all, the last Americans had left less than a week before.

Who could have imagined that three hours or three days would become more than three years of living hell as the Khmer Rouge dismantled the social structure piece by piece with a swiftness and brutality not known in modern history. This was but the first of many forced relocations for millions of Khmer people.

Even before the soldiers reached the school, the teachers and students headed for their homes. When Soeun Sieth and his two sons reached the wide boulevard they had to cross, they were pressed by the crowd. In the crush, the father lost sight of the younger child; he kept going, sure the boy would find his way.

Before Soeun Sieth and his older son arrived home, two soldiers had gone from house to house on the street ordering the residents out. Desperately afraid that the family would become separated, his wife gathered her brood about her and emerged onto the normally quiet street to find a throng of neighbors just as bewildered and frightened. They gathered in clusters to consult and console. Some returned to their homes to gather what belongings they could, packing them in automobiles or on motorcycles. Others remained on the street straining for sight of missing family members.

More than an hour passed before Soeun Sieth's wife spied her husband and son hurrying toward them. When she heard the younger boy was lost in the crowd, she did not want to move until he was safely with them. That, however, was not to be. The soldiers returned and forced everyone on the street to move in the opposite direction from the school—north toward the sports complex where several wide streets converged. From every direction people in automobiles, on motorcycles and bicycles, in carts, and on foot pushed together causing a giant gridlock. Very soon cars and motorcycles, depleted of fuel, stood abandoned, many picked over for parts.

Every member of Soeun Sieth's family wanted to push back to find the other child. But they could not do it together and no one wanted to go alone, compounding the separation. No, they would hang back until the crowds thinned and take a chance on returning to find him. They never did.

By nightfall, though few were far beyond the outskirts of the city, none relaxed in the tranquility of home. As people sat in small groups around fires cooking what food they had, a dark, eerie, vacant silence fell over the wide boulevards and tree-lined streets of Phnom Penh—deserted. As old folks too tired for the journey began to die and as babies were born behind whatever vegetation or wall afforded a vestige of privacy, window shutters on empty homes flapped in the evening breeze; lonesome dogs roamed neighborhoods in search of their owners and food. As darkness settled, people were tired, dusty, and hungry. Hindered by the congestion, few had gone much beyond the university and the railroad tracks. For this the people were grateful, as they hoped to return soon to their homes.

Once morning came, though Soeun Sieth and his family tried to hold back, soldiers herded them on to the edge of the city. Along the way they saw horrors. They stepped over bodies of people killed for countering orders to move. They watched men and women futilely pushing their sick on hospital beds. (Those who had no one to take them from the hospitals had been left to die.) They saw mothers carrying children with IVs hanging from their arms. They heard the frightened cries of small children separated from their parents. They saw old people sit down and die from fatigue. Though the family continued to move north, they still hoped to change their course and return home.

On the third day, on Highway 5 leading out of the city, Soeun Sieth and his family realized they would not return to Phnom Penh that day or the next or for a long time to come. As ordered, they marched to Chhuon's village in the northern province of Siem Reap, not far from the border of Thailand.

Pol Pot would not let them look back. The only return Pol Pot envisioned was to a time in Cambodia's distant past when it was, he believed, a self-sufficient rural society. He wanted his Cambodia to be a self-contained, giant collective of farmers, workers, and soldiers. Whatever stood between what *was* and what *would be* was destroyed. Pol Pot was singular in his vision of a Cambodia that would stand alone. Intercourse with foreigners was banned. A shroud dropped and hid the people from international view.

The Khmer Rouge regime did away with currency and bankers, schools and teachers, hospitals and doctors and nurses, industry and management, newspapers and editors, infrastructure and engineers, telephones and operators, the arts and artists, religion and monks. The structure of the family was torn apart, first by separations as the people migrated into the countryside. Separation by design followed. Beginning with the long march, leisure time was abolished. Quiet talk in restful settings, conversations that build relationships—these had no place in the new regime's scheme of things. Where one lived, what one ate or wore—these were no longer individual decisions. Angka (Committee), the watchful eye of the Khmer Rouge communist organization, would provide for individuals when and to what degree it decided. The rule of law was replaced by the bondage of discipline and terror.

The journey was long—several weeks; uninterrupted days of walking. As the rainy season began, there was little or no shelter from the weather. As a family's supply of food dwindled, they exchanged the gold, jewelry, and silk sarongs they carried for rice and other foods. Though repulsive to their taste, they caught frogs and mice and gathered vegetation they recognized as safe to eat.

As the people continued to walk, soldiers ordered men and women aside and asked about their backgrounds, ostensibly for job placement in the countryside. Others were lured away from the crowd by the promise of special work. Though some were allowed to rejoin their families and told to continue their march, others, too many to number, were herded into trucks or led into forests, never to be seen again. Wives and children, mothers and fathers reached for their loved ones until they vanished from sight—forever.

HISTORICAL ROOTS OF THE KHMER ROUGE

Any Khmer presently twenty-two years or older has lived through four governments, five names for the country,[2] and has never known a day without war. Any Khmer now forty-five or older has witnessed the country's struggle for independence from the French as well as its bondage under the Khmer Rouge and a Vietnamese conquest. Cambodia, once a large empire, dwindled to an enslaved, devastated, sparsely populated nation. In 1992 it still stood on the brink of extinction, with only a fragile peace in place.

Over the centuries Cambodia has been an empire, a colony, an independent nation, and a conquered one. In its golden time, between the ninth and fifteenth centuries, the Indian-influenced Angkor Empire reached its zenith and extended north through Thailand, west through parts of Burma, south into Vietnam and the fertile Mekong Delta, and east into Laos. It held the Isthmus of Kra that joins Thailand to Malaysia, giving the empire easy access to the Indian Ocean and the Pacific.[3] Yet the Khmer were not really a sea-faring people. With more domestic inclinations, they brought their land to life through engineering skills and knowledge. Their vast irrigation system and fertile fields provided ample food. Kings and people raised mystical temples and created fitting song and dance. But as the idyllic life lulled the Khmers, others chipped at the empire until the smaller boundaries of modern Cambodia, no larger than the state of Washington, were all that remained. From that day to this, Thailand and Vietnam, far more populous than Cambodia, have been fearsome neighbors.

Three centuries after the decline of the Angkor kingdom, Europeans were carving out their own empires far beyond their national boundaries. As the English ensconced themselves in India and reached toward Russia, the French saw Southeast Asia as their window into China and its wealth in trade. The French also wanted to stay British designs on China.

For almost a century, between 1864 and 1954, Cambodia, as a part of French Indochina, offered obeisance to France for protection of the nation and the throne. Cambodia paid dearly for such security. King Norodom, who began his reign in 1860, distrusted his Siamese and Vietnamese neighbors far more, it seems, than he did the more remote French who virtually reduced the kingdom to a colony. As the French took more and more control of the business of the nation, the king was ineffectual in his protests, as were peasant farmers who tried to revolt to prevent higher taxation and more rigid control over their land and production. In the end the king, while not condoning or even liking the tightening grip of France, did not strengthen his support for his people. He chose, instead, to maintain himself on the throne, puppet though he was. The takeover King Norodom feared by the Vietnamese and the Siamese came by the French.

King Norodom's grandson, the young King Norodom Sihanouk, bowed to both the French and the Japanese in the same way his grandfather did to the French. As a young man of nineteen Sihanouk assumed the throne in 1941, the year the Japanese occupied Cambodia. He, too, wanted protection of his kingdom and his throne not only from the French, but also from his stronger, more populous neighbors. Sihanouk believed the Japanese when they told him they would protect Cambodia against outsiders. He yielded, only to discover Japan, like France, wanted absolute control.[4]

In 1945, when the Japanese were defeated and the French regained control of Japan's surrendered colonies, the political climate of French Indochina had changed. It is from this time, the last half of the twentieth century, that change in Cambodia came less by slow evolution and more with swiftness and a searing radicalism. In Cambodia new rebel groups that did not want to be subjected to a foreign power focused on the discontent of the peasants, increasingly destitute because of high taxation and large private landowners. In French eyes, the Khmer people were incapable of becoming more than peasant farmers. In the urban areas dominated by French culture and commerce, the French elevated Chinese and Vietnamese to be merchants and administrators in what the French deemed little more than an outpost of French Indochina.

Though Sihanouk bowed once again to the power of France to maintain his seat on the throne, Vietnam was determined to free itself from French control. Vietnam's determination to overthrow the French precipitated the First Indochinese War (1945–54). During those nine years Ho Chi Minh and his well-organized Vietminh wore down the French, not, however, without generous supplies of arms from China. The Vietminh finally routed their colonial lord in the battle of Dien Bien Phu and declared their independence in 1954.

During the First Indochinese War skirmishes against the French continued in the Cambodian countryside. Khmer non-communist nationals were intent on eliminating colonialism; the nascent Khmer communists wanted more than independence. They wanted to do away with colonialism and the monarchy. Neither group—even if the two had joined forces—was strong enough to make a difference. Although they received support from Ho Chi Minh, neither group wanted to be totally dependent for arms and manpower on the Vietminh, fearing—as Cambodians traditionally did—Vietnam's taking the upper hand and ultimately ruling Cambodia. Rule by Vietnam would be comparable to rule by France. Meanwhile, as Sihanouk saw the French being defeated in Vietnam, he pressed his own case for independence.

Elizabeth Becker wrote:

> Sihanouk was uncanny. As each situation had warranted, he had willingly collaborated with the Vichy French, the Japanese fascists, and then the French colonists again. Now he was a leader of Third World nationalism because that was the path to saving his power and his country. The former collaborator was now celebrated in his own country and the world as the symbol of modern Cambodian independence.[5]

A weary France that had never regarded Cambodia as valuable in itself acquiesced to Sihanouk's urgings to free the land from its French ties.

The Geneva Conference of 1954, convened to settle the questions of both the Korean War and the French Indochina War, merely confirmed the independence already conceded by the French. Sihanouk was accorded the title of "father of the independent Cambodian nation."[6]

Both the nationalist resistance and the Cambodian communists went away empty-handed. Elizabeth Becker says:

> While their Vietnamese comrades from Paris . . . returned from their studies to Hanoi and Ho Chi Minh's "national liberation struggle," the Cambodians studying in Paris came back to a political monstrosity, in their terms—an independent Cambodia— ruled by a "democratically" elected god. Worse, the god-king called himself a socialist and enjoyed the friendship of the communist states of Asia.[7]

The Khmer communists did not simply lick their wounds; they slipped away to prepare for another day.

Even though China had assisted the Vietminh in their war against French colonialism, it did not agree with the Vietminh—that the Khmer and Laotian resistance movements be recognized as legitimate parties within their respective countries. China's Zhou Enlai feared that Hanoi's assistance of the Khmer resistance movement would spread U.S. intervention in the area and "drag China into a wider conflict." Zhou Enlai stated, "We would not like to see Laos and Cambodia become American bases. . . . That will be a threat to China's security."[8] In spite of China's efforts, the stage was being set for the Second Indochina War.

In 1955, a year after the Geneva Conference, King Norodom Sihanouk relinquished his throne to his father, became Prince Sihanouk, and formed his own socialist political party, the Sangkum Party. Sihanouk was no longer a docile nineteen-year-old king willing to give obeisance to the French to retain his throne and lifestyle. He liked power, wanted to govern rather than be titular king, and wanted to ensure he would not lose control to new enemies. The Sangkum Party, led by Sihanouk, ran in the first elections of an independent Cambodia and won handily. There was no strong opposition from the left or the right—nor would there be during Sihanouk's strong, one-party leadership as he silenced any dissent. Changes in government in this last half of the twentieth century would be by coup and military might, not by the ballot box.

Though Sihanouk was intent on keeping his nation neutral and nonaligned, in the end, he did not succeed. This policy of neutrality proved to be Sihanouk's nemesis and entangled him fifteen years later during the Second Indochina War. He made treaties with the United States and European nations while at the same time effecting agreements with China and the Soviet Union. Though the United States urged him to join the newly formed Southeast Asia Treaty Organization (SEATO), Sihanouk declined on the principle of neutrality. The United States considered this an affront and interpreted Sihanouk's decision as a procommunist move rather than an act of neutrality.[9]

As the United States became more and more embroiled in the Vietnam War, the United States put more pressure on Cambodia to side with the South Vietnamese forces, particularly in light of the fact that Sihanouk's government was receiving a significant amount of U.S. military assistance. Sihanouk first refused more U.S. aid and then broke diplomatic relations with the U.S. government in 1965, in reaction to the murder of South Vietnamese President Ngo Dinh Diem in 1963 and the introduction of U.S. combat troops in South Vietnam. At the same time Sihanouk charged the U.S. government with passing covert aid to rightist factions in Cambodia. The loss of U.S. aid had a profound effect on the Cambodian economy. Sihanouk, the people's "god-king,"[10] found it difficult to maintain his "island of peace."[11]

Due largely to a faltering economy and because Sihanouk wanted to contain the growing Khmer communist party, he appointed two of the party's strongest leaders to two important government posts—Khieu Samphan as secretary of commerce and Hou Youn, of planning. He tried to salvage the economy by nationalizing financial institutions and foreign trade.

At the same time Sihanouk allowed the North Vietnamese to build sanctuaries along the Ho Chi Minh Trail where it followed the Cambodian border with South Vietnam. He opened the port of Sihanoukville (renamed Kompong Som) to ships supplying the Vietminh troops. Though he depended more and more on China and the Soviet Union for aid, he maintained Cambodia was a neutral, nonaligned nation. As if to prove this, in 1969, despite his fear of the growing American presence in Vietnam, he renewed relations with the United States and looked the other way when American B-52s began unauthorized, secret bombing inside Cambodia to destroy the North Vietnamese sanctuaries Sihanouk had permitted.

The leaders of Cambodia's left wing received no aid, and leaders of the right decried the socialist measures Sihanouk had implemented at the behest of Khieu Samphan and Hou Youn. As the right gained strength, especially in the national assembly, the left withdrew to build up their forces. With the disappearance of the leftist leaders and the growing power of the right, the socialist reforms in finance, business, trade, education, and health reverted to privatization.

The mercurial prince continued to blow with whatever wind seemed to assure victory, playing right against left, Americans against Chinese and Soviets, Thais against Vietnamese. There came a moment when he lost. On March 18, 1970, General Lon Nol instigated a successful, bloodless coup against Prince Norodom Sihanouk. The Kingdom of Cambodia became the Khmer Republic while Sihanouk was vacationing in Paris.

General Lon Nol, Sihanouk's army chief of staff from the beginning of Cambodia's independence and more recently prime minister and defense minister, believed Sihanouk was moving too far to the left; he strongly opposed the prince's ties to North Vietnam and China. Politically Lon Nol was far to the right and gained in power as the rightist elements in Cambodia grew in strength in the national assembly.

The general was not a popular leader. Ordinary citizens wanted Sihanouk restored to power and would not accept Lon Nol's efforts to discredit him. When Lon Nol's backers began to topple statues and pictures of the prince, letting them fall in the mud—a symbolic affront to every Cambodian citizen— the people lashed out against the perpetrators. As saving face ran deep in their culture, so did saving the social structure.[12]

Lon Nol had the support of some of the elite who thought he would bring an end to the corruption rife in Sihanouk's government, would be truly neutral, and would initiate democratic reforms. The U.S. government, which backed Lon Nol, believed he would foster an economic climate in which business and trade would prosper.

Lon Nol also had the backing of the military. The Khmer Republic became a virtual military dictatorship as Lon Nol responded to demonstrations against his regime with military force. Unarmed protesters were fired upon by his troops and left to die. Their fields were burned and their animals killed.

In May 1970, the United States, an ally of the new government, took advantage of the coup: without Lon Nol's consent, it sent secret bombing missions into the countryside. As Lon Nol embroiled Cambodia more and more in the military operations of the South Vietnamese and American forces, what had been a war in Vietnam became the Second Indochina War.

Determined to obliterate North Vietnamese troops, their route to the South, and the sanctuaries that made passage possible, massive, secret U.S. bombings ravaged the Cambodian countryside during the next few years, making no distinction between military and civilian targets. The 257,465 tons of explosives the United States dropped were "half again as many as were dropped on Japan in World War II."[13] Cambodian villages in the southeastern portion of the nation were laid waste and hundreds of thousands of peasants were killed. An estimated six hundred thousand lives were lost and well over half of the domestic animals were killed.[14]

Rural villagers and farmers fled the countryside. Their homes and fields destroyed, they could not plant. The presence of landmines made it even more dangerous to remain and work the soil. With bridges and roads blown up, in some areas rural transport came to a halt. Phnom Penh, a city of five hundred thousand before 1970, swelled to twice its size and then doubled again. Its streets were filled with beggars who could not find work. Children who had attended village schools now played idly.

Cambodia's economy and political climate had been in trouble when Lon Nol took over. When he lost power five years later, the country was devastated. The new beggars in the city had been the planters and providers of the nation's food supply and of its largest export products, rice and rubber. By 1975 there was famine in the land; urban areas depended on American food aid.

Military expenditures consumed all available resources, including funds needed for business and trade development. Business and financial institutions were nationalized once again. Foreign trade was at a standstill. Freedom of speech, press, religion, privacy from search and seizure—all civil liberties were suspended. Government corruption became the worst the nation had ever known as Lon Nol and his officers prospered at the expense of the people. Even the rice given by America was skimmed off by the military before the citizens received their share.

The country was vulnerable to a Khmer Rouge takeover. The economy and the quality of life for the Khmer people were eroding at an ever quickening pace. Internally, regionally, and internationally the forces of history coalesced in such a manner that Pol Pot could impose his radical will on Cambodia's six million people.

RISE OF THE KHMER ROUGE TO POWER

The Khmer communists had formed and developed their strength slowly during the quarter of a century between 1950 and 1975. Though originally heavily dependent on the Vietnamese communists, because of ancient animosities they did not want to be integrally identified with the Vietnam communists. This fear of dominance had prompted the First National Congress of Khmer Resistance, held on April 17, 1950, exactly twenty-five years before the Khmer Rouge marched into Phnom Penh to overthrow the Lon Nol government on April 17, 1975.

Though the movement of Cambodian communists had its roots in Cambodia, it was in Paris that two future leaders had laid the foundation upon which they built the national organization. While the majority of Cambodian students in Paris were from the upper classes and were capable students, Saloth Sar and Ieng Sary were atypical. Saloth Sar, from a rural background, was a plodding student. Ieng Sary was not wealthy but he was a student. More than twenty years later, Saloth Sar would take as his *nom de guerre* Pol Pot, a name that will go down in the annals of history as one of the most brutal revolutionaries of all time.

While in Paris between September 1949 and December 1952, Saloth Sar and Ieng Sary joined in a study group with Cambodian intellectuals. Together they shared their visions and dedicated themselves to making them become reality. They wanted the French out, and they wanted to do away with the Sihanouk monarchy. They were nationalists who wanted their brand of communism to prevail in an independent Cambodia. Some in this group, such as Khieu Samphan and Son Sen, would become a part of the leadership of the Khmer Rouge when the independent Khmer communist party emerged.

As Saloth Sar focused on the need to eliminate the French and break Sihanouk's power, he wrote an essay that foresaw what would happen if Sihanouk maintained leadership. Such devastation indeed did come to pass — under Saloth Sar's leadership as Pol Pot. As he considered the ramifications of Sihanouk's being placed in a position to take credit for winning independence from the French, he said Sihanouk would

> shut up the people . . . expel those who oppose the politics of the king. Then it will lead to the dissolution of political parties that oppose the interests of the throne because political parties do not keep quiet. Finally, the politics of the king will provoke a civil war that will burn everything — even the pagodas. The monks, the people, the bureaucrats will experience the sadness of the families; the parents, the women and the children will be smashed by tanks, burned by napalm; the harvest will be destroyed.[15]

By the time Saloth Sar returned to Cambodia early in 1953, the Vietminh had declared war against the French colonialism that had been reinstated following World War II. He joined the Vietminh in their struggle against the French. Following the Geneva Conference of 1954 and Sihanouk in power in an independent Cambodia, Saloth Sar began his two-front struggle: (1) against being swallowed permanently by the Vietnamese communists and (2) against Sihanouk who relentlessly pursued the Khmer communists. It was, in fact, Sihanouk who gave the Khmer communists the name *les Khmer rouges*, the red Cambodians.

In the Cambodian countryside the fledgling communist party worked among dissatisfied, indebted peasants. Many lived in a feudal-like situation, dependent on large landowners. Others had too little land on which they could grow enough food for their families. Still others were victims of poor soil and not enough rain. When Sihanouk's army came dangerously close to annihilating the Khmer Rouge in the countryside, they moved to Phnom Penh to build the party. But in the 1960s as police repression and Sihanouk's relentless pursuit made the city unsafe for them, the Khmer Rouge began their exodus to the northeastern jungles where the party took on its revolutionary shape.

The leaders of the revolution were in place. Saloth Sar was at the head, with Ieng Sary, Khieu Samphan, and Son Sen holding other important posts. They fanned out from the jungles to win over more and more peasants and build their disciplined, guerrilla army with which they could wage a civil war.

The turn of events in Phnom Penh in March 1970, when Sihanouk was toppled by Lon Nol, furnished the Khmer Rouge an opportunity to begin the revolution. The more Lon Nol supported the United States in its war against the North Vietnamese, the more the Khmer people suffered. The destruction of vast areas of Cambodia by U.S. bombings served to convert greater numbers of the poorest and most dissatisfied peasants into Khmer Rouge sympathizers. As the numbers of the Khmer Rouge grew, so did Pol Pot's hold over them. They lived in the poverty of the jungles foraging for food, clearing the land, building crude compounds, training for combat, and listening incessantly to indoctrination.

As the American bombings increased against North Vietnamese sanctuaries in Cambodia and the Vietminh moved farther into Cambodia, its forces became the ones to engage and occupy Lon Nol's troops. Generally, when the two forces met, the Vietminh won. This left the Khmer Rouge free to strengthen their own troops from fifteen thousand to forty thousand.[16]

At the same time Saloth Sar instituted what would become the hallmarks of his reign as Pol Pot—the collectives, the forced relocations of people, and the brutal consequences for those who did not obey Angka, the watchful eye of the Khmer Rouge organization. The Khmer Rouge won over villages with assistance and promises or by force. As they brought several villages together, they instituted communal living.

Even though the peasants were cut off from the rest of civilization and even though their basic civil liberties were denied, they were free to grow their own food, or so they thought at first. As time went on, life in the jungles they cleared and the farmlands they cultivated became more and more restrictive: no leisure time, no buying and selling, no individual choice. Family structures were eliminated. There were "disappearances," disciplinary beatings, dangerous deterrents to attempted flight. Angka overshadowed the whole of life.[17]

The greed, corruption, and lack of discipline of Lon Nol, his government officials, and his troops were no match in the end to the strict life imposed by the Khmer Rouge. Haing Ngor recalls that unlike the Lon Nol soldiers, "We never heard of the Khmer Rouge stealing anything, even a piece of paper or a grain of rice. It was said that the guerrillas kept to a strict and honorable code of behavior—no gambling, no abuse of peasants and, above all, no corruption." The code read like the Ten Commandments.

1. Thou shalt love, honor and serve the workers and peasants . . . 3. Thou shalt respect the people without injury to their interests, without touching their goods or plantations, forbidding thyself to steal so much as one pepper . . . 6. Thou shalt do nothing improper respecting women . . . 9. Thou shalt not touch the people's money . . . 12. Against any foe and against every obstacle thou shalt struggle with determination and courage, ready to make every sacrifice, including thy life, for the people, the workers and peasants, for the revolution and for Angka.[18]

Under the Lon Nol government, inflation had increased markedly. Although rice was being supplied by the Americans, military officers skimmed off a hefty portion and sold it at inflated prices. They bribed anyone they could. Many others became rich and did not fight or see that their troops had adequate food and clothing. If the army leaders themselves were not disciplined, they could not expect their troops to be. They lost important battles as the Khmer Rouge moved out of the jungles and took the offensive, moving ever closer to Phnom Penh. By 1974, toward the end of the civil war, more and more Cambodians became hostages in the collectives or refugees in the city. "The choice was posed in extremes: risk starvation as a refugee in the Khmer Republic or give your soul to Angka in exchange for being fed something. Run away from the forced collectivization of the countryside so your child can starve to death in Phnom Penh."[19]

As the end came closer, the people of Phnom Penh tended to deny the impending collapse of their country. Houses shook from shelling not far from the city. As the refugees came and huddled by temples for sanctuary, the elite closed their eyes. As the economy worsened and food became more scarce, city dwellers pretended they still could turn things around. Though few knew much about the Khmer Rouge, many began to believe they would be the new salvation of the nation, especially when their exiled prince aligned himself with Saloth Sar.

Sihanouk could have remained in France. But he would not let his face be buried in the mud.[20] Shortly after the Lon Nol coup in 1970, the prince had accepted refuge in Peking—at great political and personal cost and compromise. Although Sihanouk had tracked the Khmer Rouge with such vengeance before, he now joined them against what he saw as a common enemy—the forces of Lon Nol. To give a face of respectability and trust to the Khmer Rouge, in 1975 he agreed to become the titular head of the government they imposed on "his children," the people of Cambodia. Saloth Sar, now the revolutionary Pol Pot, made certain Sihanouk had no power. But because of his presence in the government, many Khmer people gave credence to the new regime even while the actions of Khmer Rouge cadres confuted any cause for trust. Pol Pot's methods for creating his giant collective opened the people's eyes too late.

Life under Pol Pot

The boy, Chhuon, watched as people passed by his village in the north and others stopped. Neighbors' homes were bulging with people he had never seen before. One day a family of seven came to his house to stay. Since the house was not large, the family of his uncle Soeun Sieth was given the area under the house.

Before his relatives came, that space had offered Chhuon's family a cool retreat from the hot summer sun. There the family had been able to sleep in two stretched hammocks. In an additional small hammock, Chhuon had been able to rock his infant sister. Large black pots of nourishing food had simmered on raised rocks above the fire. Chickens, roosters, cats, and pigs had mingled seeking shelter.

Khmer Rouge soldiers had passed through the village, but the war had not touched their lives significantly until now. Chhuon's father, with his six buffalo, had cultivated a small piece of land in the village fields, about a mile from the house. Having planted this year's rice crop, he had daily tended the field. Chhuon had followed his father in every season. He loved the water buffalo and laughed when one of the large, strong animals rolled and stretched in the rice paddy waters. He especially liked the late afternoon during planting. He, his father, and a water buffalo—a different one each day—would go to the nearby canal. Taking the water buffalo into the brown water with them, he and his father rubbed and washed the animal with great tenderness. It was a lazy bath, deserved after a day in the fields. Peaceful and slow, life followed the seasons of planting, growing, and harvesting. There was always enough to eat.

Khmer Rouge soldiers had helped them and warned them that the Lon Nol regime would destroy them. The farmers were being taxed more and selling their rice for less. Feeding on their growing dissatisfaction, the Khmer Rouge promised them the riches enjoyed by the supporters of Lon Nol and the "pro-imperialist" Americans. The farmers listened to what the soldiers had to say.

However, as the villagers heard the stories of the people fleeing Phnom Penh, they began to be afraid. They listened in disbelief as the urban newcomers recounted the experience of evacuating Phnom Penh and of being forced from their homes and out onto the highways. They winced at tales of brutality and murder.

After the revolution life changed radically, heartlessly for Chhuon and others, even though they continued to work the same land as former generations.

Though his uncle had not worked in the fields since boyhood and the rest of his family never had, they now set their energies to this new task. Angka, with many eyes like a pineapple's skin,[21] became omnipresent, checking every aspect and movement of their lives. Some of the "old people," those who had always lived there and who had not resisted the advances of the Khmer

Rouge, were left alone. Others—who harbored relatives considered enemies of the nation—were not so fortunate.

There was an unequivocal distinction between "old people" and "new people." The former, mostly workers and peasants loyal to the Khmer Rouge, advanced the course and cause of the revolution. City people were almost always suspect and generally made subordinate to the "old people." "18 March people" had been there from the beginning. "17 April people" came under Khmer Rouge tutelage only after its victory.[22]

After Soeun Sieth and his family had lived in the village eight months, in one swift moment all the horror of Pol Pot's purge crashed down upon Chhuon and his little village. The day had been stifling in spite of the night rains. Chhuon had worked hard in the fields with his family in the full sun. Chhuon reminisced:

It felt nice to sit in a circle with my family in the evening breeze. My mother was cooking a chicken and a kettle of rice she had shucked and polished. We saw three soldiers, in the now familiar black trousers and shirts and wearing red checkered scarfs around their necks and black sandals made from tire rubber, go to our neighbor's house. Ton Pau pointed in our direction. The soldiers, each carrying an old AK-47 rifle, strode over to our circle. They were very young, two of them not more than fifteen. Their faces were blank, without life, emotionless. One of them pulled my mother from the fire's edge where she was cooking the chicken. They wanted my uncle and my father, but my mother did not know where they were. They threatened to kill all of us if she did not reveal their whereabouts. But she couldn't. She really did not know where they were.

The soldiers accused her of hiding them. They told her they were enemies of Angka, subversives who wanted to overthrow the Khmer Rouge for a government backed by the American imperialists. My mother continued to protest her ignorance. One slapped her face.

In front of my mother, my grandmother, my sisters, my aunt, my cousins, and me, they took my grandfather first. The soldier with a large scar on his face threw my grandfather to the earth and ordered him to kneel with his face to the ground. He was my mother's father. My grandmother, his wife, became hysterical, bowing in supplication, beseeching them to spare my grandfather's life. One of the soldier's slapped her face and knocked her over. The soldiers tied his hands behind his back. The youngest soldier raised an ax and brought it down very fast. He split open my grandfather's skull. One by one they killed my elder brother, a cousin, and another uncle in the same way. The bloody ax rose and fell three times more. Our screams and pleadings were without effect. The soldiers never showed a trace of emotion. We, too, learned to be silent and keep our feelings to ourselves. It was the only way to survive in Pol Pot time.

Not long after the killings, the Khmer Rouge took Chhuon from the surviving members of his family and sent him to a youth work camp. He never saw any member of his family again. Not one family, not one person, came out of those murderous years unscathed. Most have tales similar to Chhuon's.

With frenzied fierceness, Pol Pot coerced the nation into a radically and totally restructured Khmer society. It was to be a society of peasants, workers, and soldiers, all equal, utterly self-reliant, dependent on not a single outsider. Families were separated, breaking down the secure, vital core of Khmer society. Even if a husband and wife lived in the same shelter with their parents and children, they had little time together in the evening. They were so tired and malnourished, they had no energy to relate to each other. Monks were murdered; pagodas, desecrated and toppled; statues of Buddha, decapitated and shattered. Anything speaking to the Khmer soul was annihilated.

Cooperatives sprang up across the land. Unskilled people who had never built any structure before gathered wood and grass to piece together small lean-tos. Longer, open structures served for dining halls. Everyone rose before dawn and went directly to assigned work—always hard labor—digging irrigation canals, breaking rocks, felling trees, or planting and harvesting rice. Frequently, and especially as more draught animals died, men were harnessed to the plow with an ox, serving as the second beast of burden breaking ground for planting.

Fourteen- and fifteen-hour work days with few breaks were common. If the supervising soldier thought someone was not working hard enough, he would lash the back of the person until he drew blood. The food ration, two meals a day, never varied—a bowl of thin gruel and a few pieces of rice. The malnourished and overworked people changed visibly day by day. Skin clung to protruding bones; many died in the fields.

At first the laborers foraged for food—forest flora, insects, crabs in the rice paddies, mice in the fields. The one tea kettle allowed in a hut became the cooking kettle for everything. But soon harsh punishment was meted out to those who foraged—those who did not allow Angka alone to provide for them. They were accused of continuing in the privileged ways they lived before everyone became equal.

The one day a week free of hard labor was devoted to reeducation, as was almost every evening. In the same cadence night after night slogans were repeated over and over. "Long live the Cambodian revolution." "Trust Angka." Meetings closed with the Khmer Rouge anthem.

> Bright red blood which covers our fields and plains,
> Of Kampuchea, our motherland!
> Sublime blood of workers and peasants,
> Sublime blood of revolutionary men and women fighters!
> The Blood changing into unrelenting hatred
> And resolute struggle,
> On April 17th, under the flag of the Revolution,
> Free from Slavery![23]

Generally, it was midnight before the men and women were allowed to fall exhausted on their mats. Four hours later they began the same routine.

Pol Pot's genocide was against his own people, not a minority or outsiders. Between one and two million Khmer civilians died unnecessarily by outright murder and by malnutrition and unchecked disease, including malaria and dengue fever, common among those who worked in the mosquito-infested jungles. One of the worst killers of young and old was dysentery. No one had any reserves to resist it; there was no clean water to drink. People simply lay on the mats in their huts in anguish for days before succumbing to death. Others, desperate, chanced foraging for healing food for ill relatives, even though it meant dreadful punishment if caught. Tuberculosis ran rampant, untreated.

One of the cruelest sights for those who lived through those years was a soldier seizing a baby from its mother's arms and either throwing the infant in the air and shooting it or holding the child upside down and banging its head against a tree as the mother, held at bay by another soldier, became weak with overwhelming anguish. Disappearances occurred daily. One or two people, bound and led by soldiers wearing bandoleers of ammunition and carrying rifles, passed by the field workers, who in time rarely looked up. They knew they would never again see those taken deep into the forest. Some were shot. Some were bludgeoned to death after digging their own graves. Frequently the victims had been recognized and their backgrounds identified by someone in the cooperative, marking the individual for certain death. Perhaps the victim was a doctor, an intellectual, a teacher, a Lon Nol soldier — all considered enemies of the new order.

Phnom Penh remained empty except for Khmer Rouge cadres and their prisoners. The twenty thousand taken to Tuol Sleng Incarceration Center in the capital knew they would never emerge from behind its walls. The expansive grounds of Tuol Sleng, graced with ancient shade trees and broad, colonnaded verandas, had been part of a *lycee,* a peaceful seat of learning. Emptied that April day in 1975, its classrooms were filled with those classified as subversives—to be eliminated after confessing themselves traitors to the revolution. Prisoners, often so crowded they could only stand, were deprived of sanitary facilities, food, and light. Elaborate confessions extracted in the midst of medieval torture methods filled file after file. Documentation on every prisoner was meticulous and deliberate. Each was complete with a photo taken on entrance and a life history. At torture's end, many were led just beyond the city, ordered to dig their own mass grave, and bludgeoned, shot, or buried alive.

If any members of Chhuon's family survived, they lived the cruelly deprived and regimented life of the cooperative. Always guarded, intensely indoctrinated, never alone, they were stripped of every vestige of individuality and humanity.

Chhuon's life in a youth camp for boys was a horror of its own:

When I was taken from my village in 1976 along with other children, we walked for several days. I was not quite nine years old, and I had never been that distance from my home. Late one afternoon, we came to the edge of a forest and were told to build thatch huts. It was after dark when we finished. They were small, not well covered. I wanted to go to sleep immediately. That was not to be.

I learned very soon that any night we were not working under the moon and the stars, we formed a circle on the ground near the communal kitchen for education about Angka and the glories of the revolution. Over and over, night after night and year after year, we were told the power it gave to the people to become self-sufficient. Everyone had to be zealous in restructuring the society in the way Angka prescribed. No one was exempt from work. If anyone attempted to slacken work efforts or escape labor, the person received no ration. If we had any thoughts of running away from the watchful eye of Angka, we would die. Never question Angka's authority. It alone knows what is best for you.

After several hours, we were allowed to go to our huts. We had mosquito nets but nothing else. That first night we curled under the nets and fell asleep, exhausted from the long march and building our huts. Not for long, however, for we were awakened at four the next morning and told we would be going into the forest to work. All of Cambodia was to become rice fields. We would harness the water by digging irrigation canals. Cleared forests were to become new planting grounds.

The actual work of felling the trees went to the men. We boys carried logs to ox-carts driven by Khmer Rouge leaders. We cleared the forest floor, and we built roads leading out of the forest. Our tools were crude and few. Some had pickaxes and hoes for breaking and clearing the ground. Mostly we worked with our hands. We went deep into the forest and worked back toward our huts. Usually, we did not return from the forest for several weeks. We slept on the ground under the trees. If the moon was bright enough through the trees, we were forced to continue our work far into the night. Rarely were we given more to eat than some watery soup with a few grains of rice or corn. We foraged from the forest floor when we were safely out of sight of our custodian. We ate whatever we could find, especially at night when we worked since we were not so easy to spot.

I had not seen murders before my grandfather, uncle, and brothers were killed. Soon death became a common sight. Many fell sick and died. Some, exhausted, sank to the ground while clearing the forest floor. Sometimes the corpses were pulled away; often they were not. We stepped over the decomposing bodies and tried not to smell the rot. Sometimes we were ordered to dig mass graves and pull the dead into them and cover them. Others were ordered to go with a leader further into the forest. Often they were accused of stealing extra rice or failing to show up for work. Sometimes before they were taken, they were tortured in front of us or rolled in the mud, kicked, and spat upon. Our leaders wanted to show us what would happen if we failed to meet their expectations. Some of their pitiful cries for a speedy death rang in my ears for days. They could take the torture no longer. After they were led away, we never saw them again. I never became used to the death all around me. But I had learned to show no feeling, make no comments, ask no questions.

I became quite ill with malaria. I shivered from the fever. Because the forests were mosquito-infested, few escaped bouts of malaria. Even when we were very sick, rarely were we able to stay away from work. Most of the deaths among us were due to malaria or dysentery. During one period, I became so weakened from dysentery, I thought I was going to die. I almost wanted to die. Something pulled me back to life.

The months and the years passed by. We were moved many times. Sometimes we had completed a road or a project. Often we were instructed to leave the work we had begun before it was half-finished. I quit trying to figure out why the Khmer Rouge did what they did. All I knew is that if I wanted to live, I had to obey.

During the dry season of 1978, some of our leaders began to disappear. New leaders came in. Someone told us that they had been taken into the forest like so many others, tortured, and shot or bludgeoned. Some had their heads split open with a pickax, the same as my grandfather, uncle, and brothers. Then they were buried in shallow mass graves. The Khmer Rouge purges of their own had come to our area, just as they had to others. Later I was to learn that many in the eastern zone had escaped to Vietnam. Among them were some cadres who defected to the Vietnamese and would return with them later to run Pol Pot out of Cambodia.

Our new leaders kept pushing us toward the mountains. More and more groups converged from other areas. Everything seemed in disarray. Sometimes we would stop for days in one place and were told to work just as we always had. We were told to begin building a new road or cutting down trees. Nothing made sense until one day we heard artillery fire very close. Someone had told me days earlier that he heard the Vietnamese were near, but I could not believe him. Now I did. I wanted to run to them, run from the life I had been leading for the last four years. I thought life under them could not be as bad as it had been under the Khmer Rouge. But I was never able to escape, to slip away from my overseer. We marched in well-guarded lines on our way to work. We were always under the same strict supervision.

One day we quit going to fell the trees. The black-shirted Khmer Rouge cadre pushed us forward, toward the mountains that border Thailand. Artillery fire came closer daily. Sometimes we dove to the ground if we were caught in the cross-fire. Many of us wanted to run to the Vietnamese, but the soldiers in their black uniforms, short bobbed hair, and black caps gathered more and more of us together. We were emaciated from lack of food, sick and exhausted. Most of us were so thin that our skin was taut against our protruding bones. Now we were each on our own to forage for what food we could as we were pushed along in the forest toward the mountains. It was no longer possible to stop for rations. We pushed ahead day and night with little time for rest. We tripped over the bodies of hundreds of dead people.

We remained in the grip of the retreating Khmer Rouge through the forests, across the mountains until we reached Thailand. Because of our numbers and because of our skeletal appearances, the Khmer Rouge, masquerading respectability, received pity and assistance from a world that had no idea of the full horror of Pol Pot time. I was not out of their clutches yet. My reach for freedom would not come for two more years when I escaped to the KPNLF[24] area of the border where I engaged in smuggling goods between Thailand and Cambodia.

For four more years we were moved back and forth across the border. During dry-season offensives we were driven into Thailand. We returned to camps just inside Cambodia when the offensives ended—usually with the coming of the rainy season.[25] In 1985 we crossed the border into Thailand permanently and still live here in refugee camps.

Although I was no longer held hostage by the Khmer Rouge, I, and all Cambodians who amassed at the border, became hostages of another sort. Whether we liked it or not, we were controlled by one of the three Cambodian factions—the KPNLF, Khmer Rouge, or Sihanoukist—that formed to oppose the Vietnamese-backed government that captured Phnom Penh. We were controlled, too, by those who provided weapons to the factions and to Phnom Penh.

War followed us even as we ran from it. In the camps we remain in a war zone. The fighting is very close to us—not more than a mile or two away. I have not known safety since long ago when I was a small child in our village in Siem Reap Province.[26]

Shelling of a Khmer Rouge-controlled camp (Site 8). Women have taken their sick children from the hospital and are fleeing into bomb shelters.

2

Closed In

*We have . . . thrown life-belts to the drowning,
but left them in the sea.*
— *Angier Biddle Duke,
former U.S. Ambassador*

"It was culturally crazy on all social, political, psychological and spiritual levels to maintain an entire community in a state of perpetual limbo," mused a Khmer Buddhist monk on the fate of his people, following their flight from Cambodia when the Khmer Rouge were defeated in 1979 and the Vietnamese-backed government of Heng Samrin was installed.[1]

"I myself feel like a frog in a well. We cannot jump out of the well, and we can see only the walls of the well," reflected a Khmer poet who lived in Site 2 refugee camp on the Thai-Cambodian border.[2]

A woman who for more than a decade worked along the Thai-Cambodian border, where hundreds of thousands of Khmer sought refuge, likened their life at the the border to the cries of a deaf mute.

Although tragic events are a daily occurrence in the border encampments along the Thai-Cambodian border, I was deeply struck by one story . . . which I feel is symbolic of the present day situation on the border. In January [1989] . . . , the corpse of a young Khmer woman was found buried on the edge of Site 2 camp. She had been brutally axed to death. Looking around the area where she had been found, it was obvious that a violent struggle had taken place; yet no one had heard any cries for help. The reason for this became painfully clear when the woman was identified by her relatives—for she was deaf and mute. No one had been able to hear her silent screams for help. Personally, I see this as a graphic reflection of the tragic plight of the Khmer at the border, for many of them would like to escape the situation they are presently in—whether it be to flee Khmer Rouge camps with their well-documented record of human rights abuses; or the shellings at Site 2 and Site 8 camps which resulted not only in many casualties but also in creating an atmosphere of constant fear of the terror which rains from the sky without warning; or the domestic violence in Site 2—a camp described by the former Director of UNBRO [United Nations Border Relief Operation], Mr. Y.Y. Kim, as "a time bomb on a short fuse" (August, 1987). The International Community has a responsibility not only to be aware of the concerns and fears of the large majority of Khmer on the border who have no real voice, but also to actively pursue solutions to ensure the protection of their basic human rights.[3]

OVERVIEW

Three hundred and fifty thousand Khmer who fled their nation have been imprisoned behind barbed-wire in camps along the Thai-Cambodian border. They have been variously called "a community of confinement,"[4] a "dark village,"[5] a people "just waiting to die"[6]—each appellation correct. Most appropriately, they have been labeled "political pawns,"[7] hostages in a global conflict they are powerless to resolve.

Behind doors closed to the rest of the world, between 1975 and 1979 the Khmer Rouge committed monstrous atrocities against their own people and put their nation on the edge of extinction. Shortly after the Vietnam invasion of Cambodia on Christmas Day in 1978 and the installation of the Vietnamese-backed government in early January 1979, the doors of the nation opened again as retreating Khmer Rouge and wasted civilians pushed against it to get out. People of other nations were horrified, disbelieving pictures of the almost skeletal remains that tumbled over the border. A nation had survived death.

Unwittingly Pol Pot had given the Vietnamese the resources they needed for a successful invasion—some of his own leaders. Whenever Pol Pot became rankled over things not going his way, whether it was a poor rice crop or loss in battle, he purged his own troops and villagers. In 1977 and 1978, as the Vietnamese made more forays into Cambodian border areas, Pol Pot unleashed his anger on troops and civilians in the eastern zone of Cambodia because they had not obliterated the Vietnamese invaders. Whole villages and troop contingents were massacred by Pol Pot forces from the center zone. Heng Samrin, head of the Khmer Rouge Eastern Zone's Fourth Division, and a host of other eastern-zone Khmer Rouge asked the Vietnamese for help and received it. Given asylum across the border, they defected to the Vietnamese army that was preparing a major movement into Cambodia to topple Pol Pot.[8] Heng Samrin and Hun Sen, two Khmer Rouge defectors, would lead Cambodia first through a Vietnamese-backed government and then, following the Vietnamese troop withdrawal in 1989, in a purely Khmer government.

Inside the still sealed doors of Cambodia, after the Vietnamese invasion, the Khmer Rouge starved to death as their food and medical supplies dwindled to nothing and were forced toward the mountainous northwestern area. As they escaped to the western part of Cambodia, the Khmer Rouge forced hundreds of thousands of citizens, too emaciated, tired, and ill to resist, to move with them toward the border with Thailand. They marched through dank, malaria-infested jungles and across mountainous terrain. Many died on the way, their bodies simply left to the elements. Among them were people who in 1975 had been marched out of the cities into the countryside to make a new Democratic Kampuchea of workers, peasants, and soldiers. Pol Pot had failed miserably as a leader, starving, killing, and brutalizing between one and two million of the seven million he governed with villainous force and laying waste a once fruitful land. Now with its cortege of skeletal survivors, the Khmer Rouge would be the first to receive world attention and an outpouring of assistance.

When the Khmer Rouge first fled across the border mountains into Thailand, it was a defeated, rag-tag group, despised and feared by the people it had controlled during the four years of the killing fields. Most of the women, children, and old men who came with the Khmer Rouge would not have chosen to do so had they not been sick and hungry and too weak to resist. Others just trying to save their lives went with anyone who was crossing to the other side. There was not a loyal following of any significance.

In 1979 when the Vietnamese ousted the Khmer Rouge, the international community did not recognize the newly installed Phnom Penh government of Heng Samrin. Instead, Pol Pot, in exile in Thailand, was given the U.N. seat for Cambodia. In 1982 a coalition government was formed by the Khmer Rouge and the two non-communist factions—the Khmer People's Liberation Front (KPNLF), led by former Prime Minister Son Sann, and the Sihanouk faction, the National United Front for the Independent, Neutral, Peaceful, and Cooperative Cambodia (FUNCINPEC). Chinese assistance enabled the Khmer Rouge to rebuild its forces and become militarily the strongest among the three factions. The coalition did not alter the reality of the Khmer Rouge strength. Neither Prince Sihanouk, the nominal head of the coalition, nor Son Sann could overshadow Pol Pot's influence, even a Pol Pot who stood in the wings and let Khieu Samphan take the spotlight. Sihanouk and Son Sann lent respectability to the Khmer Rouge.

On the international scene, the world powers had their own agendas, generally aligning against the Vietnamese. The Chinese government, fearing a strong Vietnam on its soft underbelly, particularly a Vietnam that had "defeated" the United States, lavished the Khmer Rouge with military assistance. Knowing Vietnam's historical aspirations to be the controlling country in a Southeast Asian federation, China took no chances. Vietnam turned to the Soviet Union. As for the United States: U.S. relations with China were flowering, while the United States and the Soviet Union were turning cold shoulders to each other. The United States, having met defeat at the hands of the Vietnamese, was loathe to recognize Vietnam's puppet government as the legitimate regime of Cambodia. Another influencing country that feared or loathed a strong Vietnam was Thailand, where the exhausted Khmer civilians asked for asylum. For these three powers, the refugees became a buffer on the Thai-Cambodian border to hold the Vietnamese from invading Thailand.

The refugees became hostages as well of the three Khmer factions that received military and humanitarian assistance from the powers that wanted to impede further Vietnamese aggression and weaken the Soviet Union. Without a population of "support," none of the factions had political or economic credibility or viability. Only Khmer civilians, who could neither leave camp nor choose one camp over another one, could provide the factions with the necessary populations. Because the Khmer factions on the border were recognized as the legitimate government-in-exile of Cambodia, international humanitarian organizations had limited influence or control in the camps.

The world closed its eyes while the Khmer Rouge became the strongarm of Cambodia's coalition government in exile. Foreign involvement and influence played a significant role in sustaining the fettered status of this refugee population on the border for more than a dozen years. The breakdown of the social fabric of Khmer society that began under the genocidal reign of Pol Pot continued unabated as more than 350,000 lived in closed camps behind barbed wire, incommunicado with the rest of the world. Their lives were put on hold in a debilitating dependency on the outside world for food, clothing, and shelter.

SEEKING REFUGE

Thai Attitude toward Khmer Refugees

The people of Thailand did not welcome the fleeing Khmer. Historic animosities ran deep. Approximately eighty thousand other refugees already lived on Thai soil and were not yet absorbed into the general Thai population. This group, which had received little or no outside support, included nearly eleven thousand Chinese supporters of Chiang Kai-shek who had fled from Mao's army in 1946. Then in 1954 after the French fall at Dien Bien Phu, nearly forty thousand Vietnamese fled to Thailand. In 1959, thirty thousand Burmese received sanctuary. The government of Thailand did not want another population of unassisted, permanent aliens entering the country. There were already 160,000 who had taken refuge in Thailand following the 1975 fall of Saigon, Phnom Penh, and Vientiane, albeit financed by the United Nations High Commissioner for Refugees (UNHCR).[9]

Although Thailand had been an oasis of peace during the tumultuous breakdown of French Indochina and the ensuing Vietnam War, its relations with its neighbors were far from cordial. Thailand, like Cambodia, Laos, and China, feared a strong Vietnam that would swallow its neighbors in a forced federation controlled by Vietnam. In 1978, as the United States licked its wounds of defeat, Vietnam, still feeling its prowess in victory, felt compelled to crush the Khmer Rouge forays into Vietnam. What, thought Thai officials, was to stop the Vietnamese from overrunning Thailand as well? If they let the Cambodians enter Thailand and find refuge inland from the border, Vietnamese troops might consider themselves justified in attacking Thailand. Better for Thailand would be for the Khmer people to continue their struggle against their invaders on their own side of the border. At least the fleeing Khmer could serve Thailand as a buffer for a time.

The Thai government had no qualms about keeping the Khmer from crossing the border into Thailand, for Thailand was not a signatory to either the United Nations 1951 Convention Relating to the Status of Refugees or to the subsequent 1967 Protocol broadening the definition of a refugee to encompass not only those caught in events occurring in Europe before January 1, 1951, but also in events occurring in subsequent years and beyond Europe. The Thai government did not accede to the definition of a refugee.[10]

Nor were Thai officials legally bound to observe the rule of *nonrefoulement* found in the 1951 Convention.

> No Contracting State shall expel or return (*"refouler"*) a refugee in any manner whatsoever to the frontiers of territories where his life or freedom would be threatened on account of his race, religion, nationality, membership of a particular social group or political opinion.[11]

As more and more Khmer pressed across the border during the first half of 1979, they were as unwelcome in Thailand as the Vietnamese boat people whom the Thais were pushing back. On June 10, 1979, Thai officials made a statement that ignited an outcry from every corner of the earth, for the action uprooted the very notion of the right to first asylum of those fleeing persecution. Between forty-three thousand and forty-five thousand Khmer people — men, women, and children — who were in crude, makeshift camps on the Thai side of the border and unaware of the fate that awaited them, were gathered by Thai military and escorted on one hundred ten buses to a remote, mountainous border area. Each person was apportioned a cup of rice before disembarking the buses — not enough for survival. At gunpoint they were led to the steep cliff near the temple of Preah Vihear and back into the country from which they had just fled for their lives. No matter their pleas and cries for mercy, all forty-five thousand were forced down the mine-infested slope toward the waiting Vietnamese-backed forces. There is no count of the number who perished either by mine explosions or gunfire, but they were in the thousands. Ten thousand is considered a conservative estimate.

Word of this event as well as pictures of "a walking concentration camp"[12] seeking safety in Thailand entered homes by television and newsprint throughout the world. On the screens a parade of people with haunted, sunken eyes, shallow cheeks, skinny legs, and skin taut across rib cages raised a clamor for assistance, and an outpouring of funds softened Thai resistance, once Thai officials understood they would not suffer the burden of this population alone. Still, Thai officials wanted any assistance given to be inside Cambodian borders. Relief could pass through Thailand.

On October 18, 1979, Thai Prime Minister General Kriangsak Chamanand visited the border. He was visibly shaken by the massive suffering of broken humanity he witnessed among the dense clusters of rootless Khmer. On October 22 the prime minister announced that within forty-eight hours UNHCR-financed temporary asylum would be given to these people; near the Thai border village of Sakaeo, a small, thirty-three acre abandoned rice farm, not nearly large enough for the forty thousand people who came, was set aside by the Thai government for a transient holding center. Thai officials no longer made the assurance of resettlement a precondition of allowing the Khmer onto Thai soil. Nevertheless, after the Preah Vihear pushback, Western nations, particularly the United States, France, and Australia, opened their doors to the fleeing thousands.

Pressure remained on Western nations to take more of the Southeast Asian refugees. Not only were Khmer spilling into Thailand, but Vietnamese boat people were also seeking asylum there as well as in Malaysia and Hong Kong. As many as sixty thousand Vietnamese left their homeland in a single month in 1979.

Although the shock and the horror of the condition of the border Khmer propelled Prime Minister Kriangsak into humanitarian action that has continued generously to this day, humanitarian concern was not his only motive for letting the people cross over onto Thai soil. His own national political and security agenda played a large part in his decision to let the Khmer in. Fearing the invading Vietnamese would not stop their northward march—through Cambodia and into Thailand—he needed the Khmer Rouge and the people they held to become a viable buffer. He also needed the Khmer people who had fled but who were not under Khmer Rouge control to build a fighting capability. Never mind that the ordinary civilians caught along the border became losing pawns in a global chess game that would last for more than a dozen years.[13]

First Humanitarian Assistance Offered to the Khmer People

Neither the UNHCR nor relief organizations already in Thailand were prepared to receive the first arrivals, but they did pull staff from other operations within Thailand to service the flood of newcomers. Embassies enlisted volunteers from their ranks and searched out others willing to lend assistance to the masses pouring into the hastily constructed Sakaeo camp.

As one volunteer rode to Sakaeo in a bus filled with other volunteers, she recalled a dream she had dreamt some months earlier in which she was walking down a dirt road lined with coffins of children. When she was assigned to the babies' tent in Sakaeo, her dream became a reality. During her first day there, forty-three people died. The first child in her care who died she wrapped in a towel donated by a Bangkok hotel.[14]

Erna Hendriekson, another volunteer, became a relief worker and stayed for many years among the Khmer. "In those first days after Sakaeo opened, I came to the camp on a bus that left from the Bangkok Intercontinental Hotel at six each morning and returned at six in the evening." She continued,

That bus was filled each day with people who had heard of the plight of the Khmer who were fleeing the invading Vietnamese. Some were tourists, others were from the embassies, others citizens of Bangkok. Forty thousand refugees came to Sakaeo and thousands died. People carried the dead in black hammocks on bamboo sticks. At sunset many small bodies wrapped in black were lined on the ground ready to go to the graves. Mass graves were dug daily, burying hundreds.

I remember well the sound of the spoon scraping an aluminum plate as a person tried to get the last piece of rice. Mothers with outstretched arms made a silent plea, "Take my baby."

We could not remain in the camp at night. Anyone on an IV had to be taken off at night. People died without it.

A few months later, in 1980 after Khao I Dang camp opened, a group of former Royal Cambodian Ballet dancers lived among the 140,000 in the camp. They began practicing daily and thought it would be good if they performed in Sakaeo and lightened the spirits of those who had been forced to go there by the fleeing Khmer Rouge.

The day eighty dancers went to Sakaeo there were dignitaries present from Bangkok. As the bus drove through the gate, the dancers were light-hearted, chatting and laughing. Suddenly the bus fell silent. They saw all the black clothes and said, as if in chorus, "The Khmer Rouge."

I said to them, "I can only sympathize with you. I cannot walk in your shoes. But I have one wish. That wish is that you would try not to bring up your own children hating anyone, not to sow the seed of hatred into the heart of a little child. Hold in disdain what they have done and still do, but keep hatred from your hearts."

When they performed, Sakaeo residents climbed on the limbs of trees and everywhere to see the old traditional program that had been banned by the Khmer Rouge.

They kept asking for more. The people in Sakaeo had prepared in wood some violins and other Khmer musical instruments as a token of thanks and asked the dancers to promise to come again. The atmosphere on the bus was very good as we returned to Khao I Dang. I think the dancers were very happy.

Supported by nothing more stable than sticks or branches, ubiquitous sheets of blue plastic provided by the UNHCR sheltered thousands who poured in each day. Nearby Thai villagers were recruited to construct rudimentary housing for the refugees. Because the bamboo and thatch open-air hospital was not ready for the sick who sought help, many were wrapped in blankets and placed on the ground. It was some time before the small cots were in place: thin, plywood mattresses covered with grass mats.

Although it was early in the rainy season, torrential rains poured those first days in the camp. Some of the Khmer were so weak, they could do nothing but lie in the water. Some died just as they reached the camp; others, afterwards, face down in the mud.[15]

A second UNHCR holding center was approved shortly after Sakaeo went into operation—this one for Khmer not under Khmer Rouge control. Eight miles inland from the border, Khao I Dang opened in December 1979 and offered a safer haven from the constant shelling from Vietnamese-backed troops on the border. Unlike Sakaeo, Khao I Dang was ready when the first residents arrived, with temporary housing erected on leveled ground. Unlike Sakaeo, which had only one doctor and three nurses during its first two days of operation, a hospital with adequate staff was ready to open.

In fact, an abundance of medical personnel came to the border. The tight-skinned, wasted children and adults shown on television brought a quick response from medical professionals. A generous outpouring of funds, more generous than most crises elicit, enabled UNHCR and relief organizations to provide staff and supplies. The Khmer, who had no medical attention for five years, now had far more than did the neighboring Thai villagers.

Because of the horrifying physical condition of many of the Khmer in those early days, more emphasis was placed on the medical condition of the population and not enough on other human needs. Viewed as helpless victims, little or nothing was expected or asked of the refugees, many of whom were capable of lending a hand or became so as they received food and shelter. With so many expatriate volunteers and with the magnitude of the crisis, the need of the Khmer to be a part of the rebuilding process was not recognized. A dependency syndrome was initiated from the beginning that over the years would wear down Khmer refugees' self-esteem and the ability for self-management so necessary to human development.

As Khao I Dang swelled to 150,000 Khmer refugees, the Thai government became worried that the camps would entice more Khmer to cross the border. The prime minister feared, too, that as the numbers swelled, Western countries that were resettling Southeast Asians would cease offering asylum. In that event, Thailand would once again be strapped with a large alien population it could neither afford to care for nor wanted. In January 1980 the prime minister officially closed Khao I Dang to newcomers and placed a force of rangers known as Task Force 80 along the border to prevent further entrance of those seeking asylum. No matter what their reasons for coming—escape from the life they had been forced to live under the Khmer Rouge, famine conditions, the hope of resettlement in the West, fear of the new Vietnamese communist regime, rumor that good medical treatment was available, those who arrived at the border after January 1980 had their hopes totally dashed, as they were barred from crossing and entering either Sakaeo or Khao I Dang.

Early Border Camps

With the border's closing, the multitudes did not return inland. Just across on the Cambodian side of the border, those who had fled with the hope of being rescued from the long nightmare pitched their meager possessions under a sea of blue plastic. Others—forced to a different part of the border by the Khmer Rouge and held tightly under their control—hoped at least for food. As many as 750,000, even one million, may have sought safety along the Thai-Cambodian border in the early years after the Vietnamese invasion of Cambodia.[16]

Early in 1980 the nature of the border began to be fashioned as it would remain for the subsequent twelve years. A way of life took shape, that is very different from the form of other refugee populations, particularly the Eritreans and the Afghans, also subjects of this book. In prison-like camps, first in makeshift villages inside Cambodia at the border with Thailand and later permanent border camps in Thailand, people continued to be controlled by forces not of their choosing. Dependent on others for everything, their lives were not their own. They did not travel more than a mile or two from the border, a virtual war zone. The omnipresent military, Cambodian, Vietnamese, and Thai, dictated where and how they would live. Although they were not shut off from and unheeded by an unaware world, as they were under the Khmer Rouge, still they remained incarcerated.

Though the UNHCR continued to service those in the holding centers in Thailand (from which more than 200,000 refugees were resettled in third countries), the more than 350,000 Khmer who remained on the border for more than a decade have never been "covered" by an official protective umbrella; the option of resettlement in a third country has never been offered.

The UNHCR has not been present among those known as the border people. The organization's mandate to seek "international protection" and "permanent solutions" for refugees has not been seen as extending to internally displaced persons (those on the Cambodian side of the border) or "illegal immigrants," as these Khmer entering Thailand after January 1980 are viewed by the Thai government.

Gradually, northern Cambodia was divided up by different Khmer factions. Northeast of Aranyaprathet, Thailand, Khmer warlords ruled the Cambodian border terrain—a plain with little water and few trees. During the 1970s they had set up a lucrative black market dealing in teak, gems, gold, silver, and other goods between Cambodia and Thailand. It was a dangerous business during the years the Khmer Rouge ruled Cambodia, but many warlords became wealthy and lived in great comfort—often on the far side of the plain, in Thailand. A number of these warlords had been undisciplined officers and soldiers in General Lon Nol's army, corrupt long before the general's overthrow by Pol Pot's Khmer Rouge forces. Thousands of fleeing Khmer who were not in the grip of the Khmer Rouge went to the trading areas of the warlords and set up crude living accommodations.

During 1980 these makeshift villages, among them Bon Sangae (Ampil), Nong Samet, Mak Mun, and Nong Chan, were controlled by the various warlords. Mak Mun camp, under the control of Van Saren, a soldier of low rank in Lon Nol's army, was the worst—a pig sty in the countryside with little concern for the basic needs of the people who came to live there. Nong Chan camp, with a warlord who appeared to have more concern for the people living under him, was at the other end of the spectrum. Kong Sileah, a former officer in the Cambodian navy, led the camp and separated civilians from the military.[17]

The United Nations International Children's Emergency Fund (UNICEF) and ICRC were the lead organizations attending to the food, shelter, and medical needs of this border population until 1981. The Thai border town of Aranyaprathet, on the main trade route between Cambodia and Thailand, became the center of relief operations for Khmer located in the area. In the days before Cambodia was closed off from the world by the Khmer Rouge, the town was a railway entrance into both Cambodian and Thai trade centers. As the bulk of the camps on the Cambodian side of the border lay just north and south of Aranyaprathet, this location gave relief workers easy access to the camps. The roads from the town to the makeshift villages were generally good — paved at least part of the way or newly bulldozed by the Thai army at the expense of UNICEF and ICRC. Housing and access to goods were certainly adequate in both Aranyaprathet and the smaller town of Taphraya, forty minutes farther north. But this was no peaceable kingdom.

Convoys of trucks filled with principally Thai-grown rice and water daily plied the roads between Aranyaprathet and the border, feeding the hundreds of thousands amassed there. It was not a pure and clean distribution. Early on the warlords and military officers present determined who would receive how much and on what conditions. The major part of the food and water distributed did, indeed, go to the people, but the Khmer in charge took more than their share and did with it what they willed. A number of the leaders became wealthy on rice trading. Some of the rice was repurchased by the World Food Program, which financed it in the first place.[18]

Such irregularities in the distribution of the food posed a dilemma for UNICEF and ICRC. It is a dilemma to this day for those handing out rations to the border population. Food given by relief agencies and meant for civilians fleeing persecution is never to be targeted for the military; giving food to combatants implies alignment with a particular warring faction. Here, with the military so intertwined with and exerting control over the civilian population, it became impossible for UNICEF and ICRC to separate the military out. The only recourse, it seemed, was to refuse to distribute food to any people along the border. But such an action would leave hundreds of thousands on the verge of starvation. Also, the principal donor nations and the host government, fearing the potential advance of Vietnamese forces, wanted a Khmer military presence, such as it was, on the border. Consequently, with eyes shut on the part of the organizations in charge of the food distribution, the trucks continued to roll and give out food indiscriminately.

Food was also distributed to another group of Khmer people. When Khmer still living within Cambodia learned food was available, many brought empty ox-carts from the interior hoping to fill them with rice that they had not been able to plant or harvest in 1979 and 1980 because of drought and the continued turmoil in the country following the Vietnamese invasion. Again, the

Thai government was willing for rice distribution to be launched from the Thai side of the border. What became known as the "land bridge" began to operate in December 1979 with Nong Chan the designated distribution point for those Khmer living under the control of the warlords. Rice, and later seeds for planting, were given to individuals who came asking for them. It will never be known how much they successfully carried home with them, nor will it ever be known whether or not those to whom it was given used it solely to feed their families. Just as the warlords sought a kickback in the encampments, so too did they exact payment from those who came seeking food. And, just as some of the rice was exchanged for other goods by the village recipients, rice was also traded by the people of the "land bridge." Most of the food, nevertheless, filled stomachs denied adequate nourishment during the Pol Pot years. There will always be a percentage of food donated for relief assistance that is not used as it was intended, but the stakes in lives in emergency situations, such as the one on the Thai-Cambodian border in 1980, overshadow the loss.

Phnom Chat served as the "land bridge" for the Khmer people under control of the Khmer Rouge. Although UNICEF and ICRC had no access to these areas, they allowed the unmonitored Thai military to distribute food to the more remote Khmer Rouge camps. UNICEF and ICRC knew the emaciated state of the people and put aside their qualms and fed a population in which, most likely, the Khmer Rouge military benefited most from the assistance. No doubt, the food nourished the army and those conscripted into its ranks by the Khmer Rouge.

As the people settled into the temporary non-Khmer Rouge makeshift villages, they needed and wanted more than the bare-basics supplied for them. During the Pol Pot years they had little more than a tea pot they could claim for their own, and when the Vietnamese army invaded and scattered the Khmer Rouge, people not forced to retreat with the Khmer Rouge simply ran for their lives. Blue plastic gave way to simple huts constructed out of available materials. They wanted pots and pans, soap, clothes, jewelry—all the things that are a part of normal living, whether necessities or luxuries, that had been denied to them during the Pol Pot years. Long-hidden gold, formerly banned, surfaced and became the medium of exchange as Thai traders crossed the border ladened with consumer goods. Those Khmer who came from the interior to take advantage of the "land bridge" food distribution returned to their villages with goods to sell at inflated prices, reviving an economy nonexistent for four years. The Khmer paid dearly for what they bought since the Thai traders generally charged more than the goods were worth and frequently cheated on the current exchange rate for gold.[19] But then the traders were heavily taxed by the warlords and later by the leaders of the resistance groups controlling that area.

The makeshift villages of the warlords had always attracted bandits and smugglers. The displaced Cambodians and their gold were not exempt prey, many losing what they had so carefully concealed during the Pol Pot years.

Others lost the bullion on their way to the border, particularly in later years. Bandits attacked in the mountains and the forests and forced the Khmer to give up any valuable possessions. The robbers made certain their captives hid nothing from them. Ordering male, female, old, and young to strip, they inspected the private parts of every individual. Often when a robber kicked a man, valuables tumbled out of him and fell to the ground. The women suffered not only the indignity of a thorough body search; many were brutally gang raped as well. In the years following the initial resettlement of some Khmer in third countries, more and more of Khmer were held for ransom by bandits who would not release them until relatives sent money.

Not only did the Khmer revive the market place. In the squalid, impermanent villages the people also opened schools and overtly reclaimed their Buddhist heritage. Teachers who survived slaughter by the Khmer Rouge and made it to the camps re-created a Khmer curriculum, albeit without paper, pens, or supplies at first. The people were hungry for education and religion. Since most of the monks had been killed in Democratic Kampuchea, few were in this area. But those who were began to train young men.

Following the routing of the Khmer Rouge from Cambodia, many Khmer returned to their home cities or villages searching for lost loved ones. Among the border population many embraced family members or neighbors long believed dead. Others grieved when they received confirmation that, indeed, the ones they sought had died of starvation, disease, or at the hands of Khmer Rouge soldiers.

Political Nature of the Border, Formation of Political Factions

A major issue to be decided was the political faction that would control the people who lived along the border and were not under Khmer Rouge control. The KPNLF, an anticommunist group, was led by the former Prime Minister Son Sann who had governed under Prince Norodom Sihanouk and later broke with the prince. When he returned to the Thai-Cambodian border in 1979, Son Sann gathered a small resistance force against the Khmer Rouge. (Even then old animosities lived, as Prince Sihanouk refused to see his former prime minister when both men were in New York that year.) Among the three factions—the Khmer Rouge, the Sihanoukist FUNCINPEC, and the KPNLF— that emerged along the border in resistance to the Vietnamese-backed government of Heng Samrin, the KPNLF eventually controlled the largest number of civilians.

Gradually the warlords and their moderately equipped armies were subsumed by KPNLF leaders as the makeshift villages were consolidated under their control. Displaying a non-communist unified front, the KPNLF and the Sihanoukists began receiving "nonlethal" aid from Western nations. A new border rule took shape, and the people, willingly or unwillingly, became "loyal" members of the faction—KPNLF, Khmer Rouge, or Sihanoukist— under whose thumb they lived.

From the beginning the defeated Khmer Rouge leadership was recognized by the world community as the legitimate government-in-exile of Cambodia. Despite the fact that the Khmer Rouge didn't control the largest segment of the population, outside governments believed that only the Khmer Rouge, among the various Khmer factions, could effectively muster the military strength to repulse the Vietnamese. The Khmer Rouge government that had committed so many atrocities among its people and violated every known human rights code was given the seat at the United Nations, thereby countenancing its legitimacy. Among the international political powers, the United States and China were particularly anxious to see the Vietnamese-backed government of Heng Samrin fall to a revitalized Khmer Rouge army. The United States, of course, did not approve of Khmer Rouge atrocities or the genocide carried out during the Khmer Rouge reign, but even more reprehensible to U.S. leaders were the expansionist Vietnamese designs. Vital military assistance flowed to the Khmer Rouge from the Chinese government with the approbation of the Thai government and the Western world.

China had aligned itself with the Khmer Rouge from the beginning. It was to China that Sihanouk fled when a coup by the U.S.-backed Lon Nol government had toppled Sihanouk. It was in China that Sihanouk agreed to become titular head of the Khmer Rouge to give it legitimacy among the Khmer people as well as the outside world, never mind that nineteen members of his family met their death at the hands of the Khmer Rouge. When the Khmer Rouge fled to the border in 1979, China supplied the bulk of the military aid and equipment necessary for rebuilding the defeated troops. Food and other material aid from outside sources, including the United States, put the Khmer Rouge once again on a solid footing.

Without the assistance and the support of the Thai government, all aid would have been for nothing. But because of the Thai government's own security interests, it cut a deal with China. If China agreed to stop assisting Thai communist insurgents, who had been gaining strength, Thailand would facilitate the flow of Chinese aid to the Khmer Rouge.

Formation of the Coalition Government of Democratic Kampuchea

In 1982 two bodies, the Coalition Government of Democratic Kampuchea (CGDK) and the United Nations Border Relief Operation (UNBRO), were created that would dictate the nature of the border. UNBRO replaced UNICEF and ICRC as the organization mandated to provide crisis relief for the border people. The CGDK was born as the member nations of the United Nations, propelled by the Association of Southeast Asian Nations (ASEAN), [20] conceded that it was reprehensible for the genocidal Khmer Rouge to be the sole and legitimate government of the Khmer people. Strategically, the powers of the world opposed to the Soviet-backed Vietnamese intervention in Cambodia wanted the revitalized military strength and discipline the Khmer Rouge could offer and the arms the Chinese were willing to provide, but they could ill afford to condone overtly the Khmer Rouge's blatant disregard for human rights both in the past in Cambodia and the present along the border. Just as Prince Sihanouk had given a moral face to the rule of the Khmer Rouge during the Pol Pot years, so would a united coalition government cover over the true power accorded the Khmer Rouge by virtue of its military superiority in resisting the Vietnamese army in Cambodia.

According to the "Declaration of the Formation of the Coalition Government of Democratic Kampuchea," signed in Kuala Lumpur, June 22, 1982, "His Royal Highness Samdech Norodom Sihanouk, His Excellency Mr. Son Sann and His Excellency Mr. Khieu Samphan . . . have agreed to form a Coalition Government of Democratic Kampuchea." Sihanouk of FUNCINPEC was given the presidency, while Khieu Samphan of the Khmer Rouge was appointed vice-president in charge of foreign affairs, and Son Sann of the KPNLF was designated prime minister. The stated purpose of the CGDK was "To mobilize all efforts in the common struggle to liberate Kampuchea from the Vietnamese aggressors with the view to restoring the Motherland as a sovereign and independent country," as well as to implement U.N. resolutions in regard to the newly formed member state of that international body.[21]

From the beginning the CGDK was a loose organization of three unfriendly factions distrustful of one another. They never developed a central organization or formulated a constitution. In fact, the CGDK declaration specifically states: "Each participating party in the Coalition Government of Democratic Kampuchea shall retain its own organization, political identity and freedom of action, including the right to receive and dispose of international aids specifically granted it . . . [the CGDK] shall have no right to take any decision infringing or restricting this autonomy."[22]

They had no land as a base for governance of a population, nor could they provide for their people. They, with those they governed, were totally dependent on outside aid for daily sustenance and shelter.

Since the United Nations recognized the coalition government as the lawful government of Cambodia, in the U.N. the CGDK spoke for the border people as well as for all the people in Cambodia. The coalition government based its legitimacy on the fact that each faction controlled a population. People under their control, in essence held hostage, were their only legitimating factor. In reality the CGDK was lawful only insofar as it was recognized and propped up by nations opposed to the Phnom Penh government. As a result of the diplomatic effort to create an exile government that the U.N. recognized, the international community maintained only a limited control in the border camps because a "legitimate" government "represented" the people.[23] If the populations of each faction were allowed to leave one faction for another or go to Khao I Dang or a neutral camp or even back to the interior of Cambodia, the credibility of the factions' legitimacy would be severely undermined; therefore, each faction, with the assistance of the Thai military and no protests from donor nations, maintained domination over the population under its control.

U.S. interest in recognizing first the Khmer Rouge and then the CGDK as the legitimate Cambodian government for the sake of condemning the Vietnamese-backed Phnom Penh government is replete with contradictions. The original U.S. rebuff of the June 1979 Thai pushback of forty-five thousand Khmer, and U.S. willingness to resettle them if Thailand agreed to give temporary asylum, gave way to the stronger political pull of holding the Vietnamese at bay. When the Thais determined that the border population was not to be recognized as refugees, was not to be given the option of resettlement, and was to be kept in closed camps close to the border, virtually in a war zone, the U.S. government acquiesced because any further depletion of the border population would be a drain on the human and military resources the various factions of the CGDK needed to buffer and defend the border against Vietnamese military advancement.

Under the guise of the CGDK, the U.S. government and other nations opposed to Vietnam's incursion into Cambodia allowed this century's worst butcher, Pol Pot and his Khmer Rouge, to receive humanitarian assistance. Court Robinson of the U.S. Committee for Refugees argues that in condoning and rationalizing the assistance as a necessity to drive out the presumably worse Vietnamese, the U.S. government "hopelessly polluted our humanitarian stance. We were trapped and the rhetoric became the reality in the camps whereby we argued that no matter our stance on Cambodia, the border population should not be deprived of humanitarian aid." While the United States provided aid for political purposes, it persuaded itself that it was involved in a humanitarian undertaking on the border.

The United States, then, became the enemy to the Khmer people by allowing the Khmer Rouge to rebuild its strength and become a threat to the Cambodian nation. The United States continued to exacerbate the situation on the border because it continued its non-lethal funding to the coalition government and did not alter its policy toward Vietnam. Fear that the Khmer Rouge could take over Cambodia again permeated the border Khmer civilians.[24]

Within the camps the U.N.-recognized exile government limited the control the international community could exert on assistance designated for the civilian population. Seeing the Khmer border population as displaced people under the care and administration of a U.N.-recognized legitimate government became a convenient cover for the United States and the rest of the world to hide behind; it allowed them to simply ignore camp policies imposed by the various factions on their populations. Ignoring Khmer Rouge infractions of human rights became an unpleasant kind of necessity so long as the Vietnamese retained control of Cambodia. "In effect, the enemy of the U.S. enemy became a U.S. friend. U.S. recognition of the Khmer Rouge, in fact, made it the enemy of the border people, even though it inundated the border with humanitarian assistance."[25]

On one hand, it was U.S. policy to condemn the Vietnamese occupation of Cambodia and to resettle the Khmer on humanitarian grounds because of the abuse they suffered under the Khmer Rouge. On the other hand, it was to U.S. advantage to keep the Khmer on the border to serve as a buffer against the Vietnamese and to maintain the stalemate created by the CGDK and the Vietnamese army in Cambodia. Until 1990 there was never any serious effort on the part of the U.S. government to interrupt this stalemate.[26] The CGDK, including within it the Khmer Rouge, continued to exist in large measure because the U.S. government sanctioned its seat in the United Nations until 1990. There was no outcry that the Khmer Rouge was a threat with a potential for taking over the country again, since militarily and in discipline they were the strongest force in the CGDK. Indignation that should have boiled over in 1980 did not surface until 1990 when it was politically in U.S. interests. The refugees were never a pressing factor in U.S. Southeast Asian policy.

The refugee population had been put into a political context whether or not it chose to be. None of the three resistance factions was ever willing to abandon any of its political weight by allowing its people the freedom to choose where and with whom they would live on the border or inside Cambodia. Never were the people given a chance to say they ran because of persecution, starvation, war, or because they did not want to join a resistance. They were not given the option of a neutral camp where they could be provided with food, shelter, and medical care until such time as they could repatriate. All the people who amassed along the border, either in Cambodia or Thailand, were simply handed over like captives to the Khmer Rouge, KPNLF, or FUNCINPEC.

Khmer civilians who fled to the border did not do so for political reasons; they left in order to survive and escape from the Khmer Rouge and an impending famine in a decimated country. They had no seeds; they had no property; they had no security in Cambodia. From the beginning of the border situation, the Khmer who fled had to join one of the resistance groups, determined principally by geography. The border population was cut off. They could not return to Cambodia and they could not move farther into Thailand to seek refugee status.[27]

Although a person fleeing almost any other country in the world can petition the UNHCR to be considered a refugee, those fleeing Cambodia after 1980 did not have this option because they were the population base of the U.N.-recognized government of the CGDK. Only if they attempted a perilous, life-threatening escape from a border camp to Khao I Dang, the camp within Thailand, did they ever have the slightest hope. And that hope came to fruition only after living clandestinely for months or years, sometimes burrowing a hole below another refugee hut to hide from authorities. They had no status in Khao I Dang, not even a ration card. Over the years from time to time, amnesty was declared for those illegally in the camp and a ration card was granted, and a few were able to become legal refugees.

United Nations Border Relief Operation

In 1982, the same year the CGDK was formed and recognized, a new U.N. program, UNBRO, was organized specifically to attend to the border Khmer population. With a mandate to provide crisis relief for basic physical needs, UNBRO also supplied material assistance and technical support to Khmer-managed activities such as primary education, adult literacy, and self-reliance programs. The organization also coordinated and funded services provided by the NGOs.[28] Like the UNHCR when it was founded more than forty years earlier, UNBRO was intended to have a short life. When it was formed, no one believed the border population would remain in existence for more than a dozen years—one or two years, yes, but never beyond a decade.

Because the border operation was considered a temporary emergency situation and because of political reasons, UNBRO yielded much of its influence to individual Khmer administrators in the various factions who took on the actual distribution of food that flowed into and through UNBRO. The people who received the food understood that it was attached somehow to UNBRO, but that it was the administrators who really negotiated for and provided the food. Consequently, the various factions were strengthened by the fact that in controlling the food they controlled the population. From early on, the administrators were not held strictly accountable either to UNBRO or to the people, leaving the door open for corruption and exploitation. UNBRO found itself politically weightless.

Although founded as a neutral program to serve the emergency needs of a civilian population displaced within its homeland, UNBRO could not be a bearer of pure humanitarian aid, nor can any assistance organization working with populations fleeing occupying forces. Inevitably, a resistance force that is mixed among a refugee population will also benefit from the aid given. Although the military presence and control were blatant in the early Khmer situation, most civilian refugee populations around the world are under the influence of resistance military forces. This is certainly true of the Afghans and the Eritreans. The host governments have a keen interest in either staving off the invading power or in keeping at bay an antagonistic government.

To complicate matters, UNBRO, the assistance organization, was a creation of the United Nations. Beholden to the larger U.N. body, UNBRO was an instrument of the international political powers that recognized the coalition government as the rightful government of Cambodia. UNBRO's service to the border Khmer depended on outside decisions of nations with their own strategic interests in Southeast Asia. In addition, UNBRO like UNICEF and ICRC had no access to the three Khmer Rouge camps along the border southeast of Aranyaprathet—Phnom Chhat, Nong Pru, and Ta Prik—where the vast majority of the Khmer Rouge hostage population lived. The Khmer Rouge allowed access only to the Thai military.

Conflict on the Border—Dry Season Shelling

Like the Khmer Rouge forces, the numbers swelled within the other two border resistance forces as more refugees opposed the Vietnamese-backed Phnom Penh government. During the rule of the warlords in 1979 and until the refugees crossed permanently into Thailand in 1984–85, the border and the Cambodian interior remained rather fluid. Border Khmer in the camps would move back into the interior in periods they felt were safe, perhaps to plant rice or trade, and then return to the border as circumstances permitted. The stronger the resistance groups became, the more control they exerted over the civilian populations that were now mixed indistinguishably with the military. Leaders of the resistance groups began to curtail the movement of the population as the civilians became more important in giving legitimacy to each faction as well as providing the military with a source of food and medical assistance. Even some who returned to the border from Khao I Dang camp inside Thailand for the purpose of repatriating to Cambodia ended up in the camps and were permitted to go no further into the Cambodian interior. They were forced to remain in the camps.[29]

From the beginning in 1979 the border was a war zone where no one was safe. Because civilians and military personnel were mixed together, the Vietnamese saw the camps as fair game for shelling. Each year the fighting became most intense in what was referred to as dry-season shelling, between mid-October and May or June, when the monsoon rains once again made the northern jungles of Cambodia practically impassable for troops or tanks.

Once the shelling began, fear among the camp populations became palpable. This was a yearly event to which the people adapted. During the rainy season, muddy and slippery though the ground might be, the people situated themselves as normally as they could. At the approach of the dry season, they dug bunkers beside their homes, slept in their clothes, and wrapped their sparse possessions in a *kroma* (checkered woven scarf) and hung it on a bamboo pole, ready for flight. Camp services were cut to a minimum. Relief personnel had limited access, with the United Nations regulating who, when, and how workers could enter the camps. All nonessentials, including education and training programs, ceased. Teachers in a nine-month training program for Khmer medics, for example, could not enter the camps to teach.

Rebecca Parks, who went to the border with the American Refugee Committee in 1980 as medical coordinator and then as director, reflected in 1984:

> Five years out from the start of this relief situation, we are involved in a strange hybrid of "emergency" and "development." A child who was born in Nong Samet in 1979 is now five years old. Normally he should be offered school, literacy, and socialization. Personal and institutional role models should have already shaped his preschool years, laying the crucial foundation for the good "citizen of the world" he has the right to become. Despite every humanitarian effort, where are the appropri-

ate role models in a Khmer border refugee camp? Long-term development programs proceed within situational constraints during the rainy season— schools, women's associations, public-health campaigns. They are all interrupted with the first shell that signals the start of the dry season. Annually, and now semi-annually, our illusions of participating in the normal development of the Khmer people are shattered as we are forced to drop all "nonessential" programs and switch back to the emergency, life-and-death mode of the dry season. What about the Khmer "citizens of the world" we were developing? For now they must wait, sleepless at night, packed to leave for an evacuation site. "World citizen" development cannot continue until the rains start and the fighting stops.[30]

When the shells began to fall, people ran the three kilometers to the tank ditch, built to prevent Vietnamese tanks from entering Thailand quickly. The tank ditch straddled the Thai-Cambodian border such as it was—a mixture of an empty river basin, creeks, and canals. As they ran the Khmer sometimes saw a bone protruding from the grass or a lifeless, shattered body, clear warning to divert their path away from what was certainly a minefield. They waited at the border in hopes that the Thai military would allow them to cross in safety to temporary evacuation sites. Such displaced Khmer would remain in Thailand until the rains began. Rarely were they able to return to the exact location from which they had fled. Not only did the Vietnamese forces obliterate all structures, but they also mined the campsites, making it impossible for the former population to return. Sometimes the Vietnamese did not destroy a camp site and the people returned and stayed until the next shelling. But every year, sometimes several times during the course of the year, the people were bounced around like mailed parcels.[31] They ran with everything they had on the end of a bamboo pole, a child in one hand, another in a rag on its mother's back. Between 1982 and the 1984–85 Vietnamese offensive that pushed the Khmer permanently into Thailand, ICRC and UNBRO facilitated no fewer than eighty-five camp evacuations, sixty-five of them under shelling.[32]

At every new site, U.N. blue plastic covered the area until the people built their own temporary shelters. As the violence of war became more and more a reality of everyday life for the Khmer, instruments of war became common in the camps. There were no controls set for possession of powerful weapons among the civilians, half of whom were children. Practically every young man had a gun, many being new AK-47 assault rifles. The number of civilian gun wounds multiplied.

Whenever any of the border hospitals and clinics were destroyed, they would have to be rebuilt and resupplied. The hospitals filled with not only TB patients, dehydrated children, respiratory and malaria cases, or pregnancy complications, but also mine victims. "One thing was so common we termed it the Nong Samet syndrome," recalls Dr. Louis Braile, better known along the border as "Papa" Louis. By 1990 he had served ten tours along the border with the American Refugee Committee (ARC).

It meant that a mine injury victim was being brought into the hospital. Almost routinely the Nong Samet syndrome consisted of the patient being a young male. He would have been out in the territory just beyond the barbed wire. In most cases it seemed to be for an insignificant reason. He might be gathering wood so that his wife could cook dinner. He might be out there gathering mushrooms to eat. Conceivably, he might be out there as a part of a smuggling operation.

A syndrome is not a disease; it is a cluster of symptoms. So the Nong Samet syndrome was this young male with one leg blown off and in shock. This young male would have the misfortune of stepping on a mine. Then the explosion would occur. If someone were with him, that person would attempt to carry the victim in. Usually some place along the way a crude ambulance—extremely narrow with a hot tin roof—would pick up the victim. He would arrive at Nong Samet in shock; the litter—the canvas—would be blood-soaked with blood dripping on the ground as they carried the person. The Cambodian medics would work to stop the bleeding, put a sterile dressing over the wounds, give pain medicine, put the victim in an ambulance, and send him to the ICRC hospital in Khao I Dang. I've stood there many times watching the Cambodian medics treat these young people, and I always think how hopeless and unnecessary all this is. Bob Maat, a Jesuit brother and physician's assistant on the border, tells of a saying the people have: "You will know the Cambodian of the future for he or she has but one leg."

Medicine on the border is always a challenge. The practice of medicine is dramatically different here than in the United States. On the border, medical teams are reduced to the practice of medicine as it was fifty to one hundred years ago in the United States. Take a case of pneumonia—you take a history and you look. It takes listening, feeling, smelling, and all the rest of the senses to make a diagnosis. We did not come to build a Johns Hopkins or a Mayo Clinic along the border. It is just not that caliber of medicine that can be practiced here.

There are many situations along the border that demand additional services. When gastrointestinal disease with dehydration runs through a crowd, there is pressure for huge supplies of intravenous fluids. When the hospital receives several wounded at a time, everyone is involved in stabilizing and arranging transportation to the hospital in Khao I Dang. The state of the morale of the Khmer staff has a great effect on the practice of medicine on the border.

The medical staff had demanding jobs in the hospital, and they also had to maintain their lives and the lives of their families in very difficult circumstances. They were always surrounded by warfare and deadly disease. It was almost routine to hear artillery and small arms fire every day. Both Khmer and Western staff accepted that as the way it was. The Khmer sometimes would have information we did not have. The best sign that the Khmer medics had word that things were going to get bad again was when they brought their textbooks from their homes to the hospital and asked us to keep them in Aranyaprathet for them.

Two ideas come to my mind as descriptive of life along the border. One is that the unexpected was always to be expected. The other was the intensity of life along the border.

I cannot exaggerate the importance of the education department in the ARC program. Early on, ARC people tried their best to treat the hordes of wounded people. But they soon recognized that a small group, twenty at the most and not all of whom were physicians and nurses, could not treat all the sick people. The organization saw it needed help from the Cambodian society itself. The first step was to find Cambodians who could speak some English—ideally English speaking with some medical background as well. Such a combination was almost impossible to find. I heard only once of a Khmer doctor in the camp. The majority of Khmer physicians were killed under Pol Pot; those who survived were given asylum in a third country.

ARC began to teach those chosen basic medical care and procedures—how to take temperatures, blood pressure, and the like. Through training, they became health workers, then nurses, and finally medics. The training became more sophisticated as the years went on. By 1984 the Khmer medics had become quite capable on their own to treat diseases—especially tropical diseases they were used to. If I got malaria when I was there, I wouldn't fool around with our Western doctors. I would go to one of the Khmer medics.

Over time there was a change in what the Western staff was committed to do. The early total hands-on care gradually gave way to a Western staff in the role of teacher, advisor, and encourager.

PERMANENT MOVE OF CAMPS TO THAILAND

Medicine was practiced on the fly along the border until the 1984–85 dry season Christmas offensive. Refugees in the camps anticipated another seasonal upheaval, but not permanent relocation in Thailand. According to Brother Bob Maat, S.J., a physician's assistant at the time with the American Refugee Committee, Christmas Eve was a routine day in the TB clinic in Nong Samet: 114 patients coming for TB treatment—four were inpatients.[33] As coordinator, against all odds, Bob had worked to establish a TB treatment program that each patient could see to completion, thereby curtailing some of the TB that ran rampant among the border population.

The Vietnamese had a propensity for shelling very early in the morning, and Christmas Day, 1984 was no exception. To paraphrase Brother Bob Maat's story, Soth Sour, a clinic patient who was also a night guard and health worker, heard tank movement as early as 3:00 A.M. and shelling by 5:30 A.M. Camp residents were already on the roads leading out of the camp. They carried what they could and led some chickens and pigs as they crowded the evacuation route.

Soth Sour was in a dilemma. An elderly man, Loung Boy, with his only daughter, Khoum, had come to the clinic to seek treatment; he might have had lung cancer in addition to or instead of TB, and his respiratory functioning was severely depressed. That morning Loung Boy's daughter had already gone to the fields to gather grass. They could wait no longer for her return. Soth Sour, who was weak himself, tried to assist Loung Boy, until the elderly gentleman insisted he be left in the ditch in front of the TB clinic so that Soth Sour could go attend to his own family.

Reluctantly Sour did Boy's bidding and hoped the old man's daughter would be able to get back to the hospital area to rescue her father. Later that day at the tank ditch Sour met Khoum, who had not been able to return to the clinic. With many tears Sour and Khoum gave the father up for dead. Life was like that along the border. As the two watched with the other sixty thousand evacuees the bamboo and thatch of Samet burn in bursts of shelling, they hoped Boy had died before he burned.

But one of the rare miracles in war took place. The fire had not touched Loung Boy as he lay in the ditch Christmas Day. When the shelling quieted in the early evening, he made his way to the main hospital in the camp where people still lingered. Two days after Christmas, he was transported to the temporary TB clinic site in the new camp location of Red Hill just inside the Thai border. There daughter and father were reunited.

Exactly two months later in the early evening just after Khoum had bathed him, Loung Boy died peacefully and alone, Khoum having left her father long enough to bathe herself.

In Thailand no one felt safe under the blue plastic shelter spread at Red Hill. The dry dusty plain where the camp was located was vulnerable to the heavy shelling that continued for days following the border people's final evacuation into Thailand. This time the Vietnamese did not retreat; the troops secured the border by mining it heavily and burning every vestige of the camp sites.

Four weeks after they had crossed over into Thailand seeking safety, the Thai military ordered the sixty thousand people who had fled to Red Hill from Nong Samet to move again. As part of the preparation for the move, four expatriate nurses bagged water into two thousand plastic bags before the water ran out. Water in the border camps on the plain would remain a precious commodity.

Father Pierre Ceyrac knew how precious water was. Ampil camp was hit a few days after Nong Samet that Christmas week. When the people of Ampil crossed the border on December 31, 1984, and January 1, 1985, they had no water cans for distributing water. Father Pierre went to a shopkeeper he knew in Aranyaprathet and told the proprietor he needed five thousand jerry cans one day and four thousand more the following day. Dumbfounded at the number, the shopkeeper told Father Pierre he might have two or three hundred, but never nine thousand cans. Father Pierre does not know how the man gathered the nine thousand requested cans, but he did and the people had water.

The new location of Bang Poo was certainly safer than Red Hill as it was on the northern edge of Khao I Dang, eight miles inside the Thai border. But what the Khmer gained in safety, they lost in freedom. Bob Maat recalls:

> The move, 10 kilometers from the border, to a double-barbed-wired, moat-surrounded camp with a Thai protectorate of 400 soldiers, seemed to change everything. Surely Bang Poo was a safer haven from the enemies and robbers alike, but it also meant losses. Dependency, the curse of Khao I Dang, was a clear danger; dependency on the Thais, Thai government, Thai guards; dependency on the *Barangs* [foreigners], UNBRO, the Volags [voluntary agencies]. Not that they were ever really free in Samet, but at least the pretense of freedom was easier to believe in, even if it was false.[34]

Life in the KPNLF Camps: Site 2

This was not to be the last move for the border people. The second largest Khmer city—and the fourth largest city in Thailand—was created a little more than one mile from the border combining the old Cambodian-side KPNLF encampments—Ban Sangae (Ampil), Nong Samet, Mak Mun, and Nong Chan. Named Site 2, it became the largest camp in the history of Thailand. Site 2 is one of approximately a dozen camps technically called evacuation sites, as the Thai government never intended for them to exist more than a year at the most. From the beginning the evacuation camps have been under the close supervision of the Thai military through the Supreme Command in the Ministry of Defense, while the Ministry of the Interior oversees the UNHCR holding centers.

In 1985, 180,000 people were moved to Site 2 on the hot, dusty plain near the former Red Hill encampment. Barbed wire was placed around the perimeter of 7.8 square miles of unwanted land, bereft of ground water, and supporting only a few trees. Little planning went into the layout of the city that looked like a concentration camp. Straight roads and narrow paths were lined on either side with small bamboo houses packed closely together with no privacy.

With one of the highest birthrates in the world, Site 2's population is young. In 1990, 27 percent were under five years of age; 50 percent, under fourteen; only 7 percent were over forty-five. In addition to a high birthrate, other factors account for the young population. Many elderly people did not survive the flight from Cambodia, and many of the middle-aged were killed or resettled in third countries.

Thai Policy toward the Border Khmer

The evacuation-sites' populations have never been designated as refugees. According to the Thai government, the 350,000 border people are displaced people, *Pou Opayop*, "illegal immigrants" under Thai law. A *Pou Opayop* is one "who escapes from dangers due to an uprising, fighting, or war, and enters the Kingdom in breach of the Immigration Act." Illegal immigrants are those who enter "without passports, equivalent identification documents or visas; those without means of support if they enter the Kingdom; those who have not been vaccinated; those who are dangerous to society, or to the peace and security of the Kingdom." On all counts, the border Khmer were on shaky grounds.[35]

The Thai government determined where and how well the displaced Khmer would live. In past decades Thailand has been generous in accepting hundreds of thousands of refugees fleeing the turmoil in the surrounding countries. But in the interests of its own national agenda and security interests, in 1984–85, when the border people relocated permanently in Thailand, the Thai government implemented a policy known as "humane deterrence." They did not want the camps to become so comfortable that they served as a magnet for greater numbers of Khmer to cross into Thailand following the 1984–85 Vietnamese offensive, nor did they want the border Khmer to be too far inside Thailand so that they could no longer serve as a buffer against a Vietnamese invasion. International leaders opposed to the Vietnamese invasion were more interested in a strong resistance to the Vietnamese forces than in the people who sought asylum. Never mind that people as desperate as the Khmer would not be deterred by the prospects of life in restrictive, enclosed camps. After foraging in the malaria-infested jungles and dining on scorpions, they would seek asylum no matter the conditions, even austere living conditions with no hope of being accepted for resettlement in a third country.

The implementation of "humane deterrence" became more vital to Thailand as Western countries accepted fewer and fewer Southeast Asians. Qualifications for resettlement in the United States, in particular, became more stringent in the early 1980s. Few nations or international organizations stood in the way of Thai official actions in regard to the living conditions of the Khmer border people. Other nations were not willing to take more refugees and the United Nations made little protest, supporting as it did the CGDK, which in turn was beholden to the Thai government for a base from which to operate and a population to give it legitimacy. Devoid of political will to address the underlying causes of the outflow of refugees and with a dearth of imagination in conjuring alternatives to resettlement, the United Nations and the Western powers condoned the Thai policy toward those incarcerated in the camps.

Humanitarian Assistance and Breeding Dependency

The level of aid raised to assist the border people salved consciences as basic food, shelter, and medical needs were readily supplied by donor countries. But the quality of life crumbled for the people. Not only were the camps overcrowded and squalid; they were unsafe. At the time when Khmer civilians lived in the dangerous camps on the Cambodian side of the border and maintained contact with the interior, hope, in spite of all indications to the contrary, lingered that a political settlement between the warring factions would occur to enable the refugees to return home. By the end of 1986, when they had not crossed the tank ditch back into Cambodia for two years, hope faltered.

Keo Sakhan, a bright young man of twenty-five, is a victim of the pervasive enervation engendered by Site 2. Sakhan continues to be a part of the 12 to 15 percent of Site 2 residents who have steady jobs, but with little enthusiasm and no joy. "Once I was a medic in the hospital at Site 8," he begins.

When I came to Site 2, I no longer practiced what I had learned. What good does it do? We do not get paid since no currency is allowed to change hands in payment for work. We only receive extra rice and some dried fish, and some of that must go to the camp administrators to fill their personal store of food and to be dispensed among the soldiers fighting against the Vietnamese. No matter what position we hold and no matter how much responsibility the job demands, we all get the same allotment of extra rations.

I work now just to kill time, not to get satisfaction out of my job or to learn something new. I used to believe I would be able to take my skills back to Cambodia and help Khmer people who are ill. Now I do not know if we will ever return to our country.

When the Khmer Rouge took over Cambodia in 1975, I was only eleven. For four years I was part of a youth group. At that time I did not understand what the Khmer Rouge were trying to do to Cambodia, but I did know they were brutal masters.

As a very young child I remember Vietnamese troops coming to my small town in northeastern Cambodia on the border with Vietnam and hearing talk of communists — Vietnamese communists.

Before the Vietnamese communists came to our town, the market was very crowded, and we could buy whatever we wanted. I used to see many cars and many people. Then suddenly the town was very different. There were no more cars or taxis and the market was not so crowded. Finally the market closed and many families, like my own, had to move to another district about thirty kilometers away. Our town was later bombed by the United States.

In the new place there was no school except in the Buddhist temple. I was able to join the school and remain for four years. During that time we children learned that there were Vietnamese communists and Khmer communists. Both groups came to talk to us about communism, and Lenin and Mao.

Then in 1973 or 1974 the Khmer Rouge in our district instituted collective living. They closed the markets and the schools. There was no longer any money with which to buy goods. During that time I remember a great deal of bombardment from planes from the United States and fighting between the

Vietnamese and the Khmer Rouge. By 1975 I had been placed in the children's center and my parents were sent away to another collective to work in the rice fields.

I had never been separated from my family before. Every night I cried. So did the other children in the center. I was grouped with those who were to take care of the sixty cows and oxen. At first I really wanted to pet them; that was fun to me. But we were not allowed to do that. It was difficult for us to find grass for the animals in the dry season and in the rainy season when the countryside flooded. We were blamed for being careless with the animals and were punished.

In the evening after we finished caring for the cattle, our leaders gave some of us a saw to cut firewood. We worked until 10:00 P.M. or listened to lectures on communism feeding us what I later understood to be Khmer Rouge propaganda. At 4:00 A.M. we were awakened to begin a new day. During the flag raising in the dark we had to sing the national anthem. I always thought that was strange.

In December 1978 we heard a great deal of shelling and saw many soldiers running from the fighting and many people in the countryside preparing to flee. My group was still with the animals when a Khmer Rouge soldier asked us why we were staying. "Don't you hear the shelling?" he asked. "The Vietnamese are coming, and if you remain, they will behead you." I was trembling from fear of the shelling and was afraid of having my head cut off, so I ran, even though I did not know where my mother and father or my sister were. I had not seen them for three years. It would be two more years before I was reunited with my mother and my sister. My father was killed in the jungle.

I had a long walk from my country to the border. A Khmer Rouge soldier befriended me during my journey, so I did not really go hungry. We ate fruit from the trees of abandoned villages. In the jungle I contracted malaria; when I reached the border I was very sick. Relief workers were there with food and water. I was so happy to see the water trucks because we had had no water for several days, and I had a high fever. The soldier took me to the small open-air hospital. He left me and told me to remain there and work in the hospital. I would be safe, he said.

In 1981 when the ICRC, who ran the hospital, set up a program to train some of the Khmer workers to become medics, I joined the class. I learned more and more about medicine, even though we moved back and forth across the border during the dry-season shelling until 1984 when we were all forced into Thailand for good. Then I moved to Red Hill.

When other camps opened, I chose to go with the Khmer Rouge again. I was lured by them, I might say. All sorts of rumors floated about. It was said Site 2 was too dangerous, too close to the border, and too open to shelling. Also many robbers hid in the hills behind the camp. I was told that if I went to a Khmer Rouge camp named Ta Prik, I would be able to become wealthy as a gem trader. Rubies are found near Pailin, a Cambodian town close to the border.

There were no international relief workers in Ta Prik camp, only the ICRC. I helped set up an out-patient department. Some of the military leaders saw me and told me I was old enough to be a soldier and should go to the front to attend to the wounded and sick. My mother begged them to let me stay with her; I begged to remain with my sick mother; and ICRC requested that I continue my work in their hospital.

About that time border fighting began again. We moved to Site 8 where I worked as a medic for CAMA (Christian and Missionary Alliance), the organization that ran the Site 8 hospital. I was valuable to them because I could speak English and translate for the staff.

Not long after I arrived in Site 8, I was told again by the military that I was wanted to serve in the field, transporting medical supplies to the base hospital. The soldier also spoke of my performing operations on the wounded. I knew nothing about surgery, but they had no doctors in the field. Most had been killed by the Khmer Rouge when they were in power in Cambodia.

This time I knew I could not beg my way out. If I did not go, I would be severely punished. Even killed. Not long before, a soldier was executed in Site 8; he had been visiting his family and had not returned on time to his post.

My only alternative was to escape to Site 2. That, too, was very dangerous. Many had been caught and killed while trying. I sold my bicycle and a tape recorder to raise the money to pay a Thai escape guide. Knowing many were trying to escape, the police interpreted selling such goods as a sign that someone was planning to leave Site 8. So I stayed around for quite a while after I sold my things, continuing to work and live as I always had.

My mother contacted a Thai woman. The plan was to leave at 6:00 A.M. on a given day. At that time the Thai Task Force 80 guards raised the flag at their headquarters and sang the Thai national anthem. But that day Khmer soldiers were deployed in the area of our escape, and so we had to cancel our departure.

To the surprise of my colleagues, I went to work that day. That afternoon I went to a meeting in the hospital so the staff could see I was there. When I left, I carried only a badminton racquet so people would think I was going to play a game.

When I was out of sight, I turned toward a fence where my mother and my sister had been hiding for six hours. There was a hole nearby where we could slip through. We had arranged with our guide that if the plan failed in the morning, we would meet her at 6:00 P.M. My heart was beating very fast when we spotted the car. We ran to get in and our guide speeded from the camp. I felt very happy. I thought my troubles were behind me.

If I had been caught, I feel I would not have been killed, but I would have been jailed or sent to a reeducation camp in the forest along the border. Probably I would have been forced to serve as a soldier in a very dangerous assignment or to porter ammunition through areas filled with mines. I would have been thought of as a traitor.

After living in Site 2 for a while, I discovered that life was difficult there as well, but in different ways from Site 8. Always there is the question of food and water. The water situation here is much worse than in Site 8. All of our water must be transported in from the outside. Every morning a parade of red water-tankers comes through the gates and dispenses the water into large tin holders. With a bamboo yoke holding two jerry cans across her shoulders, my sister goes each day to the water tanks to get our allotment of twenty-five liters per person—less, really, since some is spilled in transport. In the dry season there is barely enough to drink. Often there is no water for washing either ourselves or our clothes. Some use the stagnant, putrid canal water that runs through some parts of the camp, but people, especially children, defecate in the canals.

Three-and-a-half million liters of water are trucked in here each day at a cost of about $200,000 a month. The water trucks are a vital life-line. One sure way of knowing we serve as a buffer against the Vietnamese is the cost of the water. We could live more cheaply in an area with water. But donors have given enough money to supply a camp of 180,000 people with sufficient water.

The most important event in the camp is the distribution of food, water, and firewood—really the distribution of anything. Predominantly women stand in endless lines waiting, waiting, waiting. When lines form, programs virtually shut down, but if we do not stand in the lines, we will not receive the goods. A full day's work is frequently interrupted.

Until 1988 only women and children under eight years old were allowed to receive the food rations. They lined up at the platform on the assigned day and each woman stood in the sun for endless hours until she received her ration. Men and boys over eight were not allowed to take the food because too many were military personnel, and UNBRO is not allowed to give food to the military. Many families did not receive adequate food because there were more in a family than the estimated number. Or a man may be alone. I had a neighbor whose wife died. The father and two sons were left alone. Neither the father nor the sons could stand in line for the rations, so they had to find someone who would provide for them.

Mothers became so desperate to get rations that they would insist that their young sons grow long hair, put on dresses, and stand in line for head counts when ration cards were issued. This worked until camp staff were instructed to inspect the child by lifting the dress to see whether the child was a boy or a girl. This was humiliating. Since 1988 food has been distributed directly to both women and men.

In the beginning the amount of rations given us was based on the notion that we could grow supplementary vegetables and fruit. That never happened in Site 2. The ground is too hard, the houses too close together, and although a lot of water is provided, not enough is allotted for garden watering. We have had to find other ways to supplement our rations. Year after year we have received only the rice and canned or salted fish to eat. There is never any variety.

By becoming dependent on outside donors and by having no variety in our diet, we began to gravitate more and more to the black market. Thai traders were granted entry into the camp to sell their goods, providing they paid a handsome bribe to a member of Task Force 80, the Thai guards assigned to every camp. We exchanged part of our rice and fish—what extra there was after we paid part of our rations in taxes to the camp administrators—for fruits, vegetables, clothes, or whatever we needed. Probably 150 tons of rice a week left the camp with Thai traders. Rice trading is big business on the border. Others who received money from relatives resettled in the United States or other countries were able to purchase more than most of us, but they also were taxed heavily by the Thai guards and by our camp administrators. The guards also expected payment from us for allowing us to buy from the Thai traders. On any day, if a ranger was in a bad mood or did not think a person had given him enough in tax, he might beat up the person.

From childhood we learned how to trade on the black market and bribe our way to additional food. No one learned to trade honestly. It could have been otherwise from the beginning, for the Thai villagers would certainly have benefited from legal trade, and our lives would have been so much easier. The tension and violence that resulted from trade disputes would not have been so prevalent. Also we would have been able to keep more of our own rations. Only recently in 1989 has the Thai government allowed the opening of a legal market in Site 2. Now there is an abundance of goods. The Thai traders still leave with bags of rice and tins of fish to sell to the nearby villagers, only now they do it legally.

Our not being allowed to go outside the fence of the camp indicates just how isolated we are. Under the Khmer Rouge we were cut off from the rest of the world, and now we are not that much more in touch. Incoming and outgoing mail is checked carefully and is limited. Often the money sent to us from relatives abroad is confiscated, or at least it was under Task Force 80. Legally we are not allowed to have newspapers, radios, tape recorders, televisions, telephones, or money, although some of these items are brought into the camp clandestinely. We learn much of our news from the expatriate community that works in the camps. We have a curfew after dark when we are supposed to be in our huts, but it is very dark without electricity.

Site 2 is broken into Site 2 North and Site 2 South. Until recently we were not allowed to go between the two camps without passes even though there is nothing but a guard gate that separates the two. On Sundays when we were allowed to visit between Site 2 North and Site 2 South, we had to line up in single file to go through the gate at the guard house. Many people in Site 2 have close family members who live in other camps, and they are not allowed to visit them. Some have not seen one another for years. If a person falls seriously ill and is transported to the ICRC hospital in Khao I Dang, other family members may not accompany the person for fear of defection.

Our homes are very small, only four by six meters, and six people live there. We share a latrine with fifteen other families. We hear everything our neighbors say and do. After twelve years of eating the same food and living in such cramped quarters, we argue more with our families and neighbors. In fact, the violence in domestic disputes has increased 100 percent in the last year or two. Quarrels that begin over a very small matter sometimes end up in death. Two children can be arguing over a discarded tin can and then the parents enter the quarrel. Finally the parents come at each other with axes or stones or even grenades. One day not long ago a man kicked over the water can of another man. Water is so scarce. In fighting to settle their dispute, both men were seriously injured. We can no longer cope behind barbed wire. It seems we are no longer able to live together. People explode just like a bottle of carbonated soda after it is shaken. We are not criminals and we are not the property of the resistance, even though we are treated that way.

Camp Violence and the Breakdown of Social Structures

Indeed, the border Khmer lived each day under the specter of violence. Domestic violence, the most prevalent, was not the only type the people have faced. Until 1988, Task Force 80, their "protectors," were a major source of violence. Task Force 80 was a group of poorly trained and poorly paid rangers loosely attached to the Thai military. It was a thankless job on a dangerous, war-torn, isolated, barren border. Recruits were not easily lured, and they frequently took the job out of desperation; they often drank heavily to flee the reality of the border. In 1980 when Khao I Dang was closed to additional Khmer seeking asylum, Task Force 80 was assigned to protect the border and to implement the Thai policy in regard to the Khmer population crossing Thailand's borders. Although some rangers were wounded or gave their lives in the line of duty or at least performed their assigned task with honor, others abused their power over the captive Khmer. By bribery, rape, beating, robbery, and even murder, these guards, who were seldom chastised for their crimes against human rights, terrorized the Khmer.

Trading violations frequently precipitated violent incidents. Like a drunken father who allows his child to do something numerous times and then punishes the child for the same action, so, too, Task Force 80 guards accepted bribes or looked away from trade transactions with Thai villagers much of the time. But from time to time, a ranger would attack and injure a Khmer for trading. It was a violation of camp regulations, he pointed out. Stories abound. The Lawyers Committee for Human Rights tells how a person they call Yok Khlang was badly beaten after arranging to make a future purchase from a Thai woman. She insisted Yok show her his hut so that she could collect her money should Yok not appear. He was caught while leading her to his home, was thrown to the ground, and beaten and kicked until he briefly lost consciousness. Other Khmer who witnessed the incident assured the Lawyers Committee delegate that such reactions to slight infractions were common. Few have reported such acts of violence, however, due to a fear of revenge from a ranger.[36]

It was—and is—illegal for the camp population to go beyond the barbed-wire fence around the camp's perimeter, though many risk stepping beyond to gather firewood, extra water, or wild vegetables—none in abundance on either side of the fence. The Lawyers Committee reported an incident that occurred in 1987. While a handicapped Khmer man and his pregnant wife gathered firewood just beyond the fence surrounding Site 2, a Task Force 80 guard attacked the couple, attempting to rape the woman. In his drunken rage he shot both husband and wife, killing them.[37]

Perhaps the most brutal and well-publicized incident occurred in Khao I Dang Camp in March 1986. Three Khmer men were arrested on suspicion of precipitating a raid in Khao I Dang in which one Task Force 80 ranger was killed and another badly wounded. The Khmer were brutally tortured. Their torturers placed hot irons and firewood against their bodies, set their hair ablaze, poured boiling salt water over their burned skin, shocked them with electric cables, and kicked and beat them continuously. They were denied medical treatment for many days. Although they were held in isolation, word of their torture did get out. The three were interrogated again, at times by the same guards who tortured them, to discover how word of their torture became public. They were informed they would be criminally tried and punished. The interrogators were publicly absolved from wrong-doing by their superiors.[38]

The border population suffered Task Force 80 ranger abuse for almost nine years before the Royal Thai Government agreed in 1988 to replace the unit with a better trained group, the Displaced Persons Protection Unit (DPPU). DPPU violations against the Khmer are few, and women are a part of the force, assisting in the particular needs of women.

Even now, at night when the camp is dark (there is no electricity), and empty of international personnel who are allowed to be in the camps only from 8:00 A.M. until 5:30 P.M., Cambodian and Thai bandits enmeshed in black market activity prey on the people. At one time Task Force 80 guards assisted the bandits. The camp's population trusts no one. By day spies—scouts who sneak in from the hills or resident informants—discover who has received remittances from foreign lands and who has valuables such as jewelry, tape recorders, and gold. Robbers are also aware that KPNLF soldiers on leave smuggle gems, money, silk, and other goods that they have acquired on the black market in Cambodia or have taken from newly arrived Cambodians as they pass military outposts on the way to the border camps. These goods are prime targets for thieves. The bandits often come in groups of twenty or thirty, surround an area, and attack specific huts. Most of the time the bandits' victims are left traumatized but unharmed, though frequently the women are stripped and probed for hidden valuables. Those who resist, however, are treated differently. Women and girls are raped; men and boys, beaten into unconsciousness. They kill families with impunity and do not exempt children. Some become victims of stray bullets. Most robberies go unreported, for all too often the robbers' revenge is a grenade tossed into the home of the informant at night while the family is asleep.

The hostage population of the KPNLF fears the undisciplined Khmer soldiers almost as much as they do the robbers who attack them in the night. Some of the troops practice their own form of banditry. Just as caught up in black marketeering as the hillside bandits, these soldiers use extortion, rape, and beatings to extract money and valuables from their own people, particularly those Cambodians en route to safety in the civilian camps under their control. None of the military base camps, which are in close proximity to the civilian camps, is protected by an international presence, for not even the ICRC has access to them. KPNLF military camps under the command of Chea Chutt and Liv Ne are said to be particularly lawless.[39] Few whose paths take them near one of these camps escape unscathed, and often women are held and gang raped for long periods, awaiting ransom.

Mary Beth McCarthy, a relief worker in Site 2 and founder of an Alcoholics Anonymous Center in the camp, tells one story. She does not reveal the girl's name, but says only that she "looked like a princess."

The girl was sixteen when she was kidnapped by KPNLF soldiers under Chea Chutt's command. They kept her isolated in the woods for more than six months. She was alone, for she had no mother, father, brothers, or sisters. Every night they tied her to a tree where she was to sleep while the soldiers went off to fight. During the day soldiers raped her as often as they liked and made her cook for them. When she became pregnant, she was no more use to the soldiers; so they let her go.

She came to us terrified and bruised from so much pawing. She desperately wanted an abortion, which became a conflict for me with my Catholic background. Nothing any of us could say would change her mind. She was miserable and wanted the abortion, which she had. I doubt that she will ever heal spiritually from the six months of merciless, unrelenting sexual abuse she endured under the KPNLF soldiers.

Many young girls like this one attempt suicide. One young girl was so ashamed when a Thai soldier pinched her cheek that she tried to kill herself with an overdose of pills she purchased on the black market. A woman who has been raped or who is a prostitute is shunned and not considered marriageable. Most suicide attempts are made by women and most are young women between fifteen and thirty, who are marriageable and of child-bearing age.

People along the border seek other forms of escape. That is why I started an AA Center in Site 2. I had no experience in mental health or AA, but growing up in an unrecovered alcoholic home, I knew I had to start a program to give some of these people a chance to recover and face reality. Without that, there is no real healing.

A survival state of mind prevails in the camps. The border people are concerned with getting enough food to eat for the day and getting through the night without bandits attacking them or shells hitting inside the camp. Everyone lives constantly on the edge. They want to escape, go into oblivion.

They have old memories, too, scars that have never healed. Yet they do not know how to talk about their pain. They do not understand that now they can trust people once again, that they can sit down and talk seriously about what has happened to them. Whenever a medic or someone asks a question that is troubling or embarrassing, most will giggle, afraid to answer. For too many years under Pol Pot, if a person showed any emotion, particularly when, for example, your father was being killed in front of you, you might also be killed.

When I started the center, I asked an alcoholic man who was trying to recover to be the director. As it turned out, he just sold everything I gave him and started drinking again. When the center first opened, about seventy people came; only five were alcoholic. The others thought the center might be a place where they could get money, blankets, extra rice, or just anything.

Once the purpose of the center became clear to the people, most dropped out. But during its first year, beginning in November 1988, there were about twenty-five members who were trying to recover from alcoholism. Most who continue acknowledge that alcohol is a means to forget and to get away from the emptiness of daily life.

They speak about their families in Cambodia, about family members who have died terrible deaths, about their loneliness in Site 2. They lament that they feel they have done nothing wrong and don't understand why they have to live behind barbed wire. The future looks bleak to them, for they do not see an end to their incarceration.

The program for the elderly in Site 2 referred one man who is one hundred years old. He was pitiful—a beggar who reeked of alcohol. He talked about his sixty-five-year-old wife who was dying in his house and about his second thirty-five-year-old wife who was also an alcoholic, but who was needed to take care of his dying wife. In order to keep her, he was forced to go out each day to beg for alcohol for her.

Two alcoholics from the center went to see both the old man and his alcoholic wife. When the old man agreed to come to the center, the two men got on either side of him and helped him walk. When asked by the group at the center why he wanted to stop drinking, he replied in all simplicity, "I am tired of children laughing at me and kicking me as I lie on the ground. I am tired of what I do to my family and of having no respect. I am an old man now, and I want to be a person."

It was difficult for me to convey the concept of AA to the people who came. I did not know whether they understood alcoholism as a treatable disease as most are uneducated. Because of their past, they were not able to tell their stories easily, even if we emphasized trust and the idea that telling the story was a part of the healing process. Those who come are amazed that someone wants to listen to them and help them.

I had to learn how to operate the center according to Khmer customs and beliefs, not in an educated Western way. So I asked them how they saw AA.

The group response was, "We see AA as a rice field with a water buffalo in it. The water buffalo is being pulled by one string."

A woman then asked, "Why does the earth allow grass to grow on it?" After my feeble attempts to convey that grass gives off oxygen and that people and animals need the grass or grains to eat, I saw I was getting nowhere. I asked her to explain her question to me. "The earth is the body," she replied, "and the grass is the alcohol. Why does the body allow the alcohol to take over?" The group went on to discern that the earth allows the grass to grow on it because it likes the grass and the grass feels good. It makes the earth feel better. But the grass grows and grows and starts to take over the earth, so the earth is all grass and can't see clearly. In AA they discover that so much grass isn't good for the earth. Without alcohol, flowers can begin to grow on the earth once more.

Not all the stories turn out happily. For some, the need to forget overpowers their desire to look to the future. A Khmer couple who joined AA in Site 2 recounted their story:

We learned about alcohol in Site 2. We did not drink in Cambodia. But when we came to Site 2 and could not go out of the camp anymore, we felt like caged animals, like our chickens that we put under a basket to keep them from running away. We have no freedom here.

In Cambodia we cared about trees, flowers, and the land. The countryside was beautiful and the lakes and the air were clean. We could bathe in the lakes and stand under the waterfalls. There wasn't too much industry, so the country itself was very clean. Life was simple, but we had our families and our freedom. We were happy.

Site 2 is a lawless place. No one cares about the law or each other. There is a great deal of violence, and there is little respect for others. We used to address one another with respect by addressing someone as boung; now we disrespectfully call a person aieng. No one trusts a neighbor. We have not been able to trust anyone since Pol Pot time. We never know when someone will betray us.

We do not think about the future, only about today and tomorrow. Before Pol Pot time, we made dowries for our children. We were motivated to save and care about tomorrow. In the countryside we worked very hard—seven days a week, all day. We ate very little—a small amount of rice, some fish, and some vegetables—and we bought very little. We had money, but we purchased jewels and gold to put away as savings for our children's wedding dowries. When Pol Pot's soldiers came, they took all of our gold and jewels unless we hid them. I buried mine and returned to unearth them before I came to Thailand. But on the way some soldiers stopped our group and searched us for our valuables. They kicked me and my jewelry fell out of my bottom. We had nothing when we arrived in Thailand.

In Cambodia under the Pol Pot regime, my wife and I were forced to marry.

Many people were dying from starvation or were executed. So in order to assure a population, the Khmer Rouge forced couples to come together. It did not matter whether they loved each other. The Khmer Rouge only wanted to build up their empire.

My wife began to drink in 1986 after she lost her leg when she stepped on a mine. She felt hopeless and feared she would never be able to take care of herself or her family again.

When my wife and I drank, we took all the money we had to buy alcohol. When we did not have money, we used our rice ration to make rice alcohol. The children did not have enough to eat because we took their food. We fought a lot and hurt each other.

Now that we are sober, we decided we want to marry again here in Site 2 because we love each other. We were separated when we fled Cambodia, but we found each other again in the camp. We will marry during the Cambodian New Year and start our lives over again. We want people to see that we are married and happy together.

One year after they married during the 1989 Cambodian New Year, the husband began drinking again. He began spending all of their money on alcohol and became quite violent. One day he chased his wife with an ax in his hand. She was able to escape his blows, but she was afraid to live with him. She was a victim of the increased domestic crime in Site 2. Of the striking increase in violence, Brother Bob Maat observes:

In January of 1988 the weapon of choice was a bamboo stick—people beating each other. By April the people were choosing the ax. They were killing each other with axes. By June the grenade was the chosen weapon. After an altercation one man wanted to kill his wife. When he threw a grenade, it killed his son instead. Grenades can be found everywhere and can be purchased for two or four baht (U.S. $.50 or $1.00). At this moment outside the fence of Site 2, a person could easily find one hundred.

From 1987 to 1988 the violence tripled because of overcrowding in the camps, a feeling of hopelessness of ever returning to Cambodia, being here much too long, being confined in a prison, and having no leadership to turn to because the KPNLF is broken into factions and most of the leaders are corrupt. Of the incidents 40 to 45 percent are within the family; 55 percent outside the family—robberies, rapes, beatings, killings. We in the expatriate community probably know less than half of what really happens. We are not here after 5:30 P.M. It is in the night that most acts of violence occur.

Psychological and Spiritual Needs of the Border Khmer

The wife of the alcoholic sought refuge for a time in the Khmer People's Depression Center, an oasis in the midst of the dust and turbulence of Site 2. The grounds are spacious and clean. The bamboo structures providing for patient care, clinic space, and shelves of herbal medicines are impeccably clean and offer ample room to move about. Outside there are gardens of flowers and vegetables. A bridge spans a dusty plot to give the appearance of a stream, banked on either side with delicate pink blossoms. There are benches for sitting and reflecting in the garden.

The center was founded in 1987 by Phaly and Barnabus, both of whom had fled the Khmer Rouge. "Our aim is to help people who are depressed," Phaly said.

We are not trained counselors, but we know our people and have suffered with them. We know the traditional healing methods of Cambodians—herbal medicines, massage, steaming, spiritual healing. We have Krou Khmer [traditional Khmer medicine healers] who can gather and prepare herbal medicines and others who can diagnose and treat the people who come, a massager, a healer, and counselors—both Khmer and Western. A patient with a severe problem can remain in the center for ten days. We provide a traditional house, and a garden.

Barnabus learned to be a *Krou Khmer* practitioner from his Buddhist grandfather and father. "My father planted a variety of plants and herbs to treat the villagers," Barnabus recalls.

Whenever I drink herbal teas, I have memories of my father and grandfather. Modern medicine was not introduced in our village until I was almost grown. But the people did very well on the traditional medicines. Now I would like to combine Western medicine with our original herbs so that we can meet all the needs of our people, both physical and mental.

During the time of the Khmer Rouge, modern medicine was not available. When I had malaria, I drank bitter tea, the traditional treatment for the illness, and was cured. I believe in the Khmer traditional way. Modern medicine is gained academically. Knowledge of traditional herbs is handed down from generation to generation. It is not an academic subject taught in any school; it comes from father to son, grandfather to grandson, from one generation to another.

We have gathered many herbs and species of bark, mostly from the hills behind the camp. Even with permission to go beyond the camp's perimeter, it is still a dangerous undertaking because there are bandits and mines in the hills. Still, I believe it is worth the risk to gather these things to help our people.

"Because of all the help we received and because we have our lives, we believe the center is a bit of charity we can give back," said Phaly, who continued,

In Cambodia before Pol Pot time I was a typist in the Ministry of Finance; my husband was a businessman. Like all other Cambodians, we were forced from

our home to work in the countryside. My husband and I were separated early. I was with my sister whom I watched starve to death. I carried her body by myself to her grave.

Not long after her death I was accused of being a spy for Americans. No matter what I said, my interrogators did not believe me. Some soldiers took me far away from the village into the woods. They told me to stop and kneel on the ground because they were going to shoot me.

At that time my son was three years old. He ran behind me crying, "Mother, I want to go with you. Why are they taking my mother far from me?" The little fellow did not speak clearly, but somehow his cries and his tears softened my executioner's heart. He loosened the ropes that bound my wrists behind me. Then he told me to run and never return.

I picked up my son and looked around me. The forest was so heavy, I did not know which direction to turn. We were miserable. For one week we had nothing to eat except the foliage we found in the woods. We slept on the ground. A deadly snake slithered over my leg one night. I was very afraid it would bite me and leave my son by himself in the woods. We were very quiet, and the snake went away.

Finally in a clearing in the forest, I saw an old man—Chinese perhaps. He asked me many questions, gave me some corn and rice to eat, and brought us to his house. He told me to work hard because if I did not, we would all be killed by the Khmer Rouge. Even though I was very weak, I went to the rice field every day. Then the Khmer Rouge soldiers who guarded us told me to fish and later to plant vegetables. At this time I was in Pursat Province near the western border with Thailand. When the Vietnamese came, my son and I went to Battambang city to look for my mother and father. I did not know where my husband was. Two months later I found them, and then I found my husband. We came to the border to seek safety.

When I came to Site 2, I began doing social work, visiting the very poor in the camp. In this crowded bamboo city I saw much depression, anxiety, trauma. We used to live in separate villages. We used to be civilized people with our traditions and culture. And now we are together in a crowded compound. Dirty. We have city dwellers and rural peasants. The rural people are now living in an urban environment far from their roots and their way of life. Many people hide their real identity, their real age, and educational background. The taxi bike rider might have a doctor's degree, but would never reveal it. Still we do not trust one another. We still bear grudges against each other. There is not a strong sense of forgiveness among the Khmer.

We thought the center might be a place where those who came could recover a part of themselves and their lives, a place for calling the spirit back so the person will not give up in complete despair. When the spirit is recalled, a person can become a contributing member of society once again. In the beginning, patients brought physical complaints, but very soon they began talking about their sorrows and sadness, about their emotional shock. We saw *that beyond their physical needs, we had to provide gentle care for their mental needs.*

People came with great grief—loss of family, brutal rapes, constant fear of shelling, violence, robbery. Parents especially fear losing their children, and this often results in child beating. In Cambodia the extended family is very important and children deeply respect and care for their elders. In the camps, the children rebel against their parents and do not see them as good role models. Fathers cannot work or are away in the military, mothers and fathers quarrel and physically abuse one another, fathers take additional wives. The parents are not the real providers here—UNBRO and the international organizations are.

There is a loss of cultural identity among the young as the fabric of the traditional family comes apart. There are few elders to pass on traditions, and young parents are not steeped in Buddhist and Khmer culture. Children who were born here have no memory of their homeland, and those who grow to adulthood in the camps have no knowledge of a normal life; they are unable to function as normal adults. Few have any remembrance of safety, of falling asleep in peaceful rest. Children growing up here, witnessing others getting away with dishonesty, violence, and murder, learn to respond to life in the same way.

Women make up a large portion of the camp population. Many women are single parents. The husband is either dead or at the front fighting. They are fearful of raising their children alone. In Cambodia they had a great deal of help from their husbands. Married women fear their husbands will become violent or take more wives. When the sounds of war begin before dawn and the women hear the whizzing of the shells, they worry that their husbands will be either killed or severely disabled.

These are some of the problems of the people who come to us for traditional care. The way we care for the flowers on the grounds is the way we care for our patients. Perhaps we can be a small part in bringing to life again a people and a culture that are not thriving. There is little malnutrition in the camps and the infant mortality rate is down, but the people do not thrive; they do not really live. This is very bad for our future.

Border Khmer Loss of Self-esteem

Life in the camps has left many of the Khmer hopeless of ever having control over their lives again. They feel powerless in their dependence and devoid of self-esteem and confidence as their dignity is compromised. Many hibernate psychologically from the emotional, spiritual, and physical poverty that saps their lives. They try not to experience themselves in their present situation, closing themselves in a vacuum until one day when they can afford to awaken again.[40]

Children, too, hibernate inside themselves for a time. They play-act as if they were rocks, because during the years of Pol Pot's reign, if you did not act like a rock, you could die. They have witnessed mindless, brutal killings of parents, siblings, and friends. "I don't know why the soldiers came to our village." "I don't know why the soldiers killed my mother." "I don't know why," is spoken time and time again. Children have killed because they were armed and forced to kill by the military, some as young as six or seven. Some were ordered to kill their mothers, sisters, and brothers while their fathers watched. Children have been abused, tortured, and raped. They have lived on rats and leaves. They have watched their villages burn and have walked over dead bodies as they fled for safety. Many were separated from their families.

For three years in the 1980s, Bridget Messana, a Maryknoll lay missioner, worked with children in the Unaccompanied Minors Center in Phanat Nikhom Camp in Thailand. The vast majority of children were Vietnamese boat children, set to sea by parents who hoped their children would be resettled in a Western country. The minority of children in Phanat Nikhom were Khmer; they generally were sent to the closed camps on the border. Bridget recalled a common survival action among all the children, exemplified by a Khmer brother and sister.

When I first knew this brother and sister, he was sixteen and she, seventeen. They had already spent three years in Phanat Nikhom.

During the years Pol Pot ruled Cambodia, the two were separated from their parents and from each other. They worked from dawn to dusk on projects the Khmer Rouge ordered. At one point they found each other and some relatives. Soon, however, they were pulled back to the work camps.

Shortly after they found family members for a second time, their father died of starvation. Their mother was not there, and they think she also died.

When the Vietnamese invaded Cambodia, the brother and sister walked from northern Cambodia to Phnom Penh in the south looking for their other siblings.

Although they did not find their relatives in Phnom Penh, they were taken in by a woman who knew them. When the woman went to Vietnam to find work, she found a blood uncle of the children, who kept them only a short time. The uncle sent the children to Thailand where they spent three years among the Vietnamese and Chinese.

I noticed they did not stand up for themselves, but took whatever was dished out to them by the other ethnic groups. They were particularly intimidated by the Vietnamese. They had no spirit within them. It was like the spirit had been removed. It took a long time for them to bloom. Actually, the boy never bloomed as long as I was there.

When they first came to the Minor's Center, their actions manifested an attitude of isolation that so many display when they arrive. A new minor sits on a straw mat on the floor. No one comes into his or her space. The child might remain in isolation for several hours, a day or two, or months. Gradually, a child allows others onto the mat and then moves off the mat and into the group. The girl remained a long time on the mat. Her brother never moved off on his own.

He would only let me communicate with him by holding his hand. There was no conversation between us. He did not want to talk about his past and all that he had bottled up inside.

For many children who are resettled in a third country, like the United States, the pattern continues. Social workers say they shut down inside and shut out other people by listening to loud music, pouring themselves completely into their studies, or something until they are ready to "come off the mat" into the new society. Because many foster parents do not have the patience to wait until they come out of their isolation, the children are bounced from foster home to foster home. Each time the self-imposed isolation begins again, and the children become more incapable of bonding with caring people or of expressing their emotions. They lose years of their lives in isolation because of war, living in camps, and being resettled in a third country.

Like the Israelites in the desert thousands of years ago, the Khmer ask for normalcy. The Israelites complained, "Who will give us meat to eat? Think of the fish we used to eat free in Egypt, the cucumbers, melons, leeks, onions and garlic! Here we are wasting away, stripped of everything; there is nothing but manna for us to look at!" (Numbers 11:4b–5). The Khmer, too, stripped of everything, wonder when their fortunes will be reversed; they have continued to live in fear and watch their culture and life as a people break up in the face of violence, distrust, unemployment, overcrowding, idleness, transience, lack of opportunities for technical development or study, forced dependence, and the omnipresence of a war that has appeared to have no end. They have been disappointed so many times that, even with the peace accords signed in October 1991 between the Phnom Penh government and the three Khmer factions living on the border, the border Khmer hesitate to believe the war in Cambodia has ended and will free them to go home again.

Because the basic reason for the camps is military, the people have lived as dependent hostages and have always been subservient to military priorities. Similarly, the civilian administrators are subservient to military commanders and to the Thai authorities who did not want self-development for refugees from the beginning. The close control exercised over where people can live, what they can eat, and what they can do for themselves makes the people more dependent, less able to become self-sufficient adults, less able to manage their own lives or to impart to their children how to take responsibility for their lives. There is speculation that the extraordinarily high birthrate, one of the highest in the world, is due not only to the drive to repopulate a decimated population or to boredom, but because creating a child from conception to birth is about the only part of their lives the Khmer in the border camps feel they can control.[41] Yet these children grow up with parents who are totally dependent, and they, in turn, acquire a mentality of dependency. Ask a child where rice comes from; having never seen a water buffalo or a rice paddy, the child will answer, "In a bag my mother gets from UNBRO after she sits in line in the sun waiting for it for a long time and then carries it home on her head."

Because they are military pawns to further military and political aims of the CGDK and the wider global participants and because they remain transients on Thai soil under the policy of humane deterrence, the humanitarian operations along the border have been kept at an emergency level and have never changed significantly into a developmental mode. Efforts are being made to encourage refugee self-management and to provide primary-level schooling for more of the children and secondary education for a few. There are those few who are educated to be medics in the camp hospitals and outpatient departments and who assume more and more responsibility in medical practice and the implementation of hospital policy. Others receive some administrative training. A few entrepreneurs among the tens of thousands of camp residents do acquire bicycles and become taxi drivers to the far reaches of the camps, while others develop skills in weaving, tailoring, basket making, wood carving, or jewelry designing. But even the lives of those who have been given some opportunities are subsumed under the military blanket that ultimately covers and colors every aspect of life along the border.

Camp Evacuation

Although the border Khmer have lived permanently in Thailand since 1985, they remain in a capricious war zone that continues to affect them, particularly during the dry season. Each morning on their way toward the camps, the relief workers listen to car radios to learn the "situation" in each camp. The U.N. security voice from Taphraya indicates the relative calm or volatility of the area: "Good morning. It is 8:00 A.M. Today, Tuesday, October 24, 1989, Site 2 has a Situation 2. There will be limited access to Site 2. This is Taphraya." In a Situation 0 there is no shelling near the border that would endanger the residents in the camps, while a Situation 4 signals that the interior of the camps is under fire. Situations in between caution varying degrees of danger to the camps' residents and, depending on the danger, determine the access allowed to expatriate workers, limiting it to bare-bones medical personnel and UNBRO administrators.

Evacuating Site 2, a city of 170,000 people, is a logistical nightmare, and in a barrage of shelling, there is no guarantee that the residents will make it safely to Site 3, the designated evacuation location five miles from Site 2 and only six miles inside Thailand, still within reach of artillery fire.

Andy Pendleton, who has been on the border almost from the beginning, was the UNBRO camp officer in Site 2.

Every morning for eight days in March 1989 the shelling rocked us out of our beds at 5:45, and the Thai military commander on our special radio network shouted the order to us to get to camp immediately, giving us the code indi-

cating a possible, imminent evacuation. On the first day shells were falling within four hundred meters of the perimeter. In the event of an actual evacuation it is up to the Thai government to allow the border Khmer deeper access to refuge inside Thailand, just as it was the Thai government's prerogative to allow entrance from Cambodia into Thailand during the early years on the border before the 1984–85 Christmas offensive.

Instead of running away from the shelling, which is the logical thing for a typical middle-class suburban American like myself to do, I rode into it to try to coordinate the evacuation of the second largest Khmer city in the world. I don't think any of us expatriates here are really afraid for our own lives. We are just afraid of not having the capacity to bring an evacuation to a safe conclusion.

We prepared all week long, but there can never be adequate lead time to prepare for the evacuation of 170,000 people. The first people we move to Site 3 in anticipation of severe shelling are the near-term pregnant women, the handicapped, seriously ill, and the elderly. In March 1989, they totaled close to 30,000. Full-term pregnant women are transported to the ICRC hospital in Khao I Dang. There a bamboo ward is erected for them and for those who might be seriously wounded from the shelling. Medical teams must determine priority of treatment.

The remaining 140,000 people will try to remain in their homes as long as they can because all of their worldly possessions are there in their little huts. There are 48,000 huts in Site 2. But if worse comes to worst and shells rain and people die, they will run. They are survivors. Even as shellings come closer each day, they begin the routine after the evening meal of cleaning off each plate, spoon, fork, and glass, and packing them. They begin digging bunkers either under or in front of their huts.

The ground is very hard here; it's like an airport runway. When a shell hits the ground, it explodes outward for a long distance. There is no quick escape for so many with that type of shelling; no easy way to move these civilians to safety.

Everything that comes into Site 2 comes through a life-line—40 supply trucks, 150 volunteer relief workers, a convoy of 260 water tankers. All of this must reach Site 3 as well. Water-receiving tanks will have to be moved from Site 2 to the evacuation site in phases or else people will become dehydrated. We have to have the plastic, bamboo, wire, nails, hospital areas, water stations, upgraded roads, feeding centers—all in a matter of days. Staff must act quickly as near-term pregnant women give birth en route because they are traumatized; others step on mines along the way. If all is not in place and the movement of people rapidly deployed, many can die.

We've not had a total evacuation since the 1984 Christmas offensive. Since then the civilian and military populations have been separated and civilian camps like Site 2 are less likely to be direct targets of enemy fire. But the people are still vulnerable to shells gone awry.

KHMER ROUGE BORDER CAMPS

The people living in camps under Khmer Rouge control experience all the dehumanizing aspects of Site 2 and more. Site 8, a camp of almost 45,000 Khmer civilians located about two hours' drive southwest of Aranyaprathet, is one Khmer Rouge camp open to relief workers and other outsiders, such as journalists and visitors who are given permission to enter by the Thai government. The more than 60,000 civilians in camps under the control of the Khmer Rouge live even more precariously in the shadow of war than people living in camps controlled by the other two factions.

The area surrounding Site 8 is much more fertile than the area around Site 2. There is plenty of water and space for gardens. Anyone standing on the hill leading to the mountains behind the camp can see the orderly rows of huts, many on stilts for protection against rain. Military precision permeates the camp. The discipline demanded by the Khmer Rouge of their troops and backers during the years they ruled Cambodia is now required of the civilians they control. A visitor to Site 2 or the Sihanouk-controlled camp, Site B, would note a friendly looseness when comparing those camps to Site 8.

Like the people in Site 2, Site 8 residents also live in a war zone. In July 1988 four people were killed and twenty injured as shells from Vietnamese troops on the other side of the mountains fell into Site 8. The following January two more persons were killed and two injured, while in April 1989, although shells hit the camp, no one was injured. Just one year from the July 1988 shelling in Site 8, another barrage killed nine persons and wounded twenty-seven. The Khmer Rouge permitted UNBRO and ICRC to evacuate eight hundred of the most vulnerable—near-term pregnant women, the very sick, and some of the elderly—to Khao I Dang for nearly a month, an unusual permission given by the Khmer Rouge, who fear that those who leave will not return. One was a woman who was hit during the July 1988 shelling as she and her children tried to escape the bombardment. She lost a leg.[42]

July 25, 1989, is a day Tan Lim, another woman, will never forget.

I was staying with my youngest child at the hospital when the shelling began at dawn July 22. We have become accustomed to the sound of the direction of the firing. It is clear when Vietnamese shelling is coming toward us and when our own fire is going out. When the sound is that of our own, we do not run. But this particular morning I picked up my child, even though he had a feeding tube in him, and ran to the bunker on the hospital grounds, for I knew the sound of the enemy was very close.

There is really very little protection in the bunker, which was actually a large round pipe that would break under a direct hit. We always hid to miss the fragments that could fly and kill us. As many as could crowded into the three pipes and waited for several hours until all was quiet.

Even though my child was ill, I did not want to stay near the hospital. It was too dangerous as the shelling hit very close. Several in the camp were killed and many wounded.

I took my son home, gathered the rest of my children, and ran to the foot of the mountain where it was safer. It was more likely that a shell would hit the center of the camp than at the base of the mountain, for it would have to come straight down the mountain side.

Many were there already, perhaps one thousand people. UNBRO provided plastic sheeting for us to raise as shelter. The area was not large, so we were very crowded. There was no space between families, no separation between houses, but at least we felt safe. We did not want to return to our homes because during that year many had been killed and wounded by the shells that exploded in the camp.

We remained at the foot of the mountain for several months, building more permanent structures out of whatever bamboo we could find. We collected what remained of buildings in the camp. We used the roof of the empty school; it was closed because we feared having our children separated from us in case the shelling began. We kept our belongings packed and ready to take if we had to run. Every night for more than a month we packed up our dishes and cooking utensils.

Just before dusk July 25, Choy An, a neighbor, ran to find me at the base of the mountain. "Your husband, your husband," Choy An cried. "He is at the hospital wounded very badly. Come quickly."

I picked up my smallest child and ran as quickly as I could to the hospital area. By that time a crowd had gathered around the far corner of the building. They were looking inside at a corner bed. I hardly recognized my husband when I was led to him. His face and his right arm were burned black, and one eye was dislodged. His right leg was completely blown off. Only a piece of his thigh remained.

He died a few minutes after I arrived. There was no way he could have survived. Two men wrapped him in woven kromas. They hung another cloth from two bamboo poles, making a hammock, and carried his body to our home where I washed him and prepared his body for cremation.

This war is so brutal. Will it never end? Life in a camp and always under fire is no way for my children to grow up. They have no father now, and they awake in the middle of the night screaming from nightmares. It is not safe for them to run and play during the dry season, and, when they are old enough, I do not know if they will ever be able to go to school. Children who are still young become soldiers.

I had not seen my husband for almost one year. He had come on leave, but was two days late in returning to his military camp from Site 8. I did not hear from him, but word came to me that he had been sent to Phnom Dey for punishment and reeducation. The camp is not far from here. I learned later that he had been forced to become a porter of ammunitions, mines, and rice from the military camps here in Thailand to the war front in Cambodia. The mountainous jungle areas the porters pass through are filled with mines and malaria. Not only men are forced to become porters; women are too. Some are very young—thirteen or fourteen years old. Some are children no more than seven or eight. They have to carry heavy loads. Hundreds lose their lives or limbs each year by stepping on the mines.

Punishment for refusing to be a porter might be days without food, or imprisonment in an underground prison. Some are shot and killed.

There are Khmer Rouge camps to which, even in 1992 before repatriation began, the international community had extremely limited access or none at all. The humanitarian services that are allowed are strictly monitored and controlled by Khmer Rouge camp officials. Outsiders know little of what transpires along this hidden border where civilians are forced against their will to live in tightly controlled, dangerous camps that exist only to further the Khmer Rouge military campaign against the Phnom Penh, Vietnamese-backed troops of Prime Minister Hun Sen.

Operation Handicap International (OHI), a French-based humanitarian organization that provides prosthetic devices made from locally available materials, is one of the few organizations permitted to operate at the perimeters of some of these camps. This is mainly due to the fact that large numbers of refugees under Khmer Rouge control lose limbs to mines as they porter munitions. Susan Walker, OHI's Thailand director, has had limited access to some of the more restricted camps.

I remember the first time I went into one of the most inaccessible camps where only the U.N. and ICRC went. It was 1984 or 1985. OHI was given access because there were so many amputees. My skin literally crawled as I walked into the camp. Everyone was in typical black Khmer Rouge clothing. The Killing Fields hadn't been filmed then, but it was a striking presentation. All the women wore short, severe, straight hair cuts. Faces were very serious. There were no smiles, only cold, hateful stares. The people seemed very suspicious of us foreigners.

We had to be careful not to become too friendly with our Khmer medics. Should the camp administrators observe too close contact with foreigners, the medic would be rotated to another job or would disappear. There was always someone watching us and our interaction with the Khmer workers.

I felt a reign of terror in those camps, people controlled absolutely by fear. The civilians in those camps were forbidden all outside contacts. They were not allowed to practice religion. Men and women were forbidden to marry before a certain age. They were forced to enlist or contribute in some way to the war efforts from a very young age.

I remember my first visit into the newly formed Site 8 camp after the 1984– 85 Christmas offensive when all the Khmer crossed permanently into Thailand. I was there within the first month in 1985 when Site 8 was set up. I saw civilians who had been in the remote jungle camps in Cambodia with no contact with foreigners, at least no uncontrolled contacts. During the evacuation from the Khmer Rouge-held camps, UNBRO had given colorful sarongs and different provisions to the evacuees. Men and women were smiling; they were reacting. Children were playing in the roads. "My God," I said, "this is not the same group of people." It was like they had been freed. I understood then how people can be controlled by fear.

Site 8 was set up as a showcase camp by the Khmer Rouge. Outsiders were given access to see the "new face" of the Khmer Rouge. Nevertheless, going into Site 8 for the first time convinced me that the vast majority of civilians living in Khmer Rouge camps were being held prisoners, that they would leave if they had the chance. Over the years we have seen many who have escaped from the other Khmer Rouge camps where there is only limited access — like O'Trau, Borai, Taluan, Huay Chan — or no access at all. Escapes are dangerous; many lose their lives in the attempt; others are pulled back into a life of punishment, a life of a slave.

One escape story is more remarkable than any other: A double amputee who escaped from Borai, a Khmer Rouge camp some distance south of Site 8, arrived in November 1988 at the KPNLF camp Sok Sann. The OHI staff person interviewed him because he was a new double amputee arrival. We had never seen him in Borai, by the way, even though we worked in the camp. He had been there since 1982 — a double amputee needing a wheelchair.

This man was in jail in Cambodia for two years during the Khmer Rouge years. Then again in 1982, after the Vietnamese came, he was jailed by them. After two or three weeks he escaped, and because he heard his parents were at the border in a KPNLF camp not too far from Borai, he thought he would try to find his family whom he had not seen since 1975.

He arrived at the border at Borai, the Khmer Rouge camp, quite by accident. He was immediately recruited into the army as a porter. He was in his mid-twenties at this time. One month later he stepped on a land mine and became a double amputee. He lived in Borai from 1982 until 1988.

He did not tell horrendous stories of conditions in the camp, but described a constant harshness of life and rule by fear. He lived in a small house, much too small, with six other people and the rations were never adequate. Escape from the Khmer Rouge and finding his parents were the two reasons he gave for trying to escape from Borai.

Since he was a double amputee, none of the guards would suspect that he would attempt to escape. How could a double amputee escape? He built two wooden paddles for his hands and ostensibly went into the forest with another double amputee to look for vegetables. The guards ignored them. The two men began to make their way toward Sok Sann camp. Very soon his companion gave up and returned to Borai.

After two days of travel through the mine-infested jungle with only his arms for leverage, he was exhausted. He could move neither forward nor backward. Two men from Sok Sann camp, which is twenty to twenty-five kilometers from Borai, who were out in the forest, came upon the double amputee. "What *are you doing here?''* they asked, incredulous of the person they saw before them. When he told them he was searching for his parents, the two men assured the amputee they knew his family in Sok Sann, a small camp of about eight thousand Khmer.

The two men went to tell his family and returned with his brother. They carried the amputee in a hammock to his family's hut for the reunion. One month later his sister arrived from Battambang, inside Cambodia, also hearing the family was there.

Stories like that are rare. But the lack of access to medical attention in the Khmer Rouge camps, especially those to which there is no access by either UNBRO or ICRC, is abhorrent. This particular man was without a wheelchair or prosthesis for six years after his double amputation. Borai has around 150 amputees in a population of no more than 4,000. When we began in Taluan in 1988, in a population of 6,000, there were 550 amputees—300 below knee, 200 above knee, and 50 double amputees. In the camp of O'Trau and another handicap village a few kilometers away, before the outpatient department was burned and access was closed in December 1988, the administration gave OHI a list of the number and kinds of amputees. There were 1,600 amputees in a population of 16,000—10 percent amputees.

OHI has perhaps the easiest access to the Khmer Rouge because there are so many amputees among their people. But some come from the extremely remote camps where we have no access. Even if we do an amputation, when the person is returned to the inaccessible camp, we can do no follow-up—no fitting of the prosthetic device, no education on how to live as an amputee.

The Khmer Rouge have their own hospitals in the jungles and inside Cambodia that no one has ever seen. I saw the Khmer Rouge hospitals in 1982 in the early days. They were horrifying. I don't know if they have improved.

At that time untrained or poorly trained medical personnel were doing open chest, intestinal, and brain surgery under mosquito nets in the jungle in extremely unsanitary conditions. Most of the patients I saw did not survive. They were also doing appendectomies and many amputations. Sometimes the amputations were good because they had a good deal of experience.

We've had polio epidemics in the hidden camps, and we cannot treat the children. Even in the camps with limited access, there is little we can do in critical care follow-up. During June 1989 a polio epidemic developed in some of the satellite military camps. Thirty-one children between seven months and five years of age were brought to the Site 8 hospital; we had no access to the many others who were not allowed to come to Site 8. The thirty-one children who did come stayed for a period of time in the Site 8 hospital ward—all but three who died. There was, however, constant pressure to discharge them quickly. The only way to provide follow-up for the children, some partially paralyzed, was to train four medics from the closed camps. Fortunately, two of these medics were also surgeons, so we taught them how to perform amputations as well.

After considerable negotiating efforts by UNBRO and DPPU personnel,

Khmer Rouge administrators finally agreed to allow ten thousand children under fourteen years from the military camps to come to fields several miles from any camps to be vaccinated. Rows and rows of children lined up in the hot sun waiting a turn to be immunized. Many more in the other inaccessible camps did not receive the vaccine that meant the difference between growing up healthy and whole or being disabled. It is a great tragedy that so many who could have had access to preventive health measures were not allowed to take advantage of the opportunity.

Those who contracted the disease as well as those who had received the first of the polio vaccine series were lost to us, because the Khmer Rouge relocated the camps inside Cambodia in mine- and malaria-infested jungle areas in closer proximity to the fighting. That the children became victims of cerebral malaria was evident when three hundred and fifty of them were brought to the Site 8 hospital for malaria treatment and then returned to the new camp locations.

Forced Movements of Civilians by Khmer Rouge

Fear of forced mass movements has been a component in the lives of those under the control of the Khmer Rouge from the beginning of their incarceration. Whether for punishment and "reeducation" in Phnom Dey camp, enlistment as porters of ammunition and food, or strategic relocation of base camps, civilians have been subject to arbitrary resettlement. In 1985, some months after the 1984–85 Christmas offensive, at least five thousand Khmer were moved, some coerced, from Site 8 to Phnom Dey and from there a number possibly were moved inside Cambodia. No doubt the Khmer Rouge would have liked to have moved the entire population back into Cambodia or at least away from Western influence and observation. They would have preferred to have received military and food assistance from the Chinese funneled through the Thai military, unfettered by humanitarian accountability. However, the Thai military, in this particular instance, stopped the Khmer Rouge from forcing any more people back into Cambodia.[43]

As the Vietnamese began to withdraw their troops from Cambodia in 1988, the Khmer Rouge attempted to begin building a political base inside Cambodia. They relocated thousands of their civilians from Thailand to Cambodian "repatriation villages" in highly malarial, jungle areas and to satellite base camps inside Thailand, totally inaccessible to humanitarian assistance. Between June and November 1988, at least fifteen thousand people were moved from two civilian camps, O'Trau on the northeastern border and Taluan on the southeastern border, to such Khmer Rouge-controlled areas.

Several incidents preceded further movement from O'Trau, one of the Khmer Rouge border camps that allowed humanitarian organizations limited access to civilians. The outpatient department, run by a Thai indigenous NGO, was burned in December 1988, followed by the sacking of a food warehouse. After this the camp was closed to any outsiders by the Thai military for security purposes for several weeks. O'Trau had been a camp of more than sixteen thousand in December 1988. In addition, eight thousand residents had arrived from Huay Chan, a Khmer Rouge camp near O'Trau. Huay Chan had been cut off from UNBRO assistance because the Khmer Rouge officials of the camp refused to allow a medical program in the camp, including a vaccination program, and would not give food or supply-monitoring access to the organization, one of the qualifications for providing humanitarian assistance to noncombatants. Six months later the population of O'Trau was approximately ten thousand with fourteen thousand unaccounted for.[44] They had been moved to more strategic positions with the help of Task Force 838, a branch of the Thai military that has assisted in the movement of Chinese arms and supplies to the Khmer Rouge throughout their years on the border.

In 1988 the majority of the nine thousand civilian residents of Taluan camp, mostly women and children, were forcibly moved to locations closer to the military engagements at the border. By day truckloads left with people who had consented to leave without resistance; the resisters were led at night at gunpoint to the waiting trucks. Only about one thousand Khmer were left in the camp. They were the discards, the ones no longer useful to Khmer Rouge military exigencies—the handicapped who had lost limbs in the service of the Khmer Rouge, the elderly whose age was seen as a burden rather than as a cultural resource, and the sick whose weakness was considered an impediment to the military.

The brutality of war hit the relocated civilians from Taluan in November 1988 when heavy artillery shelling struck the V3 camp to which they had been transferred. It was reported that three to five hundred had been wounded and an undetermined number killed in two days under heavy fire. Neither ICRC nor any other border agency was given access to any of the wounded. Presumably they were taken to the poorly equipped and staffed three-hundred-bed Khmer Rouge hospital at Camp 85.[45] The Khmer Rouge officials determined who would and who would not receive medical assistance in hospitals staffed by "contaminating Westerners."

Some of those who did return to Site 8 for treatment eventually told what life was like in the "hidden," inaccessible Khmer Rouge border camps. Apparently little had changed in the Khmer Rouge disciplinary tactics of "Stone Age communism" from the time they ruled Cambodia from 1975 until 1979. Everything was measured in terms of military needs. The strong and healthy received the most rations and were sent out on the most dangerous military campaigns; the less capable, enlisted as porters and laborers, were fed less. Then there were those who were counted as worthless and received what was left.[46] Living conditions were primitive at best, with no consideration given to the human needs of people. There was generally no access to medical attention in a war zone filled with malaria and mines. Children were not educated, save in learning how to handle guns and grenades. Human rights abuses were blatant; executions and extreme punishments were meted out for even minor infractions and whole populations were held hostage and exposed to heavy shelling exchanges. Steven Erlanger succinctly summarizes what went on "behind the curtain."

> They [Khmer Rouge] tell of the division of people into those useful for the war and those who are not; those whose husbands or children are fighters and those who are not; those who are trusted and those who are not; those who are allowed to re-enter the world of the Westernized camps for treatment, and those who are not; and those who are treated like human beings and those who are not, used instead like pack animals to carry weapons, food and equipment.[47]

The U.S. government condemned the forced relocations from O'Trau and Taluan, even while recognizing the Khmer Rouge as a part of the legitimate coalition government of Cambodia and knowingly permitting military and humanitarian supplies to reach them through the Chinese with the assistance of the Thai military.

> We condemn this forced relocation of innocent civilians from the relative safety of UN-assisted camps to more remote areas subject to cross-border shelling and lacking the necessary facilities for the provision of essential services.
> We have urged the Royal Thai government to use its influence to encourage more responsible, humane actions on the part of the Khmer Rouge, and we understand that they have done so.[48]

Movements of people, nevertheless, continued. By 1990, the buffer of border people was no longer vital for Thailand because the Vietnamese troops had pulled out of Cambodia in 1989 and the sporadic negotiations between the three factions comprising the CGDK and the Phnom Penh government of Hun Sen were underway. The Thai government took the stance that the CGDK was a legitimate government and could repatriate its people to the "liberated zones" in Cambodia as it willed. Relocation of refugees was no longer considered an abusive forced movement. In fact, during 1990 little was done to prevent the Khmer Rouge from moving tens of thousands of its border people back into Khmer Rouge-held territory in Cambodia.

Affect of the War on Thai Villagers

The war's carnage affected more than the opposing Khmer and Vietnamese forces and the Khmer people. Thai border villagers have been its victims as well, unintended consequences of a war. Thousands of border Thai have lost their lives, limbs, villages, and animals since the time the Khmer Rouge came to power in Cambodia. Along any border road a passer-by can see silent, deserted villages. Caved-in thatched roofs remind the observer that once a market drew neighbors together, that empty, crumbling houses once had been surrounded by children and chickens. Photos tell the story of horror—one of a man axed in half, another of a foot far distant from the body, a child blown open with intestines protruding. A mother who had been bathing her baby in an outdoor tub just moments before the blasts lay dead beside the child, only her upper torso remaining.

Military parlance calls them "affected Thai villagers." The Royal Thai government, with the assistance of donor funds and UNBRO presence, has provided new villages and assistance for many. The Affected Thai Village program came into existence in part because so much aid was going to refugees while nothing was being done for the Thai villagers who were losing everything. The relocated Thai people are safe and farther removed from the border than they were in their former villages. The new villages are orderly places. Houses are built around a square; fields spread out from the perimeter. Children are in school, and citizens contribute to the overall development of the common areas. The villages, however, show none of the diversity of shape and space nor the spontaneity of living that would normally occur physically and relationally over generations.

To the villagers who have lost their homes and livelihoods, it makes little difference if the face of the aggressor was Khmer or Vietnamese. They were at war with neither. What they want restored is the ability to work in their rice fields, keep their cattle, talk with neighbors, raise their children, and be assured that they will live their mornings and evenings in peace.

"The Khmer Rouge first came to our village in 1978," twenty-two-year-old Chamras Muksaeng recalled in 1990.

They killed twelve villagers and five buffaloes, and they burned our houses. The men remained to protect the village while the women walked to another village one hour farther into Thailand from the border.

The Khmer Rouge fell in 1979, but since then there has been shelling from time to time that has hit houses in our village. At the same time that shelling continues, so does some trade across the border. If the Khmer raid a village and take cattle from a village, they take them across the border to sell.

At night before the war we used to catch frogs near the canal. Now only the brave go there. Night is not the same and most of us do not sleep soundly. When we hear shells in the predawn, we move out of our houses and into the bunkers.

There are mines planted everywhere. The Vietnamese, Khmer, and Thai military all plant mines. No one knows where they are. No one makes a map. One area the villagers think has been cleared may be replanted. There are tons of mines, truckloads of them. When the war is over, mines will still be here on the border. Almost every day we hear mine explosions. Sometimes a person is hit; most of the time a cow is killed.

The first person from this village to step on a mine did so nine years ago. Only when a Thai military base was set up near our village did we begin to fear the presence of mines. Four people and numerous cattle have been killed by mines, and we have seven amputees. Many have left this village because of the war. Twenty families have moved deep inside Thailand far from the danger of shelling.

I am one of the amputees. Six years ago I left the village early in the morning with twelve others to go to a familiar grazing area. There was not much grass left there, for we already had been feeding the cattle in that place for five or six days. I was afraid to go, but what else could I do. We had to feed the animals.

I was the third in line when an explosion knocked me over. I felt hot all over and my shirt was torn and black. I could hardly see. I was numb and thought my companion just ahead of me had been the victim of the mine. Then I felt where my leg had been, and part of it was there no longer. My friends carried me back to the village, and I was taken in a neighbor's truck to the hospital in Aranyaprathet.

All I could think about on the way to the hospital was my father's death by a mine explosion seventeen days earlier. I did not want to die like him. As the eldest son, I knew I was responsible for the family. I could not die; I had to live.

Every day I went with my father to the rice fields and to shoot birds and catch fish. The day my father was killed, he took my younger brother, who was nine years old at the time, and my nephew to catch frogs. For the first time I did not go with him. My brother was lifted from the ground because of the explosion. My nephew came for help, but it was too late. Our father was already dead by the time neighbors arrived to carry him home.

I heard the explosion when my father stepped on the mine, but I did not realize the blast came from a mine. I thought burning made something explode. Only when the villagers said someone had stepped on a mine, did I know it was my father because he was the only one who had left the village that morning.

I became what is known as an above-the-knee amputee. It took almost two months for the wound to heal. I was fortunate that my wound did not become infected. I was then fitted by OHI for a prosthesis and was able to resume work about three weeks after I had my artificial leg. I learned how to work with it by first carrying a bucket of water and gradually was able to do more. From the first day I was fitted with the artificial limb I have worn sneakers. I do not like to wear thongs anymore, though I always wore them before the explosion.

I feared I would not be able to work again. I had lost half of myself. But there was no one else to take care of the cattle, and I was responsible for my family. I cannot carry real heavy things, and I cannot plow in deep mud.

Sometimes my mother goes by herself to take care of the cattle. I worry about her, and I fear that one of us will step on another mine. When shelling begins now, I am afraid I will not have enough time to reach a bunker. We have no where else to go, and we do not want to leave our village.

We must accept our fate very quickly. As farmers we work in the rainy season planting and growing rice. There is a system in the village in which we work together to prepare the land and plant. Every farmer must be a part of the system. The cattle must be fed. There are frogs and fish to be caught. Village life must go on.

Life is worse for us since the war. We have become poorer. It was better before because we could go nearer the border where the land is more fertile and there is plenty of water. Now we farm about two or three kilometers away from the border. The military will not allow us to go any closer. The soil inland yields only about half of what it bears nearer the border. Before the war we could produce enough for the family as well as some to sell. Now we do not grow enough for the family; we have to buy some of our food.

Young people leave for Bangkok during the dry season to make extra money. They return during the rice season. We are afraid the village will eventually disappear. We live in fear and poverty and are always prepared to evacuate. When shellings happen, we come out of the bunker only long enough to eat and work.

Refugees in the camps live artificial lives. They do not have to think if they will have rice tomorrow. It is given to them. But those of us who live in villages along the border do have to worry how we will feed ourselves. If shelling comes, the men must stay.

During heavy shelling in March 1989, a number of villages were caught in the crossfire. Narong Suwan squatted beside what remained of his home in a village less than a mile from the Thai-Cambodian border. The walls were riddled, roof beams dangled, clothes were charred beyond wearing, kitchen pans were split in half. He picked up a large piece of shrapnel, the sort that killed an eighty-six-year-old neighbor as she tried to reach a bunker, now a part of every border village home. He sat less than two feet from a crater created by the explosive that destroyed his house. A small black dog with a large sore area on his rump, bare and singed from a shrapnel burn, sat beside the man. "The dog pulled the shrapnel out of himself," Suwan commented. He continued,

When the shelling began around 6:30 in the morning only three were in the house—my oldest daughter and my two younger sons. My daughter was busy doing the laundry, and two other daughters were out gathering wood. My wife had gone to the market, and I was in the pagoda offering food to the monks.

My daughter and sons who were in the house were able to get to the bunker we dug years ago when the shelling first began to touch our village. I cannot count the times I have been to the bunker over the six years that our village has been shelled. My daughter said it was very noisy. When it became quiet again, she came out of the bunker and saw the house was on fire. She tried to bring water from the wells, and a few neighbors came to help. Many others were too afraid to come out of their bunkers.

All eight of my cows were killed. Seven were killed, and I had to kill a wounded one. I had not taken them out to graze yet. Now I have no cows to work in the rice fields, and planting begins in another month. It costs fifteen thousand baht for a pair of working cows.

My wife has not seen the house. My daughter was afraid for her to see it destroyed. She ran to the market and put her mother on a local bus passing through the town that took her to the Wat [Buddhist temple or monastery]. She is not well. I cannot imagine how she will react when she sees everything is gone.

The women and the children were moved to a school site several kilometers in from the border. We males must remain in the village to watch our belongings — chickens, cows, and houses. I fear if I leave someone will come and take what little property I have left. What will be left if the shrapnel hits the men? Sometimes the Thai military know when and from which direction the shelling will come and warn us. This time they did not.

Suwan's wife and children were taken to a hastily constructed evacuation site a few miles away from the border. With the rest of the village women, children, and elderly men, they sat on mats under the wide, white U.N. tent. They wore clothes given them by others, and they helped women cook donated food in large vats over wood fires. Women bathed their young children in the nearby *klong* (canal) and washed their clothes. "Life changed for us four years ago when our village was first hit," Suwan's wife said.

We cannot live a normal life. We are always on guard. With the Khmer Rouge military camp so near our village, we are always in danger that a Vietnamese attack on the Khmer Rouge camp may hit our village. This is the fourth time we have had to evacuate our village. Every house has a bunker under it. We do not like to think of the war, but we are always aware of it. You have to go through shelling only once to be always wary, always frightened.

We used to cross the border to a Cambodian village to visit relatives and to buy food. The noodles were cheaper. It was not far — about a five-hour walk. My oldest daughter was still small. The children would go to a movie that was shown in a field. It was more than ten years ago. Since the war we have lost contact with those relatives.

We want peace. We want the shelling to stop so we can go to work in the rice field and not run to the bunker. I hope the war finishes soon so we can live a normal life and make a living. We are Thai people. There is no war here, but we have been touched by the war.

Even some who live away from the border have been touched by the war. Sonchai Onpeng lay in the Aranyaprathet hospital, four days after he stepped on a mine. "I am the first amputee from our village," Onpeng began.

Just having artificial limbs is new to Thai villagers. Because we do not live near the border, there is no shelling in our village. Every year I go with neighbors to a certain area along the border to gather vegetables to sell. Pekwhan is well known and delicious for soup, and it grows wild. It was almost the end of the season, and we did not know there were mines in the area. We had crossed over to the Cambodian side of the border.

I am married with one five-year-old son and my wife is pregnant. We had only one hundred baht at home (U.S. $4.00). I am a seasonal worker and find only part-time jobs. Twelve bunches of pekwhan brought twelve baht (U.S. $.50). I can gather one hundred bunches in a day. My wife had not come with me that day. She was tired and remained at home.

When the explosion happened, I felt no pain. I was numb. My leg was thrown about two meters into the air, my shirt was torn, and my trousers burned. My friends who were there carried me back into Thai territory. They went to the road and asked a man on a motor bike with a wooden cart on the side to help us. They put me into the sidecart and over bumpy roads brought me to the hospital. By the time I arrived two hours later, I was in great pain. I almost fainted from the pain.

On the way to the hospital, I was very frightened, but I told myself that I was very fortunate. I had a wife, a son, and a baby on the way. But then I began to worry how I would work and wondered if my wife would leave me. That happens often to amputees. I became very discouraged.

My wife assured me she never thought of leaving me. We will live together and face the future until one of us dies. She tied a white string around my wrist to call my spirit back so that I would continue to live. A monk came and gave me his blessing so that I would have courage to fight and face the future.

I hate the war and the people who create war and cause no peace along the border. I want to call on the spirits to heal the charred earth.

MORAL QUANDARY

As years of confinement in camps lengthened for the Khmer border people, the question of continuing to administer humanitarian assistance became a moral question for many expatriate relief workers, particularly for those who worked on the border for years. The reflections of three, who will remain anonymous, explain their dilemma.

The first person looks at the border from two perspectives, the political and the humanitarian, and asks whether the continued presence of humanitarian organizations on the border prolongs the political conflict.

It seems to me that moral imperatives and moral coaxing should have some weight in how the needs of the border people are met. But politics are amoral, and we have a political situation here. The humanitarian organizations have to work within a political context. What we can do for these people is very limited. We cannot give them what they really need.

When they—and we—came to the border in 1979 and 1980, what they *needed was food and medical care. That is what we, the international organizations, can give. That is what we are here for.*

And today, ten years later, we still give them food and medical care. But that is not what they need anymore. They need a future, they need a perspective, they need a home, they need a life—a sense of life. And there we cannot help. That is a political question.

We must ask ourselves if the humanitarian aid we continue to give is reinforcing the border structure. Is it reinforcing the confinement of the people? Is it taking away a sense of life from these people? Does our presence and assistance prolong the war, or does our presence, assistance, and protection of the border Khmer still serve a purpose? If we were not here, what would life be like for them?

For some who work on the border, that sense of purpose remains very strong, particularly in remaining present among the civilian populations under Khmer Rouge control.

From the first time I went into Site 8, I have been convinced of the importance of working in and providing humanitarian services to the Khmer Rouge camps. I feel it is the responsibility of the international community to provide assistance to these camps because we are their only contact with the outside world. I believe we must not allow another Khmer Rouge holocaust to occur, which I feel is happening in the jungle camps where we have no access.

Many question our working among the Khmer Rouge. People wonder, how can we in conscience work with those killers? Those who ask that question do not realize that there are civilian populations, families caught by accident in these camps. We must make people aware of the Khmer on the border, not forget them. We do not feel responsible for those we do not see or hear about.

It is vital that we continue trying to get access to the Khmer in these camps and do something to represent them in the international community. We can make small inroads in servicing them and letting their plight become known so that one day enough people will become interested in pushing for a resolution to a conflict that has kept the Khmer people from living a normal life for more than twenty years. That is the challenge for the international workers at the Thai-Cambodian border.

For others, the presence of international relief workers has contributed to the twenty years of unrest for the Khmer.

I think when we came we did the right thing in providing relief for the Khmer people. The world responded magnificently to the crisis. I think humanitarian assistance was performed better here than in any other place in the world. And certainly our presence benefits some people—provides some with new skills and others with restored health. But the people are still here twelve years later. Why? What politics are we supporting that we let a people remain trapped?

For the powers who want to see the Vietnamese-backed government defeated, these people are simply buffers against Vietnamese incursion into Thailand and hostages who provide legitimacy to a government not one person among the border people elected. The political leaders do not care about the more than 300,000 who live in the camps or their well-being.

The border is a sick place; an evil place. The prolonged presence of the international humanitarian community has done little to alleviate the deeper suffering of these people. Certainly, they have food and shelter; they are provided with water and medicine. But the war goes on. Shells land in the camps; people are forced to move to other areas in the night when no international protective presence is there to intervene; many are executed or murdered; they are surrounded by and saturated with every form of physical and psychological human violence.

These camps we call civilian camps, like Site 2 and Site 8, are resistance camps. They exist for the military. We should call them for what they are and not continue to disguise them with compassionate words and actions under the blue flag of the United Nations.

The most that humanitarian assistance has provided for the Khmer is similar to a Band-Aid over a lethal wound. The people who have lived behind barbed wire for more than a decade have never been given the opportunity to grieve for their losses and move on with their lives. Instead, they have further lost their inner spirit and the traditions that make them a people. They try to survive and amazingly, for the most part, exhibit an astonishing normalcy in a totally abnormal situation. When, in recent years, studies were made of the psychological needs of the border Khmer, one medic tellingly observed, "We do not need psychological help; we need to get rid of Site 2."[49] Only going home can mend the broken spirits.

A Cambodian father, an amputee from a land mine, holds his small son and imagines what life in the future will bring.

Doug Hulcher

3

CAMBODIA RETURN

To tame the savageness of man and make gentle the life of the world.

—Aeschylus

On October 23, 1991, the Cambodia Peace Agreement was signed in Paris by signatories of nineteen nations: Cambodia was officially at peace after enduring more than two decades of bombings, genocide, foreign occupation, civil war, and international isolation. It is a fragile peace agreed to by the three factions of the CGDK and the Phnom Penh government. After more than twelve years of fighting, they realized that military victory would continue to elude them while the nation slid further into decline. In fact, the peace accords had gestated for two years because the four warring factions could not agree among themselves or compromise their individual positions of strength. It must be remembered that none of the three factions on the border was friendly, even though they united as a government-in-exile to rid Cambodia of the common enemy—the Vietnamese-backed government of Heng Samrin and Hun Sen. Only a United Nations-brokered and closely monitored peace held any hope for an end to hostilities.

Even as the peace accord was being signed, the sound of shelling went unabated along the Thai-Cambodian border. Jesuit Brother Bob Maat, who has worked on the border for more than a decade, is quoted as saying it was a "noisy peace."[1]

In Cambodia, the signing of a peace agreement did not assure a return to normalcy or security. The Khmer Rouge seemed incapable of letting go of their dream that one day Cambodia would embody their vision of a giant, self-sufficient collective of soldiers, workers, and peasants. To that end, even as they participated in the Paris talks, their cadres were attacking Cambodian villages and displacing hundreds of thousands of villagers, just as they had when they had controlled Cambodia between 1975 and 1979. Khmer Rouge leaders were also preparing to forcibly repatriate refugees held in their border camps to nearby, inaccessible Khmer Rouge-controlled areas in Cambodia. If they could not win by firepower, then they would attempt to do so through politics, holding a constituency hostage until "free" and "fair" elections took place in 1993.

The UNHCR's task of a safe and dignified repatriation of 350,000 border Khmer refugees will not be easy. Not only must the UNHCR contend with the Khmer Rouge's disregard of the terms of the peace accord, they also confront a land that is decimated, with almost no infrastructure in place. No more than a few schools, hospitals, roads, and bridges exist. Mines are strewn throughout the country, particularly in the area to which most of the refugees wish to return. The reintegration of the refugees will take place in a society that balances precariously between extinction and rejuvenation. It is difficult to predict the outcome.

RETURN OF CAMBODIAN LEADERS TO PHNOM PENH

Prince Norodom Sihanouk and Khieu Samphan, two of the Khmer leaders of the newly formed Supreme National Council (SNC) that will be the Cambodian governing organ under the peace accord, might well be characters representing the forces of Good and Evil in a medieval morality play. For the Khmer people, they are symbols of their hopes and fears, exaltation and anxiety as they stand on the edge of peace.

On November 14, 1991, three weeks after the peace agreement was signed, Prince Sihanouk, the god-king of light representing Khmer hopes for peace and posterity, stepped from a Chinese jet onto the tarmac of Pochentong airport in Phnom Penh to cheering crowds. Fifty years earlier he had been appointed king by Cambodia's French colonists, and almost thirteen years earlier he had fled into exile following the Vietnamese invasion of his country that routed the Khmer Rouge. The seventy-year-old Sihanouk, with garlands around his neck, pressed his hands together in *sampeah*, a prayer-like gesture that is the traditional Khmer greeting, and bowed reverently before the saffron-robed Buddhist monks and white-clad nuns. Perhaps half of the eight million Khmer people today do not know Sihanouk and visualize him only from striking billboards placed prominently around the city. The photo replicated is one taken fifteen years ago when the Prince still had black hair and great vigor.

If the majority of people were glad to see Sihanouk return, Sihanouk himself was profoundly moved to be on Cambodian soil. "I want to die on Cambodian soil. I am a Cambodian," the prince exclaimed.[2] Before his return he had voiced his fears: "I am afraid of dying or becoming senile before seeing the sun come up on the dawn of a new Cambodia and the rehabilitation of its people."[3]

The Royal Palace, from which Sihanouk had reigned for more than thirty years, had been refurbished for the prince's homecoming. When he had left its grounds in 1979, he had been a prisoner, not a ruler. After being made titular head of the Khmer Rouge during the years they controlled Cambodia, the prince and his wife, Princess Monique, were put under house arrest in the palace by the same Khmer Rouge that tortured and killed five of their children and fourteen of their grandchildren. The couple was allowed to leave only when the Vietnamese forces closed in on the capital. In the intervening years objects of art and memorabilia in the Royal Palace had been vandalized or stolen. Like the country, the shell and the shape of the palace, though battered, remained the same; inside, both needed to be newly furnished.

The revitalized Classical Dance Company of Cambodia performed ancient Khmer dances for Sihanouk's arrival. Although the prince had always encouraged the arts, 90 percent of the dancers and other professional artists had been eliminated by Pol Pot as manifestations of bourgeois elitism and capitalist imperialism, or they had fled to other countries. Only a few survive who remember the movements and the meaning of the dance and can instruct younger Khmer in this tradition.

Almost as soon as he arrived, Sihanouk began to press for the restoration of Angkor Wat. More than any other structure, the great complex of Angkor temples symbolizes all that is great in the Khmer people. During the Sihanouk era, after the French colonial rediscovery and restoration of the ruins, the complex had become a showcase to which Sihanouk proudly escorted visiting dignitaries. The Angkor era between the ninth and fifteenth centuries was the golden period of Khmer history, and for Sihanouk the more than six hundred Hindu and Buddhist structures at Angkor bear testimony to what the Khmer people might again become. To him the costly and time-consuming restoration is worth the price, for in the restoration, Sihanouk believes, the people will find themselves. Twenty years of war and neglect did to Angkor what it did to the country as a whole. In the Gallery of a Thousand Buddhas only two statues have heads.

The last time the country knew peace was under Sihanouk. The people hope that Sihanouk's presence will restore their lives as a people and as a nation. Few today seem to ponder his role in tipping the country over the edge into the hell from which it may now emerge. In his determination to maintain Cambodia's neutrality, Sihanouk had allowed the North Vietnamese to create sanctuaries inside Cambodian territory. He then turned his back when secret U.S. bombing missions destroyed those sanctuaries, causing thousands of Khmer villagers seeking asylum to bloat Cambodian cities. He threw in his lot with the Khmer Rouge when he was overthrown by General Lon Nol, and he gave a veneer of respectability to the genocidal Khmer Rouge before the world community. When Pol Pot put Sihanouk under house arrest in Phnom Penh for most of the Khmer Rouge period and killed many members of his family, Sihanouk called the Khmer Rouge "the bloodiest, most cruel and most inhuman tyranny in world history."[4] In spite of his hatred for the actions of the Khmer Rouge, he joined them in the Coalition Government of Democratic Kampuchea and from the camps along the Thai-Cambodian border waged war against the Vietnamese-backed Cambodian government in Phnom Penh. Until very recently he called the Prime Minister of this government and now vice-chairman of the SNC, Hun Sen, a "one-eyed lackey."[5] After signing the peace accord, Sihanouk joined a coalition with Hun Sen, calling him "son." Hun Sen, whose government controlled 95 percent of Cambodia at the time of the signing of the Paris Peace Agreement, in turn, named Sihanouk "head of state," a title he lost in the 1970 coup d'état.

Perhaps too much hope has been placed on one man. Though a young generation in Cambodia grew up without the theatrics and mystique of Sihanouk, though it recognizes that he conspired with the dreaded Khmer Rouge and does not regard him with the same deference as their elders, the question still remains of whether the peace can hold together without him. British Foreign Office Minister of State Lord Caithness remarked: "I would single out Sihanouk . . . as being the embodiment of Cambodia's will to survive."[6] Sihanouk has always regarded himself as the father of the nation and the people as his children.[7]

When the symbol of darkness, Khieu Samphan, the fifty-nine-year-old Khmer Rouge leader of the SNC, returned to Phnom Penh on November 27, there was no fanfare. His plane from Bangkok landed at Pochentong airport unannounced, and he climbed into a limousine with heavily tinted glass for his ride into the capital. Still Phnom Penh residents knew of his return and many gathered on the street to jeer him and throw rocks as he drove past. He was hustled into a villa prepared for him and was welcomed by his colleague Son Sen, who had returned just as furtively ten days earlier.

Within hours of Khieu Samphan's return, a crowd of thousands gathered outside his residence demanding his departure. More than a dozen persons broke into the villa and found both Khieu Samphan and Son Sen cowering, crouched in a closet on the second floor. With vengeance, the intruders pounded them with sticks and were about to lynch the two men when government troops came to their rescue. Under heavy guard Khieu Samphan and Son Sen were spirited to a waiting armored tank that took them to the airport where they boarded a plane for Bangkok just hours after Khieu Samphan's arrival.

Although the Khmer Rouge leaders at first maintained that Hun Sen had orchestrated the demonstration and later blamed the incident on the Vietnamese, it seemed clear that the people were releasing years of pent-up anger against the Khmer Rouge who had decimated their country and murdered their relatives. Khieu Samphan was a brilliant economist who had planned the organization of the pure, collective agrarian society and orchestrated the emptying of Phnom Penh. Son Sen, head of Khmer Rouge security operations, had created torture chambers like Tuol Sleng and ordered the executions of hundreds of thousands in extermination camps. It is no wonder Khieu Samphan and Son Sen wanted to dismantle these places of torture and death, now preserved as memorials to those who died at the hands of the Khmer Rouge. However, Hun Sen, whose government had set some of the torture chambers and mass graves aside as memorials to those who died under Khmer Rouge brutality, insisted this was not to be. "History is history—you cannot delete it," he said. "Whoever would like to implement a policy of destroying or dismantling these sites that mark the genocide of Pol Pot and the Khmer Rouge is implementing a new policy of genocide."[8]

After Khieu Samphan and Son Sen fled the villa, the crowds entered the residence, breaking furniture, throwing household items out the windows, and setting fire to the accumulated pile. A reporter rescued some documents from a burning suitcase. They were addressed to Number 87, the code name for Pol Pot, who, though in hiding, still holds powerful control. On one paper these words from a passage defining genocide from the United Nation's Convention for the Prevention and Repression of Genocide Crimes were underlined several times: ". . . with the intention to destroy . . . a national, ethnic, racial, or religious group." Highlighted, too, was the statement that genocide crimes are not extraditable offenses.[9] The Khmer Rouge leaders had cause for concern, since calls to try these leaders for the crime of genocide had become more intense.

In another document, Son Sen remarked on the streets of Phnom Penh, "While in the car yesterday, I noted that there were people everywhere."[10] His last recollection was of a capital emptied at the orders of the Khmer Rouge leaders, himself among them, on April 17, 1975.

THE PEACE ACCORDS

Talks that culminated in the peace accords and enabled Prince Norodom Sihanouk and Khieu Samphan to return to Cambodia began in Paris in 1989 under the sponsorship of France and Indonesia. They broke down in August with the French foreign minister stating, "Time is not yet ripe for a comprehensive political solution."[11] Neither the Khmer representatives nor the international community were ready for consensus, compromise, or reconciliation.

The process, though, continued. Early the following year the five permanent members of the United Nations Security Council—France, Britain, the U.S.S.R., China, and the United States—drafted a peace plan that proposed a transitional coalition government supervised by the United Nations until free and fair elections could be held in a peaceful Cambodia. Leaders of the four factions—Prince Sihanouk, Son Sann, and Khieu Samphan of the CGDK and Hun Sen from Phnom Penh—continued to oscillate, talking at one moment and breaking off discussions the next. In September 1990 the four factions agreed to form a twelve-member Supreme National Council (SNC) that would govern Cambodia during the transition. Slowly, painfully, and not without acrimony the Khmer leaders, with the support of the permanent members of the Security Council, progressed toward a time that was ripe for a comprehensive political settlement.

World events and new alignments affected their progress. The unraveling and economically distressed Soviet Union could no longer provide Vietnam the assistance it needed to continue sponsoring the Phnom Penh government's military needs. Although a rapprochement between China and the

Soviet Union began in the spring of 1989 when Deng Xiaoping and Mikhail Gorbachev held their first summit in thirty years, China and Vietnam remained strongholds of communism. That common bond brought China and Vietnam together over the next two years, normalizing their relations. No longer could they find cause to continue their proxy war against one another in Cambodia. Vietnam, on the verge of economic collapse, also needed to be free of the Western-imposed embargo. Ending the occupation of Cambodia was one of the major prerequisites to lifting the embargo.

The Paris accords entrust the United Nations with an unprecedented peace-keeping role. Responsibility for maintaining the peace and administering the transition period will be given over to as many as twenty thousand U.N. soldiers and civilians at a projected cost of almost two billion dollars. The United Nations Transitional Authority in Cambodia (UNTAC), in effect, co-governs with the twelve-member SNC that represents Cambodian sovereignty and reconciliation. Mr. Yasushi Akashi, a Japanese who has spent a long career with the United Nations, will head UNTAC as a special representative of Secretary General Boutros Boutros-Ghali. He sees himself as a catalyst for the Khmer people as they rebuild their country and reconstitute themselves as a nation. The SNC surrendered controlling power to UNTAC in such key ministries as defense, foreign affairs, finance, public security, and information.

UNTAC was also given the responsibility to organize and prepare the Khmer people for free and fair elections expected to take place sometime in 1993, eighteen to twenty-four months after the peace was to take effect. The importance of preparing the Khmer to participate fully in the 1993 elections cannot be underestimated as the Khmer people have never voted in a free election.

UNTAC will continue to verify the cease-fire effective with the signing of the treaty. It is also to make certain all foreign troops, military advisors, and personnel remaining in Cambodia and their weapons and equipment depart and that foreign military aid cease. UNTAC's greatest challenge is the demobilization and disarming of 70 percent of the military of the four factions and confining the remaining 30 percent into cantonments. This entails as many as 200,000 troops and at least as many militia members. During the negotiations leading up to the peace agreement, the question of disarmament loomed large, with the United States and other powers pressing for total disarmament while Hun Sen insisted on a scaled-down force for each of the four factions. His position was that the U.N. could easily monitor the demobilization and disarming of his 100,000 troops as well as the smaller forces of the KPNLF and the Sihanoukists, while the U.N. force might have neither the will nor the ability to penetrate jungle areas held by the forty to sixty thousand troops of the Khmer Rouge. Hun Sen's argument won the day, for no one wanted the Khmer Rouge to retain an independent military force.

As the need for a political solution became more apparent and after the Vietnamese troops withdrew from Cambodia, the fighting increased as the warring Khmer factions made one last effort to claim areas that would assure them of political spheres of influence. The border factions found it particularly important to control Cambodian territory to which they could either force or lure those who had lived under them in the camps.

The Khmer Rouge, militarily the strongest of the border factions, was particularly active within Cambodia following the 1989 Vietnamese withdrawal. Using their old tactics of terror and kindness, they looted, burned, and mined a number of villages while they cajoled other villagers to follow them with promises of extraordinary benefits. They murdered and maimed, displacing between 170,000 and 190,000 Khmer civilians in nine provinces.

FORCED REPATRIATION BY THE KHMER ROUGE

At the end of September 1991, less than a month before the peace accord was to be signed by the four warring Khmer factions, the Khmer Rouge announced its most blatant plan in the history of the border—to forcibly repatriate to Cambodia all forty-three thousand Khmer civilians living under their control in Site 8 camp.

Going home was something the 350,000 Khmer in camps had dreamed of for years. Only the thought of walking freely in their homeland had kindled hope in their wavering spirits.

But the Khmer Rouge plan for moving the inhabitants of Site 8 had nothing to do with freedom or choice or "going home." Many of the camp's inhabitants vividly remembered life under the Khmer Rouge during the years Pol Pot ruled. They remembered, too, being forced to flee with the Khmer Rouge in retreat from the advancing Vietnamese troops in 1979. Throughout their years in Khmer Rouge camps along the border, many had been forcibly relocated to military satellite camps closer to the front to serve the military needs of unbending Khmer Rouge leaders. They had portered ammunition across mine-infested fields, routed and massacred innocent villagers, and trembled in fear for their lives should they make one misstep before the all-seeing eyes of Angka.

In the border camps in Thailand they were incarcerated—but protected by international agencies. Many feared they would be dead in a week if the Khmer Rouge forced them through the gates of Site 8 and across the border into one of Cambodia's most malarial and mine-infested regions. Terror of a return to the killing fields gripped the people of Site 8. They would be hostage to the Khmer Rouge, serving them as an unwilling political base in the planned "free" elections.

According to Susan Walker, Thailand director of Operation Handicap International (OHI), "In my twelve years of working with the Khmer on the border, this is the worst human situation I have witnessed in a U.N.-administered camp. This is tragic given the fact that peace is within grasp and the peace accords are due to be signed in Paris on October 23 [1991]."[12]

On September 30, sixteen of the elected civilian Khmer Rouge administrators at Site 8 were "invited" purportedly to attend a meeting in the Cambodian town of Khao Din near the Thai-Cambodian border. They never returned. Instead, on October 3 they were replaced by five Khmer Rouge military personnel, four men and one woman, who declared themselves to be the new administration. The others, they said, had been assigned to new jobs in Cambodia preparing for the return of all the citizens of Site 8 to the homeland.

In the fall of 1991, one Site 8 resident, who will remain anonymous and who has sought protection in Site 2, felt compelled to tell the story of what was happening to the people in the camp. He kept a diary detailing the events of the next few weeks as he experienced them. He had lived in Site 8 for six years and had made a place for himself working among amputees like himself. Through him, they learned a trade and began to believe in themselves again. They began to believe they had something to contribute to society.

At the beginning of his diary he wrote a heartfelt poem. He chose to write his diary in faltering English he had learned from expatriates working in the camp rather than in Khmer because he wanted his message to be heard by those he believed could right the wrongs being perpetrated by the Khmer Rouge against the residents of Site 8.[13]

From a Diary of a Man

Seventeen years under Khmer Rouge,
I learned what meant by lots I knew.
When I dream up I see what's past,
Like a nightmare I come at last.

The depths of life can scarcely be told.
Let truth be true within my soul.
It's not an act but a real being;
My soul couldn't be saved just by words
I'm saying—
To know the way it is today till I am old.

My purpose of writing a short diary,
Is to tell an event when I was gloomy.
In man's value it's worth doing,
So Human Rights for all men will be respected,
It leads men forward to peace and stability.

October 3: This evening I was writing a project proposal to prepare those I work with for repatriation. I had just finished the introduction when a friend of mine got off his bicycle outside of my office.

"Terrible information. Terrible information," he said coming toward me. "We must be careful," he continued in a low voice.

"Why are you so anxious? What is the situation?" I asked.

He answered with perceptible anxiety. "I have come from a meeting with the new administrators. They are all from the military and will replace Mr. Seng Sok's administration. The sixteen administrators and section leaders who were recalled [to Cambodia] by Mr. Ni Korn, the regional commander, on the twenty-ninth, last Saturday, have been detained in Ta Chann [jail] . . . We have to pay more attention. Almost all the section leaders are already there. We are leaders of public services in the camp who someday will be forced to follow them."

It's unbelievable that these people could do such a terrible thing to the administrators, who were elected by the people in the camp, without notifying us. I dropped my pen on the paper because I felt anxious and could not conceive such a situation . . . A new man joined us and said:

"I'm afraid the ghost from the past is coming back. One of the five newly appointed administrators, Mr. Rin, was a senior officer in the Khmer Rouge when they ruled Cambodia [1975–78]. He is also the man who was our administrator when Site 8 suffered from bandits and robbery between 1985–86. I'm afraid he will allow such things to happen again, or he might use soldiers to force us to go and stay at the border where many mines were planted during battles between 1985 and 1989. It is the most malaria-infested area in Cambodia, and there is no medicine or enough food . . ."

I cannot sleep tonight. My wife is frightened, worrying that we will be dragged to the border. I sat on the edge of the bamboo bed with my thumb on my forehead. No friends visited my house in the dark as they usually do. I asked myself if I had to risk leaving the camp. What would happen if I stayed in camp and worked normally . . .? The KR used to say that all the foreign aid workers are CIA. I have worked with the foreigners for thirteen years . . . Many of them know me well.

From 1986 to 1988, a friend of mine, who worked for foreigners, was jailed with no evidence of wrongdoing. He was charged with spreading foreign ideology. I feel the ghost of the past returning.

Would this same thing happen to me? What does Human Rights mean? What is justice? I need to save myself, my family, and other people because I fear the KR, who ignore human rights and who might do something violent and stir up trouble among the people.

I got off my bed and walked to my office in order to write and ask for help . . . Two of Mr. Rin's children, the ghost from the past, were staying in the building where my office was located. I couldn't write the letter in the office, so I took some paper and a pen and returned home.

I don't have a table in my house, so I had to lie on my stomach to write . . . In the dark, my mood was mixed up and confused with many thoughts. I was so pessimistic.

At 2:00 A.M. in the quiet of night, my wife complained of pain in her chest. She has had heart trouble since the Pol Pot regime. I helped her with her breathing . . .

October 4: When I got to my office, a man came past and said, "You had better escape. You are not secure."

When I came into my office other people followed. We collected more information, both rumors and fact.

• *The camp is now closed . . . The military will no longer allow people to enter Site 8, even if they are sick.*

• *A lot of children have died during the week because of malaria. People lack food [in the KR border territory in Cambodia].*

• *The KR wants to drag us to Phnom Preuk, the area where the most fighting took place between 1985 and 1989. Hundreds of thousands of land mines are planted there, and it is full of malaria. Rumors abound that the people from Site 8 will be moved to Phnom Preuk. The military will request the U.N. and the international humanitarian agencies to follow with assistance in shelter, food, and medicine.*

• *There were a lot of [armed] soldiers coming around at the back of the camp last night. They took over all the police checkpoints.*

• *The new administration and the DPPU [Thai camp security force Displaced Persons Protection Unit] joined together for a party in the camp. We are afraid the DPPU is collaborating with the KR . . .*

This afternoon, I gave my letter to an expatriate friend who will fax it to Bangkok. It's not easy to send this letter because I trust nobody. The night is wet and darker than ever. The rain is falling heavily. How would it be if I were forced to leave camp in rain like this?

The new military administration decided to move the Site 8 population to Phnom Preuk on October 20–23. Officials from UNBRO, the United Nations, and other members of the SNC were outraged that the Khmer Rouge would make such a mockery of the proposed peace agreement just days before the warring parties were to sign the accord in Paris. While UNBRO refused to recognize the legitimacy of the new administrators, other U.N. officials protested the planned movement of the people. On October 12, S.A.M.S. Kibria, the United Nations secretary-general's special representative for coordination of Cambodian humanitarian assistance programs, stated:

> [R]eports [of the planned Khmer Rouge move] are extremely disturbing and are of the utmost concern to the U.N. Any such attempts to move those populations would be in conflict with the draft peace settlement for Cambodia . . . and would be contrary to the agreed U.N. repatriation plan . . .
>
> I would like to add that the U.N., ICRC, and some NGOs have received formal requests from a number of Khmer in Site 8 to be provided with immediate protection. I am requesting the Thai authorities to allow such special cases to be moved on humanitarian grounds to alternative U.N.-administered sites on the border for this purpose.[14]

United Nations Secretary-General Javier Pérez de Cuéllar was appalled when he learned that the Khmer Rouge planned to disregard blatantly the peace proposal and return civilians, over whom it held control, against their will to inaccessible areas in Cambodia. In fact, what the Khmer Rouge proposed, according to the secretary-general, directly contradicted the guidelines and principles of the agreements, including the assurance that the secretary-general would facilitate the repatriation of the Khmer refugees in safety and dignity. Forcible movement of the Khmer Rouge-controlled border population to uninhabitable and difficult-to-reach areas inside Cambodia flagrantly violated the comprehensive plan for peace.

On October 17 Prince Sihanouk, president of the SNC, diplomatically made clear to the Khmer Rouge that any forced repatriation was in violation of the draft agreement and the welfare of Cambodia. The prince denounced separate plans by the Khmer Rouge that were not consistent with the draft agreement to repatriate Khmer people, and which, in fact, diametrically reversed the terms laid out. The prince reacted immediately by writing to faction representatives on the SNC, directing any involved in forcibly moving any civilian-camp populations to desist immediately. He sent a special message to the Khmer Rouge representatives, admonishing them to cease any forced movements from Site 8. Repatriation must be free, the prince stressed, and the people from Site 8 and other Khmer Rouge camps must be allowed to register for the area in Cambodia to which they chose to return. The prince also notified Khmer Rouge leaders that the replacement of Site 8 elected administrators by Khmer Rouge military personnel was unwarranted, unacceptable, and not in the interests of the Khmer people, the nation, or peace.

In an October 17 press statement, the Khmer Rouge leaders on the SNC, Khieu Samphan and Son Sen, hotly denied any hint of a forced repatriation scheme in Site 8. On the contrary, Khmer Rouge leaders insisted, they had the utmost respect for the "principles of free choice of the camp population and voluntary repatriation." They pointed instead to the people's strong desire to return as quickly as possible to their homeland. In fact, they maintained, the people of Site 8 and other Khmer Rouge border camps were impatient to return home and acquire land. According to Khmer Rouge leaders, Site 8 residents had maintained close contact with relatives in the Khmer Rouge zones and had visited them many times. Further, people from Site 8 saw that their relatives lived in decent homes, had animals and adequate land for crop production.

The press statement concluded by saying:

At present, as they are aware that there will soon be the peace agreement, they most eagerly want to return home. They want, of their own free will, to settle inside Cambodia and to have lands for their families instead of continuing to wait in the camp where their future is far from certain. It was in such circumstances that the Committee of Site 8 camp have gone to the areas under the control of the Democratic Kampuchea party to look for lands along the Mongkol Borei River. All the Committee members can return to the camp whenever they want to. No one has been detained by the Democratic Kampuchea party.

Appeals for U.N. special protection by more than six hundred Site 8 residents belied the Khmer Rouge leaders' protestations of liberty and free choice. One wrote, "I don't know how I can escape from the KR. It's dangerous to stay in camp." Another pleaded, "Please help me!!!!! I cannot stay. I'm waiting for help."

Many felt that if the Khmer Rouge administrators did initiate the move, the camp residents would be powerless to resist. One said, "We cannot say no — we must go." Another explained, "If the military comes in the night to get us we cannot say NO — we must go. We are not brave enough to say no. We are afraid and don't even trust each other. We were staying under pressure of these people (KR) long ago and our fear remains."

They believed the rumors they heard. "The Khmer Rouge treat people like dogs, like animals — there are many, many children and even men and women dying of malaria and mines in the zones."

Disbelief of the purported fate of the former camp administration was prevalent. What Khieu Samphan and Son Sen told the camp population, one person observed, "reminds us of what we used to hear, which wasn't true." "I'm sure they were removed because they don't work effectively for the purpose of the KR in convening the people to start moving to the border preparing the repatriation through the KR way," stated one, while another conjectured, ". . . all the detained people are being compelled to write their autobiography of their life — like in the period with the DK [Democratic Kampuchea]."[15]

On October 6 the diarist wrote:

All around people looked very sad. No one had a smile, a sweet smile. The only words they spoke were ones of complaint about the terrible situation that is so frightening to them . . . Even though everyone in the camp is preparing for the Khmer ancestor commemoration day, Pachum Ben, *no one feels enthusiasm for it.*

Many of the camp leaders, like the diarist, feared that they would be called upon to visit Phnom Preuk and prepare the way for "voluntary" repatriation. This fear became a reality when Khmer Rouge administrators called first on forty leaders followed by another two hundred to precede the remainder of the camp population into Cambodia. Although this was not to be a "forced" move of the leaders, according to the diarist's account of two separate meetings, the administration gave them little room for choice. It seemed old words were being framed anew. In the past Khmer Rouge administrators had said: "Those who return first will be given hammocks to sleep in. Those who return second will sleep on the ground. Those who return third will sleep under the ground."[16]

According to the diarist, Khmer Rouge administrators admonished the leaders gathered at the meetings:

"If you don't help the people in the camp get out, you are traitors. You are leaders and you must go first. You cannot speak to the U.N., except to ask for help for the people, or you are traitors . . . We cannot stay here to be repatriated through the UNHCR because we don't believe the UNHCR will help us, especially with land for farming . . . We have to beware of the tricks of enemies."

When the first meeting of Site 8 leaders called by the Khmer Rouge began on October 6, the diarist observed:

All the participants were acting as brave as they could but became silent when the head . . . appeared from a nearby room. He is a handsome man with black moles on his face. His smile is charming when he welcomes us. He must be an educated man, about 42 and not very tall. He doesn't shake hands as he greets the participants, but puts both his hands [together], in the cultural Khmer salutation. Yes, he is outwardly a Khmer, but inside he is a Khmer Rouge.

The diarist recorded the pertinent points made by the administrator at the meeting. He challenged those who attended to bring to completion the mighty vision the Khmer Rouge held for the nation. "Khmer Rouge patriots who preceded you in the struggle to form a 'democratic' Kampuchea had gone 99.50 kilometers on a one-hundred-kilometer walk," the administrator admonished. "It is now up to you to begin walking the final half kilometer so we all might reach our destination." The fate of the people, the leaders were told, was in their hands, not in the hands of the untrustworthy UNHCR. The area of Phnom Preuk was ready, the Khmer Rouge insisted. The administrator continued:

"Phnom Preuk is now prepared for our people in Site 8 to settle. We have four tractors already busy working in the fields. We will build a hospital and a secondary school [with no mention of a primary school, the diarist notes]. *Because we will have enough land, the people can easily earn their living by agriculture. We can trade our natural resources of timber, gold, and gems with Thailand.*

"Now, you leaders must go, tomorrow or the day after tomorrow. I will send you for a visit to this place so that you can locate a good area to settle your people. Land will be provided them for agriculture."

October 12: [The second meeting] When there was a question about food for the population in the transitional period without support from U.N., he [the administrator] answered that: "We don't adhere to communism anymore. We prefer to have capitalism in our country. Therefore, people must buy food themselves. As soon as people come to settle at the border, they can produce crops, and begin market activity with the Thai people.

"All our seniors [the former administration] have been appointed to new positions to help our superior at the border. They are OK. Don't believe people who say those leaders are detained. It's not true. They are now studying in Bang Ken. They are preparing the hospital and other places for all people from Site 8."

Reports about the former members of the Site 8 administration, however, indicated that it was otherwise. An individual who had gone for himself to see if Phnom Preuk was ready wrote:

The situation is very bad. Even though there are three tractors clearing land, it is still full of mines. It is in the jungle and there are millions of mosquitos and no medicines. There is not enough food and not even enough water. Only those who live near the river have enough water. But the river is one kilometer away and is very small. During the dry season, it may not have very much water.[17]

A letter written to a friend who had seen the area where the Khmer Rouge intended to move the people of Site 8 warned them not to be lured by the Khmer Rouge promises:

Dear Brother: How are you all? I have just come from the first line. When I heard about Site 8, I went to Ta Chann to see if you might be detained there. I became happy when you were nowhere to be seen. Just stay in the camp and don't come to the border even if the administrators invite you to visit the area prepared for your population. I've just heard that the KR will keep trying one way or another to drag all the leaders [to Phnom Preuk] and then repatriate all the people to the border . . .

By the end of the first meeting of the Site 8 leaders with the new administration, the diarist knew he would seek protection in Site 2; he describes events that solidified his intent to leave Site 8.

October 7: I decided to go to a protection center—to safety. I don't want to stay in Site 8 any longer. At home I started to write a formal request to the ICRC delegation. My dysentery is worse.

October 8: U.N. agencies and ICRC demanded to meet the former administrators. Mr. Ni Korn refused to meet anybody from the U.N. agencies but has allowed Mr. Seng Sok and other former administrators to meet U.N. representatives. The former administrators and U.N. representatives cannot meet directly. They remain on each side of the river, which is full of running water, and talk through the radio. Ni Korn hides nearby to listen . . .

In the afternoon a soldier with a pistol came to the center . . . The supervisor came out to greet him and offered him a chair. The man refused it. He walked around in the building to see the activities and turned back to the supervisor. "It is not good, you know. In fact, you don't know what you are doing. You don't realize that the foreign ideology is being sucked into your brain. You only know that you are working for the people and our nation. But foreigners are trying to insert their ideology, which is not our culture, into your head. You may forget our loving motherland, and then you might work solely for the foreigners. Their ideas are not in the interest of our people and nation. Look!" by pointing to a foreign magazine, "it's not our culture. It might say something about the Westerners . . ."

At night some soldiers came around to sections in the back of the camp. A soldier came into section 12 and attempted to rape a girl. There were some friends of his around with guns. The police who stood guard in the section couldn't help, but the girl tried to struggle with the soldier. People felt helpless and were terrorized.

October 10: An expatriate friend visited me as usual. She told me to get ready to leave Site 8 tonight or tomorrow . . . ICRC staff was meeting with DPPU to ask for a green light for my family's departure.

We gathered our belongings and waited for approval to leave. I felt a shock in thinking about leaving Site 8. I thought of my achievements in my work here and all who trusted in me. What would it be like to leave them behind . . . I slept in my mixed up mood between exhilaration and nightmare.

October 11: My expatriate friend visited me as appointed. She looked depressed. DPPU didn't approve the transfer of my family. It said it should protect all the camp's population, not just a few families. ICRC continued to seek help for those who needed protection.

I should have helped the others to request protection, but I trusted nobody even though I knew my staff was frightened and they might need protection.

October 17: It was around 12:20 P.M. when my expatriate friend came back to my office to tell me that ICRC received approval to get my family out of Site 8, and that I had to be ready to leave at 1:30.

One hour was very short notice to get out of the camp I lived in for 6 years among lots of neighbors. It was a big shock for me . . . It was the last chance I had to decide whether to leave or not. I tried to remind myself what my fate would be if I remained in Site 8. If I stayed, my future would surely be bad.

Around 1:30 my family and I gathered at the hospital to wait for ICRC's car. I stepped out of my office thinking that I would not see this office and my people in the association again. I said good-bye to the staff I trusted with a voice touched with extreme emotion. We left Site 8 at 2:00 P.M. Finally, we are safe in Site 2.

Because of international pressure the Khmer Rouge backed down from their plan to move the entire Site 8 population into Cambodia. All but one former administrator was allowed to return to the camp, though not in their former administrative capacity. Few trusted the Khmer Rouge would not implement the plan at a later date, sometime after the peace agreement had been signed.[18]

Site 2 after the Peace Accords

While the residents of Site 2 did not have the specter of large-scale forced repatriation haunting them, their lives were not without turmoil. Teachers, medics, nurses, trained workers, the educated—those who could provide the most in building up KPNLF areas within Cambodia—were enticed by hard-to-resist promises from KPNLF leaders to repatriate them before the UNHCR plan took effect. Medics were among those most sought after. With the assurance of jobs and salaries, as well as land and protection by the KPNLF army, many found the offer irresistibly attractive. The expatriates who administered the hospitals in the camps feared for the safety of those who wanted to return and were concerned that the camp hospitals would be dangerously under-staffed for the duration.

Soldiers faced an uncertain future when peace became the practical option in response to a war no one could win. Once revered warriors in a battle for survival, they had killed for more than a decade with impunity, less than five kilometers from the civilian refugee camps housing their families and com-patriots. Some soon-to-be demobilized fighters did not lay down their guns. Instead, they lashed out against the very civilians they had been enlisted to protect during the twelve-year civil war. The soldiers, facing the prospect of joblessness and a lower status, watched as camp residents began to uncover gold and hidden goods valuable enough to trade for currency in anticipation of their return home. Joining bandits who had preyed upon Site 2 residents for years, they came in groups as large as fifty or sixty, shooting, killing, and taking hostages in order to steal the coveted goods. DPPU, UNBRO, and the UNHCR did not provide adequate protection.

During the night in late August 1991, sixty to eighty bandits rampaged through several sections in Site 2, terrorizing people, destroying their homes, and stealing their valuables. When the DPPU made no response to the situ-ation, the Khmer police in the camp fired on the bandits. They, in turn, responded with even greater fire power, killing five children and injuring at least seventeen more. In October another bandit raid left one old woman dead and seven others with gunshot wounds. Each night the residents went to bed terrified, knowing how little protection was afforded them by their bamboo huts and the camp security system.[19]

THE UNHCR REPATRIATION PLAN

For the UNHCR, the lead U.N. agency for repatriation, the threats of forced repatriation and acts of violence against Khmer civilians by Khmer military units compounded the difficulties of the already monumental task of repatriating 350,000 Khmer civilians from the border camps and 170,000 internally displaced Khmer.

As the plans for peace were being laid out in Paris, the UNHCR was designated the agency responsible for drawing up and implementing a repatriation plan for the Khmer to return to their country and their towns and villages. The projected $109 million plan stipulated that the repatriation of Khmer refugees must, above all, be voluntary and safe.

The UNHCR's first step was to register 350,000 Khmer in camps on the Thai-Cambodian border and document each refugee's statement of choice of place for return. As opposition by the Khmer Rouge to the UNHCR plan mounted, the UNHCR countered with a forceful information campaign throughout the U.N.-administered border camps. In camp video-parlors residents were presented with a film clearly depicting the steps to be taken in the UNHCR repatriation plan and calling on the Khmer in the camps to "wait and repatriate with UNHCR."[20] The film emphasized that the UNHCR plan was designed to take the refugees home safely when the conditions within the country were right, when land had been identified for them, and when land mines had been removed.

Based upon registration information, the UNHCR planned to acquire land, set up six reception centers, and plot out food distribution points where returnees could receive food and other necessities for up to eighteen months following their return, giving them the time to complete one rice-growing season.

If all went according to plan, the first buses would roll out of the camps and proceed to the reception centers in April 1992. Each week ten thousand Khmer would be processed and sent to their freely chosen destination after one week in a reception center. Repatriation of the entire border population would be completed before the 1993 Cambodian elections.

There was no assurance the plan would proceed smoothly, as the attempted Khmer Rouge forced repatriation plan attested. Daniel Conway, the UNHCR representative in Thailand, pointed out that there were actually six repatriation plans—those of the UNHCR, the Khmer Rouge, the KPNLF, the Sihanoukists, the Thai government, and the spontaneous returnees. Each faction was intent on solidifying a loyal political block to be in place by the 1993 elections. Conway pointed out, too, that there was more than one timetable that put the UNHCR in a dilemma. For example, while governments overseeing the peace accord wanted the UNHCR to have the refugees safely home in time to participate in the 1993 elections, the assurance of their safety might not be so certain since UNTAC did not plan to begin de-mining the countryside until two or three months after the April 1992 repatriation process was to begin. In addition, road and bridge repairs might well be needed before the UNHCR could return Khmer from the camps to the countryside.[21]

The UNHCR repatriation plan also required financial support. Unfortunately, donor fatigue will likely be one of the greatest impediments to carrying out the UNHCR repatriation plan and to rebuilding a decimated Cambodia.

By April 1992 the Cambodian situation was old news. Many were weary of it by the time the peace accords were signed in Paris. During the final year of negotiation, the Persian Gulf war displaced millions of Kurds and Shi'a Moslems; the cyclone in Bangladesh killed tens of thousands and left millions homeless; and the gyrations in the Eastern Bloc countries, and the economic breakdown and dissolution of the Soviet Union dominated foreign policy considerations and decisions. The UNHCR asked for a start-up fund of $33 million and by November 1991 had not received even half of it. The organization did not know where the total $109 million would come from. An additional plea for $12 million by the United Nations to assist the internally displaced Khmer fell practically on deaf ears.

In part, donor nations were wary that the peace would not hold. They did not want to invest in a failed peace that could become a more intense civil war. They had donated heavily to an Afghan repatriation plan after the Soviet withdrawal of troops from that country in 1989; yet two years later the war continued and five million Afghans remained in exile. Although we may have "won" the cold war, we could lose the peace unless we are willing to substantially invest in peace-keeping and in the reconstruction of decimated nations like Cambodia.

THE DANGERS OF LAND MINES

UNHCR officials were concerned that many Khmer civilians might strike out on their own, returning spontaneously to chosen areas, fearful that the best land available to returnees would be taken before they had a chance to claim it. The desire to acquire coveted land for their families would not deter these people from the dangers of mines, lack of food, malaria, impassable roads, and marauding groups of bandits.

One of the greatest dangers still facing all Khmer is the presence of millions of mines strewn throughout the country during two decades of war. They surround villages and are implanted in road and rail beds, footpaths, and water sources; they are buried in rice paddies. Moved by torrential rains, they are rarely mapped, and many are almost impossible to detect. They are also found in the simple, everyday living spaces of people and along their everyday paths. They are the "eternal sentinels," the enemy planted to endure long after its departure.[22] In fact, land mines have been the most lethal weapon of this twenty-year war. As the report *Land Mines in Cambodia* points out:

Unlike bombs or artillery shells, which are designed to explode when they approach or hit their target, land mines lie dormant until a person, a vehicle, or an animal triggers their firing mechanism. They are blind weapons that cannot distinguish between the footfall of a soldier or that of an old woman gathering firewood. They recognize no cease-fire, and long after the fighting has stopped, they can maim or kill the children and grandchildren of the soldiers who laid them.[23]

A number of minefields have been seeded by more than one faction. Soldiers have been blown apart while laying a new crop of mines over the old. It will take years and millions of dollars to discover and disable the mines, and because a large proportion of them will be found only by human touch, many more Khmer will lose their lives and limbs. In effect, the signed peace accord will not put an end to the war. "In the future the war will go, but the war will stay," one Khmer observes.[24]

It is estimated that during the course of the war thirty thousand Khmer have become amputees. This, in a population of under eight million, gives Cambodia the dubious honor of having the highest percentage of landmine amputees in the world. Along with malaria and tuberculosis, landmine injuries are the nation's greatest public health problems.[25] At least that many more have died from mine explosions. In the camps along the border another five thousand to six thousand wear artificial limbs and a large number lost their lives when they stepped on mines. Once the Vietnamese troops left Cambodia in 1989 and the Khmer factions began to make greater forays into the Cambodian countryside, each faction planted more mines to keep the Phnom Penh government troops from retaking the territory. From that time on, between six hundred and one thousand Khmer, mostly civilians, lost limbs and as many more died each month from mine injuries.

After repatriation, it is feared that many refugees will become victims of mines, since many of the areas they have chosen for relocation were some of the most embattled and heavily mined during the war. As they plant rice, play on the footpaths, and lead cattle out to graze, feet will make contact with a detonator. A large proportion of the victims will be women and children generally in the poorer rural areas where there is little access to adequate medical treatment. Many will bleed to death alone in the fields or herding cattle, while others will die because of the hours it takes to find even ox-cart transportation to the nearest medical facility.

The refugees, like the majority of Khmer, are largely rural people, small rice farmers. Those who have been maimed by mines will find it more difficult to fit into the agricultural rhythms and intense labor of the fields. As in other war-torn societies, the breakdown of the extended family will affect the amputees. In the poverty-stricken countryside, the able-bodied who can contribute the most in providing for the many dependents will be favored. Because most Khmer will have a difficult time providing for themselves, more often than in the past the handicapped will be ignored or abandoned, notwithstanding the fact that given the opportunity for rehabilitation and training, these mine victims can work in the fields or other jobs in the village. At the time of the peace accords only one in eight amputees in Cambodia had received an artificial limb and very few of those had access to or knowledge of rehabilitation or training programs.

Mine eradication will be costly and dangerous. Few are willing to undertake such a daunting task. A mine-clearing team funded by USAID reported to the Asia Watch and Physicians Without Borders delegation that in a one-kilometer stretch of road near the Thai-Cambodian border, they had dealt with 6,000 antipersonnel devices and 3,800 in another two-kilometer stretch.[26] There are virtually no maps to direct the mine-clearing teams, for mines were planted indiscriminately and in such profusion that few considered mapping the areas. Villages were often surrounded with mines just before the enemy forced the villagers to flee so that those who fled were likely to die in the attempt to cross the mined area. In the fields, soldiers placed mines under those they had killed so that when their comrades came to retrieve the bodies, they too were blown up. Mines, planted everywhere, were targeted at the general population, not simply the combatants.

The delegation from Asia Watch and Physicians for Human Rights sensibly proposed that mine eradication be placed under the United Nations to ensure neutrality and that no removed mines be given over to military personnel. Then they counseled:

> The cost for removing land mines in Cambodia will be proportional to the investment made in supplying mines to the combat factions. To carry the eradication program through to completion will require a large investment—many millions of dollars. Clearly, Cambodia has neither the economic nor organizational infrastructure to support such a large-scale undertaking in the immediate or foreseeable future. It must therefore fall to the international community to provide the funding and organization, at least in the short term.
>
> Since the outbreak of the Cambodian civil war nearly 12 years ago, several countries have provided military support to the four combatant factions, the Phnom Penh Government, the Khmer Rouge, Khmer People's National Liberation Front or Armee Nationale Sihanoukienne. All of these factions and their supporters have claimed to have had the future of Cambodia and the rights of the Khmers at heart. It should not require, therefore, any change in policy by those countries to fund a program so clearly beneficial to all Khmers, regardless of their politics. Such a commitment by China, the United States, the Soviet Union, Vietnam, the United Kingdom, and the ASEAN nations, all of which have been heavily involved in arming and training the combatant factions, would be likely to ensure sufficient funds to institute a realistic large-scale eradication program . . .
>
> Nations that have supplied mines to Cambodia's four warring parties have a moral obligation and responsibility to share in the costs of land mine eradication.[27]

DEVELOPMENT NEEDS IN CAMBODIA

The danger posed by millions of mines planted throughout the country is not the only stumbling block to a secure return of the 350,000 Khmer in the camps. The country remains devastated after twenty years of unrelenting war. It received no assistance from the Western world after the genocidal Khmer Rouge were routed in 1979. Instead, because of Western opposition to the Vietnamese invasion and control of the country from 1979 through the next decade, the trade, aid, and diplomatic embargo so stringently applied to Vietnam reached into Cambodia. The desired effect of the embargo was to force the Vietnamese to withdraw from Cambodia rather than to expand its frontiers. Even International Monetary Fund (IMF) and World Bank funding did not reach the country. The U.S. government's stipulation for a lifting of the embargo was, at first, the withdrawal of the Vietnamese troops. When that took place in 1989, the U.S. government protested that the monitoring of the withdrawal was not sufficient and refused to lift the embargo prior to the signing of a comprehensive political settlement by the four warring factions.

A few NGOs were allowed into the country to provide humanitarian assistance, but there was a strict line of demarcation between relief and development. While trucks and food given to the U.N. agencies were considered relief, the repair of roads themselves was considered development. Tens of thousands did not benefit from the relief because of a missing bridge or an impassable road. Although for a decade NGOs have worked wonders in small-scale development schemes under the most restrictive conditions, the monumental infrastructural development needed in Cambodia is beyond their scope.

Eva Mysliwiec remembers her first days in Cambodia in 1980 when she was part of an emergency program for the American Friends Service Committee.

The situation I found in Cambodia was still a very traumatized one. Very few people were living in Phnom Penh. There were signs of the destruction of the Khmer Rouge period as well as vandalism that occurred when Vietnamese forces came to the capital. I saw people living on sidewalks amid rubbish and furnishings. There were no private vehicles around except for the few that were brought in by the aid organizations to start the relief effort. A few people boasted old bicycles from the Soviet Union. I remember when the first new bikes from Thailand appeared and later the first motorcycles. If a new car appeared on the streets, everyone knew it.

People looked very traumatized. At that time they were still criss-crossing the country looking for relatives, looking for a place to live. Many people went back to their original villages thinking family would gather there first. In some cases they found their houses still there, in other cases not. So they went elsewhere.

The first food distribution I went to was in Svay Rieng Province. People who gathered in an open place were seriously malnourished. Sanitation problems were evident from the proliferation of skin diseases and rashes. We saw a lot of discolored hair, bloated bellies, parasites, very weak, very thin people. It was rare to see anyone looking healthy.

It was a very unusual situation for setting up an emergency program because you didn't have the kind of infrastructure you have in other countries. In order to bring anything in we first had to look at the repair of the airport and the ports. We had to bring in cranes to offload the goods, trucks to transport the goods, and typewriters and paper and pencils so people could make plans and monitor. It is very difficult to think what it meant to come from zero. There was no currency when I came. Until mid-1980 a barter system continued until a monied economy was restored. Two months later they introduced a new currency.

In the countryside people brought us to mass graves—some that were open and very fresh. We could see they were very recent, still seeing hair on skulls and arm bones tied together with rope or wire. We could differentiate children's skulls. I remember someone showing me a tree trunk where children's heads had been bashed. The trunk was caked over with blood. People used to grab me on the street—no matter that I didn't know the language—and started talking and talking in a traumatized way. I could see they were frantic trying, without understanding, to explain what had happened to them. Now people don't do that. They have suppressed it. But now and then something will happen in their lives that brings the trauma out and they burst into tears.

Slowly things came together. People began to gain a little more confidence in themselves. Services became a little more organized. People began to form families, grow crops, and build structures. Those who lost spouses began to remarry and couples began having children again. To rebuild a family was psychologically very important. Many women, though, had problems conceiving children.

Eva noted that, even more, women had difficulty raising children. None escaped the dehumanizing influence of the Khmer Rouge, whether in youth camps or in the countryside with their families. From an early age children had been instilled with a deep distrust of their elders and were expected to give unquestioning loyalty to their Khmer Rouge superiors. They learned to trust no one and became blindly obedient to the Khmer Rouge, even to the extreme of betraying their families and witnessing the resulting slaughter of mothers, fathers, siblings, and other close relatives.

So thorough were the Khmer Rouge in stamping out cultural mores that children lived in a cultural vacuum. When the Vietnamese invaded Cambodia, families searched the countryside to find one another. After a first embrace, many found their souls had been emptied and supplanted with a different world view. Families were strangers to one another. Children knew nothing of ancient traditions that bonded Khmer families to one another and to their society. Most of the children between one and fifteen had been brought up in the midst of family disintegration and the purging of all cultural and religious values. They had been surrounded by violence and corruption, and lived lives of fearful desperation.

What permitted families to reconsolidate their lives together was their mutual recognition of a tremendous need for support.

The Khmer were also hungry to learn. Before the Khmer Rouge eliminated education, most Khmer children completed at least primary school. More were beginning to attend secondary school. In Cambodia after the defeat of Pol Pot, even though families desperately needed their children to work, they sent them to makeshift schools that sprang up across the country. Classrooms were generally cleared areas on the ground under a large shade tree. A few clusters of children were fortunate enough to have a blackboard and some chalk. Very few had books or qualified teachers. The former had been burned and the latter killed during the reign of Pol Pot. Teachers taught what they remembered and began writing textbooks from memory. Some materials began coming in through humanitarian organizations, but not nearly what was needed.

The destruction was total, and the needs were monumental and clearly visible to the international community, Eva lamented. Not an area of life was untouched, yet addressing the needs within Cambodia took a backseat to politics. At times it was questionable whether the Khmer people would get aid in those early days. Negotiations between donors and even the United Nations and the ICRC seemed endless. Some aid did arrive, but, according to Eva, there was not the "kind of response such circumstances merited or that other countries have had after disasters—though it is hard to find a situation comparable to Cambodia where the destruction was so total. First food should have been provided; then the negotiating proceed."

The Buddhist monks were a source of great consolation to the Khmer people. They had been almost totally eliminated during the reign of Pol Pot. After the routing of the Khmer Rouge and the takeover by the Vietnamese, Buddhism began to reconstitute itself. In 1981 ox-carts full of Buddhist monks made a symbolic journey to Angkor Wat for the first convocation of Buddhist monks since the Khmer Rouge regime. At first the Vietnamese tolerated the monks. Then, in 1988, Buddhism became once again the state religion when the government revised the constitution in preparation for the peace talks among the four factions.

"The Buddhist monks have played a significant role in the healing process, in the process of reconciliation, and in restoring community activities," Eva continued.

Even in the poorest villages one of the first things to be rebuilt or repaired were the pagodas and temples. Even though people had very little for them-selves, they still contributed something to the village pagoda. Monks were crucial in helping the healing process. There was a great deal of depression and there is still some. People would go to the monks and talk about their hurts. Monks helped them feel they were not alone or abnormal in their thoughts and feelings.

Religious ceremonies — marriages, blessing of homes, ancestor blessings and blessings of those who died during the Khmer Rouge days — started early after the routing of the Khmer Rouge. These were very important in people's lives and in restoring some normalcy and stability.

In Buddhist culture there is a religious ceremony for the ancestor that many people have only begun to perform since liberation. They go back to their native village where their parents died, have the ceremony, and donate to the pagoda and the monks to earn merit for the parents. For many families this is quite a traumatic experience because it brings relatives from different places and there they have to look at each other and remember what happened. In some cases this was not pleasant. One might have done something at the expense of someone else. For example, someone might have withheld food or withheld help. Many bad feelings come out that people must deal with.

Eva arrived in Cambodia in 1980 at a time when the very survival of the country and its people was doubtful. The economy continued to stagnate because most of the money was channeled to the war effort — exacerbated by the gradual withdrawal of Vietnamese and Soviet support in the last two years of the war. Government troops were fighting factions that continued to be supplied by their beneficiaries — the Khmer Rouge by China and the KPNLF and the Sihanoukists by several Western powers. The denial of reconstruction aid and the embargo remained in effect. In 1990 and 1991, as the possibility for peace became more plausible, Cambodia's Vice Prime Minister Kong Som Ol spoke of the great need for immediate and significant international developmental aid if Cambodia was to absorb the 350,000 Khmer in the border camps. Last minute preparations for their return would create a new emergency. "When you prepare a dinner for your friends and invite them for seven o'clock, you begin preparations in the morning. That is what we must do," he observed.[28] As long as the embargo was not rescinded, the Khmer people could not move forward. Every sector of their economy and society felt the embargo's effect. Even in 1992 Cambodia remains "a country on its knees, on its belly," without the means to provide for its population. The 1991 per capita GNP was estimated at $110, one of the lowest in the world.[29]

Before 1975 Cambodia was largely a rural nation of rice farmers, fish catchers, and woods people. Not only could the nation provide for itself, it also exported rice, fish, and other produce. Ironically, the Khmer Rouge, intent on making Cambodia a totally self-sufficient agrarian society, ruined the very agricultural producing capacity it intended to improve; it destroyed the animals and equipment necessary to cultivate the land. In terms of the number of livestock, it has taken fifteen years for Cambodia to reach the point it was in 1969. More than half the oxen, water buffalo, and horses perished, an extreme for a country so dependent on draft animals for plowing, transportation, and as the main source of fertilizer. Without water buffalo, there is no rice. Without cattle for the ox-carts, Cambodia's rural transport system does not exist.

More insidious damage to the agricultural well-being of the country was caused by the forced migrations of so many people within the nation. It is estimated that 85 percent of the Khmer population was displaced, many of whom were relocated more than one time. Local knowledge of environmental factors disappeared with the people, as did water management techniques and appropriate knowledge of the varieties of seeds for an area. Pol Pot dreamed of a giant collective of peasants with abundant harvests. He gave birth to a wasteland.

Deforestation has wrecked havoc in the nation. In the 1960s 13 million hectares were forested; today approximately 7.5 million hectares of forest remain. Pol Pot wanted the forests cleared for planting, and today there is a strong temptation to plunder available timber for quick money, with little policy planning or funding for reforestation. Neighboring countries such as Thailand see an opportunity to purchase timber at low prices from the still relatively plentiful forest lands. With little government monitoring possible, private saw mills are springing up in the countryside. Rapid and extensive forest clearing affects the silting of rivers and lakes and, consequently, the fishing industry, one of the country's mainstays. Today the fish are fewer in number and smaller. Deforestation also affects the amount of rainfall and crop growth.

A strong agricultural and timber policy is necessary, as is the training of specialists — agronomists, hydrology engineers, veterinarians, foresters. Few survived the war, and those who did generally fled to another country, and their records, maps, and documentation were lost or destroyed.[30]

Agriculture still accounts for 90 percent of the GNP, with approximately 80 to 85 percent of the people engaged directly in agriculture and agriculture-related work. Today 64 percent of the Khmer population is female, with at least 35 percent of the nation's households headed by women and over 60 percent of the farmers women.[31]

With the Vietnam invasion in 1978–79, the new government implemented an agricultural plan that depended on the cooperation of the people. The *krom samaki,* a collective form of work, was not foreign to the Khmer. Farmers pooled resources and manpower, much as they did in former times in the villages. One might have an ox-cart, another a hoe, another an ox. Alone they could achieve little; together they could produce again. Both as an administrative and production unit, it seemed the only means of survival for many farmers who were without animals, tools, seeds, or clearly defined land for planting, cultivating, and harvesting.

Among its most important benefactors were widows and their children. Whether in rice production, fish netting, silk weaving, or other income-producing activities, these cooperative societies shared with the vulnerable groups — women, elders, children, and the maimed. When the Hun Sen government instituted land reform and privatization in 1989, the most vulnerable did not benefit. Because draft animals and tools are no longer shared in a cooperative effort, women who do not own a draft animal must pay for a half day of ploughing with one to three full days of back-breaking transplanting or harvesting of rice.[32]

Cambodia is woefully lacking in adequate health facilities and personnel. In 1975 there were 45 doctors left out of 450. Twenty of those fled to other countries. The rest had been murdered or starved under Pol Pot. During the Khmer Rouge period, hospitals, equipment, and medical schools were totally destroyed. In their place the Khmer Rouge set up small health clinics with inexperienced staff in the countryside. Rarely were they supplied with medicines, and no thought was given to the importance of maintaining sanitary facilities. By 1991 there were approximately two thousand students in all areas of medicine — doctors, nurses, dentists, medical assistants, pharmacists, lab technicians — studying at the reinstituted Faculty of Medicine at the University in Phnom Penh. Those students shared ten microscopes[33] and learned mostly by rote because few textbooks were available. There was no opportunity for specialization. In 1991, with forty dollars the minimum for survival, a doctor earned thirteen dollars a month; a nurse, seven dollars. All are overworked; in many provinces the physician-patient ratio is as high as one per thirty thousand.[34]

In 1979 when the Khmer Rouge was ousted from Cambodia, the infant mortality rate was 263 per 1,000 live births, the highest in the world. Today the infant mortality rate has improved to 133 per 1,000 live births but still remains one of the highest in the world. Twenty percent of all Khmer children die before their fifth birthday. The causes of so many deaths are preventable, given proper socioeconomic conditions. Deaths from diarrhea, tuberculosis, dengue fever, malaria, and malnutrition are directly attributable to poverty, lack of simple facilities and medicines, inadequate education in health, and generally poor sanitary conditions. The lack of a dependable source of electricity, a water supply polluted constantly with raw sewage, and overcrowded living conditions all contribute to a generally low level of health. No more than 21 percent of the urban population and 12 percent of the rural population have access to safe water.[35] Illnesses that should have been eradicated continue to plague communities. An outbreak of measles might claim fifty lives out of one hundred cases. A viable system of health care is needed throughout the country to provide everything from curative medication to staff to teach preventative community health.

In 1979 the newly formed Vietnamese-backed government found the school system had been annihilated by the Khmer Rouge who considered any education — primary, secondary, or higher — as dangerous to the collective system they wanted to build. Cherished books from homes and libraries were scattered and tossed as rubbish or used for fuel for warmth and cooking. The sacredness of the human mind was assailed and intellectuals were hunted down and eliminated. Morale, morals, and a hope for the future faded with the disappearance of educational institutions. It is said that 70 percent of the teachers were killed along with 85 percent of the students. According to a recent report "only 50 out of 725 university instructors survived, 207 out of 2,300 secondary teachers, and 2,717 of the 21,311 primary teachers. Illiteracy, after 1979, was found to be as high as 40 percent and few children under fourteen years of age had had any basic education."[36]

Only now can one find schools in which the entire class of first-year pupils is the same age. Prior to this, after the Vietnamese invasion, many of those who had lost out on education began from the beginning, no matter their age, under teachers with little or no training. One week to four months of training made one a teacher in those early years after the Khmer Rouge.

Today there is a great need for qualified people to train teachers. Books are in great demand. Four students may be expected to share a textbook and this situation may last for another four years. Textbook printing is at a 25 percent capacity.[37] There are few schools, and the majority of these are ill-equipped; few have water or sanitation facilities. Still, it is believed that at least about 90 percent of the school-age children are in primary school. However, although volunteer instructors across the nation have mobilized in an effort to eradicate illiteracy, under 2 percent of the children reach level ten.

In many ways, unless conditions change, the 350,000 border Khmer will be worse off after repatriation in their own country than they were in the camps. Medical care, education, water supply, food, and shelter, if not ample, were at least adequate and assured, and this is not always the case in Cambodia. Although better off in some of the material goods than their compatriots in Cambodia, the camp residents did not have freedom or control of their lives. They were hostages and political pawns used to advance the war and give legitimacy to the warring factions, the clients of larger powers.

The returning refugees have special needs. They need land and utensils to start over again as farmers, a reorientation to a life offering freedom of movement, encouragement as they falter in resurrecting forgotten or never-learned agricultural skills and rural patterns of life, and belief that they can reintegrate into the society of Khmer who remained inside when they fled. They must also regain the trust of the people left behind in Cambodia. Those who "have no knowledge of seeds, of irrigation, of soils and weeds, or 'reading' the weather, the upcoming monsoon and its associated floods" will have to learn. "Many youths who have lingered in idleness for . . . years in the camps" may not have the "tenacity" necessary for rice farming.[38] Adults returning to the cities and countryside will have to understand the naked reality that life cannot be turned back to another day. They will see their former houses inhabited by strangers and their family land being tilled by unknown people. All will learn to live with the shortages endemic to a country at war and closed off from the rest of the world for two decades. Children who have no sense of a homeland they have never seen or that they left too young to remember will learn of a new country.

Paramount, however, is the fact that the refugees are a relatively small portion of the whole population of Cambodia, and their biggest task will be reintegration into the whole. Inside Cambodia lives a needy and exhausted people who themselves were displaced more than once within their own country and who have struggled with little outside assistance to rebuild a life with a degree of normalcy.

Many who remained in the country believe the refugees have lived materially better off than they and will not look kindly upon special treatment for the returnees, beyond assisting them in the settlement process. The two populations, those who remained and those who fled, must meet and come together again as a nation. Lavishing excessive attention on the refugees can only provoke ill-will. Any politicization of Cambodia's reconstruction will court disaster.

In 1990 after the Vietnamese withdrawal and when the border factions began to make some inroads into the Cambodian countryside, USAID gave some $20 million for development in a KPNLF-held area in northwestern Cambodia. The money built a twenty-one kilometer road and five concrete hospitals with running water and provided training programs in animal husbandry, radio repair, carpentry, and blacksmithing for several thousand Khmer in the area. The funds also provided teacher training and school equipment such as notebooks and pencils for students.[39] When aid is not given to the country as a whole, such aid can be polarizing, political, and detrimental to the reunification of Cambodia. Multilateral and bilateral aid is needed throughout the country to facilitate, not dominate or exploit, the Khmer people in rebuilding, reuniting, and reintegrating themselves and their land.

FAMILY TRACING

Part of the work of reunification will be the joining of families separated since the time of Pol Pot. Through the tracing program of the ICRC, several thousand family members have been reunited through letters. The letters tell of simple things like marriages, births, and deaths. Almost without exception they name those family members known to have died under the Khmer Rouge, those known to have lived, as well as those whose fates remain uncertain.

For those who request ICRC assistance in locating family members and discovering whether they are alive or dead, the organization searches the Cambodian countryside. Beat Schwitzer, an ICRC delegate in Cambodia assigned to the tracing program, speaks of the degrees of difficulty in finding people:

One of the most difficult aspects has to do with name changes. It seems that every Khmer has a name and also a "nickname" that has little to do with the given name. Often parents give the child a different name than the birth name to keep the evil spirits away. Many, too, changed their names during the Pol Pot years in order to hide their identity. They have not reverted to their given names.

On the less difficult side, it is said that Khmer people spend 90 percent of their time talking about other people. If someone goes to a village where the person sought was seen fifteen years ago and then went elsewhere, there is a good chance that at least one person can lead you to the person being searched for. Village ties remain very strong. Those who were pushed from the cities and separated from one another are not so easily traced.

Soon, if the peace holds and if the border Khmer can return home, they will be seeing one another again. Most who are brought together will experience the painful joy one family found as it was reunited in Site 2 in 1990.

Two sisters had been separated early in 1975. When Pol Pot's army emptied Phnom Penh, Dani's father, a Lon Nol official, was killed and she and her mother were sent to the countryside. At the same time her sister was with her grandmother in another part of the city. From that day for fifteen years, Dani and her mother, who had come to the United States from Khao I Dang camp, did not know if Dani's sister and grandmother had survived. Through word from a Khmer family recently arrived in the United States, Dani and her mother learned in 1990 that Dani's sister and grandmother were now in Site 2.

Dani flew to Thailand for a surprise reunion. She slept little the night before and said almost nothing on the ride from Bangkok to Site 2. As the car passed Khao I Dang, tears came to her eyes as she remembered the years she had spent there. Suddenly she was in Site 2 walking on the narrow path that led to the hut where her sister and her grandmother were staying. Dani looked into the door and turned her eyes to a figure on a bamboo bed just to the left of the door. The frail figure with shaven white hair rose slowly, looking at the stranger in the door. "Is this my granddaughter? I thought I would never see you again," the old woman said with quivering lips. The two embraced just as Dani's sister emerged from the shadows of the hut and joined them.

Not everyone who finds a missing family member will want to embrace. There are old wounds and betrayals that may never mend. Others will search the walls of Tuol Sleng prison, the torture chamber in Phnom Penh where more than twenty thousand were murdered. Among the photos covering the walls of three large rooms or in the file drawers containing pictures too numerous to place on the walls, many will learn the fate of family members and finally put them to rest.

Eva Mysliwiec tells how peasants from the countryside have been coming to Tuol Sleng for years.

When peasants from various provinces in the country come to Phnom Penh, many will visit Tuol Sleng. On Sundays it is usually open to the public. On the walls of Tuol Sleng are pictures of hundreds of those who were tortured and killed. The peasants go through every single picture to see if one of their relatives is not on those walls. Even though three rooms have pictures, there are thousands of others in the files that are not made public. When visitors find a picture of one from their family they collapse from the pain.

GOING HOME

On March 30, 1992, six hundred Khmer people stood in the staging area of Site 2 camp ready to board U.N. buses that would take them home to Cambodia. Many among them had come from other camps along the border to mark the beginning of going home for 350,000 border Khmer. Seventy-five percent of those who will return are women and children, half of the population is under fifteen, and 35 percent depend on women as the sole breadwinner in the home.[40] The mixture of people from each of the three Khmer factions was to be a sign of peace and reconciliation. The truth was that just across the border Khmer Rouge and Hun Sen's Phnom Penh government troops were fighting. The cease fire was not holding.

In the decorated staging area people mingled, and Thai officials and hundreds of journalists were there to mark the event. Six-year-old Le Lim was frightened and clung to her mother's sarong. Nearby Keo Seth, who was five, wrapped his arms around one of his father's legs and buried his face in his father's slacks. Lim's mother and Seth's father clutched the few belongings they would carry with them to Cambodia. Once the buses passed through the gates, it would be no more than a mile or two to the border, but that mile would take them to a world they did not know. Lim and Seth's parents were as frightened as their children. The children were traveling to a country they had never seen and Lim's mother and Seth's father were returning to a land from which they had fled thirteen years earlier. At the time they had not been much older than the children who clung to them now. Even though they were afraid, they were also exhilarated. "I feel I will belong someplace again, and that my life will have a purpose," Le Lim's mother said.

"It will not be easy to return," Keo Seth's father acknowledged.

There are many dangers. The Khmer Rouge and Hun Sen forces continue to fight. Real peace is still a dream. I fear for my young son. He might step on a mine or become a victim of enemy crossfire. If he gets sick with malaria or dengue fever, he will not have access to the quality medical care he has here in Site 2. He could easily die.

But I want him to live in Cambodia. I want him to grow up knowing he has a homeland and feeling rooted. I think it is worth risking the dangers to give him a life in Cambodia.

I do not know how well I will be able to provide for him. Even though we have been promised land, most of the best land is already taken. There is not enough safe and fertile land for all of us who will return from the camps. I don't know how the UNHCR will be able to give us the land we will need.

I have asked to go to Battambang Province where some of Cambodia's most fertile soil is. It is also close to the Thai border. If fighting increases, I can easily take my family back to Thailand.

When I left Cambodia, I was too small to know all the skills a rice farmer must practice. But I will learn, and I will provide for my family. I feel like I have just existed here. Now I will really begin to live my life.

The six hundred Khmer boarded the U.N. buses with joy and apprehension. Crowds stood by waving them off, knowing they would board those same buses in a week or a month or several months. Some among the Khmer who boarded the buses or stood in the crowds had hoped to resettle in the United States, Canada, or France. They now accepted the reality that they would live out their lives in Cambodia, giving their best for their families and their country.

Peggy Braile, a physician with the American Refugee Committee, stood among the crowd of well-wishers. In a letter to her parents, she reflected:

Monday A.M. we watched the first buses take off for Cambodia. So far I have watched four convoys, and I am so happy to see each one leave. I know Cambodia has many problems, and life will be very difficult for the returnees. But it is time to stop having refugees here as a way of life . . .

While parts of the whole refugee camp situation were necessary to save lives, at the same time, the camps have been the ultimate welfare state. Food, water, houses, and health care are all available for free. Not necessarily in the style one would want any of those to be, but the bottom line is that rice rations are provided just for being alive. In many ways Cambodia will be a real eye-opener.[41]

Henry Kamm, a veteran correspondent, made his own observations on the returnees.

Eighty percent of the returnees have chosen to settle in the four provinces nearest the Thai border, although only 60 percent lived there before they fled Cambodia . . .

Returnees gave two main reasons for their choice of where to live. The four provinces offer the most fertile soil . . . But probably more important for refugees who are not ready to put full faith in a durable peace and who might choose to flee again, the provinces are reassuringly close to Thailand.[42]

If the fragile peace holds, learning to live in a peaceful environment after twenty-two years of war will not be easy for either those who fled and returned or those who stayed. Nonetheless, as they sow seeds in the earth to grow food, cast their nets for fish, and have babies to succeed the dead, a confidence that they are secure can emerge. They will know that it is safe to plant trees that take years to mature and they will build homes of more solid materials. They will take pride in what they produce, as did a young waitress in a Phnom Penh hotel before the peace treaty was signed. As she stood by a patron seated at a table in the hotel dining room, she picked up a small pink, tea-sized paper napkin. In hesitant English she said with a smile and great pride to the American guest, "This napkin is made in Cambodia."

There are deep hurts, wounds, and personal tragedies that call for reconciliation. Before the peace accord was signed, a group of Khmer and expatriates in the border camps proposed a peace walk from Aranyaprathet in Thailand to Phnom Penh. But the accord was signed before the walk took place. The Venerable Maha Ghosananda, a respected Buddhist monk, urged that the walk become a *Dharma Yattra,* a walk of reconciliation. He said,

I do not question that loving one's oppressors . . . may be the most difficult attitude to achieve. But it is a law of the universe that retaliation, hatred, and revenge only continue the cycle and never stop it. Reconciliation . . . means that we see ourselves in our opponent. Only loving kindness and right mindfulness can free us . . . Wisdom must always be balanced by compassion, and compassion must be balanced by wisdom. We cannot have peace without this balance.[43]

In the middle of April, the walk began. Peggy Braile recounts,

We walked the six kilometers to the border. It was a tremendous inspiration to see these ninety brave people starting on this journey. Forty monks and ten nuns dressed in white led the way, three of the monks playing Vietnamese drums, a Sri Lankan carrying a huge Dharma [reconciliation] flag.

At the border we were all allowed to cross the bridge at Poipet and walk up to the arch, the official entry to Cambodia. That was one of those mystical experiences, walking on the eastern half of the bridge, stepping a few feet onto Cambodian soil.[44]

The Khmer are a people of uncommon resilience who survived the most outrageous assault on themselves as well as foreign intrusion into and domination of their country. It is almost impossible to conceive the psychological impact of the past twenty tortuous years of war, genocide, and isolation on the Khmer people. The signing of the peace accord and the return of 350,000 refugees are only the beginning of renewal and the process of healing.

AFGHANISTAN

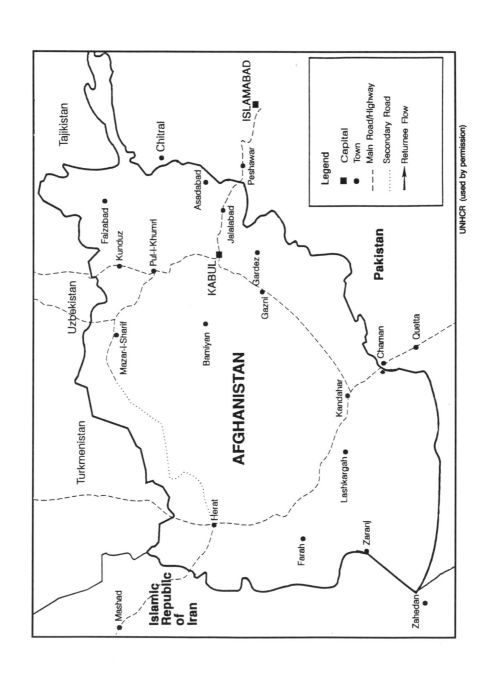

The grief of war. An Afghan grandfather mourns the death of his two grandchildren, both killed during the bombing of their village.

4

Flight Afghanistan

*Kropp . . . proposes that a declaration of war should be a
kind of popular festival with entrance-tickets and bands, like
a bull fight. Then in the arena the ministers and generals of
the two countries, dressed in bathing-drawers and armed
with clubs, can have it out among themselves. Whoever sur-
vives, his country wins. That would be much simpler and
more just than this arrangement, where the wrong people do
the fighting.*

—Erich Maria Remarque
All Quiet on the Western Front

It was late afternoon in Kabul, the 3,500-year-old capital of the ancient
country of Afghanistan. Fatima's last class of the day in the Faculty of Medicine
at the university was minutes away. It was a beautiful spring day, but this
spring of 1980 was unlike any Fatima had known in her twenty-four years.
The country was already divided and tense prior to the Soviet invasion just
last December. Now the glaring presence of troops and Soviet armaments
cast a shadow over every fragrant flower that blossomed. Less than a week
ago she had received word that her eldest brother had been arrested for
protesting the Soviet invasion. She had heard he was in Pol-e Charkhi prison,
a hole of torture and death.

Fatima reached down into her depths and back in time. Change was nothing new. That is part of the human condition. She herself was a testimony of
change in her country. Yet change had been slow and far from universal,
really not even widespread. She was an exception in her society, an educated
village girl now at the university in the nation's capital. To leave a village for
the city was unusual in itself. But for a woman to leave one for higher education was almost unheard of. The majority of women in the university were
from the urban elite. Literacy among her sex was probably no more than 1
percent.

As she thought, Fatima looked out the window at the city sprawling across

128

the valley floor and up the surrounding barren hills. The skyline was low. Mud compounds with flat rooftops gave way to stone dwellings on the hills. All had high walls for privacy and *purdah* to safeguard the tradition of enclosure of women. The question of the veil was an issue in this war and in this society. Its place and its meaning had tumbled a king little more than fifty years earlier. It had to do with the past and the future, with tradition and development, with progression and regression, with independence and its lack thereof. It had to do with a way of life that was giving way to the twentieth century. The invasion pitched questions and visions onto the battlefield rather than around tables of peaceful discourse.

Fatima looked toward the blue dome of Pul-i-Khesti Mosque that rose heavenward, dominating the landscape. Before the Soviet invasion, five times daily, a crier had called the people of Kabul to praise Allah from a high balcony in the mosque's slender minaret. The Afghans are people of Islam, followers since the seventh century C.E. of the Prophet Mohammed. Long before that and to the present, Afghans were and are a tribal people. Islam solidifies them in times of trial, but that glue will not hold them together over the long haul. They will mount *jihad* against the *kafir*. Holy war against the infidel once settled, however, will give way to tribal loyalty and internal divisiveness.

However disconnected and fractious the tribes might be, they would not tolerate an imposed government by *kafirs*. During peace time they tumbled into fratricidal wars that played like a frenzied game of *buz kashi*, the national sport of Afghanistan. Tribes pursued their own interests and clashed with one another with the same ferocity displayed on the dusty game field, where contestants whipped their stallions, lunged toward and swooped on the one who held the headless goat, prize of the game.

For now they had a common enemy, one with whom they had shared a border of friendship and trade. In fact, the whole of Afghanistan's northern border joins a large expanse of the former Soviet Union's southern border. Even the country's small northeastern tongue that licks its northern neighbor and touches China with its tip was forced on Afghanistan by the Anglo-Russian Boundary Commission of 1895-96, "so that at no point would British India and Czarist Russia touch."[1] Uzbeks, Tajiks, and Turkomen live on either side. Some among them had fled Russia in the 1920s and 1930s. Many of them would flee a second time across another border into Pakistan.

Soviet troops began their move south December 24, 1979. Moscow deployed tens of thousands of troops over the Salang Pass and into the Afghan capital and countryside. By December 27 shortly after 6:00 P.M. Kabul was under Soviet control. Babrak Karmal, leader of the Parcham faction of the People's Democratic Party of Afghanistan (PDPA), who because of factional disputes within the party lived in exile in the Soviet Union, was chosen by the Soviets to lead the nation. Less than twenty years before the Soviet invasion, Soviet money and skill had engineered the two-mile-long Salang tunnel that bores through the mighty Hindu Kush at an altitude of 10,800 feet. That tunnel made possible the highway that connects the former Soviet Union with Afghanistan's capital, Kabul.

The new road offered smooth advance for Soviet troops and tanks. Fanning out across the country, the Soviets would be sorely tested over the next ten years as they tried to crush this proud, independent neighbor. Fifteen thousand Soviet troops would die there. Afghanistan, leveled, refused to be conquered or subdued.

Historical Background

The Hindu Kush Mountains—Killer of the Hindus—stride into Afghanistan like a skeletal foot. The ankle on the edge of China narrows through Baghlan and spreads southwesterly, heel to toes across the central core of this harsh, rugged land. In many ways these towering, jagged, snow-covered mountains advancing out of the Karakoram and Himalayas define Afghanistan. Many would-be conquerors have marched into this forbidding land only to be repulsed by the terrain as much as by its indefatigable warriors. Resistance and revival are hallmarks of Afghan history.

The war did not begin with the Soviet invasion. It began far back in time. Now it was the northern neighbors who had crossed over into Afghanistan. Others had come before. This "buffer" nation has resisted outside takeovers from early times. Alexander the Great (336-23 B.C.E.) in his eastward push against the Persian Empire of the Achaemenids suffered when he met the proud independence of the fearless tribal people who lived in this land of the Hindu Kush. Alexander married Roxanne from Afghanistan to appease the resisting tribes, but the mountain tribes and wandering nomads tired Alexander's mutinous troops and finally forced him to turn back toward Babylon.[2] Had Alexander had his way, he would have moved into the Indian subcontinent on his route of conquest and expansion. What became in later times the nation of Afghanistan served as the crossroads between Persia and India.

In the thirteenth century C.E., when the Mongol conqueror Genghis Khan, described by Louis Dupree as "the atom bomb of his day,"[3] swept through this area leaving only destruction in his path, the people rose up again and revived and strengthened the Muslim influence that gained a foothold in the seventh century.

Afghanistan was never completely conquered, and it never became a colony to any invader. She had come close as the British and Russians clashed and carved their territories around Afghanistan. Afghans became embroiled in three Anglo-Afghan wars during the nineteenth and early twentieth centuries. They were fought not so much to place Afghanistan under British or Russian domination as to make the nation a buffer between British Colonial India and Russia. Afghanistan bowed to some influence, but never relinquished complete control.

Abdur Rahman, a British-chosen tyrant of a king, ascended the throne in 1880 following the Second Anglo-Afghan War. At the end of that war current

Afghanistan boundaries were drawn and the country was unified. The Durand Line of 1893 determined the eastern border with British Colonial India. Abdur Rahman was forced to accept British determination of Afghanistan's foreign policy including the carving of boundaries.

Amanullah Khan, Abdur Rahman's grandson, was determined not to be as beholden to the colonial powers at his doorstep. If the grandfather had ruled over a unified Afghanistan, Amanullah was going to rule over an independent nation. And he was going to bring that nation into the twentieth century.

To achieve such independence, Amanullah fought the Third Anglo-Afghan War in 1919, the first year of his reign. Afghans fought then as they do today. No well-heeled army marched against British troops. In fact, many people who had never before seen aircraft ducked when British planes dropped bombs on Kabul. They had nothing more than long-used, short-range firearms to aim into the sky.[4] But Amanullah had tribes fiercely loyal to their homeland who confronted British soldiers at every turn until both sides, tired and war-weary, agreed to lay down their arms. In exchange for the king's acknowledgment of the Durand Line as the official Afghanistan-British India boundary, the British bowed to Afghan sovereign independence.

Amanullah wanted more than sovereign independence from outsiders; he wanted to do away with what he considered out-moded tribal customs and bring Afghanistan into the stream of Western modernization. He dressed the part. A fairly large man with flattened, brushed-back black hair and brows, he distinguished himself with a triangular moustache angling out from his nose. He wore the latest European styles procured during visits to the West and longed to bring that lifestyle to his people. A picture taken in Europe of his queen, Soraya, bobbed hair uncovered and dressed in a short-sleeved evening gown, caused a furor when it made its way back to Afghanistan.

The king's approach to modernization was injudicious and ill-advised. He plunged headlong into initiating change, failing utterly to be sensitive to the established tribal and religious traditions of his people. The reforms that rankled hit at conservative Islamic customs—removal of the veil from women, introduction of Western dress for all, and the imposition of coeducation. Outward signs signify more deeply rooted attitudes and beliefs. Changing dress does not transform the person or society. Amanullah had little patience for the time and energy necessary to cultivate and bring about transformations at the deeper levels. He paid no heed to nurturing conditions for change and paid dearly for it. Religious revolts brought him down.

A Tajik upstart, Bacha Saqao, took advantage of the unrest in Kabul and seized the throne in 1929. Though he reverted to traditions swept out by Amanullah, his Tajik origins precluded his acceptance as ruler. After all, Durrani Pushtuns had held the throne since 1747, the foundation of the first national Afghan state. They would not lose their grip for another fifty years when Daoud would be toppled by a Ghilzai Pushtun in 1978. Nadir Shah, who had fought against the British, was now given their blessing to topple Bacha Saqao and return Amanullah to the throne.

Nadir Shah had dreams of his own. He kept the throne for himself. In his desire to have the people with him, he denounced Amanullah's reforms and abrogated all the former king had introduced. His few years on the throne were regressive.

THE ERA OF KING ZAHIR SHAH AND MOHAMMAD DAOUD KHAN

When Nadir Shah was murdered in 1933, his young son and heir Zahir Shah was only fifteen. Uncles ruled in his name for twenty years. In 1953 Zahir Shah took the throne for himself, and his cousin Mohammad Daoud Khan held the office of prime minister. Both sporadically sought reform and development in this nation of mostly poor, tribal, inward-looking, agricultural people.

Following World War II, when boundaries, alliances, and the balance of power had changed throughout the world, foreign aid became inextricably bound to the foreign policy of those powers now embroiled in a cold war. Many developing nations received bountifully from the cold warriors as they sought to bring these poor countries into their sphere of influence in the name of friendship. The king and his prime minister looked for funds beyond their borders and became willing beneficiaries from the calculated largess of both East and West. The aid would come perilously close to costing neutral Afghanistan her life.

In Afghanistan, the United States and the Soviet Union vied to finance large-scale infrastructural projects. In the rush toward modernization and the determination of the United States and the Soviet Union to outdo each other in pouring aid into Afghanistan, the human factor was forgotten. Projects frequently failed to produce anticipated fruits. "... [W]ithout consideration of the human factor, great dams simply make great ruins," Louis Dupree said, for example, of the well-funded, U. S.-backed Helmand River Valley Project.[5] Ordinary Afghans, who logically should have been the beneficiaries of the aid provided by the United States and the Soviet Union, became instead pawns in the U.S.-U.S.S.R. competition for Afghanistan.

At the same time U.S. aid was pouring in for the dam and for schools, roads, power plants, health centers, and the Kandahar airport in the south, the Soviets were providing funds and expertise for military arms and officer training as well as infrastructure construction. Educated Afghans were more and more influenced by Soviet advisors and ideas.

Daoud would have preferred to have had military aid be more equitable between the United States and the Soviet Union but U.S. foreign policy limited his options. What is known as the "Pushtunistan" question loomed large during Daoud's tenure as prime minister. The British-drawn Durand Line of 1893 demarcated the border of modern-day Pakistan and Afghanistan with little or no thought to the Pushtun people who lived on either side. The Pushtun lands were divided and their lives went separate ways—some toward the Punjab, the others toward Kabul. Daoud, fixed on this issue, wanted to pry the Pushtun lands in Pakistan back into Afghanistan. As he made noises, Pakistan used the best weapon she had, closure of the Port of Karachi to Afghan trade—export and import.

From the birth of Pakistan in 1947, U.S. relations with Pakistan were friendly. Consequently, when Daoud requested military assistance from the United States, the U.S. government said yes, providing Afghanistan would become part of the Baghdad (CENTO) Pact. Daoud refused to join the alliance and turned more and more for support to Afghanistan's neighbor to the north. Afghanistan was one among several nations whose neutrality the U.S. government construed to be pro-communist. The United States pulled back aid, enabling Soviet aid and ties to develop.

There Daoud found a government not only willing to assist, but one that backed him on the Pushtunistan question. And when Pakistan closed its borders and port to Afghan trade, the Afghans used the Soviet Union as their main conduit for goods.

Though voices cautioned against too much reliance on Soviet assistance, Daoud insisted that he simply wanted money and expertise from the Soviets. To him, it did not follow that in accepting aid, he was also accepting their philosophy. He vowed there would be no interference in the realm of governance and religion. He would not compromise Afghanistan's independence or its adherence to Islam.[6] Daoud's attitude reflected the rhetorical question an Afghan general once posed: "When you ride a good horse, do you care in which country it was born?"[7] Twenty years later, no doubt, he would have preferred to address the question differently.

During Prime Minister Daoud's tenure in office, Afghanistan was able to move forward somewhat. However, his impassioned attachment to the Pushtunistan question entangled him and encroached on time and energy that could have been more judiciously invested. Much-needed infrastructure took shape, nonetheless. Roads, bridges, airfields made Afghans more accessible to one another and to the outside world. Still, rural Afghan villagers, 90 percent of the population and mostly nonliterate, seemed more comfortable in their tradition-bound ways. While they were content with little or no change, the growing numbers of urban Afghans with progressive aspirations grew more and more impatient. Undercurrents of conflict were bound to surface between urban and rural people as well as between conservative and moderate Muslims.

Daoud's social reforms caught the ire of conservative religious and tribal leaders and their adherents. They decried him as a traitor to Islam when he pressed for an end to *purdah*, as well as for mainstreaming women in educational development and the work force. He tested the waters one August day in 1959. Each year the seats of Kabul's Ghazi Stadium filled to capacity as its citizens celebrated *Jashin Isteqlal*, the festival of Afghanistan's independence declared in 1919 when her people shed the last shackles imposed by outsiders. As the parades, contests, and fireworks got underway on the second day, Daoud and his entourage stepped into their boxes in the grandstand.

The women, dressed in colorful Western garments, had shed every vestige of the veil. The audience gasped at such exposure and recalled the former King Amanullah who fell from grace for a similar action.

Daoud knew he was playing with fire. He was accused of cozying too closely to both Soviet and Western ways, perverting the morals of the people. But he was convinced change was necessary to bring Afghanistan into the twentieth century. He was well aware that *purdah* was not a sacred tenet of Islam, but more a tradition developed over the centuries. The *Koran* enjoins only modesty of dress. Daoud saw in the enforcement of *purdah* a symbol of much that was antiquated in his society as well as a barometer for the acceptance of change. In prescribing the observance of *purdah*, men determined a woman's freedom of movement. Just as literacy is empowering, so too was *purdah's* demise. Both could open windows beyond the ignorant, circumscribed lives the women lived.

A decade after Zahir Shah and Daoud Khan took the reins of government, real power rested with Daoud. The king, dissatisfied with this turn of events, asked his prime minister to step down. March 3, 1963, Daoud acquiesced and retired to the wings to wait and observe.

Zahir Shah did not disagree with Daoud. In fact, after Daoud stepped down, the king continued to nurture progressive policies and reform. He simply felt there were other ways to achieve them in this fundamentally tribal and feudal agricultural society with little industry and few educated among the many varied ethnic and linguistic groups.

Zahir Shah was convinced that the formation of a constitutional monarchy with strong parliamentary rule could move the country forward. He walked, however, on a tightrope trying to balance the conflicting forces—the 5 percent educated elite who wanted far-reaching change instantaneously, and the 95 percent nonliterate who relied on local leaders and law, wanting minimal governance from the center. All wanted betterment, but in different ways and through different means. Divisions sharpened between conservatives and progressives; urban and rural.

The constitution opened the door to political parties, including the far left of the educated minority. The players of the revolution now stepped forward, and in 1965 the People's Democratic Party of Afghanistan (PDPA) was born. Among the thirty who were present in Nur Mohammad Taraki's home were two who thirteen years later would wrest power in the revolution from the house of the tribe of Durrani and from each other. These were Taraki, himself, who was named general secretary and Babrak Karmal, first secretary. Two others who would play major roles, Hafizullah Amin and Najibullah Khan, were students at this time. Amin reportedly became a communist while studying at Columbia University in the United States. The PDPA took advantage of unrest among students impatient with sluggishness toward progress and with too few jobs available for them after graduation.

Though the PDPA agreed to a basic agenda of land reform, nationalization of industry and import-export controls, and general education, Taraki and

Karmal battled from the beginning. Karmal, who did not wish to frighten the ruling elite, sought a milder revolution while Taraki called for radical change and overthrow of the existing government. Perhaps the differences in background and class origin heightened their contrary views. Whatever the cause, they split within two years of the party's founding into the Parcham (Flag) and Khalq (Masses) camps and formed two central committees, both bearing the name PDPA. Karmal headed the former; Taraki, the latter.

Once the constitution was set in place, Zahir Shah had hopes for a more inclusive form of government. But in this tribal land whose terrain created formidable barriers to unity, the vast majority continued to look to local tribal rulers. Though he had dreamed of advancement and transformation for his people, Zahir Shah's constitutional tribal monarchy had not moved easily into the latter half of the twentieth century. In fact, few Afghans lived with the advantages of this century. It was a bad economic time in the country as foreign aid began to slide and jobs became scarce for young and old alike. The worst drought in memory, leaving close to half a million dead and crops and livestock wiped out, was the final blow to the king's dreams of prosperity. Monarchy gave way to republic and King Zahir Shah bowed to President Daoud Khan.

July 17, 1973, the reign of King Zahir Shah and the age of monarchy ceased in Afghanistan. It was a bloodless coup. The king was on a tour in Europe when Mohammad Daoud Khan, brother-in-law, first cousin, and former prime minister (1953–63), took over. He declared the kingship ended and Afghanistan a republic. From exile Zahir Shah addressed his letter of abdication to "His Excellency Sardar Daoud Khan, President of the Republic of Afghanistan," and defined himself a common Afghan citizen of the republic.[8]

In 1978, five years after Daoud took control, the economy had made little improvement. He became embroiled once again in the Pushtunistan question, leaving other pressing issues on the back burner. Though the Soviets had supported him on this issue when he had been prime minister, they now made an about-face and urged him to negotiate with Pakistan. Daoud, wanting to depend less on the Soviet Union, began gradually to turn toward other sources of assistance. By appointing some staunch anticommunists to his cabinet, Daoud tried to reduce Soviet influence in the government, especially in the Defense Ministry with its more than two thousand Soviet advisors.

At the same time, Afghanistan's ties to the Soviet Union were difficult to loosen. After all, they were neighbors. Not only was there a growing dependence on materials for development, but also on replacement parts.[9] Almost half of the officers in the Afghan army were Soviet trained and looked toward the Soviet Union for their model. Soviet influence permeated the educated, professional circles of Kabul because a majority of those who received higher education over the past quarter of a century had studied in Soviet institutions.

Revolutions do not begin in a day; they percolate, sometimes for years. Finally, a single event provokes the conflict's first shattering fusillade. The immediate cause of the April 1978 Great Saur Revolution, named for the month on the Afghan calendar in which it took place, seems to have been the murder of a Parchamite socialist, Ustad Amir Akbar Khyber Khan. Khalq and Parcham factions united in choosing to place the blame on Daoud's interior minister.[10] Daoud planned to quell any uprisings over this matter by putting the PDPA leaders, both Parcham and Khalq, in prison.

PDPA leaders, however, were planning to oust Daoud and take control of the government. Although Taraki, Karmal, and others were imprisoned, the immediate round-up did not include Hafizullah Amin, who, though his house was surrounded by police officers, was able to orchestrate the takeover by using his young son to send the signals.

THE GREAT SAUR REVOLUTION AND SOVIET CONTROL

On April 27, 1978, Daoud went to his office as usual. As he met with his cabinet to plan the fate of the arrested PDPA members, PDPA forces were on their way to the presidential palace. Daoud did not have a chance to pass the death sentence on those he held. Instead, by dusk a blood bath had washed over the palace. Daoud and his family lay dead. Two centuries of Durrani rule ended and the one hundred-fifty-year presence of the Moham-madzai branch of Durrani Pushtuns walked no more in the halls of power.

That day and those that followed were days of quiet terror for the city. The tanks and armored vehicles that had surrounded the palace and the Afghan troops dispersed throughout the city. Though there was no widespread blood-shed, people disappeared and others fled. In Kabul, Daoud loyalists were the first to feel the effects of the president's murder. Many Kabul citizens were placed under house arrest or imprisoned. Whole families were marched from their spacious homes and taken to tiny cells in the Pol-e Charkhi prison. A day earlier many of those prisoners had been the city's elite. No longer. They replaced the now-free incarcerated enemies of Daoud.

From the day President Daoud was murdered in April 1978, events pro-pelled the country with a furious speed to days of death and destruction. The Great Saur Revolution reached out across the country. The people of Afghan-istan witnessed the metamorphosis of cold-war development dollars into funds for armaments.

Sima Wali, a woman who is a member of the Mohammadzai clan of Durrani Pushtuns that had ruled Afghanistan for two hundred years, clearly recalls the events of April 27.

We had no warning that a coup was imminent. The previous evening, people had gone about their normal routines. My family had been to a ball where many members from the extensive Mohammadzai clan were present.

The coup began early Thursday morning with many Afghans going to work as if on a normal day. Around noon action intensified. Tanks began to cause traffic jams, as people returned home for the half-day holiday. Traffic police directed tanks to the side so that buses filled with passengers could continue on their normal route.

Suddenly, about midmorning, planes began flying over the city. We thought the planes were on military maneuvers until we realized they were all headed to the heart of the city, close to the palace and the surrounding government buildings. When bombardments began, we turned on the radio, but there was no news, only music.

Later in the day, we learned what had happened. Daoud had sent word to his family, members of the royal family, and families of other officials to come to the palace where he felt they would best be protected. But the palace was the first target of the coup and was seized very early. Some of the men in the palace were armed but were defenseless against the massive invading troops.

The soldiers lined up Daoud and his family and members of the royal family. When the soldiers began firing, they aimed very low at the children, a ploy to terrorize the parents. The children were the first victims of the massacre. Over fifty members of the royal family were present. All were killed. Some of the men who were in the palace and who had guns realized before they were lined up that they and their families would not be spared. They began killing their wives and themselves so that they would not die by a firing squad or be taken to prison where they would undergo torture and horrible deaths.

The only survivor of the palace coup was the wife of one of President Daoud's sons. She was a friend of mine. Two of her teenage daughters and her husband were killed in front of her. The poor woman had the brains and blood of her children splattered on her skirt. She sustained several bullet wounds and was left for dead. Later she was taken to a hospital. Through the intervention of the ICRC, she went to the United States. She is an amazing woman who survived not only physically but also spiritually.

On the same day, soldiers began to round up other members of the extended royal family and Mohammadzai closely related to the branch ruling at the time whether or not they were politically involved. Once there were ten thousand members of the Mohammadzai clan. Now there are probably no more than four thousand or five thousand. Key ministers and government officials were also imprisoned, tortured, and killed. Women and children were not spared. Intellectuals, student activists, and religious leaders became victims of the coup.

Members of more distantly related Mohammadzai families like mine were placed under house arrest. Domestics were placed in our homes who reported our conversations and activities to the authorities. We were told not to congregate with more than four or six persons other than those who lived in the house. If we left the house for any reason, we were followed.

At the time my sister worked for USAID, and I worked for the Peace Corps. Anyone who had any connection with the U.S. government was labeled as part of the CIA. My sister was detained and interrogated several times. She was specifically asked to give information on the whereabouts of Louis Dupree, a person she did not know at that time.

People began to leave Kabul with minimal possessions and often with return tickets so that they would not be denied exit visas or have their passports absconded. Neighborhood monitoring groups reported those who sold their homes, jewelry, and other valuables as suspects. Often monitors were children trained in school to betray their parents, many of whom were imprisoned and killed based on what the children said.

As it became more and more difficult to leave the city by ordinary transportation, families began to flee through perilous, landmined mountain routes. Most urban dwellers did not know how to cross these routes. They would take other tribal members of their families with them who did know or members of the underground who volunteered their services.

A cousin who had worked for the previous government found out who from the underground could take him across the mountains if he had to flee suddenly. It was not long before he had word that he was on a government list to be arrested and taken to Pol-e Charkhi prison. He changed immediately into tribal clothes, made contact with the tribal guide, and, leaving everything behind, left with his wife.

The tribal guides never asked for money. They risked their own lives by coming to Kabul to act as guides. They defended women and children, especially those women left without husbands. There were no reports of rapes during the early period.

Not all was smooth among members of the new PDPA government. After a ten-year split, the Parcham and Khalq factions rejoined into a united front in 1977. In reality, when the PDPA took control, Taraki headed a fragmented, inharmonious group until Karmal was exiled to the Soviet Union and the Parcham faction became inconsequential for the moment. Those who wished for radical revolution were in charge. In the beginning many cheered the revolution or at least welcomed it as a promise and a hope for better economic times.

One after another, decrees were handed down and implemented with fervor. The king and all members of his extended family who had not been killed were stripped of their citizenship. The nation's flag was changed. The leaders no longer invoked Allah.

Radical land reforms turned the rural society upside down. Tribal customs and relationships were ignored as the new government took land from large landowners and parceled it out to peasants and small landowners. The Taraki government sent urban people to the countryside to enforce the changes. In doing so, the government banished the age-old form of collective government, the *jirga* (the people's assembly). It took power from the people rather than offering it to them. Old land debts were canceled and the land was redistributed, but without the personal involvement of the people. No longer permitted to manage their own affairs, men felt stripped of their honor, the most revered among Afghan virtues.

Without doubt change was needed, but the formula for creating it did not fit. Raja Anwar reminds us, "Whether a revolution takes place in a tribal society like that of Afghanistan or in the more industrialized environment . . . it cannot be kept alive in the name of the 'people' when they are neither its makers nor its beneficiaries or inheritors."[11]

Women's issues, too, were dealt with without foresight or understanding of cultural traditions among nonliterate, rural people. The decree that declared equal rights for women prohibited the bride price. Traditionally husbands were chosen for the women by the parents of both the bride and the groom. The couple had little or nothing to say about whom they would marry, and frequently the couple had never met. The bride's father was given a sum for his daughter, who would go to live with her husband's extended family. The bride price had been part of the rural social and economic system for generations. The imposition of immediate and radical change by outsiders who did not understand rural village ways summoned men to resistance and rebellion.

The *mullahs* (religious leaders) and the elders reacted just as vehemently when young urban party workers came into the villages to teach literacy to all, surely a noble undertaking in any society. However, dragging women from their compounds and demanding they come together with the men to learn was not acceptable to those who saw such action as morally reprehensible. Nor was the order to abandon *purdah* acceptable. Spontaneous armed resistance sprang up in village after village. The PDPA in its turn denounced any reaction and killed and imprisoned many *mullahs* and elders.

As rebellion increased, the Parcham and Khalq factions were fighting their own internal war. The Khalq seemed to come out the winner and Taraki and Amin were able to exile Karmal and many other Parcham members. Countless others who did not leave the country were thrown into prison. In spite of the Khalq faction gaining the upper hand, the government was not unified. It soon became evident that Taraki and Amin could not work together. Amin, with the military under his control, really held the reins of power.

Observing the rising resistance in the countryside, the Soviet leadership became increasingly alarmed. As more and more Afghans fled across the border into Pakistan and later into Iran, agricultural production fell accordingly. Taraki was summoned to Moscow. In conjunction with the Soviet government, a decision was made to oust Amin and form a government with Taraki and Karmal at the head. Learning of the plan, Amin was able to sabotage its implementation, assassinating Taraki in September 1979 and declaring himself head of state. Amin's three months of power were ruthless. Thousands were imprisoned and thousands executed. Greater numbers of Afghans fled, seeking refuge beyond their borders.

In a brief twenty months Afghanistan was on the brink of disintegration. Then on December 27, 1979, Soviet troops invaded, and Babrak Karmal (who had remained in Moscow), arrived with the troops and took control. Karmal invoked Allah, changed the flag back, and revoked the most radical reforms. In practice he made clear that "the prophet Mohammed would have to coexist with the prophet Marx.''[12] But, as the puppet of an outside invader, he would never be able to rally the people behind him. The conflict was no longer internal. For the Afghans it was time for *jihad*. The people would unite to rid their country of the invading infidel—more than 200,000 Soviet troops.

A FAMILY IN FLIGHT

Fatima was one among millions who sought refuge in Pakistan. She was forced to interrupt her medical studies, perhaps put them aside permanently, when a friend entered the laboratory in the Medical Faculty at Kabul University. "Your mother is dead," the friend notified her. "You must go to your village." Tears of loss welled to the surface and brimmed over. She had expected these words, a code. Still she dreaded them. The announced death was of another sort. It was to be her day of flight from her homeland. She had known these words were to be the sign. Her tears were genuine; they gave her convincing leave from colleagues who bade her safe journey.

For Fatima and the uncle who accompanied her, the two-day journey seemed like ten. They passed villages abandoned only days before. Blossoms still bloomed on the peach trees. Fatima wondered who would eat the ripened fruit in the summer. She pictured her own village, surrounded by vineyards, orchards, and grain fields, just around the next curve.

Never in a thousand generations could her heart be prepared for what she saw. Rubble, simply rubble. The Soviet bombers had hit their target in the early morning hours. The jagged-edged shells of the solid earthen homes stood stark under the blue sky. Roofs of mud and solid beams no longer protected the villagers' homes; what remained of the interiors was exposed to the elements. Cradles holding the new life of the village lay crushed underneath. Fresh graves scattered across the cemetery embraced the dead.

As Fatima climbed the mound of clay that had once been her own home, she saw her brown-turbaned, older brother grasp the bent, gold, jewel-bedecked ewer used for generations to wash the hands of guests and strangers welcomed into their home. He took her behind their compound. Fatima squatted beside her father, a broken man looking at the lifeless bodies of his two youngest grandchildren. Mohammad and Firouza lay side by side on a colorful quilt retrieved from the ruins. There she learned another brother, the children's father, had already been taken for burial.

In only a moment, dreams were assailed, buffeted, shattered, and scattered beyond gathering. Exploding missiles whipped the breath, the very life out of dreams. Before that day ended Fatima turned eastward toward Pakistan to find family members: from her fragile grandmother to her youngest sister, Sohaila, who had left earlier.

Proud Ghilzai Pushtuns, Fatima's family had farmed the land in Paktia Province on the border with Pakistan near the district town of Gardez for generations. Her father like her grandfather was the respected village leader. Her father had been the first to allow his daughters to attend school. Fatima and her sister Mariam were already well along in university studies. Sohaila would have completed eight years of school in the summer. This day in 1980 they set aside their books, along with the sowing and reaping of their land.

During the course of the next ten years of war, nearly 82 percent of the Gardez district prewar population of 484,000 crossed over into Pakistan — the largest refugee population from a single Afghan province. The Soviet-backed president of the PDPA, Najibullah, who replaced Karmal in 1986, came from this province. Efforts on the part of the *mujahideen* (Afghan resistance fighters) to wrest control from Najibullah's forces caused some of the most widespread devastation of this war. Hundreds of thousands of buried antipersonnel mines will continue to destroy legs and arms and lives for years to come.

The war has generated more than five million refugees since the Soviet invasion of Afghanistan. More than three million fled to Pakistan; two million, to Iran, where they remained for more than a decade. In addition, at least two million people were internally displaced and over one million have died. This adds up to approximately half the prewar population of Afghanistan.

As Fatima touched the small children, she felt the life drained from them, from their village, from their nation. Hope faltered in her heart. She remembered when each had been born, just a year apart. She had been in the village for the birth of the first — a son gently swaddled and placed in the family's rocking cradle. All the small children had gathered around, wanting their turn rocking the new baby. Since it had been a boy, there had been great celebration.

Afghan society is patriarchal. The male is the provider and the defender of the honor of the family. He is the one who works for pay, goes into the bazaar to trade, and to the city to sell crops. Only the male goes to the mosque for Friday prayers and sermon, as well as to village meetings. He determines the degree of freedom the women will have.

Women symbolize the honor of the family. *Purdah* is the means of defending a woman's honor. The veil is the curtain that safeguards her purity, and the walls of the home compound protect her from the eyes of strangers. Afghans, who are mostly moderate Muslims, were always less rigid in their interpretation and observance of traditions, including *purdah*, than more radical Muslims.

As Fatima looked at the destruction about her, she pictured the village alive as it had been less than a day ago. Its citizens were people of one clan, interrelated over generations. None were strangers. There was a rhythm to life in the village that flowed through the days and the seasons.

The homes crumbled by the bombardment had been formed from the earth — rich brown dirt from the surrounding hills gathered and wetted to mud bricks. As in most villages, a labyrinth of dirt alleys connected neighbors. Extended families lived in the same compound, separated by walls within the outer walls. Open doors made easy access.

Fatima's family compound had been larger than most because her father was the tribal leader. As a child she had watched men come and go from the long, cool guest hall where men of the village met to discuss their common needs.

Fatima remembered how in the past her mother and the other women had cooked large meals to spread before them. Kahil, a male cousin who was ten, would wrap warm freshly baked *nan*, the traditional flat, round bread, in a clean cloth and spread it on the floor of the guest hall, putting a large piece of the fresh *nan* at each place as the men gathered round, sitting cross-legged. Kahil would take the now-crushed ewer and receptacle to each person, offering soap and pouring water over the outstretched hands of each guest. Ablutions complete, other cousins would bring bountifully filled platters of steaming rice, bowls of lamb in a thin gravy, cooked greens, and carefully arranged plates of fresh sliced tomatoes, cucumbers, and onions.

Invoking Allah's blessing, the men would begin to eat. They tore pieces of *nan* and dipped them into the common platters, picking up rice, meat, and vegetables. They soaked the gravy into the bread when all the meat was consumed. The meal was complete when fresh fruit, hot green tea, and sugar-coated nuts were served. Fatima's cousin would then pass the ewer again, wrap the scraps in the cloth, and leave the men to their conversation.

The women who prepared the food were the heart of the home. Fatima's eyes filled with tears as she gazed where the kitchen had been. Actually, there had been two cooking areas, one in the courtyard for summer, another, a room just beyond, for winter. Kitchen work had begun early. Fatima recalled how all rose at dawn, responding to the first call to prayer from the minaret of the village mosque. The men performed ablutions, rolled out their prayer mats, turned their face toward Mecca, and recited prayers as they appropriately knelt, stood, and prostrated themselves.

The women prayed privately, kindled the fire with twigs and wood gathered from the nearby woods, and filled the kettle with water for tea. *Nan* made the day before was the breakfast staple. Sometimes it was deep fried and sprinkled with sugar.

She thought how the few chickens, goats, and sheep within the compound began to move about, small children scattering the hens and the chicks in early morning play, running between houses in the compound until they were called to eat.

When the men went off to the fields or to their shops in the bazaar, the women began preparations for the noon meal. Fatima recollected how as a young child she especially liked sitting beside her grandmother as she kneaded the dough for the *nan*. Rhythmically she flattened the sturdy ball, quickly tossing it back and forth until it was ready to be placed on the inverted plate for final shaping. With the heat in the deep ground oven just the right temperature, her grandmother slapped the perfectly formed dough against the inside wall. Fatima was always there to receive a bite of the hot bread just as it was taken from the oven.

Fatima remembered the sights and the smells of the bazaar. Before she was old enough to observe *purdah*, she went with her father and her brother to purchase household needs. The main highway to Kabul passed through the village. The bazaar extended for half a kilometer on either side of the main road. In the winter shopkeepers built small fires just outside their narrow wooden stalls. Turbaned heads were covered with the heavy wool blanket Afghans wear to serve so many needs—a coat in the winter, a container for supplies, a blanket to sleep on. They squatted close to the fire and conversed, hands outstretched over the heat. They drank hot tea until they were warm enough to sit inside the open stalls filled to the ceilings with everything imaginable—meat carcasses, fruits and vegetables, suitcases, colorful cloth, pots and pans, kerosene for cooking, tires. Prices were never set. Bargaining was the life of the market.

Fatima recalled her favorite stop, the almond shop—lined floor to ceiling with shelves, each arranged with containers holding every variety of almond imaginable. The shopkeeper lifted the jar Fatima pointed to, opened it, and encouraged her to taste one. After testing and then dropping the shells to the floor, Fatima selected the assortment she wanted and walked out. In the midst of the vegetable and fruit stands, the proprietor sat cross-legged above the crowd behind a large scale. He was surrounded by fruits of every kind—golden raisins, green apples, ripe tomatoes, tangerines, slender okra, apricots, watermelons, and cucumbers. Off to the side aromatic spices of splendid colors lay in large trays. When Fatima dropped fruit into one of the scale's pans, the owner placed weights in the other one. When the scale balanced, her father gave her the amount of *afghanis* required for purchase. In return the shopkeeper handed her the fruit.

The bazaar was always crowded, always busy, but somehow unhurried. Men greeted each other, hands across their heart invoking Allah, and then embracing and kissing on both cheeks. They mingled with donkey-drawn carts, goats and sheep being led to market, Toyota pickups, motor-driven rickshaws, festively decorated buses, and cars passing through on the way to Kabul or Pakistan. Only the cars seemed impatient, drivers honking horns from one end of the bazaar to the other, until they passed out of sight on their way to somewhere. Somehow the people, animals, and carts parted in a seemingly casual fashion to make way for one another's passage.

Today the bazaar was silent. Tangerines and ruptured watermelons were pitched among kerosene cans; scattered almonds crunched underfoot. Yellow mustard and red paprika were mixed among bomb fragments. Bright new bolts of cloth fluttered in the dust. Walls that had not crumbled angled precariously. Chickens and dogs foraged for food and discovered an abundance. A crater, deeper than a man, split the road, punctuating the ruin. Damage might have been comparable to the devastation of a Kansas tornado sweeping through a small farming community or a hurricane lashing a Carolina coast, where shop owners would look ahead to rebuilding; odds were improbable that such an act of nature would strike again. But the storm that pummeled this Afghan village was a scorched-earth war. Planes would return time and again until the land was almost empty of people and filled only with the rubbish of war. Many women and children who remained perished from hunger and extreme cold because food and wood for cooking and heating became virtually unattainable.

Most of Fatima's family had left for Pakistan the day before, gathering what they could carry before the village had been destroyed. This day, Fatima would join some relatives and neighbors, about thirty, who had remained behind, hiding in the nearby hills. Her father would follow his family to Pakistan later; her brother, a *mujahideen*, would return to battle. Most of the travelers going to Pakistan were women and children, characteristic of all refugee populations. One or two men would accompany them, along with a few teenage boys and elderly grandfathers.

When Fatima had departed from her village for Kabul to study in the university, there had been much rejoicing among the members of her family. Songs and laughter resounded in their compound. Her journey gave promise of a bright future, not only for those closest to her but for her nation as well. Then she had turned west. This day, as she turned east, there was no joy, no sense of promise. There was only sadness and dread of what lay ahead. Fatima embraced her father, tears tumbling over her cheeks. Would she ever see him again? Would they ever gather as a family once more in Afghanistan? Would this land, this village, one day be restored? Any hope for such a day was buried far below the anxiety and despair.

It was time to leave. Fatima took one last loving look at the fragmented homes, the splintered shade trees, and the scarred fields. She turned and began to walk toward Pakistan beside one of the six donkeys, substantial pack animals. Each was heavily burdened. A cotton quilt protected this particular donkey's back. Directly on top of the quilt was secured a burlap bag filled with grain, surrounded by tied, sheet-sized cloths filled with whatever clothes and household utensils the family had managed to salvage. Fatima's frightened three-year-old niece, Farida, grasped a bundle of cloth as she tried to situate herself on top of the burlap bag, one leg and bare foot rubbing against it. She wore a pink dress with delicate clusters of small embroidered flowers—all made by her sister, only ten. A second donkey, laden with bundles and another young niece, walked beside Farida's. Older boys and girls kept pace with the animals. Some of the girls balanced articles on their heads—a water pail, a sack of clothes. Most in that group had never been farther than neighboring villages. Now they set out to cross mountains.

War shadowed them, was their constant companion. They were haunted by what they had left behind. Some among them, particularly the young boys, had helped pull bodies from under the rubble. Others had cleaned them for burial. Now as they journeyed into the unknown, they were fixedly vigilant for mines underfoot and MiGs flying overhead.

The second day out, before they came to the mountains, they happened upon *mujahideen* firing mortar shells at the enemy. There they were, fifteen soldiers on the road's shoulder; cannons adjusted to send more fire. Coming up on the middle of a skirmish, the refugees could not move forward. Suspended in fear waiting for an all clear, keenly apprehensive of being hit, they had to wait and watch until the engagement was over.

On the third day near dusk, with little warning planes swooped low, banked, and turned. As the caravan tumbled toward shelter in a grove of trees and behind substantial rocks, three helicopter gunships approached and pelted bullets in every direction. At the approach of the helicopters, young Farida's mother reached for her daughter to pull her to safety, but not quickly enough. In stunned silence, the men opened the hard earth while the women cleansed mother and daughter for burial. The *mullah* who was with them intoned *Allah Akbar* (God is Great) and laid Fatima's niece and the girl's mother to rest.

Attacks such as the one Fatima and her family experienced took the lives of countless civilians seeking safe passage to asylum. Nomads lost their herds to enemy bombardment or to starvation. Hundreds of thousands of Afghans bear burn scars. Hundreds of thousands more lost lives or limbs from mine explosions. Some crossed the mountains in the summer without water. Dehydrated, they could move no farther and died before reaching safety. Others approached the mountains in the cruel snows of winter wearing garments too skimpy to protect their bodies.

Fatima and those with whom she traveled crossed over into Pakistan, into safety, but they were terrorized and traumatized. The journey took a week. She rejoined her mother, her sisters, and grandmother in Peshawar. Now, twelve years later, they still wait to return to their village in Afghanistan.

Afghan women refugees in Pakistan. Many women work to earn money by using traditional skills in weaving and embroidery.

Elizabeth Neuenschwander

5

Refugee Women

TO BE A REFUGEE WOMAN
is to face persecution. It is anguish over the decision to flee the land of your birth, the enveloping arms of the extended family, the way of life which has passed down from generation to generation . . .

TO BE A REFUGEE WOMAN
is to walk the miles into the country of first asylum with your culture strapped to your back, laboring under the traditions of your ancestors, charged with the task of birthing your children into an uncertain future in a foreign land . . .

TO BE A REFUGEE WOMAN
is to fear the unchecked sexual violence of war zones and to know the vulnerability of life in refugee camps . . .

TO BE A REFUGEE WOMAN
is to watch the emasculation of your husband before powers over which he has no control . . . It is to struggle to maintain human dignity and fight dependency as his confidence drains as weeks turn into months, and months to years and he is still without a means to support family and to secure their future.

TO BE A REFUGEE WOMAN
is to gaze at the severed limbs of the young and to know the mines have not stopped there. It is to look into vacant eyes and know that the violence has wreaked less obvious wounds in shattered hearts and minds . . .

TO BE A REFUGEE WOMAN
is to reach for the rice of relief when your heart aches with yearning to be planting the seeds of the future . . .

TO BE A REFUGEE WOMAN
is to watch your children growing up in an environment so unlike the dreams you hold for them. It is to see the flesh of your flesh absorbing values not your own and to be powerless to change it . . .

TO BE A REFUGEE WOMAN
is to be a majority and often head of the household, but until recently to be passed over by most training programs designed only for men while being faced with perplexing new challenges and responsibilities . . .

TO BE A REFUGEE WOMAN
is to be a woman of many colors, shapes, religions, cultures, and lifestyles, sparkling facets of the experience of women in exile. It is to know the bonds of sisterhood in the communality of persecution, the context of suffering, in the steadfast perseverance in the miracle of hope. It is to be a witness to the travesty against human life and to search for the voice of a witness.

TO BE A REFUGEE WOMAN
is to be grateful for sustaining relief but to thirst at the roots for the justice which will bring enduring peace . . . It is to reach across to the enemy as her son, too, dies in the conflict.

TO BE A REFUGEE WOMAN
is to act into hope by daring to live each day as it comes.[1]

More than a quarter of the world's eighteen million refugees are women; coupled with their children, they comprise 75 to 80 percent of the refugee population. In some refugee camps, women and children are 90 percent of the population. They are the most vulnerable of the refugees, have the fewest resources, and are regarded as the lowliest by their societies. The effect on women and children of being uprooted by war is more devastating than on any other segments of a refugee population.

The stories of flight and life in exile reveal women's fears and feelings of losing control over their lives. The courage they draw from deep interior wells fills them with a stubborn will to go on in spite of being forced into lives and actions abhorrent to them.

Sokhan related what she witnessed during the final moments of her seventeen-year-old sister's life when the Khmer Rouge killed her in Cambodia in 1977 and her own experience in 1982 at the hands of guards who were her protectors in Site 2 refugee camp on the Thai-Cambodian border. More than fifteen years later, her voice shook with disbelief.

They violated her. They violated my sister before they killed her. In front of me and in front of my mother, Khmer Rouge soldiers violated her and then, as she lay screaming on the ground trying to cover herself up, they shot her in the face. It blew into a million pieces right before our eyes. Seven years later two Thai soldiers, who were supposed to be protecting the refugees in Site 2 camp, pulled me off the road near the reservoir one evening. Each one raped me, beat me, and left me to grovel in the dirt.

Fifteen-year-old Parwin Noori, an Afghan refugee, did not experience the brutality of sexual assault. Her sense of a loss of control over her life was more subtle, yet devastating. She and the other women in the household were dying inside from a life of strict seclusion imposed on them by the male members of their household, in reaction to the threatening Western ways.

I'm afraid we'll forget how to walk. In the last two years, I have only left the apartment a few times, and I almost never walk more than eight or nine steps from one room to the next. If our neighbors see us on the street, they'll think we are bad girls.[2]

Asha, already wizened, looked at least seventy years old rather than her age of forty-five. Her husband, a *durra* (sorghum) farmer, died without medical assistance of a high fever in their small Eritrean village just months before Asha fled to the Kakora refugee camp in eastern Sudan and just two weeks after she gave birth to her third child. Six years later she was never sure from day to day if she would be able to feed her growing children.

I gathered the children and left our village because of the drought and the war. When we heard the war was very near to us, our whole village left — all except the very weak and the old. We had to leave them behind. My son Yemane had polio before we left Eritrea. He cannot use one leg and the other one is very weak. He was only four when we left, so I had to carry him most of the way.

As a widow, it is very hard for me to make a living. The rations are not enough to feed my children. I make grass mats and try to sell them, but since many others make mats, it is not easy to find buyers.

At first sun in the morning, I drink coffee if I have it, and I make tea for the children. The two girls go to the Islamic religious school, but Yemane is not strong enough to go. I prepare lunch for all the children with what I have. I never know if I will have food for them. Usually I have nothing to feed them

*in the evening. I must walk a long way for water and carry it home. I have no
donkey and no man to bring it for me.*

Thousands of Vietnamese women were abducted from their rickety boats,
raped, often killed, sometimes spirited away by their pirate captors, or made
to watch as boats still carrying their children and spouses were turned over
or torn apart, leaving the passengers clinging to floating boards, crying for
their lives to be spared. The women were helpless in staying the moment
when their children went under for the last time, succumbing to the waters.

Just as familiar are the stories and pictures of Eritrean and Ethiopian mothers
so emaciated themselves that their breasts hang wrinkled and thin like dried
up raisins. A child, on the verge of death from lack of food as well as dysentery,
makes a limp effort to suckle the dry breast, its only source of nutrition. When
the child dies and is buried in a small, shallow grave near his mother, she is
too weak to cry over her loss, yet feels deeply and forever what she was not
able to give her child—food for life. Her loss is the greater because both
causes of death—diarrhea and malnutrition—are preventable.

Each woman, whether raped, secluded, unable to feed her child, or
abducted, is a victim of war and suffers physically, psychologically, and spiritually. They have been stripped not only of their material possessions, but
also of their dignity and self-esteem. They bring with them into exile the
trauma of sexual violation, of helplessly watching children die, or of being
continually stalked by violence.

Many leave their country on a moment's notice—just before their home
is obliterated by bombs, or just after their village has been destroyed. They
have no time to gather up anything other than their children and old folks.
As they flee, they realize they will not be able to rebuild or return until
sometime in the all-too-distant future. Millions of refugee women enter
another country without father, husband, or brother—without male support.
Generally they come from countries in which the vast majority of women are
very dependent on men, especially rural women who form the largest proportion of any refugee population. Seldom do they settle immediately into
one place in the land of exile. As they move about, the first home a woman
can provide for her children is often no more than a blanket or quilt raised
on precarious sticks, and food and water are scarce. When the refugees come
in large numbers, chaos defies any quest for order.

With their lives centered around their families, caring for and nourishing
their husbands and children, they are not prepared for the tearing apart of
the very fabric of the family. Young women are not ready to accept widowhood, especially when they are left with five or six young children, yet millions
must face the reality that their husbands will never return. The widows do
not feel competent to be the chief breadwinner of the family and are threatened by such an unfamiliar role. Often nonliterate and unfamiliar with the
language and the customs of the host country, the women feel with uncommon acuity their isolation, their lack of tools, their inability to provide for their

families, and their inferior social status. Stagnation grows and perpetuates their dependency on outside sources of assistance.

Fears for family consume the refugee woman. She worries for her husband, whether he is absent in battle or present in despair. If he is a farmer like the majority and has no land to cultivate, then she must keep his spirits up and be attentive to his breaking point and his potential for violence against those he loves most if they become the symbols of his emasculation.

Besides the specter of death ever present to her and the sorrow of burying her children in a foreign land, often without the customary rites, the refugee mother worries that her young son, no more than ten or eleven years of age, will be conscripted by the army they are fleeing or by the rebels they support. A child that age schooled in the ways of war may never learn peace.

Refugee women often give birth to more children than they would in their homelands because they want to help replace those fallen in battle. They are apprehensive about raising children who survive in an environment of terror and distrust. They wonder what country the children will claim as home, the foreign land or the land of the mother's birth. They worry that daughters of a marriageable age, and many are that at fifteen, will not find husbands to care for them, as so many young men die in battle or are gone months and years to the front.

Many women echo the words of a Khmer woman living in Site 2 along the Thai-Cambodian border.

In this camp it is difficult for the women who live alone . . . Sometimes, men want to come into their houses and attack them while they sleep alone. So they must ask their neighbors to defend them when something dangerous happens.

When I get sick I have to ask my neighbors to come and help me, and when they get sick I help them too . . .

In 1983, because I had some extra money, I decided to become a [Buddhist] nun for 3 months, to dedicate merit to my relatives who had died . . . I would walk and pray, meditating and gathering all my feelings together.

At night when I am in bed, I pity my children who are small and deprived of their father and grandparents, and have no country to live in. Tears just come to my eyes without my being aware of them. People always think about their past. As human beings with brains, we cannot forget it.

It is true that I feel hopeless for myself, but I hope now for my children . . . I must send them to school to get an education for their future, as they are still small. I was fed enough with happiness . . . and I have had enough of misery in Pol Pot times, so for now there is nothing more for me to be concerned about. The only thing is my children.[3]

While these women focus on survival needs, giving up hope for their own future, they continue to hope they can give their children a future. As they live out their years in camps, many of their special needs as women, particularly in the areas of protection, education, economic independence, and health concerns, are not being met. This need not be—at least not to the extent common in camps around the world. Women of uncommon resiliency, given the opportunity, can surface from the quagmire of stagnation and dependency.

CONFINEMENT AND CULTURE

Particularly tragic is the manner in which such stagnation and subsequent dependency subtly manifested themselves in the lives of Afghan refugee women. A particular mix of war, culture, politics, and religion coalesced, placing their lives on hold in a prison-like seclusion of *purdah* behind the walls of their homes.

Soviet attempts to overthrow traditions honored by generations of Afghans generated a strong negative reaction among male Afghans. In Afghanistan, the veiling of women and a moderate practice of *purdah* were symbols of Islamic belief that Afghan men refused to abrogate at Soviet provocation. More conservative Afghan males believed that educating women and allowing them to "move freely in public would engulf the nation in sexual anarchy, destroy the family, and bring dishonor on men for failing to protect women and the family, the basic foundation of society in Islam."[4] When Soviet invaders tried to impose both the universal education of women and freedom of movement, many Afghans fled and tightened the practice of *purdah* beyond Islamic prescriptions.

In the Soviet-occupied Afghan Islamic male-dominated society, Soviet attempts to alter radically Afghan culture and traditions, particularly in regard to the liberation and education of women, were interpreted as communistic and anti-Islamic. Such a reaction to activities championing the development of women carried over into exile and became a major obstacle to those engaged in working among Afghan refugee women. Programs initiated by foreigners to benefit women came under close male scrutiny; consequently, many were never realized. Western ways, like communism, were perceived to be anti-Islamic.

As a result, both physically and symbolically Afghan refugee women echoed Parwin's fear of forgetting how to walk. Some refused these restrictions, and, in the name of Islam, risked their lives and reputations to obtain for themselves and other women the rights that belonged to them.

One such Afghan woman was Ashara. She had been missing for ten days. The last time anyone saw her was in early May 1990 when she was working in a refugee camp about ten miles from Peshawar, the main town in Pakistan's Northwest Frontier Province (NWFP) where 2.5 million of the 3.5 million refugees from Afghanistan fled after the 1979 Soviet invasion. Early that morning a driver from an indigenous Afghan nongovernmental agency (NGO) for which she worked honked his horn in front of the gate of her family's home in one of the narrow Peshawar residential lanes. She joined three Pakistani women, colleagues in the work of health education among Afghan refugee women. Each woman secured her *chader* (veil)[5] on her head and draped the right edge across her nose so that only her eyes were visible. As the hot desert air blew through the open-windowed truck, they discussed how they would proceed with the day's classes on oral rehydration.

Ashara was a nurse, trained in Afghanistan before she fled her country ten years earlier at age twenty-five. Because of the exaggerated restrictions of *purdah* for the Afghan women in exile, Ashara had not worked during her first eight years in Pakistan. Even though her nursing skills were rusty, Ashara joined the small staff of the Afghan health-care NGO and began to work in Peshawar and nearby refugee camps teaching basic health to groups of women in their homes.

In midafternoon the driver returned Ashara to her home before he dropped off the other three. That was the last time she was seen. Her fate is still not known. No one knows if she is dead or alive, murdered or held against her will. Ashara's disappearance sent waves of terror throughout the refugee population, particularly among female refugees.

The spring of 1990 was a frightful time for Afghan refugee women in Pakistan. Ashara's disappearance was one of a number of incidents that led to the practice of secluding the majority of women behind the protective walls of their compounds. No one was sure of the source of this rampage of terror. Was it fundamentalist Afghan Islamic extremists who consistently opposed any NGO-created programs for women that, they contended, corrupted the women with Western values? Was it an influential Saudi fundamentalist group that wanted to influence the form Islam would take in Afghanistan once the war ended? Was it the Pakistanis who, wearied with the presence of so many refugees in their country for so many years, wanted Afghans to end what had become a "civil quarrel" after the Soviets left and wanted the refugees to return to Afghanistan?[6] Was it a combination of the three? No one knew for sure.

The target was clearly NGOs that sponsored women's projects, particularly those of an educational or social nature. In early May in Naser Bagh camp just outside Peshawar, a *mullah* at the local mosque passionately denounced the work among widows in a million-dollar center belonging to Shelter Now International, an Australian Christian humanitarian agency. A crowd of five thousand gathered. The *mullah* charged the Christian organization with proselytizing by handing out Bibles to widows and corrupting them by giving them birth control pills and soap and allowing the widows to swing on swings provided for their children who came with them to the center. He incited the crowd until, in a frenzy, they destroyed the center as well as a nearby school for Afghan girls run by the Pakistani government. Although the director of Shelter Now hotly denied the proselytizing and birth control dissemination charges, the damage was done.[7]

A few weeks later as the director of Shelter Now was driving a truck on a road outside Peshawar a gunman opened fire. The driver and his young son escaped, returned to Peshawar, and, with the rest of the family, fled Pakistan. A letter warned that the next target would be the director of the International Rescue Committee (IRC), the largest private voluntary agency assisting refugees in the NWFP and one that has initiated multiple programs for women. He also hastily departed Pakistan, where he had worked among the Afghan refugees for eight years.

IRC's Pakistan director was instrumental in establishing both the Afghan Women's Center and the International Rescue Committee's English Language Program for Women. Both projects were threatened before he was. The Afghan Women's Center and the English Language Program for Women are housed in two large, walled, adjacent residences in the University Town section of Peshawar. To arrive at the houses, a driver must navigate to a dead end by making several sharp turns on the narrow lanes congested with pedestrians and edged on either side by open sewer canals. Several hundred women are brought there each day in school buses. The women's *chaders* completely cover them, and the windows of the buses are tinted to keep them invisible to men on the streets who might glance toward them.

In light of the violent turn of events, those responsible for the two programs questioned the women's safety if they continued to attend classes either at the Women's Center or in the English Language Program. Should anyone determine to attack or destroy either center, the women would have no avenue for escape. A driver of a van filled with women staff members had a very close call in May 1990. Late one afternoon as he turned into a street leading to one of the women's homes, several men stepped in front of the van and directed the driver to make a right turn, ostensibly because the street ahead was closed. The driver knew a turn to the right was not a detour, but only a dead end. He pushed the van into reverse and sped off into the late afternoon traffic.

Latifa and Sohaila, the two Afghan women who founded and run the Afghan Women's Center, have not escaped personal intimidation. In fact, they have endured particularly vitriolic public insults. Earlier in 1990, leaflets were handed out and posters nailed to telephone poles and public announcement boards condemning them as wanton women who lived according to Western values and not according to the teachings of Islam. Any Islamic woman so publicly reviled becomes a marked woman, an outcast in society. Even so, when the Women's Center closed its doors for a time in the spring of 1990, Latifa and Sohaila said only that the women were taking a vacation; they refused to admit fear, in spite of a 1990 religious edict forbidding a woman to leave her home unless a male in the family allowed it and accompanied her. The two women refused to admit being forced to close the center. They simply remained in seclusion in their homes until it was safe to resume the center's activities.

The war following the Soviet invasion in 1979 turned the world of every Afghan upside down. Tribal-oriented and tradition-bound, Afghans had molded a way of life through generations, the shape of which was not readily altered. But the war shattered it as millions fled the country and millions more were displaced inside Afghanistan. Bombarded villages, disruption and separation of families, heavy loss of life, homes, herds, and fields affected all.

When people are forced into exile, leaving all they have known behind and without material support, they frequently become bound to exaggerated expressions of traditions and suffocate under their weight. For strength they depend on their culture and religion. Dangling somewhere between a past they have known and a future they cannot conceive, refugees lose hope and a sense of being connected to a life that is theirs and that they believe in. They put aside goals, save that of returning to their homeland, and build a wall of defense around themselves, leaning only on what they know to be safe and true. In the case of the Afghans, when the Soviets came and bombed their villages and belittled the custom of the wearing of veils by their women, the Afghans withdrew into a protective, defensive, siege mentality; they retreated into what they knew best, the family and religion. Rather than act as they had in Kabul or in their villages, the dispersed Afghans became more conservative. Longing for the familiar in an unfamiliar place, they radicalized their cultural and religious traditions, believing that in so doing they might sense the familiar.[8] Among Afghan refugees such behavior manifested itself most clearly in the extreme enforcement of *purdah* (literally curtain) for the women.

No matter where they are, Afghans are governed by a set of cultural norms, the unwritten *Pushtunwali* — "the way of the Afghan." *Nang* (honor) and *badal* (revenge) are at the heart of this tribal code and play against each other, particularly in situations involving *zar* (gold), *zan* (women), or *zamin* (land). The defense of honor drives brother against brother, tribe against tribe, Afghan against Afghan, and Afghan against the foreign invader. The tenets of the *Pushtunwali* are as sacred to the Afghan as the tenets of Islam. Following the Soviet invasion and the flight into exile, *namus,* defending the honor of women, became a critical test of an Afghan male's ability to protect the family, the tribe, and the Afghan nation and culture.

"I sacrifice my wealth for my head, but my head for my honor."[9] Homes and herds they might lose, but not honor. In Afghan society, women above all symbolize honor; they are treasured pearls entrusted to men for safekeeping. Protecting their honor by protecting the women gives stature to Afghan men. The great bulk of Afghans did not flee their homeland until the Soviets began interfering with timeless Afghan customs regarding the status of women.

Besides their traditions, Afghan refugees brought with them their Islamic faith and lived it more strictly—particularly outwardly—as the years in exile lengthened. Although the men of Kabul, for example, had not previously worn beards or prayer caps, they began to in exile; these signs marked them as good Muslims, as did the strict imposition of *purdah*.[10] Bearing these symbols, many refugees began to live intensely the fundamentalism signified by the symbols, both religiously and politically.

Islam is political as well as religious with no separation of church and state, of religion and government. In exile, it was the conservative Muslims who amassed the greatest power when an Afghan Interim Government (AIG) in Pakistan evolved from a loose political organization known as the Seven-Party Alliance. Because its formation was at the behest of outsider governments and the AIG did not truly represent the Afghan people, many Afghans had little sense of loyalty to the AIG. Yet the Seven-Party Alliance and the subsequent government had the blessing and the backing of the successive Pakistani government leaders, from Prime Minister Zulfikar Ali Bhutto to President Zia-ul-Haq and Prime Minister Benazir Bhutto, and finally Prime Minister Nawaz Sharif. These leaders funneled the bulk of U.S. military aid through the most conservative leader of the Seven-Party Alliance, Gulbuddin Hekmatyar and his Hezb-i-Islami party.[11]

Outsiders, too, influenced the way Afghans lived in exile. Afghanistan's more fundamentalist neighbors, Saudi Arabia and Iran, poured money into the war, as did the extremely fundamentalist Saudi Wahabi sect of Islam. They wanted to influence the creation of a new government in Afghanistan once the war was over. Intent on drawing Afghanistan into the Islamic revolution, their objective was to convert the more moderate Afghan society to the fundamentalism they espoused. After all, Afghanistan has been called the "Southern California of Islam," where the people are quite relaxed in the appreciation of their religion.[12] Where better to begin such a conversion than among the refugees living in Pakistan and Iran? As groups such as the Wahabis donated larger amounts of money to the refugees in the camps, the greater became their influence among their beneficiaries. They taught their version of Islam to youth in the male schools they opened in the camps, and they convinced religious leaders of the West's profligate ways.

Afghan women found themselves caught up in the political machinations of their leaders, the leaders of Pakistan, donors with strong Islamic fundamentalist convictions, and communists who controlled Afghanistan. They became pawns of them all. It was not the women per se who were the targets of the rampage of terror in the spring of 1990. Rather it was a desire for power to control and to reshape a battered nation. Nor were the women the central cause of the tightening of tradition when they went into exile more than a decade ago. But they were the ones who felt most the austere measures it inspired. Their already narrow boundaries were further restricted. In the early years of exile, the women were in no position to question or challenge the limits imposed; their vulnerability was greater than normal, consumed as they were with fear as they tried to absorb the horror of flight and the disappearance of the life they had known.

Several reasons are conjectured for the rigid confinement imposed on Afghan women refugees. Some say more conservative Pakistani officials did not want the more moderate Afghan ways to influence their women. Still others suggest the women themselves chose to observe the strictest *purdah* out of fear of strangers and to ease the minds of their men who were fighting with the *mujahideen*.

Most, however, believe it was the Afghan men who insisted the women stay closer to home. A man's fears were allayed knowing his wife was safe and not possibly a victim of outside hostility. If she were within the walls of the home carrying out her prescribed duties, her husband did not worry as much when he was in Afghanistan fighting *jihad*. After all, in the camps and in the cities in which they settled, they were thrown together with strangers, even mixed with unfriendly tribes. Afghans had all heard frightful legends about members of other tribes who now might be their neighbors. For most men the protection of their women was a matter of honor, which in these circumstances could best be maintained if the women remained totally out of sight. For others their frustration, stemming from their inability to provide for their families, was so great that they reacted by exerting undue control over the women, restricting them beyond any bounds they had imagined. And with the increased influence of fundamentalist Islamic groups, even the husband who believed that his wife's working outside the home was in accord with the tenets of Islam feared retribution from extremists and acquiesced to the now pervasive conservative attitudes.

No matter the rationale, thousands of Afghan women who had known abundant space in their own compounds and in the fields surrounding their villages were now narrowly confined to their compounds with their aspirations severely limited. The same was true of thousands more from urban areas, whose observance of *purdah* had been minimal and whose access to a world beyond their walled homes had increased with time.

The women first experienced a sense of resignation over their loss of freedom. Most felt insecure, lacking control without the comfort of customary daily routines and knowing neither the culture nor the language of their Pakistani hosts. With their normal roles so altered or taken from them, many felt useless and became depressed. Yet for hundreds of thousands of Afghan women without extended family and friends, it was incumbent that they not quit.

The women, it seems, had to be stronger than the men. The men had lost everything when they lost their country to the invading Soviets. But the women were compelled to adjust to a world turned upside down; they held the key to the preservation of the Afghan people. Upon them depended the revitalization of the family unit, the heart of Afghan society. Upon them, too, depended the real conservation of culture without any of the props of the past.

Severe restrictions became most difficult for women who had no means to feed their families other than the rations given by international donors—rations that were never intended to be totally sustaining. The Pakistani government, which provided rations before international assistance was available, allowed Afghan men to enter many areas of the Pakistani job market, particularly jobs Pakistani men were reluctant to take. The reality, however, was that many men could not obtain jobs; others had been so badly injured fighting *jihad* that they could not work; hundreds of thousands of others had died in battle. Their obligation, according to Afghan tradition, to provide for their families became impossible to fulfill. The inability to provide for their families put both women and men in a most atypical position.

The greater curtailment of Afghan women occurred just at a time when they needed greater latitude. For women who were desperate to feed their children, strict enclosure and prohibition against selling even handiwork outside the home put many between life and death. The sort of adaptation necessary for the women to survive moved further from their reach. In many instances, if a man remained immovable and disallowed his wife's involvement in some means of providing for the family, the woman's honor might be preserved, but not her life or the lives of her children.

Although the barriers restricting women were seemingly insurmountable, there were women, both Afghan and expatriate, who slowly and patiently broke down suspicions and opened a way out of the impasse. They did this according to Afghan ways.

SELF-SUFFICIENCY OR ECONOMIC DEPENDENCE

Latifa and Sohaila were thoroughly circumspect in creating the Afghan Women's Center in Peshawar in 1989 and discussed their plans with the proper religious and political male authorities without equivocation or circumvention. Yet the center was never without serious detractors, suspicious men who were intent on confining women in their homes for their domestic and reproductive endeavors.

As administrators of IRC's English Language Program and the Women's Public Administration Program, Latifa and Sohaila saw clearly the needs of the women and wanted an Afghan institution run by and for Afghan women to help them understand the place of women in Islam and to provide the poorest women with skills for self-sufficiency.

Women of Islam, Latifa and Sohaila wear full black *chaders,* only their faces showing. Veiled, their bodies hidden from sight, the delicate print and brilliant colors of their *peran/tombon,* the traditional Afghan dress, show as they walk to a large refectory table in the center. With them at the table are other members of the center's staff, including three women who had been medical students in Afghanistan, one a graduate from the Agricultural Faculty at the University of Kabul, another a former teacher in a Kabul secondary women's school. All are dressed as Latifa and Sohaila. Just as the *chader* covers the colorful clothing of the women, the austerity of the room in the cloistered building veils the energy emanating from the women and their work.

"We are first of all women of Islam," Latifa says, "and it is upon the tenets of Islam that we have created this Afghan Women's Center." She continues,

Mohammed the Prophet was a strong proponent of women's rights. There is a story in the Hadith, *the teachings of the Prophet's followers, that exemplifies his support for their intellectual development. "When the Prophet Mohammed*

was teaching a group of men, a woman approached him, and asked, 'Are you the prophet only for men, or for all people?' When Mohammed assured her that he was the prophet for all people, she asked, 'Why don't you teach women?' Mohammed then offered to go to the women and teach them. One man protested and said the women should come to Mohammed. 'No,' Mohammed replied. 'As mothers, women have high status in Islam. I will go to them.' "

It is well known that Mohammed married a woman accomplished in business and that he was much more liberal in his marriage prescriptions than most of his twentieth-century followers. He championed the right of the woman to accept or reject a spouse chosen for her as well as the right to have a say in matters of divorce.

When I was growing up in Afghanistan, I did not think about these things very much. I had never felt confined or limited. My father wanted his daughters to have a good education through university studies.

After I completed secondary school, I applied for study in the Faculty of Engineering at the University of Kabul and graduated with a degree in that field in 1980. Shortly after graduation I started working in my first job as an engineer in a computer center. I thought about little else. By that time the Soviets had invaded our country, and everything was changing. Although I was a practicing Muslim, I did not consider the teachings of Islam in any depth. I was totally caught up in my job, my family, and my friends. I was betrothed at the time. My father had chosen a man I had known all my life. Fortunately he was of the same mind as my father and affirmed he would allow me to continue to work at least until we had our first child.

Many women traveled around Kabul unaccompanied by a male. When I went to work each day, I found the women's section of the bus quite crowded, many of them with children. Everyone talked and watched the children. There was laughter and touching, a strong feeling of community and connection. From the bus windows I saw thousands of little girls dressed in uniforms and carrying book bags, walking to school. I saw many older girls, too, on their way to secondary school. A girl's education was becoming much more widely accepted. No one talked of her education as being a bad thing.

Women's rights within the tenets of Islam were becoming more and more accepted, especially among the educated. More women like myself wanted the opportunity to work and to make our contributions to the world beyond our homes and families. We were becoming part of a larger community, no longer circumscribed to an Afghan tribe. Change was gradual but steady. We had no intention of discarding all that was good in our tradition, practices that had been a part of our culture for generations. We did not want to diminish the importance of the family in our society. Among most educated, working women, the family was still at the heart of Afghan life.

When I came to Peshawar, I was not prepared for the extent to which the fundamentalist Muslims had taken control of the life of the refugee community. The backlash against the communist unveiling of women, forced literacy classes, and coeducation was devastating. Now anyone who is an advocate of women's rights is assumed to be a communist. First we ran from the communist indoctrination; now we struggle against our own people who have become fanatically reactionary.

All of my optimism and hope for the future died the night we fled our home in the fall of 1982. Our family was considered too closely aligned with the politics of the king and Daoud. My father served as a local governor in a number of provinces before he became the provincial governor of Laghman Province near the border. During the course of the war more than 50 percent of the Laghman Province population would leave Afghanistan.

I had left Kabul and returned to Jalalabad to live with my family nine months after I began my job. When the Russians began to work in the computer center, I decided it was no place for me to work. They told me I could no longer wear my chader.

My father had been in hiding for a year-and-a-half and had not been living with my family in Jalalabad. It was early evening the night of our flight when he came to join my mother, grandparents, four sisters, a brother, and myself. My other brother was fighting jihad. We waited forty-five days in a village not far from Jalalabad until it was safe to move on. Nine of us shared one room. Frequently Soviet planes flew over. I know many people who went ahead of us came under enemy fire. Later we saw their graves as we crossed the mountains. When we finally moved on, my father remained behind in Jalalabad. In the event one of us was captured, he might be in a position to win our release.

It was night when we began our ascent of the mountains that divide Afghanistan and Pakistan. The mountain journey took six days and nights with no food, no water, no camels to carry us. My mother's delirious cries for water pierced my soul. I will never forget her anguish. We could do nothing for her. Just before dawn on the fourth day we reached the top of the mountain and began our descent into Pakistan and our life here. My father followed when he knew we were safe.

We were among the relatively few Afghan refugees who settled in Islamabad, Pakistan's capital. For two years I taught in a primary school because I could not practice my profession here. There was not a place for an Afghan woman engineer. Most educated Afghan refugee women set aside any hope of working in the field for which we were educated. Those who were studying have no opportunity to complete their studies. Here in this room you see three women who were medical students ten years ago. Probably when they return to Afghanistan they will be too old to continue their studies. Yet it is our generation that will provide the leaders to rebuild our country. So much is wasted in our lives. We were so full of optimism when we entered the university. The future was ours.

I also married in Islamabad and gave birth to two children, a son who is now five and a two-year-old daughter. In our culture it is very important to bear a son. Girl babies are still not considered to be very important. In fact, frequently when a woman is asked how many children she has, she will say, for example, two when really she has four. If she is reminded of this, she will respond, "I have two sons, but I also gave birth to two girls."

When we were granted asylum in Australia, my husband, two children and I left Pakistan. We lived there for almost three years. But my husband did not like it. He wanted to return to Pakistan to help the Afghan people. Three years ago we came to Peshawar.

Before the Soviets invaded our homeland, I thought little about my religion. In exile I have had long days and years to think and reflect. I have come to believe our traditional social and cultural ways have been mixed with the Koran to give the seclusion of women a religious context. Many things are of culture, not of religion. Much of what is done in the name of religion is a perversion of the Prophet's teachings. If more women learn to read the holy Koran, they will learn what is of culture and what is of religion and alter their lives accordingly. This is what we hoped to accomplish by starting the Afghan Women's Center.

We are Muslims; that is most important. There is a law Islam gave to us, and we want to work under that law. We do not want to stray from true Islamic teaching when we work with women.

We found this house just across from the one that houses IRC's English Language Program for Women and the Women's Public Administration Program. We advertised among the more than four hundred women who attend classes there as well as among women in camps close to Peshawar. Word spread quickly, for more than two hundred applied. We opened November 15, 1989, with eighty women, our limit. We hope eventually to have outreach centers in the camps so that we might reach at least 1,200 women each year.

Ninety-eight to 99 percent of Afghan women are uneducated. At most they attend Koranic schools for three years. [These uneducated women] give birth to almost the whole of the next generation. If many of those women could become literate and understand the teachings of the Koran, life would be very different for them and for our country.[13]

"Not many men read the holy Koran properly, for they do not want the women to become more independent," Sohaila interjects in fluent English with hardly a trace of an accent. When she left Afghanistan at thirteen, she did not know a word of English. At twenty-four she could be a master teacher. Sohaila describes the needs of the women.

Although the center is for the uneducated, educated women are interested, too. They say they do not know what the holy book really says about women.

Many women are widows. If they read the Koran, they will learn that the Prophet considers it illegal to force widowed women to marry again. Widows remarry mainly because of financial issues. They have no way to support themselves. Even if a widow does not marry and remains in the home of her husband's extended family, she frequently is treated more like a slave than a member of the family. She is forced to work much harder than the married *women in the household. The rest of the family begrudges her presence and that of her children because they are burdens.*

Even if a widow remarries, the new husband, who is often the brother of her late husband, will say he does not want her children. The stepfather will not let them into his section of the compound. A forty-five-year-old widow might be married to a teenage brother of her deceased husband. He could be twenty-five years younger than she. A widow who marries outside her extended family can lose her children to her first husband's family. This is certainly true if a woman who is divorced by her husband remarries.

It is also very important for women to become educated at this time because many of the men have spent ten years and more fighting jihad. Many were boys of ten or eleven when they quit school and trained to be mujahideen. We will need an army of educated people to rebuild our country, and we have so few now.

In our village in Afghanistan, my father was one of the religious leaders. He could read and followed everything in the Koran, including the injunction to educate women. In my village 90 percent of the school-age population, male and female, was going to school by the time we fled. We were, of course, in separate schools.

We left Afghanistan when the Soviets bombed our village. My father and my two sisters who were studying in medical school feared they would be taken prisoner by the Soviets because they were so vocal against the invasion.

For the first two-and-a-half years when I sat at home doing nothing, I began to study English. It was most difficult because we were fourteen living in two rooms. Finally, I was able to study in a Pakistani school. In Afghanistan I had completed eight years of school. Here I went to grades nine and ten. But I did not like the Pakistani schools. We spoke only Urdu and studied only the Pakistani curriculum. It was not good for me. In 1986 I came to work for IRC. When I saw the organization had a journalism class for men, I wondered why there was not one for women. I began one before I became the administrator of IRC's Women's Public Administration Program.

In the two-and-a-half years I spent confined in our tiny compound, I realized how much the women of our country had lost. We were used to space, great openness. Though larger than the majority of compounds, ours was similar to the others in our village. Still protected by the compound walls and beyond the spacious courtyard—where through much of the year we performed our household tasks and where the children played and chickens and goats roamed—lay the orchards. There were rows of a variety of trees—apple, peach, almond, mulberry. There were grapevines and a flower and a vegetable garden. We had our own well, a close source of water. We enjoyed the companionship of other women; we never wanted for something to do. Most important, we felt secure in ourselves as we shared responsibility for the household and the labor with the men.

During my first days in a refugee camp with my family on the outskirts of Peshawar, I felt my eyes were opened. The compounds were so close together and the interiors were so small. Women who had never been beyond their villages before were frightened and despondent. Many of the women and children were dirty. Some neglected their children. I thought they were living like animals. These were not the village women I knew in Afghanistan. War, flight, and the congested living on barren, treeless land had transformed them. Living with a constant sense of transience, many did not try to make a home within their compounds. They simply existed.

I began to think that if only the words of holy Koran were accessible to them they might learn all it says about women and health, cleanliness and education. If they are clean, they are a part of Islam. If not, they lose part of Islam. Knowledge frees.

Latifa and Sohaila receive the women who come by bus each day to the center. Among them are some of the most destitute and bereft of family. Once inside the compound, these women uncover their faces, revealing ages ranging from late teens to early fifties, most with strong, high check bones and wide, deep-set brown eyes. In the high-ceilinged, sparsely furnished class-room, each exchanges her heavy black *chader* for a light veil. Their clothes of many colors contrast sharply with the black *chaders*. Colorful mats circle the room. A few puffed pillows rest against the walls. Seated on the mats, they face a wall on which hang Dari and Pashto[14] alphabet charts, their life-altering doorway to the written word, literacy, and the teachings of the *Koran*. Sohaila reflects.

Without literacy a woman has no control over herself. If she is not literate, she will have no access to information. Without information, a woman cannot become a part of the decision-making process in the wider community. She will remain forever closed off to a greater part of the world.

Literacy is basic to everything in her life. Being able to read about nutrition and child health-care will contribute to the well-being of her family. Reading skills will open doors to employment opportunities. This will be particularly important to widows who, in order to retain their status in the family, must contribute something to the family. Arm a woman with education and give her literacy, and she will be able to understand her rights.

It is important not to overwhelm uneducated women with too much all at once. By gradually giving them tools to do things that need to be done, they will be able to throw off the crutch of dependency and self-confidently take control of their lives.

Much more needs to be done through Afghan women themselves. We can-not continue to depend on the expatriate community to be the teachers and managers. It is difficult to find an Afghan master teacher, for example, to train new teachers for the Afghan female community. When our people return home, the language we will speak will be Dari, not Urdu, English, or French. In administrative positions, we still may need expatriates to serve as buffers, but Afghan women are gaining confidence in these areas. We hope here to *train more women for decision-making positions. When the foreign community leaves, Afghan women will be prepared to take over.*

Besides the uneducated women, we need to concentrate on women who have had some education and those who had to forgo their university training. Educated women are so hungry to learn that they grab at whatever education opportunities are available to them, which are few, indeed.

What is most disheartening to people like Latifa and myself is the fact that so many women have been cut off from their university training. Any number of men who were in the midst of their studies have been able to complete their education either here in Pakistan or abroad. A medical student in the same class as my sister, for example, went to Lahore to complete his studies. If just ten seats a year were bought for women at Peshawar University, in the ten years we have been here, there would have been one hundred university-trained women. Unfortunately, at the present there are none.

For now, we must carefully consider the political ramifications of educating any of the women. It is a very dangerous time for Afghan women in the camps. Protecting them will cost more, and those who have the funds often are not willing to provide money for protection, particularly for women. The country of asylum should give protection, especially today when there are posters in public telling women not to work or go to school. No one seems to be taking any action when there are so many warnings against the women. Someone must know who the perpetrators are, but no one will identify them. Consequently, the women are suffering. Afghans are hurting Afghans. But the leaders of the AIG, the Afghan Interim Government, say they cannot solve the problems. If we call the police at midnight, they don't come until seven in the morning. Those who should be responsible—the Pakistani government, the AIG, UNHCR, NGOs—it seems to me, are passing the buck. No one wants to take responsibility for women; we are such a sensitive issue.

We must be low-key in all we do here at the center. All that we offer to women must be true to our culture and Islam. If our numbers grow too large, deflecting attention will be difficult. Scattering teaching sites and educating women in small groups may be the answer for now. Such a method will take forever.

At the center, not only are the women opening the world of their minds and their talents, they are also increasing their understanding of one another. Within the walls of the center, urban and rural women have come together, an unusual situation for Afghan women. Educated urban women looked with disdain on those from remote villages. They thought them stupid, barbaric, provincial, and dirty. Few urban women were willing to go to the Afghan countryside to work among rural women. Teachers, health workers, agriculturalists—all wanted to remain close to the amenities of the city. For their part, village women thought cities like Kabul were evil places filled with unprincipled women. With the walls of separation crumbled, they see each other now in a different light with far-reaching ramifications when they return to their homeland.

EDUCATION

Latifa and Sohaila were not the only women who struggled for the right of Afghan women to live according to the tenets of Islam and the cultural code of Afghans. In their midst was another, Tajwar Kakar, formerly a teacher in Afghanistan. Once she fled to Pakistan, Tajwar became indefatigable in her search for a political party or humanitarian organization to sponsor a secondary school for Afghan female refugees.

Time and again she pricked the conscience of fearful, would-be benefactors with her pleas and words, "No one has been brave enough to help the women. No one has even tried. How do you know what will happen? This is not Afghan culture; this is not how I was raised to behave in my country."[15]

Tajwar knew well what it meant to put one's life on the line, to act bravely in the face of threats and danger, even death. She fled to Pakistan only after she had been imprisoned and tortured. Tajwar's past and the suffering she endured became a prologue to her continued dedication to the women of Afghanistan.

Politics have been a part of my life since the day I was born. My father was very political; experience strengthened his views. Before I was born, he spent eight years in jail and was then forced by the provincial government to move to the northern province of Kunduz that borders the Soviet Union.

As I grew, my father talked politics continually and wanted me to listen to the issue-oriented conversations he had with his friends. Although most men opposed a female presence in such a situation, my father believed knowledge was power for both males and females.

He always opposed Daoud, believing him to be a Russian agent. But my father died in 1962 when I was in the fourth grade, a year before King Zahir Shah fired Daoud as prime minister. I remembered well my father's feelings when in 1973 Daoud overthrew the king and became president, and then himself was killed in the 1978 Saur Revolution when the communists came.

By that time I was a teacher, for my mother carried out my father's wishes that his children, my four brothers and two sisters, be educated. When I finished my fourteen years of education, I was the mother of six children. I was married at fourteen and had one child every year.

My own political activities began by my writing letters to government officials warning them of the dangers of Daoud's Soviet leanings. I did not want our young people to be influenced by the educational programs of such a regime. With the Saur Revolution, I became active in the resistance. Working with some male resistance leaders, I helped establish a village school that trained young boys in the use of arms.

With the young students in her school in Kunduz, Tajwar initiated disruptive tactics on communist celebration days. For the communists' first anniversary celebration of the invasion of Afghanistan, she gave the children balloons and small explosives to take to the parade grounds. During the parade when the balloons popped and the explosives exploded, a woman shouted, "The *mujahideen* are coming." This quickly dispersed the crowd and ended the celebration. Another parade was disrupted effectively by stinging wasps that the children let loose from jars onto the ground and that found their way under the women's dresses and up the men's pant legs.[16]

My work in the resistance, of course, was much more serious than throwing communist celebrations into disarray. As a veiled woman, I gathered information for fighters, mobilized aid for families of mujahideen, *living or martyred, and helped organize demonstrations against the Taraki, Amin, and Karmal regimes.*

My husband had no interest in politics, but he helped me, whether with writing petitions or disseminating information. There are many men like him who helped their wives take part in the resistance.

Tajwar's work led her to Kabul where she was involved in the organizational work of the resistance, helping with the 1980 uprising against the Soviet invaders, identifying informers and Soviet agents, and educating school children, particularly those she was responsible for in a large, coeducational Kabul school. She knew she might be arrested at any time and prepared her family for such an event.

When I became suspect by the communists, I was transferred to another school. Within two years I was assigned to teach in three different schools. The authorities also made me teach subjects I knew nothing about and withheld my salary.

In the schools, at least in the urban schools, the mujahideen *were little known. The communists had spokespersons who came to the schools to indoctrinate the children. The* mujahideen *had no one. In fact, we teachers were ordered to proclaim communist propaganda. Although I was cautioned against overtly educating the youth about the evils of the interloping government and the truth about the* mujahideen, *I could not remain silent. The* mujahideen, *hidden in the mountains and scattered, had so few means to become known among the students; the communists had many.*

I was arrested the fifth of Jadi [December 26, 1982], the eve of the third anniversary of the Soviet invasion of Afghanistan. It was almost midnight. I had never left my children for one night. I was torn. I wanted to do jihad. I loved freedom and wanted to serve my people in our effort to regain our lost freedom. But I wanted to be with my family as well.

When I was at home, my activities in the resistance were not a problem. My oldest daughter, Fawzia, who was sixteen, and her brother Timor helped organize political activities, persuading fellow students to demonstrate. She was young, but she could manage. Before I went to jail, I told the children, "If you want to do jihad, you must be prepared to suffer." Although I had no contact with my family during my imprisonment, I felt the children would be all right. Just before I was taken prisoner, Fawzia and Timor cleared the house of all incriminating documents.

First I was taken to Khad-e-Shishdarak prison in Kabul, a most dangerous place. I was placed in a very small room for one week. I could not lie down. I had no clothes and it was very cold. I could not talk. At night the guards turned on cassettes very loud, for it was then that they tortured people. During the day, they would not allow the prisoners to sleep. For two days they propped open my eyes and directed a strong light into them.

The prison guards buried me in the snow for one day; only my head was above the snow. Then I was held in a dark room for four days. They transferred me to Khad-e-Sedarat where I remained until my release in May 1983.

In Khad-e-Sedarat, Tajwar endured extreme torture. The invaders' treatment of women countered the Afghan code of war in regard to women and children, who were to be protected—even if they belonged to the enemy. She and thousands of other Afghan women underwent some of the most barbaric methods of torture known to humankind, to break their spirits and their resistance to the Soviet invasion of their country.

To extract a confession from her, Tajwar's torturers kicked and punched her until she bled; they beat her into unconsciousness with electric sticks, and with electric needles pushed into her fingernails, they tore her nails apart. She was told with a gun pointed to her temple that unless she confessed and informed, the guard would pull the trigger. Worst for Tajwar was the psychological torture involving her daughter Fawzia. First they told her she had been run over by an automobile and killed. Then her tormentors told her Fawzia was behind a curtain just beyond Tajwar's reach. For a week, Tajwar listened to the screams of the girl as men beat and tortured her in multiple ways. During this period Tajwar came the closest she would to writing her confession on the paper the guards had always before her.[17]

During the year Tajwar remained in Afghanistan following her release from prison, she gave birth to her seventh child, the fifth daughter, Maihan. When she heard that she would be arrested again and the baby would be punished, she would not take that chance. In the early evening, very quickly, the family of ten gathered and fled with nothing. All that had been theirs, they left behind.

"When we left Afghanistan, I felt as though someone was taking my soul. I was going with an empty body," Farida, Tajwar's second daughter, recalls.

It was evening, about 4:00 or 4:30 when I learned that we had to leave our country. I wanted to do one last prayer in our home. We all cried a lot.

The baby was only forty days old when we arrived in Pakistan. We prayed to Allah to provide enough food and life. In Peshawar we knew almost no one. My father met a friend on a street. He led us to a hotel where we stayed for two days. Then we moved to a very small house.

My sisters and I cried because we could not go to school. There was no school for girls beyond level six. We moved into the Old City, but there was no school for females there either. We watched the males go to school, and we wanted to go, too. I feared if I ever did go to school again, I would be very old when I finished.

"If I stay here one year, I will die," I thought. I only wanted to be in Afghanistan—in Afghanistan as it was before the war when we were free to be educated. I did not know the Urdu language of Pakistan. I was afraid to talk for fear the Pakistanis would laugh at me. I hardly left our house that first year.

We were very poor, for everyone in the house was jobless. It was difficult for us children to understand why we could not have what we needed. Our father had always provided for us in Afghanistan. Mother looked for a job but found nothing outside the home. She made clothes for other people at home and bought a machine for knitting. She was never able to make more than twenty or thirty rupees (between U.S. $1 and $2) a week. That could hardly feed a family of ten.

"Farida is right," says Tajwar. "My husband and I could not feed our family."

During the two years I was jobless and the girls were without schooling, I dreamed of opening a female secondary school. Before the Soviets invaded Afghanistan, many girls from early childhood looked forward to a secondary education and beyond. Many young women could read, but in Peshawar they had no books. Now they sat secluded in their homes in a foreign country wasting away their lives. Many had lost as much as six or seven years of schooling. If they continued to lose out on their education, how would they help in the redevelopment of a free Afghanistan after the war?

I went to the party leaders and to international humanitarian organizations, but no one would listen to me. Everyone I spoke with was afraid. Finally, early in 1986, I went to the International Rescue Committee, an organization that had already done a number of things for women. The director agreed to look into possibilities.

In the beginning IRC believed home study would be the best strategy. It was felt that most Afghan men would not object to home study, at least on a primary level. Secondary schooling might present a problem. Female students would be given course material in their homes and have home tutorials on a weekly or monthly basis. It was hoped this would be a first step toward opening a female secondary school in Peshawar. Nancy Dupree, an eminent Afghan scholar particularly knowledgeable about Afghan women, reflected to

Margaret Segal, who headed up the IRC's female education programs, "The very fact that you raise the question [of female education] is proof of changing attitudes, and very exciting for those of us who were threatened just for mentioning the concept back in 1979 and 1980."[18] In the months ahead, Tajwar and Margaret would learn that it was still a very sensitive issue.

In a survey Tajwar took among more than 250 families in Peshawar and the nearby camps, it was revealed that there were 61 girls who had passed the fifth grade whose families were willing for them to attend a secondary girls' school. Nine families favored home study; 30 opposed female education; 157 either did not have secondary-school-age daughters or denied having them.

Some with daughters in the schools run by the Pakistani government complained that all too frequently schools opened for girls were made coeducational and were staffed by Pakistani and Afghan men. Fathers pulled their daughters out, and the schools, in fact, became boys' schools.

Further statistics revealed just how little education hundreds of thousands of Afghan refugee girls received in the Peshawar area. Only twenty-nine girls were enrolled in the fifth grade in the Peshawar Commissionerate schools. Worse, in all other districts, only twenty-two girls were enrolled in the fifth grade. In the sixth grade there were seven enrolled in the Peshawar area, while there were none in the other districts.[19]

Such numbers did not daunt Tajwar; they spurred her to action. The real roadblock to the creation of such a school for females came from the politics of finance. Wahabi Muslims, mainly from Saudi Arabia, had already established several secondary girls' schools within some of the fundamentalist parties of the Afghan Seven-Party Alliance. In light of this fact, Margaret and Tajwar believed the climate was good for IRC's backing of a female secondary school in Peshawar. They were wrong.

Mr. Ansari, the educational president of Hezb-i-Islami, the party of Gulbuddin Hekmatyar, who had supported IRC in the development of some of its other educational programs, did everything he could to discourage the creation by IRC of a secondary school for girls. Margaret's notes best relate the political hurdles they had to jump before Tajwar's dream was to become a reality. The Wahabis, it appears, were behind the Afghan party opposition to IRC's proposal, for they did not want Westernization through education in the guise of humanitarian aid to be foisted on the Afghans. The Wahabis themselves wanted to set the tone for Afghan refugee education, for in the children they knew they held the future of Afghanistan.

Margaret recounted the political tug-of-war in her November-December 1986 reports.

He [Ansari] alleged that Tajwar . . . was procommunist. I showed him letters of references attesting to Tajwar's character [by important Afghan leaders]. He put the letters aside and said, "Anything can be forged in Pakistan."

Mr. Ansari said that if we started a school, it would be an easy target for a bomb by the KGB. Additionally, the school could become infested with spies and the political parties would oppose it . . . "I am not telling you what to do, I'm only giving you advice, and my advice is that if you open a secondary female school, it could be dangerous . . ."

According to several sources, the Arabs and Ittehad-e-Islami [fundamentalist Afghan party under the leadership of Professor Sayaf] have put pressure on Ansari to stop any activity on our part to start an independent female school.

After speaking to staff members and Afghans outside our organization, we have decided that it would be in the best interests of everyone to approach the establishment of a secondary girls school through a political party as opposed to opening an independent IRC school . . . Tajwar . . . met with President Rabbani of Jamiat-e-Islami [party].

Jamiat is a fundamentalist party that receives support from the West and several Arab groups. Three of Rabbani's daughters have attended our English Language Program and his wife is a strong supporter of Afghan women. He has presently agreed to open up a school that would be supported by us under the aegis of Jamiat . . . We would have complete control over the selection of the teachers and would form the curriculum with educators in Jamiat. Tajwar would remain as the director . . .

[Rabbani] told his educational president, Abdul Hai, to write a letter to us in support of a Jamiat secondary school funded by IRC. Abdul Hai told Tajwar that he could not do this until he proposed this plan to the Seven-Party-Alliance educational committee. Several months ago the committee signed an agreement stating that any political party that receives funding from a voluntary agency or any other foreign source for educational programming must have approval from the committee . . . Abdul Hai . . . presented the proposal for a Jamiat female secondary school to the committee. The majority of the members . . . voted against it. Abdul Hai . . . told Tajwar that he was sorry but there was nothing more he could do.

We have discovered that Mohammad Jan Ahmadze, who is the director of the finance department of Jamiat, has been putting considerable pressure on Abdul Hai to do whatever he could to stop the establishment of a Jamiat secondary girls school. We have also found out that Ahmadze and Ahmad Shah from Ittehad-e-Islami, an Arab-linked party, went to educational president Ansari from Hezb-i-Islami and coerced him into trying to stop IRC from establishing a secondary girls school . . . [T]he Arabs are exerting whatever influence they can to stop Western organizations from participating in the field of Afghan education.

It is also of interest that Tajwar's husband, who works for Mohammed Jan Ahmadze in the finance department of Jamiat, has had his salary decreased by a considerable amount. It is of even more interest that none of the educational projects that are supported by the Arabs has ever been brought to the "official" attention of the Seven-Party-Alliance committee. Also, none of the party schools that IRC supports (InterParty schools) was ever brought before this committee for approval. We got support from political parties by talking *individually to the presidents for education. To the best of our knowledge, no party ever used the committee to get support for a project. Thus we think that Abdul Hai brought the female project before the education committee knowing that it would fail. He was then able to tell Rabbani, who supports secondary education for women, that the project was voted down.*[20]

Fortunately for Tajwar and the girls who would become the first students in the school, President Rabbani of Jamiat conceded that the committee vote was of little consequence. What Tajwar needed was a letter from him, which he delivered.

Lycee Malalai opened March 1, 1987, shortly after a bombing brought on by tension over the Geneva Accords talks then in progress. Several Pakistani school children were killed.

The school's name honors an Afghan heroine who, during one of Afghanistan's nineteenth-century wars with the British, stalled the Afghan soldiers' retreat and, sword in hand, spurred them to victory saying:

> Are you not men? Are you not Afghans?
> If not martyred in Maiwand—
> I swear by God, I keep you from shame.
> If not victory—
> What is our work?
> We have been suckled by the milk of Afghan women—
> Why should we not be victorious?
> God is great![21]

The school might well have been named for one of the thousands of Afghan women who died from the fire of Soviet arms. There is the story of a gathering of school girls in Kabul who, when they encountered young Afghan soldiers loyal to the Soviets, taunted them by offering them their *chaders* saying that they, the soldiers, were in truth girls as indicated by the way they obeyed the Soviets. The young Afghan soldiers opened fire on the crowd of Afghan girls, killing and wounding many among them.[22]

Twenty girls came to Lycee Malalai on opening day. Wary at first, others followed. By the second month there were thirty-five. By the second year there were one hundred, and the school grew to two hundred young women, with a long waiting list. In the beginning there were no Dari textbooks. Tajwar and her staff tirelessly searched many months for textbooks they could translate for the twelve subjects offered in grades seven through twelve. At times they felt they would never be able to provide them for the students. Finally, they did gather the sixty books they needed and had them translated.

The school was never without its detractors; it was always a point of controversy in the community. But young women graduated and hoped that someday they would be able to continue on with university study. Without that option, they felt they had met another dead end. Some dropped out of

Lycee Malalai because they felt even completing secondary education was fruitless since they could not attend university.

Lycee Malalai did not close during the tumultuous spring of 1990. They were close to the end of the school year and played it out. Tajwar was no longer there. Her continued controversial political activities, now advocating the return of King Zahir Shah, once again put her on the move. For her own security and the security of her family, the Kakar family packed up and departed—this time for Australia. There, at least, her daughters would be able to pursue a university education so that when they returned to their home-land, they would be better prepared to help rebuild the devastated country.

EMPLOYMENT

Nuria, an Afghan refugee woman, had not experienced the terror of Pesha-war, for in Quetta, a city far south of Peshawar, the atmosphere was much less volatile. Fewer than one million refugees lived in the area, and Quetta was not the seat of the AIG. Nevertheless, on this spring day in 1990, she looked both left and right before she stepped from the door of her home toward the waiting Catholic Relief Services truck. Her brown *chaderi* com-pletely concealed her; the cloth grill covering her face allowed her to breathe and see. To Nuria, wearing the *chaderi* was as foreign as the country she had been living in for ten years, and the reason she wore it now bore little relation to the religious rationale for *purdah*. She wore it out of fear of recognition, not out of respect for tradition. She was working outside her home, traveling long distances to different refugee camps each day—a dangerous practice in light of the growing conservatism.

When she left Lashkar Gah, the city of her birth in Helmand Province in south-central Afghanistan, she was broken in spirit. She had lost her father, her home, and her profession. Her father, a prominent engineer, had worked for the American company that built the Helmand River Valley Project to harness the spring flood-producing waters of the Helmand and Arghandab rivers and to make the surrounding land more productive. He had provided well for his family and encouraged his daughters to seek higher education.

Nuria's father may have paid with his life for his involvement with an American company, for after the Soviet invasion of Afghanistan such people were suspect, particularly the well educated. One night not long after the Soviets came, there were sharp raps on the door. When her father responded, the military police pulled his hands back, bound them, and led him into the darkness. The security this woman had always known in the arms of her tightly knit family evaporated in the air.

The family received no word of his whereabouts. They did not know if he was dead or alive. They did not know if he had been killed and his body mutilated and thrown into an unknown mass grave or if he suffered depri-vation and endless torture in some prison. Nuria was determined to make every effort to find him or learn of his fate. After exhausting all local possibilities, she traveled to many other prisons in the country without finding a trace of him, not even receiving the small comfort of having someone tell her they had seen him. Her final stop was Pol-e Charkhi prison in Kabul. She knew that Babrak Karmal, the Soviet-backed leader of Afghanistan, had released a number of political prisoners in a gesture of good will when he took over the government from Hafizullah Amin in 1979. She hoped her father would be among them. But people in Kabul who knew him did not give her even a flicker of hope. She never found him.

Nuria returned to her home in Lashkar Gah, and for a time continued to teach, as she had since graduation from the university, until she knew she was suspect by the Karmal government.

I was doing my job teaching Dari in a secondary school for women. The presence of soldiers or government police became a common sight in the building. They came into our classrooms and observed our teaching as well as the conduct of the students. Few girls were taken to prison, but a number of their brothers were taken from the men's schools and incarcerated or murdered. Others lost their fathers just as I did. Thousands of people innocent of any crime faced firing squads. Entire families were put under house arrest. Some children were sent to schools in the Soviet Union. All were urged to inform on their parents. I could no longer trust my students for fear one would inform on me. It did not matter to the authorities whether what they said about me was not the truth.

Finally, I resigned because I refused to disseminate the soldiers' propaganda. Many times they asked me why I did not teach the songs and the slogans they gave me. I said to them, "I am a language teacher. That is what I teach, nothing more."

She left the large, walled family home with her mother, sisters, and other relatives for Pakistan in 1981. Nuria and her family journeyed to the rugged area of Quetta, where Nuria worked among some of the most needy of the refugee female population.

Not only did I flee my homeland, but a way of life as well. In Lashkar Gah I had a profession and was able to travel freely between my home and the school. I wore Western clothes; never did I wear the chaderi. I felt no constraints. Even the fact that I was not married, generally a stigma in our society for one my age, was not a problem.

Here in Quetta, however, I felt pinched in every way. When we arrived, we moved into very small quarters with other relatives. There are twelve of us living in a home not one-third the size of the home we left behind. There we were only seven living together. Here we have no space.

Not only was the living area small, the women were confined to their quarters. Suddenly, my freedom of movement was taken from me. I was not allowed to work or go outside without at least wearing the chader, a covering less severe than the chaderi. *Always I was accompanied by a male. Even when I did go out, I did not know the language of Pakistan.*

I became very depressed. I felt like I was imprisoned. I was so homesick and worried constantly about the fate of my father. He was a tall man, a strong man whose merriment enlivened our family. Yet I would dream of him bound, weakened, and very sad. To this day, I still cry out in my sleep and awaken in a cold sweat. Will we never see him again? Will our family never be whole? Will we forever remain in a foreign land?

As Nuria herself felt impotent in staying her own stagnation, she became more and more depressed. Like many other women, she felt powerless to release her life from being on hold.

By 1988, seven years after her flight from Afghanistan, Nuria's uncle and brother were experiencing great difficulty in providing for the twelve persons who lived together in their small quarters in Quetta. Work was not always available and their remuneration was meager. Anguished because they could not provide adequately for their women, the two men acknowledged their need for Nuria to work. Through connections, her uncle found a job for her with one of the NGOs sponsoring a women's project.

Elizabeth, the woman leading the women's program, was one of the refugee women's greatest advocates. For more than thirty-five years this Swiss woman, now in her sixties, has been a champion of poor women in many underdeveloped countries. The last six years have been spent among Afghan refugee women.

''What about the women? What about the women?'' has been Elizabeth's clarion cry. She never failed to raise this question when the NGOs of Quetta met to discuss their work with the Afghan refugees in the area. Over the years she has searched out many of the poorest refugee women and initiated them into income-generating projects they can do in their homes.

In the beginning it was not easy for her to convince the *mullahs* and the tribal leaders that the sewing and quilting projects would not bring harm to the women or dishonor to the family. Elizabeth knew well that one of the most painful aspects of exile for Afghan men has been to accept the need for their women to work for compensation.

I went to many camps at first in the Loralai district, about a five-hour drive east of Quetta. ''No, no, no,'' the mullahs *said to me when I proposed sewing work for the women. Some threatened to burn the home of any woman who agreed to participate in such a program. I knew it would not do to argue with them. I had to be sensitive to their customs. I thought of the many thousands of refugees in this area. Surely I would find some leaders willing for their women to learn machine sewing.*

Finally one listened to me. I said to him, ''You know we have a program for poorer women. We would like to teach them sewing to make school uniforms for UNHCR. The women can even earn a sewing machine for half price, five hundred rupees rather than one thousand." I asked him if he might be willing to supply a place for the poorer women to gather and a chokidar, a watchman, to guard the premises. To my surprise, he made all the arrangements, and we began our first training course.

After we started, another leader came to us and said, "We also have a space—not in this camp, but in the next one. Come to us. We also have poor women, and we can provide a chokidar." That is how it went. The word spread, and more leaders came to us asking us to provide training for their women. That first year we trained 209 women in two camps near Loralai.

In one of the camps women walked as far as three miles to reach the meeting place. Suddenly, after meeting for two years, they stopped coming. The mullahs, for unknown reasons, changed their minds and said the women could no longer come. That did not happen too often, but the women have to obey the men's wishes. Even a young boy no more than seven or eight, if he is the eldest male in the household, can either approve or disapprove of a woman's request to become a part of a sewing group, train to be a traditional birth attendant, or even go to the camp's basic health unit when she or her child is ill. We took material to them and formed a group in a family compound rather than in a center. The men bring the finished product to the center and take new material to the women. The men also receive the payment when they bring the completed items. I never know if the women even see the money.

Each year UNHCR commissions me to make thousands of school uniforms and quilts. I purchase a number of portable sewing machines and distribute them among the women. The machines become theirs when they pay for them by completing so many uniforms or quilts. Other women earn their machines by doing traditional Baluch embroidery.

It was not easy for Elizabeth to reach the Afghan refugee camps. That section of Pakistan is not unlike the American southwest, except the roads are not super highways or even comparable to old Route 66. On twisting mountain roads not wide enough for two automobiles and with innumerable, unprotected hairpin curves, overloaded buses and trucks defy any oncoming vehicle. Too many fall into the yawning valleys. The physical condition of the roads is not the only danger travelers encounter. On the road to Iran, travel is precarious with desert and sand-dune land harboring roaming bandits.

To get ahead of the heat and complete a full day's work after the four- or six-hour journey, Elizabeth's workday began at 5:00 A.M. She set out for Surkhab, Mohammed Kheil, Loralai, Chagi, Malagagi, Girdi Jungle, or Zohar Chah—remote places all, but home to hundreds of thousands of refugees.

Nuria accompanied Elizabeth to those no more than two or three hours away from Quetta, for her brother and uncle would not allow her to spend the night away from home. Early each morning Elizabeth's white Toyota pickup truck wandered through the maze of narrow paths bounded on either side by sewer drainage ditches to the house where Nuria lived. To avoid drawing attention to Nuria's daily departure, the driver did not honk the horn. He waited for her to open the door cautiously, step out fully covered in her brown *chaderi* and into the truck's cab. Nuria felt alive again in a job that afforded both purpose and challenge.

Stone and sand, sand and stone—that is all one sees approaching the Mohammed Kheil camps. The sand is coarse and rocky; the stones are large and sharp. There is not a blade of grass. The truck rocked and swayed as it followed a path up and down gullies. This moonscape was seemingly void of people until tattered tents and mud compounds could be seen on the horizon. On the outskirts of the tented and mud village, a group of turbaned men with picks and shovels were digging a grave in the already large cemetery. They would make a rounded mound and raise some colored cloth on a tall stick to mark another who died in a foreign land.

Outside the walled compounds a few children played; two women surrounded by children washed clothes in the shallow, muddy water of a gully. Even in the tented area without the privacy of walls, few people were evident, due in part to *purdah* and to the heat.

Tents eventually gave way to the mud compounds. When the people realized they would not be going home in the foreseeable future, they built less transitory structures, though still not permanent enough to give the appearance of rootedness. To many nomads in Mohammad Kheil, tents were familiar dwellings. But their traditional tents were of goatskin, not tattered canvas or cloth. They had space as far as the eye could see and abundant herds. In the camps hundreds of tents stood side by side; there were no animals—at most a goat or two and some chickens. They lived as intact families and clans, leading their animals to high mountain areas in summer and back to lower, warmer climes in winter. That life was no more. They lamented their loss of open space and freedom to move. They lamented their dependence on rations and outside assistance. Their animals provided skin for their tents, meat and yogurt, wool for their clothes. There was always sufficient firewood to gather and sources of water to wash and drink. They traded animal products for any commercial goods they might need.

Although the nomadic people were latecomers among Mohammad Kheil's refugee population, the war disrupted them from the beginning. From 1980 to 1986 they moved constantly within Afghanistan, fleeing the fighting, seeking safety from Soviet strafings and bombing raids. As the years passed, they were reduced to utter poverty, many with no alternative but to beg for sustenance. They brought with them the horrors of flight. Their stories of loss ran together in a swelling dirge.

The women of Elizabeth and Nuria's newly formed sewing group, as if a chorus, mourned their losses. "Our men went off to war; our men were killed. Only the old men remained. As we moved from place to place, our children and animals caught the enemy fire," told one.

"I was injured." "I was shot." "I was burned." Around the room several women lifted an arm or raised their skirts to reveal their scars. "There are bullets in my body that still hurt me," one disclosed. While another in resignation remarked, "I have too many children to care for; I cannot go to a doctor. Look at my legs; look at the scars. I cannot walk well anymore."

A spokeswoman for the group continued,

Once we decided to come to Pakistan, it took us four months to make the journey. If we had any animals left, we rode on them. Others we ate. Still others starved because we had no food. Can we ever be nomads again? How will we ever rebuild the herds? Too many men are dead. Women alone cannot be nomads. As soon as our sons are old enough, they, too, go off to the war and die.

It is difficult to get enough to eat. My husband fell in a well and broke his hands and his back. He cannot work, and the rations are not enough to feed nine children and a sick husband. All the children are not ours. My husband's brother died in the war. His wife went back to live with her parents, but she left their three children with us. Another woman died and left her children with us as well.

There are so many like me. Tatia's husband was injured in the war. He lost an arm and his eyesight. Anni's husband went to Iran five years ago to find work. She has not heard from him since. She must support their five children. Other men are diseased. Some women are married to very old men who cannot find work, no matter how hard they look. They have been nomads all their lives; they know no other work. Many men do not even receive rations for their families because they have not pledged support to one of the political leaders. You must belong to a political faction to get rations. Also, many of our women are widows without rations. Sometimes Saeed's brother will give her some wheat. Khadija, though, does not have family who will give her anything. Often she must beg for food. Sometimes she will break nuts for the shopkeepers in the bazaar. She collects paper from rubbish dumps to sell for fuel and finds old scraps of cloth to make clothes for her children and mats for them to sleep on.

We are totally dependent on the men for rations. The women do not get ration cards and cannot collect the wheat and the oil. Those who have no man to look out for them must depend on the leaders. For many reasons, some just do not get rations.

Sardar's husband is now going to take a second wife, much younger than Sardar. He will favor her and the children she will bear him over Sardar, we fear. She will need a second sewing machine, for her husband will surely give the one she has now to his new bride. I'm sure the two wives would not like to share a machine.

Many have sold their daughters in marriage, even at ten years of age, for several thousand rupees. That money goes very quickly and the other family demands they turn the girl over to them. It is very difficult to survive.[23]

These fifteen women have never used sewing machines. Elizabeth and Nuria are there to distribute the portable machines to the women and teach them how to use them. The women gather outside one of the tents. One by one their names are called to receive a machine. It is a proud and happy moment for them as the designated male leader distributes them. The silver metal of the case glints in the sun as a woman opens it to lift the machine and admire it. Each woman places her machine on a space cleared of rocks and stones and squats in front of it. The wheels turn; the needles move up and down. Then it is time to learn to thread the machine. Hands rough from years of tying tent ropes, gathering firewood, milking goats, and spinning wool awkwardly move the thread through the small holes and wires until it reaches the needle. Thumbs, dry and split, direct the thread through the eye of the needle. They are ready to sew. First attempts result in a mass of tangled threads and heavy sighs of exasperation. Soon, however, they catch the rhythm, and the laughter and relieved talk rises into the air. The men present were certain the women could care for goats; they were just as certain they would never learn to sew. Perhaps now some of the women will be able to afford better nourishment for their families.

Elizabeth and Nuria move on to a quilting group in one of the mud villages. The women in this particular group were village women, wives of farmers and shopkeepers—stationary, not on the move as were the nomads. They, too, live with the same hardships and memories—of villages bombed until no more than four families survived, of husbands killed or maimed and no longer able to provide, of confinement to their compounds year after year, of anxiety over not being able to provide enough sustenance for their children.

Today, though, is payday. In the quilting center, a large room made from mud, ten finished, colorful quilts are piled on the dirt floor, swept clean every morning by the women of the center. Six women sit off to one side, a quilt spread across their laps as they complete the finishing touches. Their fingers move quickly as they talk. In 1990 almost six hundred women Elizabeth has trained produced approximately twenty thousand quilts, with a total income of more than 350,000 rupees (U.S. $20,000); each woman earning close to six hundred rupees (U.S. $35). As each woman comes forward to collect her pay, she squats beside a purple-ink stamp pad. Slowly, she rolls her thumb from right to left and puts her thumb-print in the square next to her name that Nuria points out. The thumb-print is her signature. These women can neither read their names nor write their signatures.

In the back of the pickup are two large rolls of raw cotton, stuffing for the next order of quilts. There are bolts of colorful material, too, bought cheaply in quantity after much bargaining. Supplies are not easy to obtain. The logistics of any undertaking among the refugees is tricky at best. The cotton comes from the Punjab in eastern Pakistan. The driver must cross the country on poor Pakistani highways in an enclosed truck to purchase the cotton. There is always the danger of bandits stopping the truck to abscond with the finished products. Once purchased and brought to Quetta, finding safe storage is difficult. Most supplies and completed products are stored in private houses. For further protection of themselves and the goods they transport, on the roads beyond Quetta the expatriates who work with the refugees travel with *levies,* armed security escorts.

Most of the refugees in the mud villages of Mohammad Kheil have lived there for ten years or more. Approximately forty-two thousand refugees live in Mohammad Kheil's five camps. In the host country there is no land to till or ground for grazing open to the refugees, nor will leaders of the Pakistani government allow their guests to acquire land. The government wants to safeguard the land for its own citizens and also does not want to stir any sense of permanency in their guests. They want the Afghans to return to their homeland.

Because able-bodied men who are not fighting *jihad* are barred from earning a livelihood from the land and because inadequate rations make additional income a necessity, they seek the few casual labor jobs available in construction or seasonal agriculture on Pakistani farms. Some who were proprietors in their village bazaars in Afghanistan have set up shop in camp bazaars, hiring others to assist them. A number have become truck drivers, while others have found positions with international NGOs.

As more and more women become widows, those men in the extended family left to look after them and their children find they cannot provide for them. Certainly women left without any males suffer the most. Some lose as many as three generations of men—father, husband or brother, and son. Still the women support the men's role in *jihad,* challenging the men to be brave and chiding them if they cower.

In the face of destitution, an increasing number of men allow their women to work for remuneration. In fact, as Elizabeth and Nuria move from one group to another, they often are stopped by a leader of another extended family who implores them to form a sewing or quilting group among his women. "When there is no food on the table, men quickly open the door," one woman observes.[24] In reality, a relatively small percentage of the 3.5 million refugees are reached by NGOs that have involved themselves in women's projects. There are never enough funds or people or markets for the NGOs to expand according to the constantly growing needs. Yet without the income generated by women, which can provide proper nutrition and attention to their special health needs, women's and children's lives are often in jeopardy.

HEALTH

Nineteen-year-old Zarghuna was in labor, the third time in as many years. She had not come to full term so the child would be born six weeks prematurely. Her father-in-law had gone to ask the traditional birth attendant, the *dai,* to assist in Zarghuna's delivery. It had been a difficult pregnancy for Zarghuna who had been sick for months and had gained little weight. Her color was ashen and she was constantly weak. Now, during her labor, some of the women of the household gathered in the room with Zarghuna to lend their support while others tended to the children.

It was a cold, overcast December day; little light came through the small window carved in the mud wall. There was no stove for warmth in this room, only in the main room. Zarghuna shivered under the quilt spread over her. Once the *dai* arrived, there was little time for preparation; Zarghuna's water had broken. Fully clothed as she was under the quilt, with the assistance of the *dai* and her mother-in-law, the young woman rose from the mat and squatted over a shallow hole dug in the floor for the birthing. As she pushed, a tiny head and then the body of a male child emerged. In the tradition of their village, the *dai* picked up Zarghuna's shoe from the floor, turned it over, and placed the umbilical cord across the shoe's sole. She severed it with a razor blade taken from her pocket. The child wailed to life as it was lifted and then washed. The baby's father, a *mujahideen* fighting *jihad* in Afghanistan, would welcome a male child when he returned from the front. The first child had been a boy as well, but the second, a girl.

Zarghuna, exhausted, held the child but a moment before her mother-in-law lifted and carried him away to tightly swaddle him during his first days of life, an ancient custom. Two other women remained in the birthing room to watch the covered Zarghuna. As they watched for the next two days, they could see she was losing rather than gaining strength. When she began to hemorrhage late the third day, there was little the women could do to save her. Zarghuna died that night leaving three young children for their absent father. The baby died during his first year of life, succumbing to an upper respiratory tract infection, not an uncommon ailment in the camps.

Wanting to aid the war effort in whatever way they can, women see their role as replacing the population killed off by the war, either directly or in illness. It is particularly important for them to give birth to male children, who can continue to protect and defend the honor of the country. Little attention is given to the physical and emotional strain too many pregnancies have on women or to the strain of caring for fragmented families.

Too frequent pregnancies take a heavy toll on a woman's body, particularly a woman in exile who suffers deprivations she would not in her homeland. There is no time for a malnourished woman to replenish and rebuild her body sufficiently to carry another child so soon after delivery. Like Zarghuna, many women give birth prematurely because they cannot sustain two lives at one time. Underweight and underdeveloped babies put an additional strain on the mother's ability to feed the infant. Babies like Zarghuna's, orphaned at birth, are at much greater risk. Small mounds of stones that mark infant graves continue to multiply. A report from the 1988 International Consultation on Refugee Women bares startling statistics. "In a population of 15,000, 450 women will be pregnant at any one time, [and] there will be 600 deliveries per year. Of this, 2 women can be expected to die in childbirth or as a result of the pregnancy, 50 children will die before their first birthday, 24 of these before 1 month and 9 of these deaths will be from neonatal tetanus."[25]

It was spring in this remote refugee village. The earth and the air were warm again. Over the four months since Zarghuna's death, other mothers and their infants who died in birth had been buried in the camp's cemetery near Zarghuna and her child.

A truck kicked up dust as it passed the cemetery, leaving a cloud over the graves. It meandered into the mud village, stopping at a small compound in view of the burial ground. Two Pakistani women—Saeeda, a doctor, and Rama, a mother-child health (MCH) trainer—who had come from the town of Hangu, stepped down from the truck and passed through the low entrance of a compound gate.

The area was immediately filled with chattering children. The children of every camp gathered whenever a truck brought outsiders, and each pushed to the front to shake the stranger's hand. Veiled women from adjoining compounds also found their way into the courtyard. Men shooed the children away from the serious women's business about to take place.

Bakhtawar, a large, tall woman—the lady of the house—greeted Saeeda and Rama with a smile that surfaced her own interior beauty. Four other women came forward to welcome the guests.

These women were traditional midwives, *dais*. They were not young, but not as old as were many of the midwives. In traditional Afghan society, midwives are chosen from among these elder village women because an older woman has more freedom of movement and can move from house to house to attend births. Having passed her own child-bearing years, she is venerated in the family and the community as one who has given offspring, the ones who then will create the next generation of Afghans. These midwives had gathered for a class in birthing that would, hopefully, prevent some of the untimely deaths of women like Zarghuna. After all, it is estimated that among Afghan women between the ages of sixteen and forty-five, 40 percent are pregnant at any given time.[26]

Like income-generating programs and female education, creating preventative health classes had not been easy. Saeeda voiced the frustrations:

In Islam there is no directive against women learning. On the contrary, it is encouraged. However, during the time of the Soviet occupation, the Soviet attempt to overthrow long-standing tradition was seen in conjunction with their push for propaganda-loaded education for both males and females. At the same time, although the Soviets intended it as a means of liberation and unthinkingly coupled it with education, taking away the woman's chader was, in fact, the removal of a symbol of the Afghan's Islamic belief. Both men and women, especially those in villages, resisted the changes forced upon them. They would not accept education that issued from a force which so opposed their basic beliefs, their freedom, their value systems.

In the refugee setting they lived reactively, hardening their traditional practices until, in reality, the freedom for which they had fled was further curtailed. At least until recently. It has taken more than ten years to begin to break down some of the barriers the men placed on the women as a consequence of the war. Now they find themselves moving away somewhat from their distrust of education, partly because Pakistani women share their Islamic beliefs, yet also encourage education. Seen in this context, the women are becoming more receptive to new ways that still respect their deepest values.

Inside, the mud hut was cool and very clean. As in every Afghan refugee home, colorful quilt-like mats were lined on the dirt floor against the walls — as were large, stuffed pillows. On the wall hung a poster of a snow-capped mountain scene near Lake Louise in the Canadian Rockies, a place as foreign to these village women as the dusty refugee village in Pakistan. Still, the mountain scene reminded them of their mountain-valley village in Afghanistan, now obliterated by Soviet bombs. At the far end of the room on a low table were two cream-colored trunk-like containers, vessels of the family's possessions, covered with bright, printed pieces of material.

In the center of the room, three metal washbasins had been placed in preparation for the day's lesson. Water was heating in a tea kettle resting on a small kerosene burner. Rama, the MCH trainer, opened the blue flight-bag she carried and took out the necessary tools for the day's lesson on child delivery; she placed soap and clean rags near one of the wash basins.

This day Bakhtawar would play the role of the midwife. She pulled her black floral-print veil behind her head, rolled up the heavily embroidered sleeves of her traditional dress, pulled up the long, flowing skirt, also embroidered around the edge — colorful in gold, red, and purple — and tied it behind her. Under the dress, her rose-patterned baggy pants were full around her legs and tight at her ankles. Her large bare feet were the color of the dirt floor.

She poured some water into one of the basins and squatted before it, taking the bar of soap, scrubbing her hands and arms three times. Each time she rinsed with heated water from the kettle. As she stood, she raised her arms — elbows bent, palms toward her face — and held them out from her body, avoiding contact with anything or anyone to keep them sterile.

She walked over to Mastana who would role-play the pregnant woman. When Mastana was comfortably settled lying on a clean plastic sheet, taken from the flight bag, Bakhtawar squatted beside her and examined her stomach. It was time for her to deliver.

Next Rama pulled from her bag a skeleton pelvis and a cloth doll wrapped with a rope representing the umbilical cord around its neck. While Rama held the pelvis and the doll on the interwomb side and pushed the head through the cervical opening, Bakhtawar gently brought the baby forth into the world, unwrapped the umbilical cord from around the neck, and completed the delivery. Tenderly and with surety, she took the small, purple rags she has sterilized in the boiling water and wiped the blood from the baby's face and body.

Suddenly, the baby was no longer breathing. With Bakhtawar giving mouth-to-mouth resuscitation, the child began to breathe again and lived. Everyone in the room broke into congratulatory chatter for a successful delivery. Then they gathered in a circle to complete the class with an evaluative discussion and preparation for the next time they would meet.

In the nonliterate world of these women, simple drawings portraying procedures became their textbooks and their tests. Such drawings were the media of instruction used by all community health workers among the camps' populations. A sketch of a mother breast feeding her child or of a mother feeding a child a variety of basic foods helped those instructed retain what was learned. When medications were dispensed at the basic health unit (BHU), pills were placed in a small paper container on which was printed pictures of a sun rising just above the horizon, a full sun at high noon, and a sliver of a moon and stars. A pen mark by the proper picture indicated the time of day the medicine should be taken.

Earnest learning and giggles mingle as evidence that this was not only a serious class that expanded their world but also a social occasion for these women who had lived in strict seclusion for almost a decade.

After the class was over, Bakhtawar's twelve-year-old son gave each woman hot tea with sugar in a small juice glass, an Afghan tradition. For Saeeda and Rama's pleasure, as the women fell into talk of weddings, babies, and cooking, Bakhtawar opened one of the foot-lockers and lifted out a cloth-tied bundle. She placed it on the floor in the center of the circle and untied the knot. As she folded back each corner of the cloth, she revealed intricate beading and brilliant colors. On the first dress sleeve was a round beaded star of white, red, and blue with a small, round mirror in the center. Gold bric-a-brac covered the edge, interspersed with the colorful beading. Velveteen pieces of gold, purple, green, and red made up the rest of the lower sleeve. These met the black of the rest of the dress. A beaded breastplate as brilliant and varied as the sleeve was the centerpiece of the dress. The other sleeve complemented the first and the bottom of the dress was also decorated elaborately. This was Bakhtawar's wedding dress, preserved and carried from the decimated village and life she left behind.

At present, there is a growing awareness among refugee women and girls of their special health needs and an effort to prevent so much needless suffering and preventable death. Theirs is a monumental task fraught with obstinate barriers, not the least of which is the glaring lack of women in decision-making positions, from top-level international offices to the camps themselves.

Upgrading the skills of traditional midwives is but one of the efforts of international agencies to improve the health of Afghan refugee women and children. Among most refugee populations such development endeavors are slow in coming as the agencies tend to focus principally on relief. Generally, health education programs reach the female population much later, often because of their low status in society and inhibiting cultural factors.

The chief obstacle to better health care for women has been the lack of female health workers and female doctors. In very traditional Afghan households a woman's husband would go to the male doctor to describe his ill wife's symptoms. Based on the husband's description, the doctor would make a diagnosis and prescribe a treatment that the husband would communicate to his wife. In other cases, the woman might go to the camp's basic health unit, but she was not allowed to disrobe for examination or allow a male doctor to see any part of her body uncovered.

Gradually, however, particularly with the presence of more Pakistani female health workers, health care among women has improved with far-reaching consequences. In many cases the BHUs provided the first health care for these women. The men needed and wanted women to be healthy, charged as they were with child bearing and child rearing. Because the BHUs were one of the few places women could legitimately go beyond the seclusion of their homes, they became social gathering places. The BHU woman's court-yard filled early each morning with women eager to talk and children ready to play.

Such gatherings provided a real outlet for women. Perhaps this was the closest these women would come to special days in their home villages and towns when they gathered at the baths or in secluded gardens with picnic meals in hand for a day away from their normal routines. They wore their finest clothes and bedecked themselves with jewelry.[27]

It seemed to the health workers that the BHU courtyard was a perfect place to encourage women to become better attuned to health issues peculiar to themselves, such as nutrition.

The vast majority of Afghan refugees did not arrive in Pakistan in a state of starvation as did, for example, hundreds of thousands of Eritreans when they crossed into the Sudan in 1984 or Cambodians when they fled into Thailand following the fall of Pol Pot in 1979. Nor have the Afghan refugees experienced outbreaks of savage epidemics of cholera and typhoid as have so many refugee populations. Like the Kurds who fled into Iran and Turkey following the 1991 Persian Gulf War, they were relatively healthy when they were forced to flee from their homeland. Unlike the Kurds, who were not welcomed by Turkey and who waited in inclement weather and appalling conditions on cold mountainsides while the slow, bureaucratic machinery of assistance edged into action, the Afghans were taken into Pakistani homes, often Pushtun tribal kin, or were provided early on with basic necessities.

Still, few refugees around the world escape the plague of malnourishment, and the Afghan refugees are no exception. Less desperate but more subtle, their lack of proper and adequate nutrition has, nonetheless, serious effects. What the women lack affects the fetus in the womb and the newborn as it grows—the future generation of Afghans. Without adequate food, the child's weight is far below normal, bones and organs do not grow or function prop-erly, and mental abilities are stunted.

Cultural factors play a role in an Afghan woman's diet. Traditionally men and boys are served first. Guests also take precedence. Women and girls receive what remains. In normal times when crops are plentiful and animals are healthy, there is plenty for all. In fact, women pride themselves in managing food supplies astutely for the months when the ground lies fallow.[28] In exile with meager rations supplemented rarely by chickens and eggs, goat meat and milk, or fresh fruits and vegetables, women suffer most from the lack of adequate nourishment and often live on a diet of bread and tea.

More than 60 percent of Afghan refugee women are anemic.[29] Without sufficient iron, for example, women hemorrhage more readily in childbirth and die, as did Zarghuna. Without sufficient iron women are tired, weak, and without energy. Active children wear a woman down further and frequent pregnancies take a costly toll on her body. She does not have the energy to do all that is required in a household with many dependent upon her. To collect the daily supply of water and firewood is arduous, for most refugee homes do not have wells and often the source of water can be at a great distance over rough, stony paths and in intense heat.

Because of improper nourishment, many women do not lactate, and their babies do not receive the vital fats, minerals, and vitamins they normally would receive from the mother's breast. The powdered milk given to many refugees around the world lacks these nutritional additives so necessary to proper growth. Many children, particularly the underweight and protein deficient, may need supplementary feeding that can be dispensed in BHU clinics. Weighing and recording the weight of the child each month can make the mother more aware of the development needs of her child.

Although the women's courtyards in the BHU of Afghan refugee camps appear to be bursting with people, only a fraction of the women actually take advantage of the care provided. Hundreds of thousands are never reached. Through home visitation outreach, lady health workers (LHW) go from door to door to offer more women particular care. Pregnant women are of special concern. The visiting health workers must first convince the woman and her husband of the importance of monitoring throughout pregnancy and following delivery.

Health workers would like to see more women visit the clinics from the beginning of pregnancy through the postpartum stage to ensure proper attention to their special needs. Simple immunization against tetanus could save many. Outbreaks of polio and measles can be prevented; fortunately, because refugees are concentrated in large clusters around the world, high percentages of these populations are now being immunized.

Not more than a handful of Afghan women ever have the luxury of a hospital for their obstetric/gynecological needs, particularly for high-risk deliveries. Through the foresight and persistent appeal of Dr. Hussain Momand, one such hospital came into being as an outpatient facility in Peshawar in 1984, opening with two female doctors, one male doctor, and four nurses. A year later a labor room and five inpatient beds were added, and a surgical unit opened in 1986. Today it has grown to a fifteen-bed hospital, small by any standards for the needs of the world's largest refugee population.

A great but preventable killer in the camps, especially among children, is diarrhea, particularly during the dry, hot season when flies are abundant and water supplies are low. A mother's knowledge of simple preventative steps can save the life of her child. Many fear feeding a child during bouts with diarrhea, dehydrating the child even to the point of death. Learning the benefit of continued feeding through oral rehydration can make all the difference for the child. Something as simple as digging the latrine, which always attracts flies, far enough from the living quarters can prevent many dysentery-related deaths.

Malaria can be controlled as well by precautionary measures. Women and children are generally the water bearers as well as the ones who wash the clothes. Avoiding stagnant waters where malaria-carrying mosquitoes multiply is one means of staving off this killer.

Prior to the war, access to health care in Afghanistan was extremely limited; most villages had nothing comparable to a BHU. But then in Afghanistan, people did not live in such congested areas, and latrine placement and stagnant waters were not so much a concern. Space, clean water, and adequate food were natural inhibitors of illness. Readily available health care in the Pakistani camps themselves has afforded many Afghans with new insights into simple preventative health measures. What Afghan women have gained through health education is limited by Western standards and little in the light of all they have lost. But some of women's most basic health needs have nonetheless been addressed, and the new insights and practices can be taken with them when they return to Afghanistan.

FEMALE REFUGEES AND POLICY DEVELOPMENT

The fact that refugee women have lived through the crucible of war and its horrors sets them apart from all other women. War is a crucible in which many witnessed children, husbands, and relatives being killed; others were injured or maimed themselves; some survived imprisonment, torment, and sexual assault; millions fled their bombed-out villages, towns, and cities. As a consequence, their needs are different from women in general. So, too, what they require to sustain life differs from the needs of the male refugee population. Yet the importance of this factor is generally lost or dismissed as inconsequential. Until recently, those charged with distributing refugee assistance have paid little attention to these devastating ramifications.

Anders Johnsson of the UNHCR points out that the United Nations 1951 Convention Relating to the Status of Refugees was obviously written with the male refugee in mind. Within the definition of a refugee, only the male gender is used.[30] Mr. Johnsson further observes that "not a single woman was to be found amongst the plenipotentiaries who met in Geneva in 1951 to draw up the Convention Relating to the Status of Refugees."[31]

All too often the particular needs of refugee women are not taken into consideration by refugee workers who receive the masses tumbling across a border. In a crisis situation, the people of the host country and those present to give humanitarian assistance see numbers more than individuals, people more than female, male, old, young. Relief workers know how to work in emergency situations—that is their expertise. They bring some order out of chaos, sorting out the sickest and doling out survival portions of rice and grain.

If women, who are the sustainers of culture and the nurturers of children, are to survive and give life to children and the spirits of their men, and if they are to live, not simply exist, in their radically altered circumstances and perform roles they have never before hazarded, their special needs must be addressed. If the stagnation of dependency and despair swallows them, others will be consumed as well. Only a development mode of action rather than one of relief can stay the effects of stagnation.

Not until thirty years after the 1951 Convention Relating to the Status of Refugees took effect, were advocate voices for refugee women heard. Undaunted through the years, their voices became stronger in the 1980s. The male-oriented, male-managed policy-making bodies began to listen. Today incremental changes are slowly finding their way into discussions about and actions on behalf of refugee women. In 1990 a woman was appointed to the newly created post of senior coordinator for refugee women in the office of the UNHCR, reporting directly to the deputy high commissioner. Today, a woman, Mrs. Sadako Ogata, is the United Nations High Commissioner for Refugees. Women's advocates and the office of senior coordinator for refugee women campaigned for specific measures in the areas of protection, education, economic development, and health, and established two very important underlying principles.

The first principle is fundamental, setting the foundation for all that follows. Refugee women are among the most valuable resources to be tapped in any refugee community; to fail to benefit from and make use of what they have to offer is to diminish what is done by humanitarian organizations for the good of all refugees. These women are vibrant, capable, thoughtful, resourceful, and resilient; they are not—as they are frequently stereotyped—passive, marginal, or inept. They are wives, daughters, mothers, grandmothers, and professionals, who generally lived self-sufficient lives with their families, contributing to the management of households, farms, and jobs. They made decisions in the interest of those closest to them, profoundly affecting their present and their future.

Before the war these women were food managers and producers; they worked in tandem with their husbands in the production of goods for market. The formation and inculturation of children largely fell to the mother. The health of the family rested with her. As wife and mother she was the backbone of the home. Other women, mostly urban women like Latifa, Nuria, and Tajwar, were engineers, teachers, attorneys, administrators, doctors. Although they leave much behind when they flee, refugee women bring their skills, education, knowledge, culture, experience, plans, and visions for the future. In exile, the women are most responsible for the reestablishment of the family.[32] Though sapped by the trauma of flight, there is within the women sparks of energy that can be ignited. In the voice of an anonymous refugee woman, "Consider us not only as we are, but also as we were."[33]

The second principle involves the creation of programs by the UNHCR, NGOs, and governmental organizations such as the United States Agency for International Development (USAID) and the European Economic Community (EEC). According to advocates for the integration of women into every aspect of program development, women are to be considered in all programs for refugee communities and are to be a vital part of their planning, design, and implementation. Women and programs for women are not to be isolated or segregated from the mainstream. It has been recognized that "programmes which are not planned in consultation, and implemented with the participation of half of the target population (the women) cannot be effective, and could, inadvertently, have a negative impact on the socio-economic situation of this 'forgotten' portion of the population."[34]

Women can best assess their own needs; but only if they are fully incorporated into the planning and implementation of programs, can they be assured of full access to programs and opportunities offered to the refugee community. Previously programs without strong female input benefited men at the cost of women. If the women participate in all levels of planning and implementation, economic and educational doors will open to them, their protection will be better secured, and community health care will include their special health needs. The more involved the women become in shaping suitable programs for themselves and their children, the greater will be their self-esteem, well-being, and contribution to the refugee community at large.

In addition, women need to participate with men in planning the construction and maintenance of shelter for the family as well as in distributing food to various segments of the society. Access to fuel and water is important to women, as they are most frequently gatherers of both. Other basic concerns such as consideration of sanitation and privacy in the placement of latrines would likewise benefit from their input. While respecting cultural traditions, women need to be assured such traditions will not be abused to deny them access to resources and opportunities.

Involving refugee women in planning programs for refugees requires an increase in female staff members at all levels among both refugee populations and expatriates. International organizations that service refugees must place more women in managerial positions so that half of such positions are held by women, so as to ensure that the different needs and roles of women in refugee populations would be addressed in developing specific projects.

The area of female protection is a case in point. In flight, women who are separated from their families and from male protection are most vulnerable to rape and physical violence. The plight of the female Vietnamese boat people in the face of pirates exemplifies this in the extreme. Once in the camps, women are vulnerable to aggressive sexual attacks by camp administrators and guards as well as male refugees. Many are forced to give sexual favors in exchange for survival rations for themselves and their children.

Even though males are the perpetrators of these sexual assaults, the majority of protectors for female refugees are males. More female protection officers are necessary as are female counselors who can understand what the woman has experienced as a victim of a sexual crime and who can educate her in protection measures. Most refugee women fear taking their stories to male officers or counselors and so remain silent. As a result, often the criminal is not apprehended, charged, or convicted and is, in fact, allowed to strike time after time.

More influential women are needed also to speak on behalf of women in the areas of education, employment, and health. Whether it is a question of food distribution and nutritional balance to combat malnutrition or the use of food as a political weapon or primary health care through the education of women home visitors and traditional birth attendants, women can best assure that the particular needs and interests of refugee women are met. The development of immunization programs, gynecological services, formal and nonformal educational opportunities and skills training, or access to work and fair compensation all require women in leadership positions, particularly refugee women.[35]

In this day of "donor fatigue" and budget constraints, resources for development among refugees grow more scarce yearly. Funding for simple relief and survival items, such as shelter, food, water, clothing, and protection, is difficult to raise. Still the donor community must pay attention to the special needs of women refugees and allocate meager resources to meet these needs that have been neglected for so long to the detriment of refugee populations as a whole.

Women remain the backbone of the refugee community and the nurturers of the future generation being born in exile. Just as they are the ones who must reestablish the family in exile, so too will they be the ones to re-create the familial environment on return to the homeland. Whereas dependency and marginalization during exile will only weaken their ability to be intimately involved in the rebuilding of their community once they return home, empowering and encouraging them to develop their potential in the midst of their refugee lives will enable them to participate fully in re-creating and enhancing the lives and the land from which they fled.

The education of Afghan boys is often limited to the skills of war. With no other classroom, how will they be trained to lead a country at peace?

6

AFGHAN RETURN

Human beings are like limbs embodied in one
* entity.*
In essence they are created from the same
* ingredient.*
Perchance mishap strikes one limb;
Others will be affected simultaneously.
You who absolve yourself from the suffering of others
Are not worthy of being called a human being.
* —Sheikh Maslahuddin Sa'di*
* Ninth-Islamic-Century Persian poet*

POLITICAL DETERRENTS TO PEACE IN AFGHANISTAN

On April 27, 1992, Sebghatullah Mojaddidi, elected head of a fifty-member interim Islamic ruling council for Afghanistan, left Peshawar, Pakistan, where he had lived in exile throughout the Afghan war. He left for Kabul, the capital of Afghanistan and his departure coincided with the fourteenth anniversary of the bloody Saur Revolution of April 27, 1978. That revolution toppled President Mohammad Daoud from power and led the way for the Soviet invasion of Afghanistan in December 1979.

A dramatic chain of events between April 16 and April 27, 1992 launched Afghanistan into a new phase of its history and brought the country to a crossroad. It can come to peaceful terms with its make-up of multiple ethnic and linguistic groups and degrees of Islamic tolerance or it can continue strife that will bring the country to ruins. On April 16, President Najibullah was ousted because he lost the loyalty not only of his Kabul troops, but also of troops throughout the countryside who defected to rebel commanders, particularly to Ahmed Shah Masud, a renowned Tajik *mujahideen* commander in the north. The way was clear for a *mujahideen* government to form, leaving in tatters the U.N. plan that special U.N. representative Benon Sevan had worked on for four years to bring to the verge of inauguration. In the end

Afghans were going to work things out in their own way.

Years of negotiations and seemingly unrelated world events influenced the outcome of the war in April 1992. Ten years earlier, in 1982, three years after the Soviet invasion of Afghanistan, the United Nations, through its representative Diego Cordovez, initiated the first talks between Pakistan and Afghanistan on the question of their interference into each other's affairs, particularly the issue of Pakistan as conduit of arms for the *mujahideen*. At the same time the issue of the Soviet invasion of Afghanistan was on the table. Each year the U.N. General Assembly condemned the invasion.

Six years later the talks bore fruit and the Geneva Accord, a bilateral agreement between the Republic of Afghanistan and the Islamic Republic of Pakistan, was signed by the two parties. The agreement took effect May 15, 1988. The Geneva Accord dealt with matters of noninterference and nonintervention, with the respect of each one's sovereignty and territorial integrity, refraining from armed intervention or destabilization. It also dealt with the voluntary return of Afghan refugees who were residing in Pakistan. The official witnesses and guarantors to the Geneva Accord were the government of the Union of Soviet Socialist Republics and the government of the United States.[1]

The question of the return of refugees, however, would not have been significant had there not been a bilateral agreement between Kabul and Moscow. The Soviet Union agreed to a U.N.-monitored incremental withdrawal, beginning in May, of 110,000 Soviet troops that had been fighting in Afghanistan since the Soviet invasion in December 1979.

The accord was ambiguous at best. Even though Soviet troops would no longer be present, the Soviets could still assist Najibullah's government as it chose. According to the accord, Pakistan was no longer allowed to give material support to the *mujahideen*, but there was nothing to prohibit the United States from giving them assistance. Both the governments of the United States and the Soviet Union continued their aid, lethal and nonlethal, to the *mujahideen* resistance and the Soviet-backed Kabul government respectively. At the time, both the United States and Soviet Union indicated to the United Nations, however, that if one ceased its flow of military armaments, the other would do likewise. In spite of the rhetoric, both superpowers heavily stockpiled their clients with additional weapons before signing the accord.

It took less than a year for the Soviet troops to withdraw. Almost immediately after the last Soviet soldier returned to the Soviet Union, Mikhail Gorbachev proposed an arms cut off to both sides and encouraged representatives of the *mujahideen* resistance and the Soviet-backed Najibullah government[2] to form a coalition government until U.N.-supervised elections took place in Afghanistan. Gorbachev even suggested the return of the deposed King Zahir Shah. By this time the Soviet Union knew it could not afford to finance its Afghan client much longer. Soviet domestic problems would have to take precedence.

Neither the *mujahideen* representatives nor the Bush administration would consider the offer. U.S. government officials did not believe Najibullah could survive without the presence of the Soviet military. At the time of the Soviet withdrawal, an American embassy official called the Kabul government "a house without girders."[3]

Throughout this East-West proxy war being fought on Afghan soil, the U.S. government wanted the Soviet Union to capitulate, as the United States had been forced to do in Vietnam. Although this became a reality as Soviet troops withdrew from Afghanistan, U.S. officials still believed that the *mujahideen*, with continued military aid, would soon overthrow the Kabul government. In this case, there would be no need for concessions or a coalition government.

The *mujahideen* representatives refused to deal with Najibullah. They had not been signatories to the Geneva Accord, an agreement between the government of Najibullah and Pakistan. They stood firm in their conviction that they could overthrow a government installed by the Soviet "infidel." They held President Najibullah responsible for the bloodshed and the brutal tortures and deaths of so many Afghans over a thirteen-year period. Najibullah had been the head of Khad, the Soviet-controlled and financed secret police in Afghanistan. The *mujahideen* refused to compromise on what they had fought ten years to secure—an independent Afghanistan under Islamic rule.[4] Above all they had fought to uphold *namus* (honor): to negotiate with the "infidel" Soviets would betray that honor.

Out of an estimated 1978 population of 15 million, more than 1.5 million Afghans had died, more than 2 million had been injured, 5.5 million had gone into exile, and more than 2 million had been internally displaced during the decade from the Soviet invasion in 1979 until the withdrawal of Soviet troops in 1989. At least twenty thousand to twenty-five thousand of Afghanistan's thirty thousand villages had been laid waste, totally reduced to rubble. To the *mujahideen* fighting *jihad*, all those killed, injured, or displaced were martyrs and revered compatriots whom they would not betray by consorting with the enemy.

After the departure of Soviet troops, the Soviet-installed government still remained. Though the *mujahideen* continued to fight to oust Najibullah, the war changed from a war on the invading "infidel" to open strife among leaders of the *mujahideen*. The dissension among them was not evident as long as they were unified against a foreign invader. Once the Soviet troops withdrew and they turned their attention to deposing Najibullah, the fractious nature of the various *mujahideen* parties became evident. They began fighting each other as well as the Soviet-installed government in Kabul, with radical fundamentalists against the more moderate Islamic groups. What had been a war for the survival of an independent Islamic Afghanistan quickly became a civil war, and disunity among the *mujahideen* made it easier for Najibullah to retain control of the government.

The *mujahideen* had no formal, internationally recognized government-in-exile, such as the Coalition Government of Democratic Kampuchea. Leaders of various parties, representing seven among a number of Afghan resistance groups, had formed a loose alliance in 1985 and served as the channel for receiving and disbursing armaments and other goods that came from their allies, the United States, Saudi Arabia, Pakistan, and Iran. Commanders leading *mujahideen* forces inside Afghanistan were aligned with one of the parties, as were refugees in Pakistan. The leaders of the alliance, who resided in Pakistan, not Afghanistan, ranged from radical Islamic fundamentalists such as Gulbuddin Hekmatyar to traditional moderate Muslims such as Sayuyed Ahmad Gailani.

Immediately after the Soviet withdrawal in 1989, with pressure particularly from Pakistan and the United States to form a provisional government, the Seven-Party Alliance was formed and became the Afghan Interim Government (AIG) based in Peshawar, Pakistan. Conspicuously missing were representatives of the Afghan Shi'a Muslims who had taken refuge in Iran. Even though the AIG leaders had been ostensibly elected by a representative *shura* (an assembly of the people), they were not representative of the majority of the Afghan people, either in Afghanistan or in refugee camps in Pakistan. The leaders of the Seven-Party Alliance assured their elections by inviting to the *shura* people who supported them; few independent political thinkers were invited. The *shura* was held in Islamabad, the capital of Pakistan, rather than in a liberated area of Afghanistan. Neither the civilian population nor the commanders inside Afghanistan wanted a government so far removed from the people and with little understanding of their lives in Afghanistan. Most believed each party had its own agenda at heart with little concern for the national interest. Many maintain that outside powers, not the majority of Afghans, legitimized the Seven-Party Alliance and allowed it to operate. In essence, the interim government was another foreign-installed government. Created on an emergency basis, the interim government depended on outsiders for its existence and continued military support. Their differences were so great, that the AIG, in its formal capacity, disintegrated within a few years of its formation.

The U.S. government allowed Pakistan to funnel weapons and funds through Alliance leaders of its choosing from the beginning of the war, recognizing that the United States could not nourish a government hostile to Pakistani interests. Inadvertently this policy strengthened the power of Afghan fundamentalists. Under then President Zia-ul-Haq, who died in April 1988, Pakistan chose to support the Hezb-i-Islami party under the leadership of Gulbuddin Hekmatyar. This choice was unfortunate for the majority of Afghans who are moderate Muslims. Although not the choice of the majority of Afghans, Gulbuddin Hekmatyar and the Hezb-i-Islami party could best meet Pakistan's needs. Pakistan needed an Afghan government that it could depend on not to let the old border disputes fester between Pakistan and Afghanistan. Pakistan was much more concerned with its relations with India than with Afghanistan; there was a real potential for serious military actions with India over the question of the control of Kashmir. Pakistan's government could not afford to risk problems with Afghanistan. One observer noted, ''In opposing Communism, the United States and its allies created a monster for Afghanistan in the form of Islamic extremism."[5]

Hekmatyar, who denounced America and the evils of Western society and who sided with Saddam Hussein in the Gulf War, was assured of the best weapons, and he funneled them to commanders he preferred. The commanders who lead the *mujahideen* in Afghanistan belong to one of the seven political parties, if only to be assured of receiving arms and military equipment. They are an independent assortment of warriors who otherwise profess little allegiance to the Peshawar-based interim government, and, in fact, have been critical of the AIG for basing itself in Peshawar rather than in territory held by the *mujahideen*. While the Najibullah government held most of the cities, the *mujahideen* controlled the countryside.

Following the Soviet troop withdrawal, the U.S. government, Pakistan, and Saudi Arabia, not accepting further conciliatory overtures from Mr. Gorbachev and believing the Kabul government would fall, urged the rebel forces to begin to attack the cities. The siege on Jalalabad, a government stronghold near Pakistan and an important stepping stone to Kabul, which lies only 125 kilometers west of Jalalabad, revealed clearly the lack of cohesion and central planning among *mujahideen* forces. They could not form a united front.

On March 6, 1989, less than three weeks after the departure of the last Soviet troops, resistance forces began their assault on Jalalabad with long-range rockets. Four months later, more than five thousand were dead, mainly civilians. Seventy thousand Afghan refugees fled to Pakistan, setting up new tent villages near older refugee villages. Other Afghans took refuge in Kabul, joining the two million internally displaced throughout the country who faced starvation. Although the rockets had been aimed at urban military objectives, many missed their targets and caused major destruction in other parts of the city. The Kabul forces retaliated by carpet bombing rebel areas in the vicinity.

The U.S. and Pakistani military still believed that, given time, the resistance could overcome the Kabul troops. They urged AIG leaders to press for an attack on Kandahar, a strategic city in southern Afghanistan. Knowing of the devastation and numbers of casualties in Jalalabad, the commanders leading troops near Kandahar refused AIG orders to attack. All had relatives and friends in Kandahar and did not want to be responsible for their deaths.

Over the next two years, the rebels took the smaller town of Khost, south of Jalalabad, and they fired rockets on Kabul and other cities, while the Kabul military laid waste more of the countryside. The rebels refused to negotiate with Najibullah, and the Soviet government hesitated to let him go, fearing the installation of a radical fundamentalist Islamic government that could threaten the Soviet Muslim states bordering Afghanistan.

By the fall of 1991, the Bush administration and some factions of the *mujahideen* were seeing the situation in a different light. Almost two years had passed since the Soviet troop withdrawal, and the antagonists were no closer to a military victory. The United States and the Soviet Union were still pumping in hundreds of millions of dollars each in lethal and nonlethal assistance. Until 1990, when it reduced the amount considerably, the U.S. government had provided about $250 million annually. It is estimated that the Soviet Union poured in $250 to $300 million monthly to maintain the Najibullah government and the army.

But Najibullah held out and built an effective fighting force that the *mujahideen* could not topple. Even after the Soviet and U.S. governments agreed in September 1991 to a mutual embargo on arms to both sides and disentangled themselves by January 1992 from the ongoing warfare, the question of who would govern Afghanistan remained the source of conflict. The two powers hoped their actions would persuade other nations to cease providing arms to either of the warring sides; they also hoped to convince the Kabul government and the *mujahideen* to accept a political settlement rather than continue a war neither side was able to win.

The adversaries, though, certainly did not lack weapons. Reportedly, both sides had stockpiled enough military hardware to last for over a year. Pakistan, it was believed, would continue to supply the resistance, especially the extremists. Saudi Arabia, particularly the Wahabi sect of the Sunni Muslims, would continue to pour money to rebel groups under their influence, for the Saudis wanted to influence the nature of the Islamic government Afghanistan would form. Iran, too, was becoming more active in trying to influence Afghanistan's political future and assuring a significant role for Afghan Shi'a Muslims in a newly formed government.

Even without these sources, the Afghan rebels could still survive for an indefinite period, as the rebel-held Afghanistan countryside produces the world's second largest source of opium; exports amount to nearly two thousand tons annually.

Najibullah, too, depended on outside sources other than the former Soviet Union. India and North Korea appeared to be those most likely to assist the Kabul government. It was in India's interests to support the Kabul government, for India was one of thirty nations that did not censure the Soviet invasion. In addition, India has a continuing conflict with Pakistan over Kashmir. Besides searching for outside sources to assist him in the continuation of war, Najibullah offered a plan for a coalition government, even to the point of his stepping down and offering leadership to Prime Minister Fazal Haq Khaliqyar in a government that would include *mujahideen*.

In the Afghan countryside, commanders became more and more independent from the party leaders in Pakistan, and the sharp differences between them were evident. War-weary, some made agreements with government troops for a cease-fire in their territory. Other commanders began to form their own governments in areas they controlled and make some attempts at reconstruction. A number of commanders from various political parties came together to discern what sort of government they could forge to replace the AIG that was crumbling in Peshawar, far removed from the turmoil inside their country. Through joint efforts, they planned to become militarily more cohesive and more coordinated in reconstruction plans.[6] Other more extremist groups continued to bombard cities like Jalalabad in Nangarhar Province and Gardez in nearby Paktia Province while government forces retaliated with heavy bombings and artillery fire. Both sides scattered villagers and city dwellers alike; once again many refugees crossed the border into Pakistan and others sought refuge in the overcrowded cities. On both sides tens of thousands of civilians were affected by the continuing warfare. The counts of dead and wounded rose, and human rights violations by both armies went unchecked.

Opting for military victory over the Najibullah government, Masood Khalili, a political officer in the Jamiat-e-Islami party, asked:

How can people in the West expect us to make peace, a coalition, with Najib? It would be like rewarding Hitler at the end of the Second World War by making him president of Germany. When Najib was head of Khad, he was listening to the tortures, the shouts, the screams and cries of thousands of men, women and children. Someone who can hear this and allow it to continue is a bloody, cruel person, a war criminal . . .

It will be difficult [to depose Najib]. Najib still speaks through the barrel of a gun. At the same time, he uses the Afghan people as a kind of shield. Kabul had 2.5 million people, and only about 5,000 of them are Communists, traitors. If we fire 5,000 rockets into Kabul we might kill 25,000 people, and maybe 200 of them would be our enemies. It is a terrible dilemma.[7]

The war continued to fragment Afghans. Conflict increased among leaders of the AIG and between AIG leaders and the commanders who became increasingly independent, but also among the various ethnic, tribal, and religious groups, even at the village level—Tajiks against Pushtuns, tribal chieftain against tribal chieftain, clan against clan, resistance group against resistance group, Sunni against Shi'a, fundamentalist against moderate. Without a political settlement, it seemed the nation would disintegrate and chaos would reign.

In November 1991, after the failed Soviet putsch in August 1991 and before the demise of the Soviet Union, a delegation of Afghan resistance leaders living in Pakistan and Iran, headed by Burhanuddin Rabbani of the Jamiat-e-Islami Afghanistan party, met in Moscow with then Soviet Foreign Minister Eduard Shevardnadze. This first face-to-face dialogue between the two adversaries ended on a somewhat positive note. In a joint declaration, they agreed in principle to the transfer of state power in Afghanistan to a transitional Islamic government. The agreement was based on the U.N. comprehensive peace initiative of May 21, 1991, which Benon Sevan, U.N. special representative of the secretary general, had been urging for four years. The U.N. plan called for a political resolution to the fourteen-year conflict, the creation of a "transitional mechanism" to prepare the country for U.N.-supervised general elections, a cease-fire, and an inter-Afghan dialogue under U.N.

guidance. The dialogue would include the Kabul government, *mujahideen*, Shi'a Afghans in Iran, former King Zahir Shah and his supporters, and other independent Afghan parties. This would be followed by U.N. mediation of the final terms of a peace agreement. The Afghan party leaders said they could be ready to hold elections in two years. Jointly, Shevardnadze and the Afghan leaders who were present condemned the 1978 Soviet invasion of Afghanistan as "illegal intervention."[8]

Although the dialogue between the Soviets and the Afghan resistance delegation went smoothly for those who participated, it did not ensure peace. Three of the AIG leaders refused to be part of the Afghan delegation, including Gulbuddin Hekmatyar, the powerful, radical fundamentalist leader of the Hezb-i-Islami party who sought total elimination of the Najibullah government in Kabul. Hekmatyar stated: "In our country a coalition government is impossible because sooner or later it will show its ineffectiveness and inability to stabilize the situation. I'll never accept one government imposed on us by foreigners."[9] He did not consider himself part of an imposed government, even though the AIG—never popular among Afghans—had been formed outside Afghanistan and was dependent on outsiders for both its creation and continuation.

The unexpected demise of the Soviet Union and the creation of the Commonwealth of Independent States had a dramatic impact on Afghanistan. With the disarray and calamitous economic situation in Russia and the other members of the newly formed commonwealth, Boris Yeltsin and other commonwealth leaders were unable to address the political or financial needs of the Najibullah government. Unless Najibullah gained considerable backing from India, his government would fall, not because of the sword, but because of empty coffers.

If Najibullah fell in this manner with no comprehensive peace agreement, there was a strong likelihood that a radical fundamentalist Islamic government would replace him. If a fundamentalist like Gulbuddin Hekmatyar took control of the government with the backing of Pakistan and Saudi Arabia, all political opponents would be eliminated and strict Islamic law would be ruthlessly enforced. The lives of many would be in danger, particularly the more Westernized urban population.[10]

The majority of Afghans and the international community did not want an extremist regime, either Islamic or Marxist. At the time it seemed that pressure must be brought to bear on the *mujahideen* to talk with persons more palatable to them than Najibullah in the Kabul government and come to an acceptable agreement for a U.N.-sponsored transitional government. The alignment of moderate *mujahideen* and members of Najibullah's Watan party could prove a stronger force than Hekmatyar. Former King Zahir Shah, who reigned for forty years before he was overthrown, might be a respected neutral figure who could head a transitional government until fair elections could be held. Early in 1992, the major foreign powers involved in Afghanistan agreed that Zahir Shah, like Sihanouk in Cambodia, might be the best head of state in an interim government. The citizenship of the former king, along with other family members, was restored. Although Hekmatyar opposed the return of Zahir Shah, most Afghans, it seemed, saw wisdom in accepting the proposal as their only way out of the war. The newly formed Central Asian republics expressed their approval of the idea because they wanted peaceful borders open to trade, and they did not want an extreme fundamentalist Islamic government close by.[11] Restoring Zahir Shah's leadership would not be the ultimate solution, but at least, many Afghans believed, it would pull together disparate groups going off in all directions.

A second significant effect of the collapse of the U.S.S.R. was Pakistan's decision in late January 1992 to follow the U.S. and former Soviet governments in cutting off all military aid to the *mujahideen* and in deciding to back the U.N. peace plan. The U.N. plan called for a ceasefire and a negotiated settlement by bringing together in Vienna in April 1992, 150 Afghan representatives from around the world to form a group of thirty to thirty-five that would summon an assembly in Afghanistan to function as an interim government until a *Loya Jirga* (a traditional gathering of tribal leaders) could be called and free elections held.[12] Pakistan's support of this plan meant that Pakistan no longer favored the installation of a fundamentalist Islamic government in post-war Afghanistan.

Pakistan's decision was primarily economic. It is in Pakistan's economic interest to develop strong diplomatic and economic ties with the Central Asian republics, formerly in the Soviet Union, of Turkmenistan, Uzbekistan, Tajikistan — all moderate Muslim republics that fear an extremist Islamic Afghan government. A railroad running through Afghanistan connecting all the Central Asian republics to Karachi, Pakistan's main port, would be an economic boon to Pakistan. In addition, Pakistan hoped to mend its frayed relations with the United States over the question of the development of nuclear weapons, and convince the U.S. government to lift its embargo on military and economic aid to Pakistan. Again, economic considerations took precedence over religious ones.

From January 1992, events moved at lightning speed. Najibullah and the *mujahideen* had both lost the military support they had depended on for so many years. Afghanistan, the last battle ground of the cold warriors, had to play itself out without U.S. and Soviet props. Najibullah, long the adversary of the United States, seemed to be grasping at straws in the wind when he appealed to the United States for support against a potential radical Islamic fundamentalist takeover of Afghanistan that would ensure the continuation of civil war for years to come. Without Moscow, Najibullah did not have the funds to pay his troops or keep the Afghan economy afloat. He could not even feed his people. By early March, the man who had been Moscow's chosen leader also agreed to step down, step out of politics, and transfer power to the U.N.-proposed interim government.

Najibullah made a final great tactical error that had more to do with ethnic matters than military. In the northern reaches of Afghanistan that border the

Muslim Central Asian republics and are largely populated by Tajik and Uzbek ethnic groups, Najibullah decided to replace one of his most loyal generals, Rashid Dostam, an Uzbek, with a Pushtun. Without pay and seeing the writing on the wall for the Kabul government, Dostam and some other generals defected with their troops to one of the most revered *mujahideen* commanders, Ahmed Shah Masud.

Masud, who belongs to the Jamiat-e-Islami party of Burhanuddin Rabbani, has left Afghanistan for Pakistan only once (in 1990) since the war began. No commander has had greater staying power in the front lines than Commander Masud. Soft-spoken, he is a brilliant strategist and statesman, well read, and articulate. A native of the Panjshir Valley (Five Lion Valley) north of Kabul, he is known as the "Lion of Panjshir."[13] Not only did he unite the north militarily against the Soviets, he also established a government administration and social services such as schools and hospitals for the civilians in his embattled area.

Other disaffected government troops began defecting to commanders in other parts of the country until their strength was great enough to cause the fall of Najibullah on March 18. He transferred power to four generals and tried to flee the country, but was blocked by Dostam's forces who controlled the airport north of Kabul. While Najibullah's wife and three daughters waited in India, where they had gone a month earlier, Najibullah took refuge in the U.N. offices in Kabul. He, who had ordered the torture and death of so many Afghans, would not easily be exonerated or given safe passage.

It was not a united army of Afghans who marched toward Kabul. In fact ethnic and religious dissonance finally plunged hostile factions into open conflict. The two figures who represented the points of controversy were Commander Ahmed Shah Masud and Gulbuddin Hekmatyar, leader of the Hezb-i-Islami party. Masud was a moderate fundamentalist Muslim from a minority tribe, the Tajik. Or, as one person observed, "Although a fundamentalist, his Islamic vision is moderated by the more relaxed Tajik culture and centuries of persecution by the Pushtuns."[14] Hekmatyar espoused a radical Islamic fundamentalism and represented the majority Pushtun tribe.

Afghanistan is a melange of ethnic, linguistic, and sectarian groups. For two hundred years the Pushtuns had been in control of the government of Afghanistan. The minority groups that had fought against the Soviets for the survival of Afghanistan with as much fervor as any Afghan wanted fair recognition and equal voice and representation in post-war Afghanistan. The most esteemed commander, after all, was a Tajik. Among ethnic groups, Pushtuns represent 50 percent of the people; Tajiks, 25 percent; Uzbeks, 9 percent; Hazaras, 12 to 15 percent; and others, 1 percent.[15] Linguistically, they are divided by Pashto speakers, followed by Dari, Turkic, and others. About half speak Pashto as their first language. Religiously, they are divided mainly between Sunni Muslims at 64 percent and Shi'a Muslims at 15 percent. Only 1 percent of the population represent other religions. However, the great divide within the Sunni Muslims is between the moderates and the fundamentalists. And within each of those groups, there are degrees.[16]

To make a point, General Dostam and *mujahideen* commanders in the north who are mainly Uzbeks and Tajiks urged, almost insisted, that U.N. special representative Benon Sevan meet with them in the northern city of Mazar-i-Sharif, Afghanistan's second largest city and a stronghold of Uzbeks. Sevan, knowing there was no longer a chance to establish a broad based, U.N.-monitored transitional government, went to meet with the generals and commanders. Masud, himself, had said, "The situation has changed. I think there is no need to create a neutral government. It is better that a *mujahideen* government comes to power."[17] Sevan's talk conveyed a profound sense of urgency.

The biggest problem is national union. This is the reason I stress that unless you first start thinking as Afghans and less about your ethnic backgrounds, things will not get better. They will get worse. I think everybody should think seriously of a cease-fire and stay in place so there is a dialogue . . .

If there is a march toward Kabul, you are going to have lightning. I think that we have to avoid this by putting up lightning rods. I think you should first talk to each other. Talk first, establish a government, then you walk in as a free citizen of Afghanistan. Otherwise, you go back to the mountains . . .

First and foremost you are Afghans, then Tajiks and Uzbeks. You are all Afghans. The time is the most critical in history to think and act with authority. There are almost two million dead and two million disabled. Afghanistan has the highest rate of child mortality.

For God's sake, sit down and talk. Don't go in and then start talking because then it's too late. There will be a lot of foreigners who will take advantage of you.

We are prepared to help you, but over my dead body will I allow the United Nations to interfere in your fights.

There's one thing I want to tell you. None of you scares me because I am not an Afghan. But just as you have lots of cooks from outside, you have a lot of assistant cooks who serve their masters well.

One thing. Afghanistan is no longer what it used to be. It's like a volcano. Even when it dies down, it's like lava. It takes a long time to cool.[18]

Nevertheless, Masud and Dostam marched south and took up their position in Charikar, about thirty-five miles north of Kabul. Hekmatyar and his troops settled at his headquarters in Logar Province just south of the capital. Masud did not want to storm Kabul. Hekmatyar threatened attack by April 26 if Dostam and all who had consorted with Najibullah's government remained in collaboration with Masud.

Meanwhile, in Peshawar, party leaders of the main *mujahideen* factions met and agreed on the formation of a provisional government of fifty members headed by Sebghatullah Mojaddidi, a theological scholar from the mystic Sufi sect of Islam and a moderate in his religious thinking. He had left Afghanistan in 1973 because of his opposition to the spread of communism in Afghanistan.

In Pakistan, though he had little military strength, he had been chosen to head the Seven-Party Alliance (AIG) formed in 1989 in Peshawar.[19]

As the motorcade carrying Mojaddidi and some members of the provisional government advanced to Torkam, the last stop in Pakistan, and across the Khyber Pass into Afghanistan, fighting between the forces of Hekmatyar and Masud developed and increased. Civilians in Kabul lost their lives, and the daily routine of Kabul citizens was interrupted, though many tried to maintain a semblance of normalcy. Once the remnants of the former Soviet-backed government handed over the reins of power to Mojaddidi, no one knew what the future would hold. For the moment there was little that the new government could do except to try to return services like electricity to the city of Kabul and get its economy operating again. They had little access to the rest of the country. In many places, ad hoc governments of commanders and elders were attempting to put order into war-torn areas. Late in May 1992, Hekmatyar and Masud met face to face and agreed to a cessation of hostilities, at least for the present. All that seemed clear at that point was that Afghanistan would have an Islamic government, though, true to Afghan tradition, probably not a strong central government. "No one likes to be told how to pray," Thomas Friedman observed.[20] How moderate or how strict the Afghan government ultimately will be depends on who wins this round of the ancient, fractious, and frenzied Afghan game of *buz kashi*. An old Afghan saying, "We are sleeping without shoes today," means that, indeed, not much has changed. And yet everything has changed in an Afghanistan where all the disparate groups must discover how to live together peaceably.

RECONSTRUCTION NEEDS

After thirteen years of war the country is devastated. *New York Times* correspondent John Burns's perspective is particularly fitting.

I saw devastation that went far beyond anything I had seen in half a dozen other distant wars. In Darwaza-i-Mashad, the oldest section of the 2,500-year-old city of Herat, every building for miles was destroyed. In streets that had been thriving when Alexander's army passed through three centuries before the birth of Christ, nothing remained but rubble overgrown with weeds. A Russian military interpreter who had worked in the country throughout the Soviet occupation quietly wept as he looked over the devastation. "Look what we have done," he said. "My God, how can we be forgiven?"[21]

Refugees will return to a country where at least 80 percent of their villages have been destroyed; the land is pocketed with bomb craters and strewn with mines; burned-out tanks, downed aircraft, and wrecks of jeeps and trucks line roads woefully in disrepair. Schools, hospitals, and other public buildings have been reduced to rubble. Buildings and equipment not laid completely to waste have been stripped of any usable pieces of equipment or furnishings.

Fruit orchards and wooded areas have been cleared. Land not tilled for more than a decade will need preparation and no machinery is available.

With more than half its population in exile, killed, maimed, or internally displaced and with the countryside in ruins, the movement of 5.5 million refugees from Pakistan and Iran is a daunting assignment for the UNHCR, the U.N. organization mandated to this task. Both the United Nations and the NGOs working in Pakistan foresaw the need for rehabilitation of the country-side before refugees in massive numbers can return. In 1987–88, there were clear pockets of peace in Afghanistan and opportunities for NGOs to provide tangible assistance. Once the Soviet military began to withdraw and the hope for repatriation of refugees became imminent, U.N. agencies and NGOs began to implement cross-border operations, a number of which were supported by the United Nations and USAID.

In May 1988, then Secretary General of the United Nations Javier Pérez de Cuéllar created the Office of the Co-ordinator for United Nations Humanitarian and Economic Assistance Programmes Relating to Afghanistan (UNOCO) to oversee the relief and rehabilitation of a country in ruins. He appointed Prince Sadruddin Aga Khan to head the organization. Better known as Operation Salam, UNOCO called for a budget of $1.2 billion over the first eighteen months, followed by an additional $840 million for the following three years. In itself, UNOCO was nonoperational; implementation of relief and rehabilitation projects would go through other U.N. organizations, such as the UNHCR, UNDP, WHO, WFP, UNESCO, and UNICEF, and through NGOs working in Pakistan and Afghanistan. UNOCO's reach was to be greater than any one of the organizations, for it planned offices not only in Kabul, but also in Moscow and Tehran. Its goal was to ensure that organizations did not duplicate projects in health care, agriculture, food assistance, vocational training, rebuilding of schools, hospitals, and other public buildings, road construction, reconstruction of communication systems, emergency aid to the most vulnerable, or training Afghans for administration and work in various operations. Operation Salam was to be a purely humanitarian operation, neither influencing nor taking political sides.

Along with most of the international community, the United Nations envisioned an imminent return of hundreds of thousands of refugees in the spring of 1989, in time for planting. The hope of UNOCO was to precede repatriation with some basic reconstruction of the country's infrastructure. Operation Salam wanted to take advantage of pockets of peace, called "zones of tranquility," which existed inside Afghanistan in areas where fighting had not taken place for a year or more, to help shore up peace through humanitarian activities. UNOCO administrators maintained that with no let up in the provision of arms and deadly equipment for the continuation of the war, Afghans seemed to have no alternative but to continue the conflict—unless the world community proved its interest by contributing to peace through humanitarian activities.

But donors were leery and unwilling to invest heavily in a country still at war. Even after the Soviet withdrawal of troops in February 1989, the country was not at peace and refugees refused to return, lacking the prospect for peace incentives for the warring parties to end the conflict. As the war dragged on and internal Afghan party and tribal conflict escalated, donors were less and less prone to allocate money for rehabilitation. Operation Salam fell far short of its original hopes and expectations, and, in fact, was used as a negative example in early reconstruction considerations for Cambodia.

Afghanistan and the fighting *mujahideen* faded from front pages, and the country had less and less strategic importance to the U.S. government, particularly with the breakup of the Soviet Union. Future U.S. involvement in the rebuilding of Afghanistan is unknown at this time. The Soviet Union, intent on assisting Afghanistan to rebuild, had originally pledged significant sums to UNOCO, but, given its subsequent demise and economic plight, it is questionable what the new commonwealth will contribute to the reconstruction of Afghanistan.

The NGOs, for their part, were not necessarily in coordination with UNOCO. Most NGOs envision their mission as one of rehabilitation, not of development, a task for which they are not equipped professionally, financially, or materially. While NGOs proposed to create conditions conducive to refugee repatriation, significant development was the task of large bilateral donors.

Even with rehabilitation tasks defined, implementation would not be easy. Travel inside Afghanistan was difficult, some areas were almost impossible to reach, and communication with other parts of the country or with Pakistan was almost impossible. Both access roads and appropriate means of transportation were needed. Living conditions were pitifully crude. Security could not be assured for anyone who crossed the border into Afghanistan.

Even though there were areas in the country that were no longer battle zones, it was premature for agencies or donors to think of long-term development projects. Afghanistan lacked both a stable government and a stable economy, and the war had not ended. Their best hope was to return the people of Afghanistan to a prewar standard of living and to lay a foundation for something enduring, particularly in agriculture, health, and education.

Agricultural surveys revealed the need for an increase in food production, which was far below the prewar level. There was not enough food inside Afghanistan to support those living there, much less a doubling of the population with the influx of returning refugees. The price of available food was so high that most could not afford it, particularly in cities like Kabul. Fertilizer and seed varieties to increase the yields by 100 percent were needed. Forty percent of the cattle and 70 percent of the sheep and goats had been killed or had died of starvation. Herds needed to be replenished for people to start over again, and this was particularly true for the nomads. The irrigation system that had served generations of Afghans was virtually decimated.

Hospitals had been laid waste and needed reconstruction. During exile, many Afghans had been trained by NGOs as basic health workers, and some had received nurse's training. Among those trained in Pakistan, some health workers were willing to return to Afghanistan to begin training Afghans there for the same medical roles. Vaccination teams from the French organization AVICEN traveled to many parts of the country to immunize people and educate them in the need for and benefits of immunization against certain diseases. They reached thousands, even though at times members of a team had to overcome people's long-held perceptions. In one village no women would be vaccinated because they believed that they would become nonbelievers or they could no longer bear children or that they would bear twins or triplets.[22]

The International Rescue Committee (IRC), a New York-based NGO that operates world-wide and has been the largest and one of the most productive NGOs among Afghan refugees in Pakistan, conceived its rehabilitation program for Afghanistan following the signing of the Geneva Accord in 1988 and began its implementation the following year.

The majority of the people in IRC programs were refugees in Pakistan from four nearby provinces in Afghanistan—Paktia, Paktika, Nangarhar, and Logar. The devastation of the war turned some areas in these provinces into moonscapes. Without prior rehabilitation, the area could not support any returning refugees.

IRC chose not to have a major presence as an organization in Afghanistan. Instead, its personnel worked through *shuras*, village or district administrative councils comprised of tribal leaders and elders. Before any organization could enter an area, trust had to be built, based on a respect for Afghan culture by the outsiders. For Afghans this takes time, and only when an organization is invited by the local *shura* can serious talk begin as local elders present the most pressing needs of their area.

As the war progressed, military commanders had become more involved in the administrative councils. In areas where commanders were strong and did not agree with the elders, it was necessary to make some adjustments in needs assessments. Such a situation was difficult for an NGO like IRC that preferred to work through a unified group of Afghans. War changed not only the landscape, but lines of governance as well. Elders who had lost power to commanders wanted it back. Commanders justified their right to power, arguing that they had fought for the people and deserved to represent them. Elders countered with the argument that they were the ones who enabled the commanders to fight. All the complexities of Afghan tribal society, including family ranking and patronage, came into play as negotiations for rehabilitation projects took shape.

After needs were determined, contracts were drawn up between IRC and the local *shura*. The *shura* was then empowered to implement the project. Money for the project was given to the *shura* in installments and technical advice was offered where necessary. However, responsibility for the project rested with the *shura*; it was up to the Afghans to complete the work, not foreign NGO personnel. In Pakistan, IRC established the Shura Management

Training Unit to train Afghans for management of the projects.

None of the IRC or other NGO projects was grandiose. They were, however, critical to Afghanistan's reconstruction. Within the four Afghan provinces of Paktia, Paktika, Logar, and Nangarhar, backed by money from various U.N. organizations, IRC contracted with various district *shuras* for the provision and distribution of vegetable seeds, wheat seeds, and fertilizer. Contracts were signed for a number of irrigation repair projects, erosion control work, construction of grain and seed storehouses, and road surveys. Farmers requested a livestock vaccination program, since disease was rampant among the greatly reduced livestock population. IRC encouraged Afghan farmers, under trained technicians, to establish village wood lots and conserve other wooded resources to promote soil conservation and reduce erosion and flooding. Tree nurseries were established on the Pakistan side of the border for the transfer of saplings at a later date. IRC ran a dental training program for Afghan paramedics as well as microscopists. Its vaccination program reached thousands, and training sanitarians would later enable Afghan people to have access to a clean water supply, adequate latrines, and control of insects and rodents.

Refugees, too, benefited from cross-border projects. For example, in one IRC project refugees made large quantities of gabion boxes from wicker or metal. Constructed to carry or protect something, the boxes were needed throughout Afghanistan for water diversion, erosion control, road and bridge building, and other agricultural and construction projects that require the shoring up of dirt.[23] These boxes were built by 150 refugee families living in camps in the Hangu-Thal area. Selected by IRC, the first designated families were among the poorest families and those least able to support themselves. However, once the Afghan camp leaders learned of the generous compensation given for gabion building, they applied pressure to broaden the criteria to include tribal and political factors.[24]

As in Cambodia, so, too, in Afghanistan, the proliferation of mines will continue to kill and maim Afghans for years to come. It is said there are two mines for each Afghan. With an estimated prewar population of fifteen million that calculation puts the number of mines at thirty million. It is said that one in ten children is disabled.[25] Some observers consider these conservative estimates.

Mine clearance began in 1989 under UNOCO and it was financed by USAID. De-mining teams from Australia, Canada, France, Italy, New Zealand, Norway, the United Kingdom, and the United States arrived in Pakistan and set up training centers near Peshawar in the Northwest Frontier Province and Quetta in Baluchistan. Several thousand Afghan males were trained in mine clearance as well as in how to recognize and mark minefields and mines and how to escape from mined and booby-trapped areas.[26]

The Royal Thai Government donated a team of dogs trained to detect mines and other explosives up to a meter deep, including those that have been in the ground for many years. Each dog, on an average, can find five or six mines a day; some find as many as fifteen or sixteen. Early in 1990, the first team of twenty-two Afghan de-miners, eight instructors, and the dogs went for a forty-five-day de-mining mission. On 135 kilometers of a roadbed near the Afghanistan-Pakistan border, the team removed a total of 1,068 mines or almost 8 mines for every kilometer of road. Generally, when mines were very close together, the de-miners could clear one hundred meters a day. If the mines were not close, they could clear up to four kilometers in one day. After clearing the 135 kilometers, the de-mining team stood on the border and watched as the first truck—carrying a cargo of petroleum—rolled down the road.

WOMEN IN POST-WAR AFGHANISTAN

One Canadian team of female instructors trained Afghan women in mine-awareness. Operation Salam hired Crystal Ashley, an American woman working with the IRC, to coordinate mine-awareness training for women. According to Crystal,

The greatest difficulty in pursuing mine-awareness programs for women is getting permission from the male hierarchy in the camps—the elders and mullahs. One of the most tragic legacies of this war is the association of education for women and children with Sovietization. We send trained Afghans to the camps to talk with the elders and mullahs, explain why we are doing mine-awareness training, and ask their permission to educate their people, not just women, in mine recognition and about the ramifications of their proliferation.

When it became a question of women receiving such training, one mullah voiced the stand of many. "We will let our women and children blow up before we educate them in anything." The trainer to whom this was told placed the responsibility on those leaders to educate the women. This they did, and because Afghan leaders themselves and not foreigners planted the suggestion that they set up their own training program with no outside interference, the men actually did begin training the girls under ten, and then the girls under fifteen. Finally they began gathering all their women kin—mothers, aunts, sisters—and had them congregate in the mosque where the leaders trained them. We were told such numbers of women would never be gathered in a mosque.

When the Afghan hierarchy understands the importance of mine recognition and how to avoid coming in contact with mines, they are not so resistant to disseminating the knowledge.

I went to a camp with one of the Canadian women deminers to ask questions and try to get a grip on the information absorption level of the refugee women in the camps who had been hearing the mine safety information. I expected them to give simplistic responses, for we had been told the message we were giving to the men should be considerably reduced when we trained the women since they would not understand such technical information. What we found, much to our amazement, was that in talking with and asking questions of 150 women, they gave us much more detail than we had asked for. They had very accurate retention of the shapes, sizes, and colors of the mines and even the danger radius. They knew what to look for, and they showed us how to mark them. They took us outside to demonstrate with rocks. To one demonstrator, other women standing around her warned, "No, no, no—not that close. You're going to blow up." They grabbed their children telling them, "If that were a real mine, you'd be dead now." They were so serious and so eager that they competed with each other to give us the information. These are ladies with no education in the formal sense, yet, as an educator myself, they confirmed for me what I believe about the human mind. It is a sponge, no matter if it is neglected for a long time, especially when the information is so relevant. In this case, the lives of the women's husbands and children are at stake. They are enthusiastic about teaching others. "Our sons and our husbands are the ones who are going back and forth between here and our homeland. They are the ones who are in danger now," they told us.

Women and children are the ones who will be most affected by the devastation—economic, social, spiritual—of the country. It is they, as well, who will feel the most constrained should a radical Islamic party take control of the government of Afghanistan. While there are moderates who want to incorporate women more fully into Afghan social and economic structures through education, professional employment, and political pursuits, including the franchise accorded in the 1964 constitution, conservatives would revert to strict *purdah* for females, keeping them uneducated and confined to their homes. A prominent political leader summarized this conservative approach. "We shall make you [women] ministers—of your own households."[27]

War has altered Afghanistan so that its society will never again be the same. For practical and ideological reasons, it will be almost impossible to maintain a society that secludes and excludes women from its mainstream. Urban educated women, both those exiled and those who remained in cities like Kabul and Kandahar, will chafe against such constraints, for they know that their talents, so critical to particular aspects of reconstruction, should and could be used to help rebuild their country. Women—including those who are educated and those whose education was interrupted when they went into exile—want very much to be involved. During exile many women entered a seclusion greater than they had ever experienced and now want to return to their careers and studies. Those educated women who remained in Afghan cities during the war and continued with their jobs and schooling cannot now conceive of reversion to the strictures of *purdah*. Because of interrupted lives and the fighting, death, and maiming of so many males, many of these women have not married. Many women will protest if older or less educated marriage partners are imposed on them. They envision an open and tolerant Islamic post-war Afghan society in which women are accorded the equality pronounced in the *Koran*. For most Afghan women, the primacy of Islamic teaching and motherhood will continue to carry the highest value, but they will look to a more moderate interpretation of the former and altered personal expectations for the latter.

Eighty-five percent of the Afghan population was rural in prewar Afghanistan, and most Afghans will return to the land. In the rural areas in particular, the stability of the extended family always ensured women's security. The underpinnings of that family stability were loosened by the war and, so too, the security of women, particularly widows, the severely handicapped, and wives of totally disabled husbands. Whereas rural men and women complemented the other's work in the production of crops and the care of animals, millions of women will have lost their spouses and there are so many widows that it will be difficult for the extended family to care for them and their children. They will need to have a source of income that will enable them to be financially less dependent on relatives or independent from them through activities such as management of poultry projects; growing vegetable gardens and processing of the products; planting and caring for tree nurseries, especially fruit trees; supplying milk from milch cows; and engaging in a variety of needlework endeavors from tailoring to handicrafts. Through initial small loans, many will succeed in becoming self-reliant. Their contributions will be indispensable in the rebuilding of Afghanistan.

A significant number of educated women who spent years in exile became aware of the great social needs in their country, and their experience as refugees has enkindled within them a desire to be of service to Afghans less educated and less fortunate than they.[28]

Nasrin is an educated Afghan woman who is determined to help rural widows when she returns to a post-war Afghanistan. During her ten years in Pakistan as a refugee, Nasrin worked with rural women, mostly widows, training them in traditional handicrafts. She came to know their strength of character and discovered robust personalities among them.

I will help widows and the rural poor of Afghanistan when we Afghans go home because I hope to live up to my mother's dreams for me and because I am a graduate of the Faculty of Agriculture of Kabul University.

My mother, who is sixty-nine years old, is my greatest source of inspiration. My father died when I, the youngest of nine children, was less than a year old. Our relatives did not agree with my mother's choice to remain a widow and tried to remarry her.

Mother had made a promise to my father that she feared she would not be allowed to honor if she were to marry again. My father wanted all of his children to be educated, males and females. She wanted to complete that hope of his.

After my father died, my mother sold everything she could—jewelry, ornaments in the house, anything that would bring some money. She worked at night sewing and doing beautiful traditional embroidery to decorate peran/ tombom, the Afghan traditional dress, for others. All the time I was growing up in Kabul, we had no money and only a small house.

We did not have shoes or nice clothes. On most days when we came home from school, there was nothing for us to eat except bread with salt and pepper and tea. Sometimes a neighbor brought fruit for us to eat. But when my uncle, who physically abused my mother because she would not live as he wanted her to, brought fruit for his children, he never gave any to my mother. My mother fought for her children, and every day, she told us to be brave.

When my oldest sister graduated from the Faculty of Engineering several years after my father's death, she helped financially, as did some of the others following graduation. Three brothers became engineers—one in geology—and the other became a teacher. Two of my sisters are doctors—one living in Canada, the other one in Hangu—one is an engineer living now in Peshawar, the other is a teacher who is jobless living still in Kabul.

Three of my brothers were taken to prison in 1978 during the Taraki period shortly before I finished my schooling in the Faculty of Agriculture at the University of Kabul.

After two of my brothers were taken to jail, soldiers searched our house a number of times and questioned why we never attended committee meetings. My third brother was arrested following a math exam he was taking at the university. Soldiers called out his name in the classroom, but his friends said he was not present. The soldiers left a letter for him which his friends gave him after class. The soldiers were watching, and three of them took him, put a cloth over his face, forced him into an unlicensed car, and sped away. When Babrak Karmal was installed as president after the Soviet invasion, he released a number of prisoners. We waited for our brothers, but not one was released. We have never seen them since.

When I graduated, we cried because not all of my brothers could celebrate with us. My mother bought nine bracelets, one for each child, the day of my graduation. She went with them to my father's grave, placed them there, and cried for joy that she had completed the mission he had given her.

Now my mother is happier, for she is proud that her three sons did not give in to the Najibullah regime. She knows they would not be soldiers in Najibullah's army. Because of this, she can rest. Also, now many of her relatives are jealous of her because almost all of her children have good jobs. Their children, particularly their daughters, who were not so well educated, cannot provide for themselves.

In Pakistan my mother frequently whispers to me, "Please do not forget your father, your mother, or your country. If you like your mother, please help widows. If you like your country, help your poor people."

I am glad I have a degree from the Faculty of Agriculture, for I can help many widows and poor women when we return to Afghanistan and begin to rebuild our country. Originally I wanted to study agriculture because I wanted to be a man. As a child I did not like to wear girls' clothing. I liked either engineering or agriculture, but by the time I entered the university, the Faculty of Engineering had been closed because of the coup and the political situation; so I chose to study agriculture.

In the student body in the Faculty of Agriculture I was the only woman among three hundred male agricultural students. "You are the class mother," the teachers said to me. Today it is different in the university because the majority of students are women. So few men can be educated because of the war. This is one reason why it is so important for women, especially educated women, to play an important role in the reconstruction of Afghanistan.

In Kabul before I came to Pakistan I felt free. I did not cover my face and did not hesitate to work in an office or attend classes with men.

When I return to Afghanistan, I want to obtain a higher agriculture degree so that I can be better prepared to work with women who have been left alone or whose husbands are so maimed that they cannot work in the fields.

I want to go out in the countryside, but I will go only to one of the freest provinces like Ghazni, Badakhshan, Balkh, Herat, Helmand, or Kandahar. I will help women with poultry and vegetable projects. I want to open a clinic for diseased plants and a veterinary clinic for chickens. I want to work with fertilizers and seeds that will give greater crop yields. I want to help farmers who have no knowledge of the land or who have forgotten their knowledge. For so many years the men have been mujahideen, fighting a brutal war. Young men who were boys when they went to war know how to shoot rockets and how to fight, but they do not know how to work the land. They are ignorant of the science of agriculture.

The war, though, is far from over. Life only becomes more difficult and dangerous in Afghanistan. I have secretly returned to Kabul several times. Today in Kabul a banana costs forty afghanis, a loaf of bread forty-eight. Before the war bread was never more than six afghanis. I stood in line from 5:00 A.M. until 7:00 P.M. just to buy bread. Bus fares have risen from one afghani to ten. Many people are living without food, clean water, oil, light, and electricity. Thousands continue to leave. When I was last there four hundred men, four hundred women, and one thousand children boarded trucks bound for Pakistan.

I do not know what the situation will be when the war finally ends. Much will depend on who gains power. If the extremists control the government in Kabul, women who have been used to certain freedoms will find it very difficult to observe strict purdah once again. In all likelihood, I would not have the opportunity to go into the countryside and work professionally in my field of agriculture. That is a very difficult thought for me to consider. Here in Pakistan, I have worked among very poor women, but not in agriculture. Instead, I have taught them handicrafts— the kind that I learned from my mother who did handicrafts for so many years at night to educate nine children.

CHILDREN OF THE AFGHAN WAR

Children are the most tragic consequences of any war, and the war in Afghanistan is no exception. "It is children who pay the heaviest price for our shortsighted economic policies, our political blunders, our wars."[29] More than half of the Afghan refugee population is composed of children, as is the case with most long-term refugee populations. These children have been robbed of their childhood and the normalcy of living in their homelands, whether they have crossed borders, become internal refugees, or remained in their disrupted or threatened villages and towns. They are immersed in wars they neither created nor understand. Their reintegration into a post-war society will be difficult.

In many countries, an entire generation of children has become the victim of war. They are among the most vulnerable and most at risk of any children in the world. Frequently they preface their hopes for the future with, "If I grow up . . ." rather than, "When I grow up . . ."

On a level, barren area below a mud refugee village in Pakistan, five tents served as the school for a small minority of the Afghan male children who lived in the refugee village on the hillside above. Run by one of the seven parties of the former AIG, a strong political philosophy and devotion to *jihad* permeated the curriculum. Early each day the more than one hundred young males, ranging from five to fourteen years, emerged from the tents and lined up in military formation. At the command of the leader, they broke into groups and ran together around a large track-like circle. They performed numerous drills until they were called back to attention in their original lines. On a particular morning in April 1989, four young boys, between five and eight years old, came forward to the front of the lines. For ten minutes, with great fervor, they chanted phrases to which the rest of the students responded. It was a chant for Islam, for the *mujahideen*, for victory over the evil Soviet "infidel." It was a promise to fight *jihad* and give their lives as martyrs if called to avenge the deaths of so many of their fathers, brothers, and uncles. Among the students, fifty-five had lost their fathers in *jihad*, an honor among the Afghans. No wonder they lifted their hands high in a sign of victory at the end of the drill.

Like most Afghan children, Mohammed learned very early the concepts of war and the enemy. Much less of his mental and emotional energies were expended on thoughts of peace and friendship. Through ideological training, both sides of the conflict vied for the minds and hearts of children.

Back in the tented classroom where the boys studied Pashto, mathematics, science, and the *Koran*, Mohammed, who was eight and one of the drill leaders that morning, was asked what he aspired to be when he grew up. He responded without hesitation, "A doctor to heal all the war wounded." In reality, there was little chance he would be able to study beyond age fourteen and a high probability that he would become one of the war's casualties.

Mohammed received more education than most of the refugee children, and certainly more than those children who remained in Afghanistan. Nearly 80 percent of all educational facilities in Afghanistan were destroyed as the war ravaged towns and villages. Education for youth in the countryside and villages totally collapsed. Only the schools in government-controlled areas remained open. By 1989 the number of primary schools dropped to 210 from 1,154 in 1978. High schools dropped from 163 to 44 in the same period.[30] A small percentage of Afghan children received more than a few years of education before the war, but for both refugee children and those who remained in Afghanistan, education for those who attended schools changed radically. Inside the country, Soviets brought their system and philosophy of education, including the forced education of girls, much to the distress of their parents. In Pakistan, schools run by the Pakistani government for refugees offered a Pakistani curriculum, including Urdu, the official language of Pakistan, rather than either Pashto or Dari.

Mohammed was two when his village was bombarded. His parents and siblings survived the bombing, though a number of relatives did not. It was late fall 1982, and as they crossed the snow-covered mountains leading into Pakistan, Mohammed's brother, Hassan, who was then five, stepped on a mine that shredded both legs and charred his stomach. His mother staunched the bleeding and carried him the rest of the way. Nightmares plagued Hassan, and Mohammed feared his open aggression. Among Afghan children, there are hundreds of thousands like Hassan, and millions more around the world among refugee and internally displaced populations who have known intimately the trauma of war.

Dr. Azam Dadfar, an Afghan physician, is the only psychiatrist among three and a half million Afghan refugees in Pakistan. He treats thousands each year, even though he has only a small staff and minimal funds. He insists that the psychological attention given to multiple psychosomatic disorders among the Afghans or any refugee population is not a luxury. Victims of the brutalities of war deserve an opportunity for treatment.

Dr. Dadfar, himself, was incarcerated in Kabul's Pol-e Charkhi prison from November 1978 until January 1980. Even the lack of space was a form of torture. The prison was built for five thousand, but by the time Dr. Dadfar became an inmate, the population was three times that. He understood personally the stress and trauma of torture, for he was tortured for prolonged periods over the course of fourteen months.

Many children who have experienced extreme war trauma are resilient, though scarred for life, while others wither from the internal havoc that war creates. Dr. Dadfar worries about the next generation that knows nothing but war and wonders how to deal with the psychological effect of the war upon it. Before children's eyes parents and siblings have been arrested, murdered, or mortally wounded by enemy fire. In flight, many children have themselves been captured, bombarded, orphaned, or wounded. Some children who were pressed into service as combatants were made to kill and even dismember their own parents.

Children live in poverty and insecurity. In refugee camps, fathers are absent from the majority of households because they are fighting or dead. The majority of the children do not have access to education, and many do not receive adequate health care or proper nutrition. Their development needs are not really addressed to the extent they could be.

Frequently mothers who are severely traumatized migrate twice, Dr. Dadfar says—once from their homeland and then into themselves.[31] Because mothers who withdraw are no longer capable of meeting their children's needs or interacting with them, children, particularly the very young, fail to thrive. Even children who are physically healthy fail to respond to the world around them. Parents who can no longer cope under the stress of war react violently against their children, who then become victims not only of an impersonal war, but also victims of their source of security in a world that appears to have gone completely out of control. A parent's powerlessness and lack of self-confidence shatter children's levels of trust for those who should be their protectors and providers.

Stories of children of war abound. Their pathological reactions to aberrant situations are entirely normal. In the dehumanizing world of war, mental and physical traumas break them. They see only a shaky present and a dark and violent future. They find little motivation to excel or to have normal dreams and aspirations. They live in constant terror, fearing a knock on the door or the sound of bombs exploding around them. They watch brothers and fathers leave for the front, knowing they may die, and they are aware that they may be saying good-bye forever to a close family member. These children of today will be tomorrow's adults.

A seventeen-year-old was eye-witness to the bombardment of his home and village. As he looked on from his nearby hiding place, eleven members of his family perished. Later he and several others stepped on mines when they were caught in a Russian ambush, and they were either disabled or killed. He cringes now at the sound of planes, is aggressive, irritable, and prone to nightmares.

A child of seven was a victim of an air raid while crossing the mountains to reach Pakistan. Her mother, one-year-old sister, and grandfather were killed before her eyes. She has chosen mutism and has not spoken since the incident in 1987.

In 1986 a fourteen-year-old, whose brother joined the *mujahideen*, was seized by Khad agents who surrounded and searched his family's home. He, as well as two cousins and two neighbors, were beaten by the agents in front of their families. In turn, the families were beaten in front of the children. He continues to be deeply depressed, cannot sleep easily, and has multiple somatic complaints.[32]

At an early age many children were taken from their stable environments of the extended family and placed in day-care centers where they were indoctrinated in an ideology foreign and abhorrent to their parents. Planeloads of children were transported to the Soviet Union for a Soviet education in which birth language, traditions, and ideals were discredited and disavowed. When children were taken from their schools and put on planes, parents were not notified and did not know where their children were. A resistance commander reacting to the Soviet education strategy said, "They saw that they couldn't conquer us, and they realized that there is no way to change the people. That's when they decided to take the children, because they think that they have 'empty brains.' "[33]

Other children were trained for the battlefields. On either side, it is not unusual to see a line of young Afghan boys positioned in a trench and aiming AK-47 assault rifles at a practice-target enemy. Many are not more than ten or twelve years old. They learn quickly to dehumanize the enemy, seeing in front of them not a person, but only a stone or a board—no face. They can even kill a person who has been a neighborhood friend only a short time before. Some are trained to be spies, for young children are less suspect than adults. Few can articulate the ramifications of what it is that they are about. They espouse, mimic, and act on the rhetoric fed to them by the warring parties.

Booby-trap toys have disabled and disfigured hundreds of thousands of Afghan children. They were attracted to a doll, a pen, a plastic butterfly, or a watch on the ground that exploded when they picked it up. Many lost hands and sight, and will live the rest of their lives with scarred faces from severe burns, while others will live among the multitude of leg amputees from anti-personnel mines.

On November 29, 1989, the United Nations General Assembly adopted the United Nations Convention on the Rights of the Child, the international legal instrument of guarantees of a child's human rights. Sixty-one nations signed. States which accept the convention are "legally accountable for their actions towards children."[34] According to the convention, every child has the right to life that includes more than mere physical survival. The child has the right to intellectual, spiritual, and moral development in a family and a society conducive to and encouraging such growth. All children, including orphans and disabled, are to be protected from physical and mental harm. All children have the right to an education, adequate health care, and the time and space to play. No child should be tortured and none should be actively engaged in armed conflict before the age of fifteen.[35] Each child has the right to develop his/her own capacities and to live in and build a world at peace.

Millions of children who are born into and develop in the midst of armed conflicts are denied these fundamental rights. Long after hostilities cease, these same children remain stunted and deprived of life beyond simple survival. In countries as decimated as Afghanistan, Cambodia, and Eritrea, education and access to adequate health care and nutrition take second place to the mon-umental tasks of reconstructing the shattered physical infrastructure. The children of Afghanistan, Cambodia, Eritrea, and dozens more countries have been formed by war with little control over their lives and their worlds. These children of war will return to lands they do not remember or have never experienced and will find, at least initially, little sense of normalcy.

One person warns, "The suffering of children is a dragon seed, and we will harvest it later on."[36] Will this generation of children create new hostilities or will they forge a new and peaceful vision when the present wars end and they are able to go home? There are scores to be settled. Will these take the form of violent revenge? Or will the children be able to echo the voice of one child?

> It's impossible for everyone to die [in a war] . . . My family survived. And those of us still alive also have learned to love. To have been so close to death and survived, we think, "I will come back and give." I don't know what has saved our lives, but sometimes I feel that there has been some miracle that has happened. Or sometimes I think it's luck. But I also believe that there are some people who give luck. My great-grandmother is still living, and she often prays for me and says she hopes that my ancestors will look after me.[37]

ERITREA AND SUDAN

LIBYA

ARAB REPUBLIC of EGYPT

RED SEA

CHAD

NORTHERN

NILE

DONGOLA

SUDAN

BERBER

AD DAMER

EASTERN

PORT SUDAN

DARFUR

KORDOFAN

Omdurman KHARTOUM

ERITREA

KASSALA

GENEINA

EL FASHER

EN NAHUD

EL OBEID

EL GEZIRA

EL HASAHEISA

WAD MEDANI

ED DUEIM

EL GEDAREF

NYALA

KADUGLI

ED DAMAZIN

Blue Nile

ETHIOPIA

BAHR EL

GHAZAL

WAU

UPPER

NILE

White Nile

MALAKAL

CENTRAL
AFRICAN
REPUBLIC

RUMBEK

BOR

EQUATORIA

YAMBIO

JUBA

YEI

KENYA

ZAIRE

UGANDA

| Paved Roads |
| Secondary Roads, Unsurfaced |
| Railways |
| Rivers |
| Airports |
| Regional Boundaries |

UNHCR (used by permission)

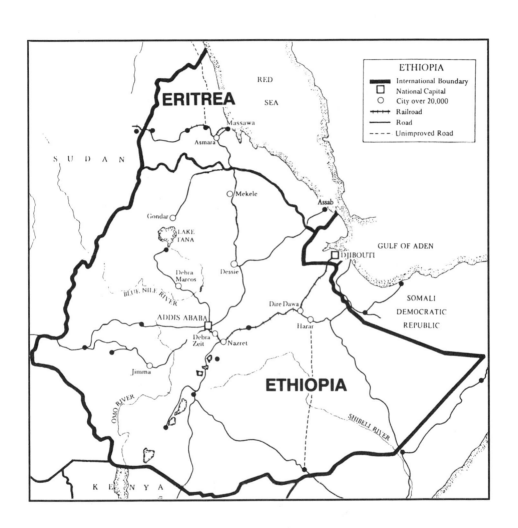

ETHIOPIA

International Boundary
National Capital
City over 20,000
Railroad
Road
Unimproved Road

ERITREA

RED
SEA

SUDAN

Massawa

Asmara

Mekele

Gondar

LAKE
TANA

Assab

GULF OF ADEN

DJIBOUTI

SOMALI
DEMOCRATIC
REPUBLIC

Debra
Marcos

Dessie

BLUE NILE RIVER

Dire Dawa

ADDIS ABABA

Harar

Debra
Zeit

Nazret

Jimma

ETHIOPIA

OMO RIVER

SHIBELI RIVER

KENYA

Eritrean refugees on the move, living in tents fashioned of whatever is available along the route.

7

FLIGHT ERITREA

To go into exile is to lose your place in the world.
—Jean-Paul Sartre

Tall and straight and dignified, Danait is a beautiful Eritrean woman. She rose from a simple wooden bench to join the circle of six of her compatriots in an Eritrean dance, and as she did so the nobility in her movement and face evoked the richness of the ancient civilization from which she sprang. The dancers lowered their bodies to the earth and rose again in time to the music. In the dim light Danait's features were more pronounced, framed as they were by her hairstyle and white traditional dress. She lifted the white, embroidered scarf from her shoulder, fanning it as she immersed herself in the movement.

Danait and her compatriots were not in their homeland. It had been twelve years since she had walked on its soil. This night they were on the roof of the home of a Senegalese family who worked among the six hundred thousand Eritrean refugees who had fled to Sudan. Danait was one of those refugees.

The occasion was a party in honor of the fourth birthday of the host's daughter. Among those celebrating were Sudanese, Egyptians, French, Swedes, Australians, Japanese, Thais, Senegalese, and Americans—all in Sudan as a part of the refugee relief effort. Under the desert night sky the guests ate dishes from many lands, talked in several tongues, and danced to different sounds. Significantly, the circle dance of the Eritreans expressed the unity of purpose amidst such diversity. Its almost ritual movements of rising and falling embodied, too, oneness among Eritreans in their sure and steady pursuit of self-determination in the governance of their land.

As she ate, Danait spoke of her homeland and of her profound sadness in being so close and yet not being able to return. On holidays and during parties like this one, she felt her loss most deeply. She had not seen her aging parents since she had left. But she and they had survived the longest running war in Africa.

For thirty years Eritreans and Ethiopians clashed for either liberation or secession, depending on one's perspective. Most of the world knows tiny Eritrea as the famine-stricken northern-most province of Ethiopia; few are aware of the long-standing war. Even though the people of Eritrea have disparate religious, ethnic, and linguistic roots, they were one in identifying themselves as Ethiopian colonials held in bondage.

Eritrea contains no more than one-tenth of Ethiopia's fifty million people and the same fraction of its land mass. Part of the Horn of Africa, Eritrea's coastal plains stretch seven hundred miles along the Red Sea, a vital life-line to otherwise land-locked Ethiopia. For this, Ethiopia continued to war against a much smaller and less well-equipped army of determined men and women. In this David and Goliath struggle, it was not sheer doggedness that kept the Eritreans going; it was a resolute commitment to self-determination. Harboring no doubts of the legitimacy of their task, they were ready to continue the struggle for as long as it took.

Danait was not always political; probably she would not have been had the war remained on the periphery of her life. But the conflict sucked her into its center and catapulted her into the tempest that swept across her homeland.

World events in the year of her birth dramatically influenced the course of her life and the future of Eritrea. Danait arrived on the cusp of the old and new order. It was 1952 and post-World War II boundaries set by the victors federated this former Italian colony with Ethiopia, a nation then friendly to the West and strategically important. Because Ethiopia's Emperor Haile Selassie wanted incorporation, not simply federation, the arrangement was doomed almost from the beginning and immediately spawned sporadic violence. The dissolution of the federation took place in 1962 when Danait was ten.

Born the third of seven children—four male, three female—in a village not far from the Eritrean capital city of Asmara, Danait lived in relative peace during her early years. Her father was a small farmer, a vegetable grower in the Eritrean highlands. He was a Coptic Christian, as were the majority in the highlands, in a mixed culture of Christianity and Islam. Her family was neither wealthy nor poor. They lived simply among people whose village roots took hold generations before.

Ordinarily village children completed no more than primary school, if that. Most were needed to work the land or herd the goats. An exception, Danait received a more extensive education. Before she completed secondary school in Asmara, Danait could speak six languages. Tigrigna, her native language, and Arabic, the language of Islam, are the two national languages of Eritrea. Tigray was spoken by Eritrea's closest provincial neighbors, and Amharic was the national language of Ethiopia. She studied English in school and spoke Italian as did many in this former Italian colony.

By 1974 when she was studying for a degree in public health in the university in the Ethiopian capital, Addis Ababa, radical changes were taking place in her country. Not only were Eritrea and Ethiopia locked in battle, the forty-four-year rule of Emperor Haile Selassie came abruptly to an end. Eventually Mengistu Haile Mariam out-maneuvered other contenders for head of state and gained control of the Marxist-oriented military government that toppled the emperor. Still the Ethiopian government asserted historical claim as ancient as Sheba and Solomon to the area of Eritrea with passage to the sea.

COLONIAL BACKGROUND

Rulers of Ethiopia know from early history that loss of the sea can be the ruin of a realm. As far back as the first century B.C.E. the Axumite kingdom that spread across present-day Ethiopia and the coastal region of what is now Eritrea collapsed when it lost access to the sea. Though the monarchies of this early kingdom had openings to the sea, they never ruled the whole of present-day Eritrea. Nor did the Abyssinian rulers between the thirteenth and nineteenth centuries; they ruled Tigray and southern Eritrea, but never the whole. Still, the two twentieth-century heads of state justified their hold over Eritrea on the basis that both Axum and Abyssinia encompassed the entire area. They argued that at the end of the nineteenth century, Italy, when it took control of Eritrea, colonized a part of Ethiopia.

It is clear that between 1889 and 1950 Eritrea was not a part of Ethiopia. Europe was busy with its "scramble for Africa" and Eritrea fell to Italy. Like the other colonial powers, Italy's expansionist interests included expropriation of land as a source for raw materials and a market for Italian goods. Eritrea served as a place for Italy to settle its surplus population and enhance its economic interests at the expense — as usually happens during colonization — of the colonized Eritreans. Italians settled as large landholders on the most fertile land and used the Eritrean peasantry for labor. Eritrean land ownership was negligible and strictly controlled. As the Italians established their domination, they developed an industrial base in the cities and roads and railroads for internal linkage and access to the Red Sea ports of Assab and Massawa, again finding a cheap source of labor among the Eritrean population. In fact, the development of industry and infrastructure in Eritrea far excelled Ethiopia's. The Italians restricted the education of the people and stressed Italian language and history. Only the lowest government positions were offered to Eritreans. Rigorous segregation separated the two peoples. Any seminal dissent was quickly quelled.

Eritreans were conscripted to wage Italy's battles in its reach for more land. Italy wanted the whole of Ethiopia and attempted a takeover shortly after Eritrea became a colony. The Italians were routed in 1896 by the Ethiopians and retreated to Eritrea. They did not meet defeat easily, and by 1935 Mussolini was ready to try again. Moving north from Italian Somaliland and south from Eritrea, the fascist leader crushed Ethiopia. Coupled with its hold on Somalia, Italy controlled much of the Horn of Africa for a short time.

In 1941 British invasion forces from Sudan, Kenya, and India expelled the Italians from the Horn. Haile Selassie, who had been driven from Ethiopia by

Mussolini, was restored to the throne by the British, and Eritrea and Italian Somaliland were placed under British trusteeship. Eritrea's fate would not be determined for another decade.

By 1940 when Italy joined the Axis powers against the Allies, the Italian population in Eritrea had swelled to sixty thousand. The British inherited this population. The British, like the Italians, did not encourage partnership or leadership on the part of Eritreans. Such a typical colonial attitude, of course, affected British administration of the colony now under its control. Because the Eritreans had been denied more than basic education and job opportunities under the Italians, the British found few who could fill more skilled positions. In fact, the British encouraged a number of the remaining Italians to continue with their business and agricultural enterprises. Conqueror and conquered seemed to work in tandem.

As long as the war continued, the economy prospered. During these years, the British administrators eased colonial constraints somewhat and unwittingly initiated a climate for dissent that was unleashed at war's end when an economic bust followed the boom. When the British cracked ever so slightly the doors to educational opportunity and allowed the formation of trade unions and political parties, Eritreans legitimately took advantage of the springboard.

During the war when factories were being built, job availability continued to draw peasants into the cities from the countryside. Such movement was necessary because the Italians continued to hold much of the choice land and were allotted more by the British. In addition, the number of peasants who forfeited their land swelled with the imposition of heavier taxes. At war's end factory closings compelled many to return to the countryside where land was no longer available. Unrest and rebellion were not long in coming. Dissent among the more politically conscious urbanites and workers rose as the economy stagnated and increased taxation stretched them to their limits.

Eritreans, well aware that their future was at stake, formed parties with that future in mind. Unionists, largely Coptic Christian church leaders and former Eritrean nobles deprived of their land by their colonial counterparts, believed union with Ethiopia would enable them to lay claim to what they had lost. Two separatist parties formed and united a short time later. The Moslem League drew mainly on the faithful who lived in the western lowlands, while the Liberal Progressive Party attracted primarily Christians from the central highlands.

POST-WORLD WAR II DISPOSITION OF COLONIAL ERITREA

At the Paris Peace Conference in 1946 at the end of the Second World War, the question of the disposition of Italy's colonies was left to the Big Four (United States, Soviet Union, Britain, and France) of the Allied powers. Great Britain and the United States had the most at stake strategically. Both opposed Eritrean independence. Ethiopia wanted outright annexation.

Britain's foreign minister proposed division. According to the Bevin-Sforza

(British-Italian) plan, the western and northern parts would go to British colonial Sudan; the southern and coastal regions would belong to Ethiopia. The important ports of Assab and Massawa would be in friendly hands with Ethiopia's alignment to the West. Such a division, the British believed, would bring Muslim Eritrea under the Muslim rule of Sudan; Christian Eritrea, under the Christian rule of Ethiopia.

The Four Powers, in the end unable to agree except that there should be no partition of Eritrea, abdicated resolution to a United Nations Commission of Enquiry on Eritrea composed of representatives from Norway, Pakistan, Guatemala, Burma, and South Africa. Although the delegation traveled throughout Eritrea and held hearings among various political groups to consider the welfare and desires of the Eritrean people in regard to their future, geopolitics influenced the outcome more than the wishes of the Eritrean people.

The importance of the Red Sea to Western interests in general and U.S. interests in particular overshadowed recognition of Eritrean wishes. Already the crude oil of the Middle East was a consideration. Eritrea with its ports so near Saudi Arabia would be a fine place for refineries as well as for naval and communication bases.

On December 11, 1948, U.S. Secretary of Defense James Forrestal wrote to Secretary of State Dean Acheson.

From the standpoint of strategic and logistical considerations it would be [of] value to the United States to have refineries, capable of supplying a substantial portion of our aviation needs, located close to a crude supply and also close to areas where naval task forces would be operating and where airfields would be located, yet far enough removed to be reasonably safe from effective enemy bombing.

With respect to the Middle East, refineries located in Italian Somaliland and Eritrea would meet the foregoing conditions . . . [T]herefore, as long-range provision of potential military value, it is believed that concession on rights should be sought for United States interests to construct and operate refineries in Italian Somaliland and Eritrea. These rights should include necessary transportation and port concessions, together with air and naval base rights and communication facilities.[1]

Ethiopian Emperor Haile Selassie promised these in return for military and economic assistance if Eritrea came under Ethiopia's rule.[2] John Foster Dulles, secretary of state in 1952, said in a speech before the U.N. Security Council: "From the point of view of justice, the opinions of the Eritrean people must receive consideration. Nevertheless the strategic interests of the United States in the Red Sea basin and considerations of security and world peace make it necessary that the country has to be linked with our ally, Ethiopia."[3]

British coloration of circumstances made it seem that Eritreans were not capable of surviving economically, politically, or socially as an independent nation. The visiting delegates witnessed large segments of the population unemployed and in a high state of tension because of the shut down of much of the British wartime industry. Eritreans had access to only the most menial government-related jobs and none had been prepared for national leadership. Coptic church leaders and large Eritrean landholders, calculating the bounty they would receive from union with Ethiopia, played their role in assuring there would be no independent Eritrea. They initiated campaigns of intimidation against separatists, hoping to frighten them into submission. Church leaders denied sacramental access to those Eritreans who did not support union. They were not allowed to receive communion, nor be married, baptized, or buried with the blessing of the church. Landowners tightened their grip on peasants who rose in rebellion. When the U.N. Commission arrived, unrest triggered by such actions convinced the visitors that, indeed, Eritrea could not govern itself.[4]

Eritrean Federation with Ethiopia

On December 2, 1950, Eritrea's fate was sealed. U.N. Resolution 390 A(v) came just short of annexing Eritrea to Ethiopia. It was to be an "autonomous unit federated with Ethiopia under the sovereignty of the Ethiopian Crown." According to this arrangement, the "institutions, traditions, religions and languages" of the Eritrean people were to be respected and safeguarded. Self-government over internal affairs was to be accorded, insofar as it did not encroach on the prerogatives of the Ethiopian empire.[5] The Eritrean government was accorded power in Eritrea's domestic arena, while the Ethiopian crown held sway in all federal and foreign matters, including currency and finance, defense, foreign affairs, and interstate commerce, including control of the ports.[6]

The resolution cited that due consideration would be given to "the wishes and welfare of the inhabitants of Eritrea, including the views of the various racial, religious, and political groups . . . " Ethiopia was charged with ensuring "human rights and fundamental liberties," such as equality before the law, education, freedom of expression, religion, and peaceful assembly, and freedom from unlawful detention.[7] But the resolution also assured recognition of Ethiopia's legitimate, historical claims to the land to the north and its need for access to the sea. These claims became the key consideration in determining Eritrea's future.

The question of Eritrean self-determination was never an issue. Eritreans had no voice, no formal vote, in the choice of their future. Independence was not really a consideration as the U.N. Commission drafted the resolution. Haile Selassie resolutely inaugurated Ethiopian sovereignty and firmly maintained that Eritrea was an integral part of the empire seized by Italy. In retrospect, talk of the "wishes and welfare" of the Eritrean people was hollow. Even when the British flag was lowered on September 15, 1952, and the Eritrean flag was raised alongside the Ethiopian flag, the majority of Eritreans believed they had merely changed their colonial dependency from one country to another. Had the spirit and the form of the federation been observed, however, and given a chance to flourish, Eritreans may well have adjusted to living as an "autonomous unit" of the Ethiopian empire. Ten years later, though, on November 14, 1962, formal annexation officially abrogated the federation and any semblance of self-governance. Eritrea became the fourteenth province of Ethiopia.

ABROGATION OF THE FEDERATION

Nullification of the U.N. resolution was gradual but systematic and measured. Emperor Haile Selassie never intended autonomy for Eritrea; he would abide nothing less than its total absorption into Ethiopia. The Conquering Lion of the Tribe of Judah, Haile Selassie I, Elect of God, King of Kings, Emperor of Ethiopia[8] would abide no challenge to his control. The democratic thrust of the Eritrean constitution remained foreign and unacceptable to the autocratic emperor who took his title seriously. As early as 1955, the emperor's representative in the Eritrean capital said: "There are no internal or external affairs, as far as the office of his imperial majesty's representative is concerned, and there will be none in the future. The affairs of Eritrea concern Ethiopia as a whole and the emperor."[9]

Rights accorded Eritreans by the U.N. resolution and the subsequent federation constitution were undermined by the Ethiopian government almost from the beginning. Though the emperor's representative was to have little voice in the Eritrean assembly, he rigorously influenced those who would hold office in the Eritrean assembly. His base of support remained with the Eritrean Coptic church leaders and large landowners who had most to benefit from stronger ties to Ethiopia.

An unintended consequence of Italy's colonial development was the unity it accorded Eritreans. Roads and railways linked urban and rural areas. Peasants forced from their land by large landowners or who refused to live a life of feudal serfdom frequently moved to the cities in search of work. There they came in contact with urban workers dissatisfied with the menial positions they were allotted by the colonizers. Peasant bands in the countryside linked in rebellion. In the early days of skirmish just after federation, Emperor Haile Selassie regarded such groups as no more than "a handful of bandits from the hills."[10] *Shiftas* he called them. He pursued them and all others who tried to frustrate his design for absolute control.

A policy of terror and intimidation ensued. Imperial forces brutally quelled protesting and striking students, workers, and teachers. Many were beaten, arrested, and held without legitimate charges. Labor unions and political parties were banned. Industries were closed; others were moved to Addis Ababa, the Ethiopian capital. In the countryside villagers who assisted rebels were executed. Villages were destroyed; crops, burned and animals, slaughtered. Such actions had the opposite effect from that intended. Nationalist fronts grew and Eritreans became solidified in their commitment to self-determination.

One by one the rights guaranteed to the Eritreans were violated, then rescinded. In 1957 even the right to speak their own language was crushed. Amharic, the language of Ethiopia, officially replaced the Eritrean national languages of Tigrigna and Arabic. Ethiopian law superseded Eritrean constitutional law; the Ethiopian flag, the Eritrean colors. Imperial forces spread throughout Eritrea in the name of defense.[11] Finally, on November 14, 1962, the chief executive of the Ethiopian-controlled Eritrean assembly was said to have announced, "The statement I am going to read to you is the final issue of the Eritrean case, and there is nothing you can do other than to accept it as it is. We have rendered the Federation null and void and are henceforth completely united with our motherland."[12] Ethiopian troops surrounded the assembly hall.

It seems there was no official recourse for Eritrea as the emperor's government chose to abrogate the federation. Nothing in the original U.N. resolution of 1952 creating the federation anticipated or specified sanctions against such a move by Ethiopia. The document did stipulate, "The United Nations Resolution of Eritrea would remain an international instrument and, if violated, the General Assembly could be seized of the matter."[13] However, this did not guarantee Eritrea's autonomy within a federation, and the United Nations did not take action.

Neither the U.S. government nor the members of the NATO alliance had any reason for championing the Eritrean cause. With the Red Sea safely in friendly hands, there was no cause for alarm among Western powers. Through the twenty-five-year 1953 Mutual Defense Assistance Agreement between the United States and Haile Selassie's Ethiopia, the emperor received the military and economic aid he sought while the United States secured and expanded its presence at its intelligence-gathering Kagnew Communications Center and in coastal naval and air facilities.

FORMATION OF ERITREAN LIBERATION FRONTS

Many Eritreans, despairing of U.N. intercession, now saw armed resistance as their only recourse. Forming a united front against a common enemy was not easy in an area inhabited by people without common ethnic, religious, or linguistic bonds. The multiple Eritrean fronts that emerged finally combined into two, the Eritrean Liberation Front (ELF) and the Eritrean People's Liberation Front (EPLF); they fought a bloody civil war of Eritreans against Eritreans in the midst of their mutual battle against two successive Ethiopian governments.

A large number of Eritreans of the Islamic faith had gone into exile in Egypt and Sudan. One group comprised members of banned labor unions, students, teachers, and others who had fled the expanding oppression of Haile Selassie's government. Their numbers swelled after a general strike was crushed in

1958. During the same year five young Eritreans formed the Eritrean Liberation Movement (ELM) to oppose the suppression of Eritrean rights and the gradual negation of Eritrea's autonomous status.[14] The ELM was a short-lived organization, soon denounced, disarmed, and superseded by a more influential band of exiles.

An older group of Eritrean Muslims in exile in Cairo formed the ELF in 1960. They had led the separatist movement in the 1940s and saw armed conflict as the only resolution to Ethiopia's destruction of Eritrea's autonomy. Inside Eritrea, ELF membership and a nascent guerilla army were built largely from western lowland, nomadic groups. Mostly Muslims, they looked to Arab countries for assistance. Conservative in their approach, the ELF wanted to retain their ethnic and religious characteristics. Beyond their determination to end Ethiopian rule, the ELF had little to offer in regard to a plan for a future, independent Eritrea. Nor did the ELF build an effective military machine. Their forces were divided into five zones, with commanders acting independently of one another.

As their ranks and the diversity of membership increased, latent problems surfaced. Students, workers, and Christians from urban areas who tended to be more radical in political and social orientation found themselves in the minority and often suspected by the ELF leadership. Distrust of Christians ran particularly high because so many Coptic church leaders had pledged their loyalty to those who supported union with Ethiopia when the future of Eritrea was being decided a decade earlier. To many ELF members, Judas-like Christians betrayed the Eritreans to the Ethiopians. As ideological differences intensified, splinter groups formed their own resistance associations. One emerged strong enough to confront the ELF.

The opposing EPLF espoused a philosophy of radical social transformation of society and a secular nationalism that embraced the multiplicity of ethnic groups and religious persuasions. Through an intense program of political education, they sought to imbue their adherents with strong political convictions. In a free, independent Eritrea they envisioned national unity that encompassed their diversity. Nationalization of the bulk of the economy and industry, land reform that allowed for more equitable distribution, equal rights with particular attention to women's rights, access to education and public health, and political power in the hands of many through a people's assembly were some of the goals of the EPLF. They saw clearly, as well, the need for unity in their military organization.[15]

So different were the two factions in approach to revolution and in their goals that after more than five years of angry confrontations a bitter civil war broke out in 1972 between the ELF and the EPLF. Before, during, and after the internecine conflict, both parties continued to fight first against the forces of Haile Selassie and then against the Soviet-fortified troops of Colonel Mengistu Haile Mariam.

When two fronts emerged in competition with one another, the emperor took advantage of the overt division between the ELF and the EPLF to solidify his control of Eritrea. In addition to taking several thousand Eritreans prisoners, the emperor's troops continued attacks on Eritrean villages.

Just as in the 1950s during the federation, so now there were Ethiopian reprisals against civilians believed to be harboring and assisting those who opposed government policy. Villages were burned and civilians were killed. In 1967, following a series of attacks by the ELF in which some Ethiopian officials were killed, Ethiopian forces struck with a vengeance. Employing a scorched-earth policy, Ethiopian troops routed villagers from the rubble of their razed and looted villages and massacred them by the hundreds. Aerial raids pounded a widespread area for days, decimating herds and charring crops and fields. The stench of napalm permeated the air. This offensive generated the first large mass of refugees as more than twenty thousand Eritreans fled to neighboring Sudan.

The Eritrean people did not cower. The ruthlessness of the Ethiopian attacks further strengthened Eritrean resolve to free themselves from what they perceived as colonial status. More and more people joined the march for liberation and self-determination. Their resources were small. Because few countries were willing to provide arms or other assistance, both the ELF and the EPLF built their arsenals from captured enemy weapons.

As many as three hundred villages were attacked in the 1967 offensive. In some villages, leaders were summoned and summarily executed. In other villages, citizens were packed into the village mosque and brutally killed. Those who escaped fled to the hills for protection in caves or to asylum in Sudan. When those who sought protection in the hills returned to bury the dead, they found only charred remnants of their homes. The Ethiopian army achieved its intent to terrorize. Comparable attacks occurred over the next twelve years. Hundreds of thousands — mostly women, children, and old men — were killed or fled to Sudan, swelling the refugee population to the limit of that country's ability to receive them. Others returned to their villages to rebuild, hoping the soldiers would not mount another assault.

The Eritreans were not the only national movement seeking independence from or greater autonomy within Ethiopia. Much of the clamor arising from the multiple ethnic groups stems from the nineteenth century when they were overpowered by the Amharas, the dominant though not the most populous ethnic group, and brought into the expanding Ethiopian Empire. The creation of liberation fronts was a more recent development in their quest for self-determination. Besides the ELF and EPLF, three other groups have been the most active. The Oromo Liberation Front (OLF) and the Western Somali Liberation Front (WSLF) cover most of southern Ethiopia east to west and have clashed off and on with Ethiopian troops since the 1960s. Tigray, the heart of the ancient Axumite Empire, flanks on Eritrea's southern border. Longstanding animosity against succeeding Ethiopian rulers climaxed when Haile Selassie imposed Amharic as the official language on the Tigrayan people. The Tigrayan People's Liberation Front (TPLF), with its goals of self-determination and social transformation, became most active after Mengistu came to power.

If, then, Eritrea were allowed to determine its relationship to Ethiopia, the emperor and later Mengistu would lose more than Red Sea ports. With others clamoring for autonomy, the whole of Ethiopia could fall apart. A nation would dissolve.

DOWNFALL OF HAILE SELASSIE

Although Haile Selassie was determined to crush the Eritrean rebellion, his own grip on the absolute imperial power he had exerted for almost half a century began to loosen. Unrest and dissatisfaction with his policies on several fronts coalesced and gained momentum in the early 1970s. As is often the case, the first voices of dissension rose from the university campus, in Addis Ababa. There students from all parts of the empire verbalized the cultural, regional, and ethnic hopes of many of Ethiopia's seventy nationalities.

Haile Selassie's ability to silence opposition failed utterly when it became known in 1974 that a famine had killed between two hundred thousand and three hundred thousand Ethiopians. For two years the emperor had denied the famine. In fact the emperor used food as a weapon by denying access to food to civilians who lived in areas where the resistance was strong. Word of its devastation began to seep through the shroud of silence. Still, the emperor went beyond denial and prohibited the organization of relief efforts when the extent of starvation became known. Ethiopians began to take action. Students rioted, teachers struck, and soldiers mutinied. As demands and demonstrations increased, so did measures taken to quell the unrest. On the university campus in Addis Ababa, security forces swiftly and mercilessly crushed student cries of outrage against the government's disavowal of the famine. Clubs split heads of protesters. Some lay dead. No one was allowed to channel relief to the starving masses.

As dissatisfaction grew in a number of provinces throughout the empire and as impassioned strikes and demonstrations in the capital became more fiery, Haile Selassie's dependence on his military intensified. But events also raised disaffection among the troops.

On September 12, 1974, Emperor Haile Selassie, the Lion of Judah, was deposed by junior officers of the imperial army and driven from his palace in the back seat of a battered Volkswagen. The constitution that had extended absolute rule to him was scrapped; it had not lifted the majority of Ethiopians out of abject poverty nor had it eliminated the feudal land system. Haile Selassie died one year later at age eighty-three, still under arrest. Few who served him escaped with their lives.

RISE OF COLONEL MENGISTU HAILE MARIAM

When the military coup of September 12, 1974, brought the Provisional Military Administrative Council (PMAC), known as the Dergue, to power, many Ethiopians hoped that the autocratic, power-buttressing centralization of Haile Selassie's rule would give way to a less authoritarian, more independent government. The appointed chairman of the Dergue, General Aman Michael Andom, was a native Eritrean who favored negotiations with the ELF and EPLF and possibly the return of Eritrea to its federal, autonomous status. This encouraging sign was dashed within two months, with the execution of Aman.[16]

Colonel Mengistu Haile Mariam, who replaced Aman, had no room in his scheme of power for an independent Eritrea or a decentralized nation. The term *empire* was struck from the records, but the shape remained. Peasants who had hoped to gain land under the new regime were quickly disenchanted. To them, Mengistu's nationalization of all the land gave them no more access than they had had under the emperor's claim to imperial ownership. The new land policy served to heighten the restive spirits of the peasantry.

Colonel Mengistu had his hands full, attempting to retain command; to solidify control, he initiated radical measures. Persecution and incarceration of dissidents were widespread. His program of resettlement served to break up rebel groups, while his villagization scheme centralized peasants under the watchful eye of Mengistu's troops, weakening any influence and recruiting capability of national fronts. Ostensibly the first program was created to diminish the potential famine in certain areas by removing peasants from overused lands to areas of fallow land. The government purported to gather peasants into centralized villages to enhance social services and better their lives.

By 1976 the Dergue had unleashed its maniacal rampage of "red terror." Thousands of students and workers were caught up in its furious slaughter. Suspected political opponents were imprisoned, tortured, and often killed without trial. In the countryside peasants who struck out against Mengistu's land reform policies met the same fate. In a single day thousands of civilians in Asmara were killed when Ethiopian soldiers let loose a barrage of fire in the streets.[17] The new government was relentless in its pursuit of total control.

DANAIT, A VICTIM OF THE WAR

Though Danait stood on the fringe, not totally absorbed in student dissent, she was moving into the web of revolution. It did not seem long ago that she had walked beside her mother and father as they planted cucumbers, eggplant, tomatoes, melons, and all variety of vegetables and fruits. When harvests were bountiful, her father arranged the produce with pride in the ox-cart, lifted Danait and her sisters and brothers beside him, and drove to Asmara to set up a stall in the capital's largest market. With some of the money, he bought colorful material for clothing, kerosene for cooking, a gift for their mother and grandmother.

There was never an abundance of money. Quite a large sum was always set aside to pay taxes whether to the Italians, the British, or to the empire of Haile Selassie, for all the land was his. The use of the family land had been extended to their kinsmen for generations. Nevertheless, feudal lords held control and the right to tax. The majority of peasants lived their entire lives indebted beyond their ability to pay. These extremes of indebtedness, however, did not plague Danait's father.

As a child, Danait knew great stability within her family and in her village, a contrast, to be sure, to life all around her. Actually, she lived a rather favored life. In the late 1950s she attended primary school; not more than 5 or 10 percent of primary-age Ethiopian children had the opportunity to attend school. In the 1960s she was among the 2 percent with a secondary-school education. By then the number of children receiving primary education was growing. Although relatively few continued to receive an education, those who did were well educated. Living near Asmara, education was more accessible than it was to lowland nomadic people or to those who lived greater distances from the cities. Often children had to walk six, eight, even ten miles to the nearest school. Education itself was free, but the books, clothes, and pencils cost so much that few peasants and herdsmen could afford them, putting education out of their reach. Later on, during Mengistu's government, even the limited educational system crumbled.

By the time Danait entered secondary school in Asmara, language was an issue. Amharic, now the official language, replaced Tigrigna as the language of instruction. The Eritrean people did not formulate their memories of traditions and culture in this foreign tongue. For the Muslims, the prohibition on teaching Arabic, the language of Islam, reached to the core of their being.

Students in Eritrea rose up in protest when Amharic replaced their mother tongue. Danait and her classmates resented not only the requirement to study in this foreign language, but also the fact that to enter the university in Addis Ababa, they had to pass an Amharic language examination, even though the language of instruction there remained English. Eritreans who could not master Amharic had to forgo university studies. It was not until Danait reached the university that she became aware of the serious social and political implications of the denial of the right to speak one's mother tongue.

Nor did Danait understand the limiting aspect of attendance at the university in Addis Ababa. It was the only university in the empire and very, very few were offered entrance, particularly Eritreans who challenged the emperor's claim to their land. The emperor did not allow university-level education in Eritrea. He viewed literate Eritreans with suspicion and did not want them to be highly educated. As she left her village and Asmara for the Ethiopian capital, Danait felt that her world was expanding to horizons that she had thought impossible. Few of the women she had known knew the world beyond their village—certainly not beyond Asmara. She had been an outstanding student and had excelled not only in Amharic, but also in English, the teaching language of the university. She was ready to study public health and nursing.

It was late 1969 when Danait arrived in Addis Ababa. The federation had been abrogated seven years earlier. Eritrea was now a province of the empire, no longer an autonomous unit. Two years earlier the series of ruthless attacks on Eritrean villages sparked support for the growing liberation movement. Small cells of rebellion formed on the university campus. Other ethnic groups voiced their growing dissatisfaction against policies of the emperor. During her first years in Addis Ababa, Danait felt the unrest and observed the demonstrations, but she was not an active participant.

It was almost the end of her third year of studies when Danait stepped more surely into her own future. She met Tamrat, a fellow Eritrean from Asmara studying economics. He was twelve years her senior. Tamrat's original hopes were to become a secondary teacher in Asmara. But his life took other turns. His father, a teacher in the Eritrean capital city, was part of the unorganized minority of the Christian intelligentsia that championed separation from Ethiopia. Suspect by Muslim separatists and out of step with the thinking of Coptic church leaders, few men in the position of Tamrat's father vocalized their desire for independence.

As a younger man, Tamrat, like his father, had stood in opposition to the majority of highland Eritrean Christians. He had wanted to play an active role among those seeking self-determination for his homeland. He, too, had been suspect by the Muslims who belonged to the burgeoning ELF, yet, until the EPLF had formed, he'd had no other organization to which he could turn. He had not sought membership immediately, attaching himself, instead, to like-minded urban, Christian proponents of an independent Eritrea.

In 1966, four years after Haile Selassie had absorbed Eritrea into his empire, Tamrat and other members of his group linked up with the increasing number of Christians who were joining the ELF. Up to this point the emperor had looked contemptuously upon the ELF Muslims. He began to take it more seriously when Christian membership mounted. Only then did he order his troops to launch devastating attacks on the Eritrean countryside, displacing thousands of people and creating the first large wave of fleeing refugees.

That same year Tamrat journeyed south to Addis Ababa to study economics at the university. Convinced of the need for a total—social, political, and economic—transformation of the empire, he wanted to be a part of the change.

During hours of political discussion over coffee, he found compatriots dissatisfied with the organization and aims of the ELF and linked himself with those wanting to form a splinter group. The older leadership, they felt, had too much of their own self-interests invested in the front to make it a viable, growing movement.

Danait went north to Gondar Province late in 1973 to study for a second degree, in midwifery. She and Tamrat continued a courtship, making the four- to five-hour journey between Addis Ababa and Gondar frequently during that year, before he accepted a study fellowship at Harvard. They dreamed of a future together in a free Eritrea and saw the possibility for its becoming a reality as more and more Ethiopian citizens became disillusioned with the absolute power of Haile Selassie. The demise of the old feudal order, they believed, could only enhance Eritrea's future.

Neither Danait nor Tamrat was in Addis Ababa when the end of the empire finally came. Tamrat had left for Harvard and Danait continued her studies in Gondar. Tamrat, who after completing his work at Harvard went for further studies in Germany, watched from afar the tightening grip of Mengistu's government and realized that Eritrea's hopes for a peaceful, negotiated settlement were dashed. The struggle that had begun twelve years earlier would continue, with no peace in the foreseeable future. Still, he knew the liberation fronts would take advantage of the new government's need for time to solidify its hold over the nation. He hoped, too, that a truce between the ELF and the EPLF in their civil war would last and would strengthen the Eritreans in their common battle against the new regime.

Though Danait's concerns were with the plight of the people, her mind and heart were on things less political. A little less than a year after the coup, she completed her midwifery course. More importantly, she and Tamrat were going to marry in early 1976. She had much to plan, Eritrean weddings being long and festive. She was anxious to return to her family and her village to make preparation and to establish herself in her profession in Asmara where she and Tamrat planned to live.

As she sat on the wooden bench at the birthday party on a roof under the clear Sudanese sky, Danait spoke of the nightmare that began for her the day she left Gondar for her home in Eritrea.

I was aware of the potential danger I could encounter if I returned to my home. Those of us living outside Eritrea, particularly in cities like Addis or Gondar, witnessed the lengths the Mengistu regime would go to secure power over the whole country. We watched fellow students taken into custody and imprisoned. Others disappeared. Although we did not know their fate, we felt sure most of them were not alive. I was warned not to travel to Eritrea. Anyone who made the journey from the south to the north was suspected of being an informer against Mengistu's military government. Still I could not believe anything untoward would happen to me. I was not an informer. I was a public health nurse and a midwife, and I wanted to return home to prepare for my marriage. Why would anyone suspect me?

As Danait settled into life in Eritrea with her family, she was convinced that she had no reason to fear for her personal safety. She did not consider herself politically active. Nevertheless, war was all about her.

Early on, the new regime focused its war efforts in the Eritrean highlands, particularly in areas around Asmara. Dergue troops routed people from their villages and left a path of destruction in which homes lay flattened and burned and animal carcasses grew cold and rotted. In some villages soldiers gathered villagers together, pulling out some to be murdered in front of the rest. They planted mines in the fields to ensure the remaining villagers would not till the land again. In 1975 tens of thousands more Eritreans either fled to the hills or across the border into Sudan.

Danait continued:

I found my village intact when I arrived, but people lived in fear. They did not know when our village would be terrorized by the Dergue. Three of my brothers and one sister had joined the EPLF and were fighting in the highlands. My parents had no word of them for many months. Mengistu's government placed a curfew on Asmara when he first came to power. Then he proclaimed a state of emergency over the whole of Eritrea, just as Haile Selassie had. We were losing our freedom of movement, our freedom to speak our mind, our freedom to associate with whomever we wanted. He told us he wanted peace and offered a plan while he was gathering a massive number of peasants to confront our army. Of course, we did not believe him. He had announced at one point that the different nationalities in Ethiopia would have the right of self-determination and then sent his troops in to quash any aspirations we might have to choose the way we would live.

During the first weeks and months after her return, Danait could not envision what lay ahead. Fifteen years later, she still found it difficult to speak of the next two years in her life. Her response to the unspeakable horror that ensnared her was the profoundly simple question, "What good is war? Does the continued killing of men and women make us more human?"

She continued,

I moved to Asmara shortly after my return. There I took a nursing position in a government hospital. After a few months, I set up a private pharmacy in the central market. I made certain I did everything according to government prescription. I did not want to tangle with any of Mengistu's men. In spite of my caution, they suspected me. After all, I had come from Addis and I did have brothers and a sister fighting with the front.

It was chilly but sunny that early morning in April. Tamrat was to return in less than three months for our wedding. With his Ph.D. completed, he was thinking more and more of a career with the World Bank. My heart was happy about our future. I parked my bicycle beside the pharmacy. The street was already alive with sounds of opening doors and shopkeepers putting out their wares, greeting one another as they did. I remember clearly grasping the padlock that secured the door. It was a common lock—silver and squat. I do not know why I thought of it at that moment as a symbol of safety and at the same time one of the loss of freedom, of dread and death.

The thought passed out of my mind as I arranged the stock on the shelves. From the corner of my eye, I saw the color of khaki. I turned slowly and saw three Ethiopian soldiers standing there, uniformed, each with an AK-47 rifle slung carelessly over his shoulder, a bandoleer of bullets spanning each chest. I do not remember well my movements or theirs from that moment as I was marched from my store. I felt the gaze of other shopkeepers as my captors pushed me into their battered automobile. All I really knew was that I was their prisoner. I was bewildered as much as frightened; they had no cause for seizing me.

Prisons in Asmara were full—overflowing—at this time. The Dergue took so many of us. Mariam-Gimbi owned a large villa in Asmara. He was a gynecologist, a person who brought life into the world. How could such a person's home become a place of the most brutal torture and death? Most of us thought of it as a museum, so great was his collection of art. The soldiers took his home, looted it, and held him a prisoner inside. He eluded his guards and escaped. They brought more and more prisoners to the residence until it was as full as any in the country. This is the prison they brought me to.

Men were in one area; women, in another. Only thin walls between several rooms separated us in a hastily constructed building for the prisoners. Most of the time we were so crowded there was room only to stand. We could not sit or lie down. I shared a room—Room 8—with more than 250 women. We were always thirsty; we had no place to relieve ourselves. The human stench became almost unbearable. Sick women, pregnant ones—no one was given special attention. The cry of a newborn child was pitiful to hear. Usually the cry of life offers joy and hope. Not in Mariam-Gimbi. If one among us died, her body might not be removed for hours. And when it was, the body was tossed into a holding area until enough were amassed to take to a common grave beyond the walls of the prison. Anyone taken to Mariam-Gimbi rarely emerged alive.

So many lives were wasted by Mengistu. Of those in my nursing school class, no more than ten of thirty are alive. I have seen only five. I do not know if the other five are alive. I know twenty are dead. He killed the intellectuals, doctors, nurses, and educated people. He does not know that skill makes a difference in saving or losing lives, in building or destroying a country.

There were many types of torture. All hours of the day and night we heard groans and screams of pain. We tried to remain silent in front of our tormentors; sometimes it was not possible. Our torturers came drunk in order to have the courage to inflict such great pain. My first of many interrogations occurred two days after I was taken to Mariam-Gimbi. As they tried to pull information from me, they inflicted a common torture. My torturers forced me to kneel in a fetal position so they could bind me and string me up off the ground. They beat my feet until they ballooned with water. When they let me down, I was forced to walk on gravel and pieces of broken glass. The water pockets on my feet burst open causing my feet to bleed. If I fainted, the soldiers kicked me and pulled me up, ordering me to continue walking. They pulled my toenails and fingernails out.

There was a well six meters deep in what had once been a beautiful garden. Prisoners who underwent this torture were first bound—hands and feet—and tossed into the well like a stone. Once a person was drawn up from the water, the torturer tried to make the person talk. If he or she would not, the person *was once again tossed into the well. The person became so full of water that the stomach burst and blood and water came out when he or she was brought again to the surface. At one point the prisoners began to drown the torturers. Consequently, the well was closed with heavy wiring.*

One of the most gruesome and dehumanizing forms of torture involved pushing an individual's head into a latrine filled with vomit and feces. The person could not breathe and took in the human waste.

My torture went on for a year. I do not know why they ended it. No one ever knew. I remained a prisoner, while at the same time the authorities ordered me to work in a state hospital treating Ethiopian war-wounded. Even though I could not walk well, I was forced to be on the floor long hours every day. If my toes bent down, I could not move them back to the correct position. The pain was severe.

Danait knew little of the course of the war during that year. Colonel Mengistu inherited all the unrest created by Haile Selassie, and Mengistu's nationalization policies intensified the conflicts. Just as all the land belonged to the emperor during the reign of Haile Selassie, so too, it belonged to the state under Mengistu. The use of the land was dictated by his government.

During the period the new government was forming, the national fronts struck in Eritrea, the Ogaden, Tigray, and in the southern provinces of the Oromos. Most made considerable gains. By 1977 the EPLF and ELF controlled all of the countryside and all but a handful of cities in Eritrea. They even surrounded the provincial capital of Asmara and partially surrounded the port city of Massawa. Both sides knew the capture of Asmara and the main port cities would bring about the liberation of Eritrea.

That same year Mengistu ordered the U.S. government to close its base, Kagnew Station, as he moved closer to the U.S.S.R. The arrival of Cuban advisors and Soviet military equipment confirmed the alliance. In this case the United States and the Soviet Union simply exchanged client nations. When the U.S.S.R. began aiding Ethiopia, the U.S. began selling military equipment to Somalia.

At the same time Eritrea took advantage of Mengistu's need to organize his new government, so too did the Western Somali Liberation Front (WSLF) in the Ogaden. With assistance from Somalia, the WSLF unleashed a major military offensive against Ethiopia. Mengistu's troops, who met hostility both from the north and the south, were losing. Only when thousands of Cuban troops and hundreds of millions of dollars' worth of powerful Soviet military equipment rolled into Ethiopia did the tide turn for the Ethiopian military. With a quick defeat of the WSLF in the south in 1978, the troops turned full attention on Eritrea. That same year, with thunderous fire from Soviet ships in the Red Sea into Massawa and with cluster bombs filled with napalm, Mengistu's Cuban-augmented forces regained control of Eritrean cities, but they did not defeat the Eritreans. The war for self-determination marched forward into its sixteenth year. Floods of new refugees crossed over into Sudan; others fled to the mountains. Danait said,

I learned later from my parents that Tamrat continued to write. He did not know I had been imprisoned. Finally my father wrote Tamrat and told him I had been taken to Mariam-Gimbi. My father warned him it would endanger them and me if he continued to write. When Tamrat received this news, he gave up all hope of my being alive. No one came out of Mariam-Gimbi.

Tamrat lost all interest in his future. He could see little significance in having achieved a doctoral degree, nor did he see any purpose in pursuing his financial career. He had dreamed of providing well for us and for the children we would have. Now that dream had been dashed. There were a number of Eritreans in Cologne, many attached to the Eritrean Relief Association [ERA], the humanitarian organization founded to assist the large portion of the Eritrean population displaced by the war. Tamrat volunteered his assistance and offered his financial expertise full time to the ERA. He worked first in the Cologne office and later in the main office in Khartoum.

Then there came a day like one at the end of a great habub. When the land is very dry before the rains have come and the winds are fierce, sand and dust are raised from the earth above the highest altitude a small aircraft can climb. Stinging sands lash against your body as you strain not to topple with the wind's fury. Such a habub began to diminish for me the moment the hospital's supervisor informed me I was to attend a six-week public health seminar in Nairobi. No one else, he told me, was qualified.

At that moment I knew I would either escape to freedom or die. My brother who lived in Italy knew someone in Nairobi. Through a colleague in the hospital, one on whose trust I staked my life, I sent a letter to him. I arrived in Nairobi not knowing if he had received it. Three weeks into the seminar my brother's friend invited me to dinner. I gave the Ethiopians responsible for me at the seminar the address and location of the home my brother's friends had given me. He, of course, had given a false address, an address of a family in an entirely different part of the city—people who had never heard of my host.

My brother's friend drove me northeast, out of Nairobi into the countryside. He could not travel far with me that night. After about two hours he left me with a small supply of water and food, and his blessings. I walked to the border of Sudan. For all the days I remained in Kenya, I lived in dread of being captured. On the morning of the eighth day, I arrived in a small village. The family who offered me bread told me I was in Sudan. The moment I discovered I had crossed the border, I knew my life was spared; my fear evaporated.

The village family cared for me for more than a month. I journeyed on to Kassala town, a crossover point for many refugees from Eritrea and Ethiopia. There I registered as a refugee and remained until I was accepted into West Germany a year later.

My first task was to learn the German language. I studied intensively for eight months. I became a citizen of Germany and worked as a licensed nurse

in a small, well-run private hospital. It was a very comfortable environment, and I earned a good salary. Though my body and soul were healing, I was restless. I grew to know some of the Eritrean community in Frankfurt and became more involved in their fund-raising efforts to help the EPLF in the war efforts. Several years after I arrived in Germany, I decided to attend a rally of Eritrean refugees being held in Bonn. Someone told me Tamrat was in Germany. But he was a part of my past, not my future. Still, I hoped I would see him. Six years and so much change—would we know each other?

The rally was large—about two thousand attended. For four days I looked for Tamrat. We did not connect. On the last evening as I walked to the car, I caught a glimpse of the profile of the person unlocking the door of the car parked just behind us. I knew those features so well. I could never forget them. Tamrat and I married a few months later.

At first when I came out of prison and for many years after, I did not believe I would be all right—mentally. But now, years later, I see I am. The human person is strong. For a long time I dreamed of prison and feared at night that soldiers would come and take me away again. Because of prison, I despise soldiers. Tamrat is very good and tells me to put the past away.

All those years he had put his heart into the Eritrean effort by doing financial work for the ERA. He was totally dedicated to the cause of winning the right for us Eritreans to determine our own form of government. By that time, he was working mainly out of Khartoum. All who work for the ERA volunteer their time. As the breadwinner, I continued to practice nursing. But it was time to return to Africa.

Spiritually, I did not feel right in Germany. I was comfortable and fairly well off. Wealthy in comparison to all in Eritrea. I knew I could no longer remain in Germany. I wanted to be among my people. Now we are here in Sudan. Tamrat lives in and travels from Khartoum to all parts of the world for the ERA and its financial needs. I am here in Gedaref doing my nursing in the Tawawa refugee settlement and earning a salary for the two of us. Tamrat and I see one another only on weekends either here or in Khartoum. But we are very happy.

In Tawawa Danait worked among Eritreans who had fled in the first wave of refugees in 1967 as well as among those who had come as recently as September 1990. She returned to Africa in the aftermath of the great drought of 1984–85 when international attention first focused on tiny Eritrea. Danait and Tamrat hoped to return to Eritrea to work behind the front.

THE ERITREAN WAR FRONT

In Eritrea the EPLF created an invisible world. Under the barren, rocky earth, life pulsated with indomitable, driving energy. Before dusk a scouting sortie could detect no life below, so devoid it seemed of human presence. Close to the ground all manner of sounds rose from the earth as Eritreans continued to dream and struggle for a transformed social order.

Near Orotta, a northern Eritrean town close to the Sudanese border, war wounded were carried to a 1,200-bed hospital that ran three-and-a-half miles underground. Nothing was wanting. A soldier with a face shattered with shrapnel or a limb dangling loosely by a thread of flesh could go there and be made almost whole again. With generators humming, highly educated Eritrean surgical teams, many European- or U.S.-trained, worked through the night in modern operating rooms. Modern X-ray equipment and skilled radiological readings guided the surgeon's practiced hands. From plastic drip bags manufactured in the EPLF pharmaceutical laboratory, dextrose and salt coursed down through the tubing and into the anesthetized soldier's veins. The intravenous solutions were made in a bunker constructed from three sea cargo containers. Women in labor also waited in a converted sea cargo container to bring new life in the midst of so much death. In another bunker raw materials for wonder drugs such as penicillin and tetracycline as well as aspirin and vitamin C were transformed into tablet and capsule forms.

"Vodka-Cola" trucks[18] was what someone named the reassembled trucks that plied the hundreds of miles of Eritrean-built roads over mountains and formidable terrain. Nothing was wasted by the Eritreans, nor was abandoned equipment left to rot, no matter its national origin. In the case of these trucks, Soviet and American parts were easily combined or interchanged in the underground repair shops. Everything that could be was recycled. With no set uniform, only black plastic sandals identified every Eritrean soldier. Sandals beyond repair were returned to the bunker factory and recycled into granules. New pairs were made from "a 50-50 mix of new granules and recycled granules."[19]

A passion for education was evident everywhere. Schools were created in caves, in front-line trenches, between leaning stones and under thorn-bush- and eucalyptus-branch-protected bunkers—anywhere that was out of sight and safe from strafing MiGs and armored tanks. No matter the probability for a weak child to live another year, that child learned among the others in their makeshift, well-camouflaged classrooms. Discarded brown paper package wrapping was their only writing paper. Textbooks for a wide spectrum of courses were printed underground. In front-line trenches when the battle slackened, soldiers set Kalishnakovs beside them and opened English grammar books.[20]

Just beyond the rubble of abandoned villages, mounds covered with dirt, rocks, tree limbs, and brush concealed homes of those who had not fled. Holes in ceilings provided fresh air and the earth was carved into sofa forms; empty ammunition boxes served as tables. At dusk when the people emerged from the earth, children shouted and played while their parents tended to gardens planted in bomb craters. No one was ever distracted enough to miss the sound of an approaching MiG. Nerves were poised for flight.

Food was always scarce behind the two hundred-mile fortified trench that the EPLF created in 1978 after massive gains made by the Soviet-supported

Ethiopian troops. Mengistu used food as a weapon by not allowing as much food coming into the port of Massawa to be directed behind the front as to the government-controlled areas. Bombings, at first limited to two specified times each day, became more frequent as the war wore on. Because of bombardments, Eritreans were not able to spray what crops they had with pesticides. Increasing numbers of locusts ate away the protective camouflage of twigs and branches, exposing Eritrean women and children to enemy attacks.

Food came from across the Sudanese border through the determination of the ERA and the material assistance of USAID and other donors. By means of trucks, camels, and donkeys, Eritrean volunteers made the cross-border operation effective, reaching an otherwise inaccessible and starving population. The food relief was minimal and many succumbed to starvation while others manifested stunted growth of mind and body resulting from malnutrition.

Mengistu Haile Mariam increased his war of terror, massacre, and deprivation to flush out the rebels and subdue what he claimed to be a recalcitrant Ethiopian province. The more he ravaged the land and the people, the more determined Eritreans became to defeat the person who made Ethiopia and Eritrea one of the world's poorest areas. Eritreans who settled abroad gave time and money to the effort. At home, women comprised 33 percent of the fighters.

Eritreans exiled in Sudan did not escape war totally. There was little peace in the Horn of Africa, and Sudan was embroiled in its own civil war. As long as the cold war continued and U.S. and U.S.S.R. proxy wars were fought in the Horn, exiled civilians from Eritrea, Ethiopia, Sudan, and Somalia mixed in miserable circumstances. Hope for homecoming, however, never faded as the months of exile turned into years and the numbers of refugees increased.

8

URBAN REFUGEES

*In our sleep, pain that cannot forget falls drop by drop upon
the heart and in our despair against our will comes wisdom
through the awful grace of God.*

—Aeschylus

When asked why Sudan had such a generous policy in accepting refugees, Fadil Dieb, the former deputy commissioner of refugees, responded immediately with three reasons. "We are Islamic, and the holy *Koran* admonishes us to take in the stranger. We are Africans, and attending to the downtrodden is our custom. We have been refugees before and we may be again in the future. We would want someone to take us in."

Hundreds of thousands of refugees from Eritrea, Ethiopia, Chad, and other countries bordering Sudan have benefited from its open door. For many years Sudanese generously opened their doors as wide as any country in the world to those seeking asylum from neighboring countries. Time and again, in the most difficult circumstances Sudan has given asylum to those seeking it. *Laji*, the Sudanese term for refugee, means "downtrodden." That generosity was tested from late in the 1960s to the present as waves of refugees poured in by the hundreds of thousands from Eritrea, Ethiopia, Chad, Uganda, Zaire, and Somalia, fleeing to escape war and famine. At the end of 1990 Sudan still hosted more than 725,000 refugees. Seven hundred thousand of the estimated total were refugees from Eritrea and Ethiopia who began arriving in Sudan in large numbers in 1967.

In 1990 only 370,000 refugees were officially registered under the UNHCR umbrella and were, consequently, eligible for protection and material assistance from international donors.[1] Another 355,000 spontaneously settled without registering when they crossed the border into Sudan. They were not officially recognized as refugees and therefore did not receive either the protection or the benefits afforded those who had registered. These unregistered refugees tried to eke out an existence either in the limited, poverty-plagued agricultural or pastoral areas along the Ethiopian-Sudanese border or went to

243

A young Sudanese girl who is internally displaced. She uses a few drops of precious water to wash herself in front of her family's hut.

the cities and lived clandestinely trying to find work in spite of governmental barriers.

Most of the refugees, registered or spontaneously settled, were from rural areas. They were able to adapt to the rural settlements developed for refugees by the Sudanese government. But refugees from urban areas found it difficult to adapt and tended to drift to Sudan's larger cities like Khartoum, Port Sudan, Gedaref, and Kassala. Many Sudanese feared they would encroach on an already tenuous job market and government officials wanted all refugees to live in designated refugee settlements. Sudanese hospitality and generosity extended only to refugees who registered and conformed to explicit regulations.

Unregistered urban refugees were not the only displaced people who crowded into large Sudanese urban areas. In Sudan today there is another population with a story to tell, for these people have received no generosity. They are the more than two million displaced southern Sudanese who have fled to the north from Sudan's brutal nine-year civil war. Since the war was renewed in 1983, the Arab, Muslim north has been fighting to impose Islamic law and politics on the predominantly black, Christian and animist south.

Sudan not only received refugees, it also produced millions itself during the 1980s as the north-south civil conflict escalated and became intolerably brutal. A principal weapon in this civil war has been the withholding of food from civilian populations, causing them to flee in search of food to survive. Of the 4.5 million southerners who either sought refuge in the neighboring countries of Ethiopia, Uganda, Zaire, and the Central African Republic or were internally displaced, approximately 2 million took shelter in large northern cities such as Khartoum and Port Sudan. Others fled their villages to cities in southern and eastern Sudan. Unlike their registered refugee counterparts from other countries, internally displaced Sudanese have received little or no assistance or protection from the government, the international community, or ordinary Sudanese citizens. In the world today, there are twenty to thirty million internally displaced people in more than twenty-five nations. They outnumber those who seek asylum by crossing a border, but they benefit from none of the protective legal instruments in place for those who flee to another nation.

Khartoum, the capital of Sudan, is unique in that it hosts tens of thousands of spontaneously settled, unregistered refugees from Eritrea and Ethiopia and more than 1.5 million southern Sudanese. There, as well as in other Sudanese cities, unregistered urban Ethiopians and Eritreans live as precariously as do the southern Sudanese. The host, the government of Sudan, welcomes neither population, for Sudan's refugee policy calls for rural or semiurban settlements in areas specifically set aside for the purpose of housing all who seek asylum in Sudan. Refugees without special work permits are unrecognized and unassisted. Alternately ignored or harassed by the government is the internally displaced population from the south, who belong predominantly to the Dinka and Nuer tribes, the backbone of the rebel Sudan People's Liberation Army

(SPLA). As Sudan cries "too many, too long"[2] and tries by various methods to rid the larger Sudanese cities of both populations, the refugees and the internally displaced struggle to survive side by side.

BACKGROUND TO SUDAN'S CIVIL WAR

Sudan is the largest country on the African continent and its nationals are among the poorest and least literate in the world. Spreading out over one million square miles, twice the size of Alaska, the vast majority of its twenty-four million people have lived with a per capita income of less than four hundred dollars per year for more than a decade, and pestilence of biblical proportion—famine, floods, locusts, war—has battered both the country's fragile economy and the land. The war between the north and the south has been particularly devastating. Since independence from Britain in 1956, Sudan has been embroiled in civil strife for twenty-four of its thirty-five years as a sovereign state. The eleven-year hiatus from gunfire and military maneuvers occurred between 1972 and 1983.

Like most of the civil conflicts on the African continent in the second half of the twentieth century, the roots of Sudan's civil war lie in its colonial past. The country's early history set the stage for animosities between the predominantly Arab Muslim north and the minority African Christian and animist south when Egypt invaded and subdued Sudan in 1821. Under British tutelage and funding, Egypt opened trade routes in northern Sudan and paved the way for unprincipled plunderers to move into the south and take not only material goods and natural resources, but also humans whom they arrantly sold into slavery.

In 1881, the same year that Britain occupied Egypt, the Sudanese, led by Muhammad Ahmed the *mahdi* (religious enlightened one), rose up against their conquerors and defeated them in 1885, killing the Egyptian-appointed British governor of Sudan, Charles Gordon. In 1898, thirteen years later, Horatio Kitchener, then British governor of Sudan and commander of the Egyptian army, defeated the Mahdist forces in the Battle of Omdurman. Britain and Egypt signed a "condominium," effectively giving political power in Sudan to the British. For twelve years, 1924–36, after some Egyptian troops in Sudan assisted a Sudanese separatist group seeking independence, Britain ousted the Egyptian army and ruled Sudan alone until 1936 when Egypt and Britain once again joined in governing the nation, with British occupation agreed to by both parties.

The British had separate policies for northern and southern Sudan. The focus of economic development was on the north and the seat of government remained in Khartoum.[3] Under the "southern policy," however, the south was virtually ignored economically, politically, and socially. What negligible attention was given in health care, education, and community development came through missionaries who were encouraged to go there by the British. Christianity rather than Islam was promoted, as was English rather than Arabic.

Tribal diversity precluded the threat of a united opposition to British rule in the south, lack of education among most of the southern people prevented development, and the absence of good transportation ensured isolation. But unrest prevailed throughout both north and south, and Britain acceded to Sudan's push for independence in 1955. On January 1, 1956, Sudan became a sovereign nation.

The seeds of civil war, though, had already taken root, and independence did not forestall its escalation. The British had calculated that Uganda would incorporate southern Sudan into its territory, leaving northern Sudan to develop on its own with its Islamic cultural identity. They were mistaken. After independence, when the north and the south became one nation, the north was no more cognizant of the developmental needs of the south than the British had been, nor were northern officials willing to incorporate more southerners into the administration of the country. When the British had "Sudanized" the government in 1953, only four posts out of eight hundred went to southern Sudanese.[4] After the British flag was lowered in 1955, no more went to the south.

In fact, the north tried to impose both Islam and Arabic on Sudan's southern population. Such actions became the immediate cause of the seventeen-year north-south conflict that had festered for years and finally broke out in 1955. Several hundred thousand Sudanese died as the south sought independence. Peace was attained on paper in 1972 with the Addis Ababa Agreement, according the south limited regional autonomy with its own government and parliament. But the underlying hostility and the intrusion by the Khartoum government into the constitutionally given powers of the south remained an impediment to the building of a true federation.

By 1972 Sudan was under the rule of its fourth government since independence less than twenty years earlier. Colonel Jafaar al-Nimeiri had taken power in 1969. Although Nimeiri achieved peace for a time, his actions renewed military hostilities in 1983. In the intervening years between the peace accord and the outbreak of new hostilities, Nimeiri launched some of the most ambitious and most flawed development schemes, moving during his sixteen years as head of state from socialist nationalization of the economy to capitalism. Neither brought prosperity to the nation. Instead, the country was plunged into a debt of $8 billion, exacerbated in part by the 1973–74 oil crisis. Total Sudanese exports did not meet the interest payments of the debt. While a few of the powerful lined their pockets with gold, the majority of Sudanese went to bed hungry and much of the money intended for development was squandered. Nimeiri, who wanted to make Sudan the "breadbasket of the Middle East," ignored all signs of an impending drought in the mid-1980s. Blinded to the reality of the economic plight of the nation and to the proportions of the drought of 1984–85 that took at least 250,000 Sudanese lives, he continued to plot grandiose schemes for development using low-cost petro-dollar loans.

The southern Sudanese gained nothing from the plans of the Nimeiri government and remained deplorably underdeveloped. In fact the government's attempt to exploit southern resources was one of the causes of the renewal of armed civil conflict. Nimeiri sought to place the rich southern oil fields within the northern sphere of influence and to divert Nile waters away from the south, both without proper compensation or recognition of southern claims.

Nimeiri rescinded recognition of the regional autonomy for the south that had been agreed to in the Addis Ababa Treaty of 1972. Distrustful of a united south, he split the area into three independently governed regions and imposed Arabic as the official language. In response to the economic and political actions taken by the Khartoum government, a sizable number of soldiers from the south mutinied and followed a new leader, Dr. John Garang, a former Sudanese army colonel and an agricultural economist with a doctorate from Iowa State University. With his leadership, they formed the SPLA in conjunction with the Sudan People's Liberation Movement (SPLM). Theirs was not a separatist movement as had been true of the southern troops of the earlier civil war; rather, the troops under John Garang sought full incorporation into a democratic nation that recognized the rights and equality of all citizens. Such recognition would have to include the repeal of the Muslim *shari'a* laws, institution of a secular constitution, and economic development of the south. Economic neglect of the south by the Khartoum government and domination of the south by the northern Arab-Muslim majority were no longer acceptable.

What finally led to armed rebellion was the introduction of the "September Laws" by the Nimeiri government in 1983. The strictest form of *shari'a* (Islamic law) was placed on both the north and the south—Muslim, Christian, and animist alike—and Islamic taxes were levied. Under *shari'a* a person could be stoned or flogged or sentenced to the amputation of one or more limbs or even crucified for a multitude of infractions and crimes—from consuming alcohol to murder. If the government wanted punishment imputed, the courts complied whether or not the action merited such harsh retribution. What was a crime under Islam might not be for adherents of Christianity or traditional religions. Yet Islamic law governed all, at least on the books.

In 1985, after once again raising food and fuel prices, Nimeiri was overthrown by the military and went into exile in Egypt. The people had risen in protest, particularly trade unionists, professionals, political activists, farmers, and intellectuals. Very soon the military gave way to democratic government and Sudanese citizens voted into power a coalition government headed by Sadiq al-Mahdi, who had been the leader of the Umma party from 1964 to 1969 and prime minister from 1966 to 1967. It was Sudan's first election in seventeen years. In 1985, because of the war, thirty-seven of the sixty-seven southern constituencies could not vote; subsequently, the SPLA refused to vote. As a result, the north dominated the government.

The war and a worsening economy plagued the prime minister's administration. The two were intertwined, as the government diverted funds from the social needs of the people to the military to finance the war. When he took office in 1985, Mahdi, his Umma party, and the Democratic Unionist party (DUP), a moderate party in the coalition government, favored settling the civil war. Mahdi and John Garang were negotiating a settlement in August 1986 when, after the International Committee of the Red Cross (ICRC) had airlifted emergency relief into a government-held town, the SPLA shot down a civilian plane, killing all sixty people aboard. Negotiations ceased and the war escalated. Following the breakdown of negotiations, Mahdi shifted from his alliance with the DUP and joined forces with the National Islamic Front (NIF), the fundamentalist faction in the coalition. Together they pursued the war with greater vigor and enforced *shari'a* more stringently.

As Mahdi escalated the war, the SPLA and DUP leaders drew up and signed a peace plan in November 1988. The signatories to the "November Plan" offered a cease-fire, the freezing of *shari'a*, and called for a constitutional conference of all parties in Sudan — north and south, rebel and government. At first Mahdi would not present the plan to his cabinet, and the parliament rejected it, favoring the objections of the fundamentalist NIF party to the abolition of *shari'a*.[5] In protest, the DUP bowed out of the coalition.

Under pressure from the army, the Sudanese population, and Sudan's greatest benefactor, the United States, Mahdi once again sought peace. In the south the army was losing the war, and in the north civilians protested the state of the economy. In the United States media attention was given to the massive starvation of the people in the south. The use of food as a weapon by both sides brought an outcry from the American public, which called for the president and Congress to withhold funds and pressure the Khartoum government to allow relief food and medical supplies to reach all areas of the south and to negotiate for peace with the SPLA. Up to this point, the Mahdi government had deliberately not requested famine relief for the south, which was the stronghold of the SPLA, and the U.S. government and other Western donor countries had acquiesced to the policies of Sadiq al-Mahdi's government.

In the south John Garang's forces controlled the countryside and surrounded the garrison towns held by the army. Little or no food could get into these towns, and the SPLA threatened to shoot down cargo planes airlifting supplies to these government garrisons. The government military forces gave the prime minister an ultimatum — either supply the troops with adequate personnel and arms to achieve victory or settle the war with a peace agreement. Otherwise, the army determined, the prime minister should step aside. Mahdi decided to pursue peace.

In March 1989, when the prime minister agreed to the proposed "November [1988] Plan" of the SPLA and the DUP, the DUP and NIF changed places — the DUP returned to the government and the NIF walked out. Under no conditions would the NIF agree to the abolition of *shari'a*. NIF party members would call for a revolution before acquiescing to an end of Islamic law in Sudan.[6] A cease-fire was agreed upon and *shari'a* was to be frozen.

Mahdi was to meet with John Garang on July 4, 1989, with September 18, 1989, as the day set for the convening of the constitutional conference.[7]

For some months there had been speculation of an imminent coup, and the prime minister had taken precautions. On June 29, 1989, Prime Minister Mahdi and his wife were attending an evening wedding, the celebration lasting until early morning on June 30. As the couple was about to leave the party, aides notified Mahdi that their home was surrounded by soldiers.[8] Shortly thereafter, Mahdi, apparently after he jumped from the second-story balcony of his host's home in an attempt to escape, was arrested and taken to Khartoum's main jail.

In a military coup, then Brigadier Omar Hassam Achmed al-Bashir (later designating himself lieutenant-general) became the head of state of the seventh Sudanese government since the nation's independence in 1956, thirty-three years earlier. The little-known officer, a paratroop commander who had fought in the south, said his top priorities were to end the war and revive Sudan's failed economy. Unlike the military coup of 1985, led by General Abdel Rahman Suwar al-Dahab, whose intention was to turn his government over to a democratically elected one, Bashir retained power for himself and his Revolutionary Command Council (RCC). His government was not to be a transitional one. From the beginning, when he declared himself prime minister, defense minister, and commander-in-chief of the armed forces, he had no intention of relinquishing power. To ensure his hold on the government, Bashir suspended the constitution, dissolved parliament, banned political parties, forbad civilian association meetings without government permission, shut down the free press, declared a nationwide state of emergency, and set a curfew.

The Sudanese people hoped that this government would indeed pull the country out of its intractable economic chaos and unresolved war. As the new ruler lashed out against government corruption, hoarding, and black marketeering, he opened warehouses filled with goods held back from the market to keep prices high. Anyone caught selling goods above the government's official low prices could be jailed. There was to be no leniency. For a few weeks there was an abundance of goods in the *souk* (market), with people able to buy sugar, kerosene for cooking, and fuel for automobiles. As suddenly as the goods appeared, they were sold.

After the hoarded stores of supplies had been consumed, nothing remained to sell as the new government had done nothing to turn around either the economy or the war. With an inflation rate of 80 percent, there was no plan for economic development, and, by November 1989, there was an official determination to conclude the war by a military victory rather than the hoped-for negotiated settlement. In fact, there has been speculation that Bashir's coup was supported by fundamentalist Muslims in order to sabotage any plan for peace. Many businessmen with no incentive to remain in their country left, while hundreds of thousands more southerners trekked to northern cities or sought asylum in neighboring countries before they starved to death.

Throughout Sudan, shelves were bare, cooking kerosene extremely scarce, gas lines formed for miles if any fuel reached the pumps, the debt rose to $13 billion, and the war ground on at a cost of $1 million a day. In Port Sudan, Sudan's only deep water port on the Red Sea, transport trucks sat idle, loaded with essential goods but without fuel. The drivers lined up the trucks—fifty or sixty of them—near fuel pumps. Night after night they slept under the flatbeds, hoping that a delivery of gasoline would allow them to transport their goods to Khartoum. Most of Sudan's imports arrive by sea and are carried by truck on the one tarmac road leading south to Kassala, west through Gedaref, and north to Khartoum. When the trucks did not roll, none of the cities received supplies.

FOOD AS A WEAPON OF WAR

Under the leadership of both Prime Minister Sadiq al-Mahdi and Lieutenant-General Omar al-Bashir the war in the south has been one of the most vicious and deadly on the African continent. Following the August 1986 downing of a civilian aircraft by the SPLA, effectively halting the proposed ICRC airlift of relief supplies, Sadiq al-Mahdi struck back with a blatant and vengeful use of food as a weapon, and the SPLA reacted in kind. Neither side relented until early 1989. In 1988 alone more than 250,000 southern Sudanese died from starvation as the military leaders on both sides refused to allow food to reach civilian populations believed to be loyal to one opponent or the other. One hundred eighty thousand of the dead were said to be children.[9] Only a few thousand were members of the military forces. The greatest numbers were women, children, and the elderly who, like the Khmer people, became defenseless pawns in a war in which the leaders on either side cared little for the ordinary people. Humanitarian needs ranked far below military strategies and international diplomacy.

The majority of the six million southern Sudanese, including the SPLA leader, John Garang, belong to the Dinka tribe. Extremely tall and proud by any standards, the Dinka are the cattle herders of the south, feared by many other neighboring tribes. The war and the drought of 1984–85 had already weakened them and killed some of their herds. With rains and a normal harvest they could have survived, but the war-induced famine that followed devastated them.

Three southern provinces, Bahr el Ghazal, Upper Nile, and Equatoria, were the hardest hit by the war-induced famine. Bahr el Ghazal's population is almost exclusively Dinka; Equatoria's and Upper Nile's, a mixture of tribes. As the SPLA's control of the countryside increased, the tactics of the Sudanese military hardened, particularly in the government-held garrison towns. In addition, the government began forming militias by arming Arab tribes—Baggara, Misseirya, Reizegaat, Murahaleen—with AK-47 assault rifles, giving them license to track down and terrorize their traditional tribal enemies, particularly the Dinka, with impunity.

Retaliatory massacres by militia were not uncommon. One such reprisal followed an SPLA attack on the army garrison at Safaha on the border between Bahr el Ghazal Province and Dafur Province. Members of the Reizegaat militia stormed the Dinka village of Ad-Dhein, burned the church, rounded up six thousand civilians, and forced them into the railway station. There members of the militia opened fire on the civilians, killing scores of people. At least five hundred Dinka were burned alive in the railway police center. Others fled toward the empty rail cars on the tracks. Before the village people were able to start the locomotive, the armed attackers set fire to the first car, burning to death more than two hundred Dinka who had sought safety within. After the train's engine was started, people in the other cars were able to escape to a town further north, leaving their village and their homes behind with nothing but the clothes they were wearing.[10]

A second massacre occurred a year later south of Khartoum. Southern Shilluk tribal people, who were farmhands, had labored in the area and lived peaceably with their Arab employers. Eleven, who were Christians, refused to work for another Arab farmer until after their Christmas celebration. The farmer called on local police to force the farmhands into submission. The police refused and a fight ensued. The Arab farmer was killed and the eleven Christian farmhands were arrested. When the farmer's driver returned to his village and informed the family, they gathered an armed militia, traveled to the village, and opened fire on defenseless men, women, and children. It is reported that at least seven hundred Christians died. Even those who sought refuge in the police station were slaughtered after the policemen were removed from their post. Others who tried to swim the Nile to escape drowned. The killings spread to other small surrounding villages of the Dinka, Nuer, and Burun tribes. Hundreds of bodies were bulldozed into mass graves. Most of those who survived fled, seeking asylum elsewhere.[11]

Food supplies were also jeopardized by the scorched-earth tactics used by both the SPLA and the government military, which burned villages and fields, frequently killing many villagers and their cattle. The northern-based government hoped that depopulating the south would bring victory. All over the south, people were on the move, seeking safety, but rarely finding it either in northern cities such as Khartoum, another country such as Ethiopia, or other locations in the south. It has been reported that up to 85 percent of Sudan's southern population was displaced.[12] As starvation increased and as more people became desperate for food, thousands more died.

Among the 350,000 who fled to Ethiopia, numerous survivors recounted stories of passing villages and finding nothing but strewn, disconnected bones of humans who had starved without leaving home and who, after dying, had become food for hyenas and vultures. Along the way the survivors saw individual skeletal remains of those too weak to continue the journey.

Those who headed for southern towns or north to Khartoum and Port Sudan encountered similar situations. Arab militias struck many vulnerable groups, particularly parties of women and children who had been left heads of households.

Akub fled with her two daughters, nine-year-old Baketa and ten-year-old Abuc, after their village near the southern town of Wau had been looted and burned. "The soldiers came in the late afternoon," Akub began.

They were heavily armed and made us give them all the food we had in our home. They did the same to our neighbors. Then they began to take every-thing—our clothes, jewelry, money, whatever we had. Next they lined up the men who were present in the village and shot them. My husband was among them. I saw him fall from the gunfire. They killed our cattle and burned our homes.

After they left, we had nowhere to go. That night we slept in the brush near the village, and the following morning we started walking north. We had heard that many were going to Aweil because there was food and shelter. But by the time we arrived Aweil was so crowded that people could not find places to sleep. Many children were dying, especially from measles and diarrhea.

With four other women from our village, I decided to try to go further north. That was the biggest mistake of our lives. But what were we to do? We had to find food to survive.

A large group of Arab militia surrounded us. They dismounted their horses and pointed their rifles at us. We were five women and sixteen children. There must have been forty of them. Not one of us, women or children, was left untouched. They raped the women and the girl children over and over and beat the boys. Baketa has never spoken since that day. It is as though her spirit departed. I cannot see life behind her eyes, even though they are open.

When we were sold to Arab farmers, we were all separated. Baketa stayed with me, but Abuc was sold to another farmer. I have never seen my child again. Every day I worked in the durrah fields and did work for the farmer's wife. One day when her husband was away, she told me to run with Baketa and try to get to Khartoum. It would do us no good to try to return to Aweil or Wau, she said.

Now that we are here in Khartoum, our lives are no easier because we live on a garbage dump under a burlap bag. We are always afraid soldiers will bulldoze our camp and we will be forced to move again.

Tens of thousands of the refugees who did reach southern towns like Aweil, Abyei, el Muglad, el Meiram, Wau, Juba, and Torit did not find sanctuary or sustenance. One hundred thousand sought refuge in Aweil; seventy-five thousand walked to Wau. One hundred people were dying each day. In the summer of 1988, in the government garrison town of Aweil where thousands of Dinka had fled, almost every child under five died during a measles epidemic. The civil war made it impossible to immunize the children against the disease. Planes carrying the vaccines were not given permission to land, and in Aweil and other towns, hospitals were nothing more than empty structures without beds, bedding, or medical supplies. What doctors there were could give scant medical care to the multitudes who needed a physician's attention. Nearly eight thousand refugees died in this town because food and medical supplies could not reach them, and a large proportion of them were children. In many towns and villages virtually all children under the age of three died, for they were the most vulnerable. Far more girls died than boys, because when choices were made of who would live and who would die, the girl children were seen as the more expendable. Extreme malnutrition was common. Throughout the south, nearly one out of every five children died before the age of one. Mothers had no milk and there was no other food.

In the displaced persons area near el Meiram, 3,600 people died in a space of four months between June and October 1988. According to an Africa Watch Report:

> These figures imply death rates at almost incredible levels of 7.1% per week, or one percent per day [a higher rate than that of Korem feeding camp in Ethiopia during the 1984 Ethiopian famine that gained world wide attention and response]. 10,000 people died in Abyei between January and October. Relief agencies have estimated that a total of 30,000 displaced people died from famine in southern Kordofan in the summer of 1988, under the eyes of army garrisons, while wagons of relief grain stood idle in nearby railway sidings.[13]

In some instances where food was available, merchants, unhampered by the military, would sell grain for as much as 400 to 1,000 percent profit. Emaciated mothers holding dying, skeletal children watched their children succumb to purposeless yet deliberately intended deaths. Desperate parents might sell a child, most frequently a girl child, for as little as five dollars to Arab tribesmen, believing that perhaps the child would have more of a chance of access to food and, consequently, be more likely to survive. Others sold a child to ensure their own survival, at least for the moment. Some were drawn to towns by rumors of food, only to find there was nothing. Others, too hungry and too afraid of armed attacks, stayed behind. Before trees were stripped of leaves and before wood for fuel became impossible to find (or inaccessible to the mine-surrounded towns), parents boiled leaves and lily pads to stave off hunger. Adults frequently went two and three days without any food. Food became the obsession of people whose lives revolved around seeking nourishment.

The government continued to deny there was a famine and refused Western relief workers access to the devastated areas. The U.S. government and other donor nations maintained their conciliating manner toward the Khartoum government, allowing Sudanese officials to determine relief needs. Western relief workers who saw what was happening could do little to respond to the needs of a starving population, for they were allowed to remain in the country only as long as the government permitted. They feared that if they crossed the government in any significant way, they would be expelled and the little they were doing would be negated. Some relief agencies were expelled from the south in 1988.

While tens of thousands died from starvation, the rebels and the government troops both continued to obstruct the delivery of emergency relief. The army insisted that any convoys include relief and commercial trucks and that they be escorted by the military to ward off rebel attacks. Rebels insisted that such convoys were little more than camouflage for transporting military weapons and supplies for the government soldiers in rebel-encircled towns. Time and again SPLA soldiers blew up escorted convoys. Just as frequently the government refused to give relief trucks permission to proceed, pleading that the rebels would abscond with the food en route. Sometimes the government held convoys for months before allowing them to proceed. Transport by air was equally difficult. John Garang stated that he would shoot down any aircraft attempting to land in Juba. The airport was closed for more than a month, depriving the people in the city of much needed food and medical relief.

Bishop Paride Taban, the Catholic bishop of Torit, related his experience of traveling the short distance between Juba and Torit with a convoy under attack.

In 1988, I traveled with a convoy to Juba and then to Rome. When I came back from Rome, I found it was impossible to return to Torit, because the road was mined. I got a message that many people were dying; so I pushed the government for a military convoy to carry relief food. Many advised that the convoy would be destroyed. I decided to go anyway. There was a convoy of nearly 100 lorries—60 relief lorries and the rest were military. In the convoy accompanying us, there were nearly 1,000 soldiers. The road was so mined that we couldn't travel on it. So the lorries had to go through the bush, and we had so many ambushes. Eighty-four miles took us 31 days in which over 30 lorries were destroyed by the SPLA and by mines. Over 100 people were wounded, and over 50 people died.

After 31 days, with the balance of the lorries, we managed to enter Torit alive. We saw many wounded people. Every day we had to bury people either blown up by anti-personnel mines or killed in ambushes. When we arrived with the balance of the food in July 1988, we found three priests had remained in Torit town. They were very tired from burying people, using road graders. The food helped the people to survive. After the SPLA closed the way, we made an appeal. I asked the commander to let those who do not fear the SPLA move out of the town because there were too many people in the town.

By 1989 the situation was desperate. Many soldiers even were dying. Norwegian People's Aid wanted to parachute food and the government refused. Only the government could parachute food for the army—only one kilogram of food for 15 days for a soldier. Yet they would parachute arms for these soldiers who were dying of hunger. On February 26, 1989, the SPLA took over the town of Torit. Many soldiers fled and many died on the way to Juba or Uganda of hunger, thirst, or ambush.[14]

When food did reach the government garrison towns, the people did not receive the bulk of the relief. "We are dying like animals, without being counted," the Episcopal archbishop of Juba lamented in November 1988. "Children, pregnant women, old people are dying."[15] The bishop of Torit counseled his people to prepare their souls for death[16] at a time when several military planes either landed in Torit and Juba each day or else made air drops bringing military supplies and food to the troops.

What was worse was the fact that the military cargo that reached Juba and Torit contained bags of grain that went to the Arab merchants who lived in the towns rather than to the civilians. In turn, the merchants sold the grain to anyone who could pay the exorbitant price demanded, often the equivalent of several months' wages. The merchants and the army personnel who connived with them made handsome profits while the hostage civilian population ate leaves and waited to be buried.[17] If any grain dropped inadvertently from a merchant's bag, riots broke out as people pushed to gather whatever they could. Desperate, they scraped the dust for every spilled kernel and picked them up one by one. Children vied for the meager offerings, with the older and larger ones knocking down the smaller and younger boys and girls. Few had any source of fuel for cooking the few grains and leaves they could gather. Coal had to be imported and not many trees remained. People were reduced to digging the roots of trees for fuel.[18]

Given the opportunity, ordinary civilians foraged for food in the area surrounding Juba's perimeter or attempted to plant gardens. Usually the government soldiers, who probably numbered close to ten thousand in Juba, would not allow them to leave for fear they would join up with the SPLA. The civilians were held captive, in the belief that the presence of so many southern civilians would deter the SPLA from engaging in massive shelling of the town. The SPLA, in turn, ringed the perimeter with mines to keep the military inside the city. Civilians were squeezed between the two forces. They could not plant, purchase grain, forage, or seek safety elsewhere. Anyone attempting to leave might be killed or at least forced back.

Late in 1988 the massive starvations of southern Sudanese came to the attention of the Western public through the media. At this time, as the U.S. government and other donor nations pressured Prime Minister Sadiq al-Mahdi to change the course of the war and as a public outcry grew against the crimes perpetrated on the Sudanese people, Sudanese government and SPLA leaders agreed that international relief efforts could become operative in the war zones.

UNICEF created Operation Lifeline Sudan (OLS), an unprecedented humanitarian relief effort to reach both sides in the conflict, and by early 1989 the relief operation was supplying food and medical supplies to the most devastated areas of southern Sudan. James Grant, who headed the program, remarked, "Never before have we seen a situation of civil conflict where the two major parties agreed to one common plan of action and [have] gone on to agree to corridors of tranquility down which relief convoys, unescorted, can pass freely."[19]

Before the rainy season began in June, at least sixty thousand tons of food had been delivered in three provinces—Upper Nile, Bahr el Ghazal, and Equatoria. Much had come over land in large convoys of trucks from Nairobi. One story clearly describes the unprecedented cooperation between the government and the SPLA. A train with one hundred cars filled with food and medical supplies was destined for Aweil in Bahr el Ghazal. En route the train stopped for refueling at a small government-held town. Because it was so long, the end of the train remained in an adjacent rebel-held area. Government soldiers protected the part of the train in its territory while rebel troops protected the remaining cars in the area under their control. The train reached its destination safely.[20] Such cooperation between April and September 1989 was not unusual, for there was a virtual cease-fire in effect. Access to relief food, coupled with a lessening of the famine, enabled more Sudanese to escape the severe malnutrition that had caused hundreds of thousands of deaths the previous year.

Neither the easy access nor the cease-fire lasted for long. Massive and deliberate starvation tactics began once again. As the peace talks were about to convene in June 1989, a U.N. plane was bombed as it delivered food to Torit. It was speculated that the purpose of the bombing was to sabotage the peace initiatives. By the end of that month, Bashir's coup had taken place. Shortly after taking control of the government, Bashir scuttled all peace initiatives.

Throughout 1990 and 1991 Bashir's government did all it could to hamper UNICEF's efforts to get food and medical supplies to a south growing more desperate by the month. Even though Bashir contended that he wanted Operation Lifeline Sudan to continue, once the cease-fire was no longer observed, he banned flights of planes carrying relief supplies to rebel-held territory. Even when goods began to flow, government troops and armed Arab tribal militia pillaged relief trains. Barges were attacked as they flowed up the Nile. Trains and barges were delayed as much as a year, while the government and the SPLA argued that most of the food would be distributed to the other's enemy. Planes of the United Nations and the ICRC were strafed. Relief workers were denied travel permits and forbidden to carry two-way radios that kept them in contact with Khartoum. One plane granted government permission to fly was shot down. Three relief workers from *Médecins sans Frontières* lost their lives. Other workers, now unable to communicate with Khartoum headquarters, left their isolated posts, especially when fighting resumed. Once again, villagers and townspeople in the south had only limited access to food and medical assistance. People who had sought and found relief assistance in towns in 1989 returned the following year only to find no food was available.

The SPLA retaliated against the government by attacking relief operations as well and by more tightly encircling garrison towns filled with defenseless civilian hostages. In addition the SPLA called for the civilians held in these towns to come out into the countryside, even though they were powerless to feed them, leaving the remaining military vulnerable to SPLA siege.

Operation Lifeline Sudan had hoped to initiate a second phase of its operation, with a goal of development rather than simple relief. It sought to deliver seeds, tools, and working supplies so that in the less war-torn areas of the south, Sudanese could begin feeding themselves again. It wanted to assist the Dinkas and other cattle-herding tribes to rebuild their herds. The OLS's hopes were dashed. Instead, in 1990 and 1991 in the face of a war- and weather-induced famine that threatened to be greater than the 1984–85 Ethiopian famine, people in areas not directly under fire who had any seeds, tools, or cattle sold them, and abandoned their land—once again becoming supplicants to the international community.

The United Nations always operates within the sanctions of a government recognized by the United Nations, and the ICRC must have its personnel present for the distribution and implementation of goods that it provides. In addition, the Red Cross charter requires absolute impartiality in the service of rivals in a conflict. Both the United Nations and the ICRC were stymied by the recalcitrance of the Khartoum government to allow either group to operate freely in the best interests of the southern civilians. When the Red Cross was forced by the circumstances of war to suspend its flights or take its personnel out of an area, thousands of men, women, and children were adversely affected. For example, without a representative present, available Red Cross animal vaccines could not be distributed and the cattle could not be immunized. Likewise, hospitals could not be resupplied if Red Cross personnel were not present for monitoring purposes.

In 1990–91 as the specter rose of a new drought and of war-induced famine in the Horn of Africa, more than eleven million Sudanese from all parts of the country were at risk of starvation and in need of more than a million tons of grain for survival. In spite of a donor-weary world skeptical of its ability to reach those who were in need, about half of what was required was available for delivery, but much of it was not allowed to move.

The story of the silver and white Red Cross II barge exemplifies the political and military machinations preventing delivery of donor goods. The government of Norway gave the ICRC a large barge capable of carrying sixty metric tons of supplies (at one-eighth of the cost of airlifting food) through even the tropical, swampy, crocodile-, snake-, and mosquito-infested Sudd, a section of the Nile where the river breaks up into twisting, stagnant streams. With transfers of food from the barge at strategic points to convoys of trucks, food would become available to some of the most inaccessible war zones, particularly areas in Bahr el Ghazal and Upper Nile. When the Khartoum government heard about the presence of the barge, leaders forbad its movement outside government-held territory, so suspicious were they that the barge operators would deliver not only food to rebel areas but also tanks, missiles, and guns. To the bewilderment and consternation of the people of Bor, a small town in the south of Upper Nile Province, the $1 million barge remained tied to Bor's dock, unable to be loaded with food and medical relief that could help save millions of lives.[21]

In addition to impeding delivery of available assistance, Sudan's leader, General Bashir, refused to acknowledge publicly that there was a food shortage in the country. He boasted, instead, the advances in self-sufficiency among his people. He defiantly stated that even if there were a famine, he would not reveal this to an interfering Western world. Without the proclamation of a food emergency or a request for outside assistance, donors stood by with hands tied. Bashir was so obsessed with winning the war that in 1989–90 he sold almost all Sudan's grain reserves to gain foreign exchange for financing his $1-million-a-day war.

Clearly Bashir was and is blatantly violating the human rights of a large number of Sudanese citizens. Yet behind the shield of national sovereignty, he is able to retreat from responsibility to the people and to the international community's cry for access to those dying as a result of his policies. Sudan's problems are internal, he contends, and he challenges anyone who would interfere in the nation's sovereign, private affairs. According to Bashir, the enactment of domestic policies is his prerogative, no matter how they affect the citizens of the nation.

Bashir considers those outside his control as sympathizers and supporters of the rebel forces. Whether or not the civilians caught in the vise of the opposing forces want to declare loyalty to one side or the other, they are marked by each side as friends or enemies and suffer the consequences of attack, with little help from either the government or the SPLA.

At the heart of this situation, as in many situations around the world where massive numbers of people are internally displaced by civil strife, is the concern for national sovereign rights over human rights. Sovereignty carries responsibilities. Citizens of every nation have the right to expect protection from their government. Is there a point beyond which a government can go in abusing those citizens it is bound to protect without some outside intervention? Can a ruler kill citizens with impunity?

In 1992 the Refugee Policy Group of Washington, D.C., convened a conference dealing with the issue of the human rights of the internally displaced. Tellingly, the report stated:

> Answering these questions is certainly made more difficult by an international system that is built more upon sovereignty than upon the rights of the people in the countries concerned. Respect for sovereignty has been the cornerstone of the United Nations system and the basis for the provision of humanitarian aid to beleaguered populations. Time and again, respect for sovereignty has taken precedence over the equally compelling obligations of states to provide humanitarian assistance to persons at risk and to promote observance of human rights . . .

The vast range of human rights agreements, signed and ratified by U.N. member states, not only oblige governments to protect the human rights of their citizens, but also require other governments to review their records . . . When governments seriously violate them, they open themselves up to criticism and potentially to international actions.[22]

While refugees who have crossed an international border are given safe haven by legal international instruments that define them as a people with rights and that assure protection, the internally displaced have no legal recourse. The internally displaced have fled their homes for the same reasons as those who cross borders, except they have remained within their own country. They are citizens of sovereign nations, and few national leaders would consider allowing outsiders to impinge on their sovereignty. To them, unrequested interference from other nations smacks of a new colonialism. Organizations like the United Nations, the ICRC, and NGOs are in a country like Sudan only at the sufferance of the recognized government. They must tread lightly when it comes to actions that might give Bashir cause for expelling them. Humanitarian organizations must consider the impact on those they are trying to benefit. If they assist civilian victims in a conflict situation regardless of objections of a leader like Bashir, they must weigh whether they will endanger even more lives than those they want to assist. At the same time, the humanitarian organizations feel a moral responsibility to work toward a cessation of the conflict or at least negotiate for neutral corridors through which food and medicine can reach those citizens in danger of starvation and death. In some cases "voluntary agencies have taken the position that humanitarian concerns must take primacy over state imperatives and that governments forfeit their sovereignty when they refuse to meet the humanitarian needs of their population."[23]

Until there is a public outcry against the repression of a class of people and for the implementation of a legal mechanism to protect and assist them, governments like Bashir's will continue to impose order on the people. As long as multilateral assistance, condoned by the U.S. government among others, continues to flow into Sudan through the World Bank and the International Monetary Fund, Bashir's government is able to maintain the capacity to wage civil war. Incredibly, Western donors threatened to suspend humanitarian relief to Sudan. Such an action would only increase the number of civilians threatened with starvation. Cutting multilateral aid rather than the humanitarian assistance to civilians would be a more logical sanction. What is needed is a trenchant look at donor policy and strategy that supports regimes that abuse their people.

INTERNALLY DISPLACED IN KHARTOUM

Because of the intensity and the viciousness of Sudan's civil war and because of the new and ravishing drought, hundreds of thousands of Sudanese remain on the move in 1992. Since 1986 it was in the economically exhausted cities in the north, particularly Khartoum and Port Sudan, that at least two million internally displaced Sudanese sought refuge. There they poked sticks into the dry ground and covered them with discarded burlap grain bags, empty cardboard boxes, or whatever refuse they could find in the surrounding garbage dumps, and called it shelter.

The first Sudanese seeking asylum in Khartoum were Arab victims of the 1984 drought. Officials were not disturbed by their presence, for most found lodging with relatives, and, as they were Arabs, they would not "contaminate" the Islamic foundation of the city. But in 1986 both Christian and animist southerners began to appear. At first groups of male children appeared on the streets. When parents were no longer able to provide for the whole family but wanted the male children to survive, they urged their sons to go where the parents believed they could find a source of food and work. The children did not speak Arabic and had no relatives in Khartoum who could harbor them. They lived on the streets, begging and covering themselves with sand to ward off the desert cold during December nights. By 1988 many parents in the south could no longer feed themselves; those who did not die of starvation sought refuge elsewhere.

They gathered by the tens of thousands. By 1990 forty-eight shanty towns, each populated with 10,000 to more than 100,000 victims of civil war, ringed Khartoum, at the confluence of the White Nile and Blue Nile. The city's population doubled and then tripled.

On November 12, 1990, ten-year-old Katarina Deng stepped out of her family's burlap shelter. It was already hot even though it was only six in the morning. During Sudan's dry season temperatures soared, and the fifty thousand displaced people living in Khartoum's Hillat Shook camp, officially a city garbage dump, were crowded so closely together that there was no cooling breeze. This particular morning Katarina held something very precious in her hand—a yellow, plastic watering can half full of water. It had cost her father a great deal, but the family had not had sufficient water to drink or wash in for many days. Katarina stretched out her left arm and sparingly sprinkled water on her skin. She set the can on the ground and rubbed the water up and down her arm until it was dry. Picking up the can, Katarina repeated the careful bathing until she had covered her body. She disappeared again under the burlap the family called home. The dust that swirled both inside and outside the hut would wipe away the water's cleansing, cooling effect. Still, she appreciated it for the moment.

Later that morning government officials came to Hillat Shook, announcing that all residents were to evacuate the camp by the next afternoon. Those who lived in the camp had less than twenty-four hours to gather their meager possessions and find somewhere else to live in the already crowded "unplanned" areas of the city. Katarina's family and the other residents knew that they would have no grace period. Before people could pack all their belongings, city police arrived on the scene and set the "carton" village ablaze. By evening it was a giant empty lot of ashes with no trace of human dwellings, crude as they were, and only a trinket here and there in the dust to remind passers-by that thousands of refugees had been ruthlessly dislodged.

It was not the first time Katarina had watched her home burn. She came from a Bahr el Ghazal village of farmers who had been swept off their land by marauding militia armed by the Sudanese government. The soldiers had destroyed crops, killed the cattle, and looted and burned the village. Katarina's father had lost a source of income when his cattle were taken, and he had lost also the bride price for his daughters, for the dowry was cattle. Dinka never killed their cattle and a man's worth was gauged by the number of animals he possessed. Throughout the war, government troops encountered civilian populations far more frequently than they did rebel troops. Katarina and her family learned that civilians like themselves were fair game for the government's scorched-earth policy. They felt they had little or no protection from the SPLA who were supposedly fighting for them.

The burning of their village had taken place in 1986. At least their family was intact as they made their way north to the government garrison town of Aweil. By the time Katarina and her family arrived, the town had swelled from fewer than twenty thousand to more than sixty thousand. It was difficult to find room in the squatter areas on the town's fringe.

Through the following year, Katarina, her parents, and her two elder brothers watched helplessly as four other siblings died—two slowly and painfully of starvation, and two in the measles epidemic that swept the town when ICRC was unable to gain access with vaccine. Sick and weak herself, Katarina did not know if she and her other siblings would survive. She had watched many graves being dug. It was said that one man dug eight hundred mass graves because he was one of few survivors who had the energy. Day after day Katarina noticed fewer and fewer small children. All of them were dying.

Her father thought the only chance the family had for survival was to try to reach Khartoum. At least there would be no bombing; perhaps there would be more food and jobs so that he could provide once again for his family. The city would be strange to them, as none of them had ever traveled more than a few miles from their village.

It was not easy to leave Aweil. Rebel forces had surrounded the town with a ring of mines. Yet with no food or water reserves, weak from malnourishment, the family made the two-month trek from Aweil to Khartoum. Only the hope for food and work kept them from giving up.

One month after arriving in Khartoum, they were not certain they had made the best choice, as Khartoum experienced some of the worst flooding in its history. For two days in early August 1988, rain poured, never letting up. Media attention resulted in an outpouring of donations for the inundated city, but since no funds were specifically earmarked for the displaced, the Mahdi government ignored their needs and allotted the assistance as it chose. There was nothing for the displaced to do but wait until the sun dried the slippery, red mud.

Now two years later, with Hillat Shook in ashes, they searched for a place to spend the night. They followed the crowds walking south. Hillat Shook had stood south of the heart of the capital on the eastern side of the airport and had been peopled by Dinka and Nuer tribal people. The two tribes had not always had the best relationship, but for now they were victims in a common war. Once again they would be located in one of the "unplanned areas," only farther from the heart of the city. These areas lacked an infrastructure, and there was little or no access to the public transportation her father and brothers needed to search for casual work in the city.

Katarina and her family crowded into one of the most squalid of the forty-eight displaced persons' camps that ring Khartoum. They gathered sticks. They found some discarded U.S. food-aid burlap bags and some plastic. Those who could find USAID plastic were fortunate, as it might last for a year. Ordinary plastic holds for two or three months at most. Out of these materials they put together a shelter on land where there was no water, no sewage system, no latrines, and certainly no medical clinic or school. Next door to Katarina's hut a family constructed its shelter from discarded Ethan Allen furniture boxes. The residents designated a site as far removed from the huts as they could for a latrine. The designation made little difference, for it was too great a distance for most to walk to, particularly for the children and elderly. After the residents had constructed their own dwellings, the Christians among them built a church out of cardboard.

The family was reduced to purchasing water from a northern Sudanese who charged more than most of the destitute southerners could pay. Each day young men led their donkeys hauling oil drums filled with water to the many camps. Because there are more than 1.5 million internally displaced southern Sudanese in the Khartoum area, the water sellers know they can charge high prices and make a large profit from those who could find a way to pay for the water. Rarely could Katarina's father afford to pay. Although most of the people lost everything before coming north, what they did manage to hold on to they were forced to sell to purchase food and water.

Using food as a weapon of war was not unique to the government's tactics in the south. Food and water also served as powerful instruments of control in the northern cities. As a means to coerce the unwanted multitudes, the Khartoum government manipulated access to food and water for more than two million southern Sudanese who had fled to northern urban areas. Bashir made water almost impossible for many to obtain, and when he did allow food aid to be distributed, none was to be allotted for males of any age under any conditions. No services were provided, no amenities tolerated.

In none of the settlements were the squatters allowed to dig deep wells. Shallow ones were sometimes permitted, though that water, which was never sufficient, was easily contaminated and spread disease within the camp. The farther away from the heart of the city they were forced to live, the more expensive the water brought by donkey carts. The government frequently placed limits on the amount of water that could be sold in the settlements, interdicting sellers at will. Rarely did the people in the camps get ten liters a day as recommended by the World Health Organization. They were fortunate to get two or three. Finally, when there was not access to sufficient water to prevent dehydration, the displaced had no option but to move on. Many had to leave the Khartoum area.

Another tactic used by the government was to round up and forcibly remove internally displaced such as Katarina and her family. During Sadiq al-Mahdi's government the *kashas* (round-ups) were fairly straightforward. The people simply were moved forcibly to another location, and their former settlement was looted and then bulldozed or burned. Such removals were done quietly, without notice. International organizations were not given warning. If NGOs had been working in a settlement that was razed, they discovered the destruction only after the fact.

Sadiq al-Mahdi and Omar Bashir both justified the removals by invoking the national constitution's article that gave all citizens the right of freedom of movement except "for reasons of security and public health." According to the rulers the displaced fit into both categories.[24] When the southerners first began coming in large numbers, the government feared their mobilizing a rebel force right in the capital. The government was also concerned that the purity of Khartoum as the Arab capital of Sudan would be lost. They did not want to be forced by the presence of so many ethnic groups to recognize that the country was multicultural. Customs practiced by the southerners not in accordance with Islamic *shari'a* gave the Khartoum government the excuse it needed for pushing them out.

The sites were populated mainly by women as heads of households and their children. The men who were present very often could not find work, or at least not steady and lucrative enough work to provide for their extended families. The women, as was their custom for generations, brewed *merissa* (sorghum beer). In their home villages, it had been brewed primarily for family consumption. Now the women sold it to supplement whatever they or their husbands could earn. Degradated and in violation of cultural mores, a number of women turned to prostitution for survival. Both activities were in clear violation of *shari'a*. Often not only were the offenders prosecuted, but also the entire settlement of tens of thousands was punished by the destruction of their huts and forced relocation.

In addition to being subject to arbitrary removal under the constitution, the displaced had no legal right to reside in Khartoum. Only "planned areas" in the city were recognized as legal areas for residences. Such areas had been or were scheduled to be supplied with water, sewage, electricity, and roads. None of these areas was available to the displaced; if found there, they were considered illegal squatters and could be removed. So, too, they could be uprooted at will for squatting in "unplanned areas," territory unapproved for living.

Under the Bashir government, the policy became more confused and complex. When Bashir first came to power, he assured the displaced he had no intention of forcibly removing them, though he would "encourage" them to go elsewhere. He particularly "encouraged" all households with able-bodied men to move to a rural, desert area where, the general stated, they could become self-sufficient in growing crops. However, one observer remarked that the land was so bleak that "not even a locust could survive."[25]

Government leaders then devised a scheme whereby agricultural and production areas were to be set aside in farming regions in the north of Upper Nile Province to allow the displaced to become self-sufficient. On paper the government policy appeared to have at heart the interests of those who would be affected, promising provision of basic needs wherever they were to be relocated and making every effort to resettle them as close to their homes as possible. Official statements appeared innocuous, even kind. The government's intent was to provide the displaced with "basic factors of production, trusting the displaced's ability to rely on themselves and to contribute to the building of a new Sudan." For those who did not choose to go to agricultural or production sites, the government would "pave the way" for their return home.[26] Although officials protested that no displaced would be moved by force to these new areas, squatters were given a ten-day ultimatum to leave their present sites and informed that they were to be moved to a "temporary site" before further relocation. A Khartoum militia had been armed and was ready to enforce government policy.[27] No one knows how many displaced people were affected by this plan, for movements under this scheme were carried out quietly. The situation became more confused when government officials stated their intention to transport a large proportion of the displaced now in Khartoum back to their homes in the south. Never were the needs or desires of the displaced taken into consideration, nor the dangers that they would face when they were returned to a war zone.

From the beginning NGOs were given little or no access to the hundreds of thousands of southern Sudanese seeking relief in the north. Cracks did occur periodically in the armor of the Khartoum government, and in 1987, when the first flooding occurred in the capital, Sadiq asked for assistance for all people in Khartoum. That was not the case the following year when more devastating floods engulfed the city. Indigenous NGOs like Sudanaid and the Sudan Council of Churches (SCC) seemed to be able to move among the displaced with fewer repercussions than expatriate humanitarian organizations. But even Sudanaid and the SCC had their problems.

Following the 1989 coup of Bashir, all humanitarian organizations were monitored much more closely in their work with refugees and the internally displaced. Sudan's generosity to the hundreds of thousands of foreign refugees, primarily Eritreans and Ethiopians, who sought asylum within its borders was made possible in large part by its congenial working relations with the UNHCR and voluntary organizations. In Bashir's early days, the work with the refugees was not curtailed to a large extent, although regulations in a military state made life more difficult and precarious for any outsiders who chose to remain. Travel permits became more difficult to obtain, not only for expatriates but for refugees who worked for Western NGOs. Along the highway between Port Sudan, Kassala, Gedaref, and Khartoum, military personnel at checkpoints took their jobs much more seriously. Sometimes it became a game of cat and mouse, a matter of subterfuge to get around the tightening laws. Eritrean refugees who either forgot or did not have a permit and were traveling on business for an NGO would slip out of the vehicle they were traveling in before reaching a checkpoint, disappear into the crowds in the adjacent truckstop area, emerge a mile or so farther along the road, and climb back into the NGO vehicle waiting on the other side of the checkpoint. "We are making tricks," became a common phrase of those involved in such subterfuge. The currency rate of exchange for NGOs was far lower than for ordinary travelers to Sudan, about 25 percent of the real value of the dollar. The exchange rate was so bad that an ordinary truck battery replacement might cost as much as one thousand dollars.

Access to the displaced became more and more difficult after the newly installed Bashir government scrapped the peace plan. Tssega, an Eritrean refugee who worked for the SCC in Khartoum, became caught in the strangling regulations imposed by government officials. Tssega was part of a team working among the displaced in the camp where Katarina lived with her family. The two women had much in common. Although Tssega had obtained a refugee permit from the Sudan government to work in Khartoum and was considered to be a registered refugee, she had not always been. She lived clandestinely in Khartoum for a number of months. She understood how unbending the government could be toward people it regarded as illegal urban residents like Katarina and her family.

"When I began working for the Sudan Council of Churches, I never dreamed I would be working with the displaced southerners from Sudan's own civil war," Tssega recalls.

It has been frustrating and rewarding work at the same time. We never know when the Khartoum government is going to ban our presence in the displaced camps or how they will impede our work. Nor do we know when we go to a site whether some or all of the people will have been removed. Today the displaced are seen as more alien to the Sudanese than we Eritreans. The concern about the presence of strangers has shifted to the southerners.

As a refugee I understand many of their concerns and fears. They have passed through the same traumas as we. In a way the displaced are crossing a border coming from the south to the north. The north is alien for them. The environment, weather, language, religion, customs, traditions—all are unfamiliar, all are barriers to their being welcome in the north.

The vast majority of them do not speak Arabic, and most of them are pastoralists, not urban dwellers. Many from the villages have never seen cars or a tarmac road. Some get killed simply because they do not know how to carry themselves around in a town.

I worry a great deal about the breakdown of the families. Families are torn and scattered, both among refugees and the internally displaced. A friend of mine is a good example. Her mother is in Asmara, her sister in Finland, a brother in California, and another sister in Rome. My friend in Khartoum failed the resettlement process. She could not convince the authorities that she and her sister in Finland were siblings, for when they crossed the border they changed their names for security reasons.

The feeling of living a temporary existence has a detrimental effect on the structure of the family. No one sinks roots. Every shelter has a transient air, as though those who live within will depart momentarily. Yet this temporariness can last for years and years.

The displaced enter into illegal means for making money by brewing beer, gambling, hustling illegal goods, or working as prostitutes just to make ends meet. They go through much degradation. At home they are independent; they have a patch of land and some animals. Here they have nothing.

The deleterious effect on the children living in such abnormal conditions is critical. A father who cannot take care of his family and sees his wife earning whatever the family has frequently resorts to heavy drinking. Children witness and become objects of the violence that often accompanies the drinking.

It is very depressing to make visits to the slum areas where they have built their shanty towns. As many as fifteen people live in an area no larger than four by four meters. When we made our health survey in one of the fringe camps, most of the children were malnourished. Many of them weighed 85 percent or less of weight for height. But though malnourishment deprives children of energy, they do not seem to lose their spirit. Whatever the displaced earn in wages, it seems they can't give their families more than one substantial meal a day. Many cannot even give that.

Those of us who are refugees know we are in bad shape. Yet for the displaced it is worse. The fact that they are Sudanese hinders them from getting special care from the U.N. or international organizations. No one can plead their case. Those NGOs like SCC who do have some access to the displaced find that it is really beyond their capacity to do anything that will really make a difference for them. No help we give shows any remarkable effects. They need more help than any NGOs can give.

Tssega did not want to be in Sudan; she did not want to live in Khartoum where life was very difficult for refugees. But she could not go home to Eritrea, and she certainly did not want to live in the rural refugee settlements, where she had lived when she first arrived in Sudan.

The Sudanese policy toward refugees is [and was] to locate us in refugee settlements far enough from the border that the Eritrean and Tigrayan military do not make the camps their base. Almost all of the settlements are rural in nature because most of the refugees came from the countryside. Living in rural settlements where refugees are given five feddans [about five acres] to farm made life for those of us who came from urban areas extremely difficult. We knew nothing of farming and in the camps there were few jobs for us. Sudan wanted refugees to become self-sufficient. How could we when we did not know how to farm? Some of us were fortunate enough to get office jobs with NGOs working in the settlements. I was one of the fortunate ones.

Still, life in Um Gargur camp was difficult for me to endure. I was used to a city and talking with educated people. The isolation was the hardest for me to bear. The rural settlements are far from the main road. Anyone coming to one must drive miles across flat desert sand, much of the way on land where no roads have been carved out. Suddenly in the distance, one can see thousands of tukuls [grass huts] rising out of the earth. There in some of the poorest land in Sudan, hundreds of thousands live.

It is true, the Sudanese and international donors have been very generous with us refugees who had to leave our homes in order to live. There are many projects in the camps which help us, and most can become at least partially self-sufficient. I do not believe that there will ever come a time when all can take care of themselves completely. There is not enough land to grow all the grain and vegetables a family needs, and other jobs do not pay enough to live completely independently. A man who tends another's goats gets no more than ninety Sudanese pounds a month. That is not even ten dollars.

There are many widows in the camps who must try to sell nuts in the market or weave mats to sell. Very few are able to exist on their earnings. Most of them are not able to make even as much as the goat herder. Small children of those widows have little energy because they do not have enough to eat. I worked with many of these women in the community outreach program sponsored by the NGO I worked for in the camp.

Eight years was much too long for me to live in Um Gargur. I decided to go to Khartoum and hope I could find work there. In the camp I was a registered refugee and had all the benefits offered to us as well as a job through which I earned an income. But I needed the city; the isolation got the best of me.

In the city I was an illegal immigrant because Sudanese policy did not allow for refugees just to live at will in any of its towns. Only the settlements had their blessings. Refugees, though, take care of one another. I had a sister in the city and some other friends. Five of them lived together in a cramped room. They took me in.

The owner of the house we lived in had divided it into many small single-room living areas, all opening onto a common, dirt courtyard. We were six people in a six-by-nine-meter room. There were only three narrow beds and no kitchen. Sudanese who rent and live in multiple houses generally have access to the use of a refrigerator, heater, fan, and other electrical equipment. Most refugees are not allowed to use those appliances. Even when we had a fan, we had to turn it off after 5:00 P.M. During the hot summer months, we brought our mats into the courtyard to sleep. We cooked on a small kerosene stove in the courtyard and kept a small refrigerator in our room. The rent was S£ 300 (U.S. $25), each contributing S£ 50 (U.S. $4). When I first came, I did not have a salary. The others were making between S£ 150 (U.S. $12) and S£ 300. What was left from the rent went for food and transportation.

My friends had moved often. Two of them, shortly after coming to Khartoum, were awarded UNHCR scholarships to continue university studies at Ahfad College in Khartoum. Even though they felt like the luckiest refugees in the city, they still found it difficult to live. Mariam said they were not living; they were surviving. Sometimes they ate; other times they did not. Most of their money went for rent. They received S£ 90 (U.S. $7) per month for food, rent, school books, clothes, and transportation. They lived in a small room with three other people.

One landlord told them they were making too much noise and must move. Three others raised the rent so high they could not pay. That is a problem for all refugees in the city. Landlords charge us more rent than citizens of Khartoum and raise it at any time. Too often we cannot pay the higher rent. The landlord knows that he will be able to rent to someone else at the higher price. They seem to care little whether we have a roof over our heads. We are at their mercy because in theory there are no urban refugees. Legally we do not exist because we should be in camps.

When my friends were studying they had to think too much about accommodations—whether they would be evicted again and again. It was difficult for them to concentrate on their studies. They are very bright, but they did not do as well in school as they were capable of doing because they had so many other things on their minds. I think they did very well under the circumstances. Their worries often kept them from sleeping; electricity frequently was cut; the library was a great distance from them; landlords were always after them.

We have moved several times since I came late in 1985. During the floods in 1987 and 1988 we moved from place to place. Everyone—Sudanese citizens, refugees, the displaced—was affected by the floods. Now we have lived in our present room for one year.

I was fortunate enough to get a job with Sudan Council of Churches soon after I came to Khartoum. Then I was able to obtain an ID card and a work permit. It was no longer necessary for me to live in hiding. We cannot go anywhere without our ID card. If we do not have it, we can be put in jail. Women frequently must pay in sexual favors to be released. Just as we are at the mercy of landlords, so too are we at the mercy of the police. Jails in Khartoum are dingy, dirty, and frightening.

Shortly before I came to Khartoum, when Nimeiri was still in power, some of the worst kashas (refugee round-ups) took place. A large proportion of Eritreans are Christian. When they were gathered in church, government officials found that to be a convenient time for a round-up. They were taken to jail and held there for several days. They were fined for as much as S£ 500, which very few could pay. Most of the time, the prison officials released the captives without payment. They knew they could not keep so many confined.

Still none of us ever feel secure from day to day knowing that at any time we can be picked up.

From time to time new registrations are called for. We have learned the importance of IDs, work permits, travel permits, and any kind of certificate. Refugees are conscious of the need to keep such documents in a safe place. To remain in Khartoum each person must give proof of a job and salary. That, then, is taxed. Most Eritreans will take whatever jobs they can find, skilled and unskilled—construction workers, housemaids, drivers, janitorial, office work. If when we register we do not have jobs, we are subject to being returned to settlements. Many avoid registration fearing they will be sent to a settlement.

Khartoum saw its policy of registering urban refugees as legitimate and beneficial to the refugees. Officials wanted a standard process to identify who was in the city. According to the government, round-ups and jailings were not intended to drive refugees out of town but to keep order and peace. Registration was difficult, for most Eritrean refugees who came to urban areas had crossed the border into a town and were never officially registered in a reception center with the UNHCR or the Sudanese government. The government argued that it could protect only those refugees who were registered, who had legalized their presence in Sudanese cities. Those who had not and who were not working had a negative impact on an already overcrowded and overburdened city. Sudanese officials maintained that most Eritrean and Ethiopian refugees should be in settlements except for the very few with work permits. It was better to locate people in designated areas for control and assistance, the government maintained. *Kashas*, from time to time, weeded out those who taxed urban services without contributing to a city's economy.

DEVELOPMENTAL RELIEF IN REFUGEE-AFFECTED AREAS

As the refugee population grew, the Sudanese population, particularly urban Sudanese, grew more and more resentful of the presence of refugees. In devastating economic times, the average Sudanese urban citizens perceive the refugees to be the cause of their problems. The lack of fuel, bread, sugar, and flour is directly related to the presence of the additional population of refugees and displaced southerners.

Gedaref, a city that is a six-hour drive southeast of Khartoum on the road to Port Sudan, became particularly volatile. The area surrounding Gedaref is rich agriculturally, and in good years the city's market has an abundance of produce. But both economic and environmental catastrophes severely affected urban and rural people alike. Because seasonal farming jobs had been plentiful in the Gedaref area during years when there was no drought, a number of Ethiopians and Eritreans had settled there. Not only did they not always get along with one another; they frequently had altercations with the Sudanese population of the city. Fighting was common, and the citizens of Gedaref protested their presence. Rabaa, an area in Gedaref heavily populated with refugees, mainly women and children, was known as a center of prostitution and *merissa*, the local beer. As Gedaref citizens increasingly vented their anger over the presence of refugees, claiming the refugees were taking their jobs and causing rents and food prices to soar, the authorities took action against the people of Rabaa for the violation of *shari'a*.

In 1979 Rabaa was burned after rioting broke out, purportedly started by a fight between a Sudanese and a refugee. Eight people were killed and three thousand refugees lost everything—houses, clothes, jewelry, cooking utensils. They were not considered official refugees because they were not registered. They were moved to a football field where they remained for almost four days, given bread and tea for sustenance. After having lived and been gainfully employed in Rabaa for as long as five years, they lost their homes and access to their jobs.

As a result of the Rabaa riots, the Sudanese government created semi-urban settlements located fairly close to Gedaref and yet far enough removed to keep the refugees separated from the people of the city. Tawawa was one of these settlements. Close to the tarmac road, Tawawa became a showplace for visiting diplomats and journalists. Its population was fluid. Officially there were around seventeen thousand registered refugees. In reality approximately twenty-five thousand to thirty thousand lived there, many on a nonpermanent basis. Because it was the camp most frequently visited by outsiders, the people who lived there were provided with many more services than were those in most of the camps. Consequently, they became more dependent than the majority of Ethiopian and Eritrean refugees who had been given asylum in Sudan. Access became more difficult to both the city and to the surrounding countryside where mechanized agricultural jobs were plentiful in season, particularly as Sudan's economy worsened and scarce fuel limited transportation. Young, able-bodied refugees had nothing to do. The rate of fighting, stealing, and killing escalated in Tawawa as the refugees' responsibility for their own lives diminished. Prostitution and *merissa* brewing increased accordingly.

Among Sudanese cities, Port Sudan, located on the Red Sea, seemed to be an exception in its treatment of the spontaneously settled refugees and the internally displaced. Perhaps the people of Port Sudan were more accustomed to outsiders since it was Sudan's only port where ships of all nations entered with goods. People from other countries, particularly from India, had lived there for years. It was not the seat of government, so the concern for maintaining a pure Islamic society was not as pronounced. In addition, many of the early refugees who settled in Port Sudan were from the same Beni Amer tribal group with the same roots and language. The Beni Amer lived on both sides of a generally porous national boundary, and when they began crossing into Sudan from Eritrea in the 1960s, they found refuge with relatives and mixed in with the local population. Then Port Sudan was a town of sixty thousand. By the 1980s the city had grown to 500,000 and a mix of people, especially Christians from the Eritrean highlands, began to arrive in large numbers.

As troubling economic times worsened, refugees and the internally displaced became scapegoats for all the ills befalling the city. Overcrowded schools and hospitals, the lack of clean water and sanitation, high rents, roads in disrepair—all of this and more were blamed on the influx of refugees. The vast majority of both refugees and internally displaced lived in squalid conditions in squatter villages circling the edge of the city. Their cramped quarters were constructed from burlap, plastic, and any discarded wood they could find. A number of them were located on garbage dumps where goats grazed on the refuse.

Several NGOs, local and expatriate, saw the growing problem and tried to address the roots of some of the most pressing problems of the economically and ecologically distressed area. Ockenden Venture, Euro-Action Accord, Sudanaid, the Comboni Fathers, and the Jesuit Refugee Service were particularly involved with both the dislocated and the poorest local population. Their aims were twofold: to assist refugees and internally displaced to become self-sufficient, and to introduce small-scale development projects that would benefit the local citizens living in affected areas. This latter was important so that xenophobic tendencies toward the dislocated might lessen and so the refugees could be integrated into the community. By helping these people become self-reliant, the larger community might begin to look upon them as people who could contribute to the society.

Early on Ockenden Venture involved itself in the construction of schools as a community enterprise, a cooperative effort among refugees and local Sudanese. The school project would benefit the children of war who had few options offered to them except the gun and military engagement. With additional classrooms, the burdensome refugee and internally displaced children, who shared facilities with Sudanese children, would place a lighter burden on the overcrowded facilities. Adults, too, would benefit since refugees, who could not own land and did not have a host of employment opportunities, would be offered a means of employment, involvement in the community, and a sense of pride.

Late each afternoon just before dusk, about a dozen men, both refugees and Sudanese who were often accompanied by their sons, gathered at a school construction site. They were fathers of the children who would attend the school they were constructing. Even though most of the men had already worked one or two jobs during the day, they came each evening to build the school. Cement blocks were piled near the almost completed outer frame of the school. Some men stood at the top of the front wall of the structure, waiting for others to lift the next block to them. They were almost ready to build the side walls. They would shape windows and doors, and after they had built the roof, they would construct the wall that would separate the two rooms, each of which was built for sixty to eighty students. When the school was complete, there would be four two-classroom buildings, a structure for the latrines, a water shelter, and a small structure that would serve as an open kitchen. Others built benches, writing tables, and desks for the teachers. While

Ockenden Venture provided the materials and the refugees, the labor, the Sudanese government provided the teachers. The school would be open to both Sudanese and refugee children.

Just next door, a group of students sat on the ground surrounding a teacher sitting in the midst of them on a simple wooden chair. For now that was their classroom. There was no blackboard, very little paper, and few textbooks. Students followed the Sudanese curriculum, learning Arabic rather than their mother tongue and Sudanese history rather than Eritrean. Still, they were learning, and this was important to their parents. At home, parents tried to keep alive the culture, language, and history of their ancestors.

Not far from the school site, other men had completed construction of a community center to be used by all ages, both sexes, and from morning until night. Here preschoolers played with wooden educational toys constructed by disabled refugees and Sudanese. The wooden toy boxes were filled with building blocks, toy vehicles, simple jigsaw puzzles, board games, dominoes, and skipping ropes. Educational toy catalogues provided ideas, and the disabled adapted them to the children's needs and available materials.

The community center provided a place for adults, particularly women, to attend literacy classes and receive instructions in making handicrafts that could be income-generating projects. Sudanaid offered health and nutrition classes as well as immunizations for children. Young boys played volleyball, soccer, and board games. There was space for supervised study halls where students received help in troublesome subjects. Residents of the squatter settlement where the community center was located volunteered in overseeing the various activities and protecting the equipment.

Euro-Action Accord, like Ockenden Venture, works with both nationals and refugees, giving loans for building small income-generating businesses. When the organization came to Port Sudan in the early 1980s, it found the Sudanese as poor or poorer than many of the refugees. Both lived on the margins of life in squatter settlements with only the barest necessities. The greatest need Euro-Action Accord identified was for credit assistance to start small businesses and train management. Very early Euro-Action Accord personnel observed ordinary people, the handicapped, and elderly men and women sitting on the ground selling small items they had placed in front of them—cigarettes, candy, razors. Euro-Action Accord grouped them into three or five or more people so that they could buy their wares at lower cost and in bulk.

Once the organization began to give small loans, the recipients opened tailoring shops, tea shops, and grocery stalls. Women purchased sewing machines and materials for handicrafts. Men bought carpentry tools, donkeys, and water tanks. Staff and people seeking loans discussed together what was best for each to purchase and made contracts.

Large organizations like the UNHCR, UNICEF, and Oxfam provided large orders for chairs, shirts, dresses, and a variety of other goods produced by these small businesses. Defaults on several thousand loans were negligible.

The same held true for home improvement loans. Without loans families could not afford to protect themselves and their children from the rain, dust, and desert sun.

More and more the organizations developed on-the-job training programs—mechanics, carpentry, welding, fitting, plumbing, tailoring, radio, tape, and watch repair, typing, secretarial skills, bookkeeping, and a host of other skills. Euro-Action Accord began to focus on group businesses and cooperatives in 1989. The organization gathered together fishermen, carpenters, bakers, millers, bus drivers, and others jointly to plan, finance, and initiate a variety of businesses. There were successes and failures. A variety of problems slowed and discouraged some projects. Those who purchased a bus did not repay their loan because the bus broke down and the owners did not have the money to replace parts. As sugar and other foodstuffs became more scarce, bakers could not produce their products. Because of the Sudanese economy, carpenters lacked work. Since none of the businesses could legally operate without a license and since the Khartoum government denied licenses to many, even though the group had organized and was ready to work, it could not do so without the proper documents. A number of groups waited as long as two years to obtain a license at a cost of S£ 110. Some simply gave up trying. Others who had the good fortune of receiving a license and setting up a business were shattered when their sites and inventory were destroyed by people who opposed the operation of businesses by refugees and the displaced. The refusal of the Bashir government to encourage such projects and its heavy investment in the military caused promising projects to crumble.

The Comboni Fathers and the staff of the Jesuit Refugee Service wanted to offer refugees the opportunity to dream dreams other than those of war. What they had to offer was education to the future leadership of a country no longer at war. The staff of the Comboni school did not see education as a luxury; education offered possibilities for the future. More than 60 percent of the Comboni school student body in the secondary school were refugees. A JRS community center afforded supervised study and extracurricular activities, while rustic wooden structures in the center of some of the most squalid settlements offered preschool children the opportunity to develop motor skills and learn basic language and numbers. A cargo container from the Port Sudan docks still serves as a clinic in one of the slums.

Wafaa came from Cairo to work with the children in the slums for the JRS. As she created kindergartens in several areas, she hoped to involve mothers in the education of their children.

Most mothers have so many children and are so busy preparing food and carrying water that they have little time to involve themselves in the education of their children. These women from the south who have no real education themselves want very much for their children to be educated. Only one or two mothers can sign their names. Because they have suffered in the war, they want a better future for their children. That is why they try very hard to pay the S£ 10 monthly fee, or at least half of it.

Many of the children have health problems. They do not have clean water or sufficient nourishment. One meal a day is standard for many. Because they are undernourished, the children frequently do not get enough exercise. They do not have the energy to play as normal children do. Many of the homes have no tables or beds. Living conditions are very poor.

Families move often. One day the children will be at school, and then we never see them again. Many mothers find that they must keep older children home to care for the younger ones, sometimes for a year or more. Perhaps a child began school at five, but was removed and returned only at seven. That child lost two years of education.

Home situations frequently inhibit a child's capacity to learn. Two children live with their grandmother. She is almost always drunk. The children have never seen their father, and their mother died two years ago.

Pots for water are generally empty and most days they receive no more than one skimpy meal. The sheets and mattresses are black with dirt.

The little boy is particularly sad. He never smiles and tends to worry about everything. Because his grandmother is so irresponsible, he must look out for his sister. He is not a child anymore. He is like an old man.

As the Sudanese economy worsened in the late 1980s and the early 1990s, jobs became more and more difficult to find for those who had been trained in a skill. Refugees once again became the scapegoats for the ills of the society, and the displaced southerners complained that the refugees had access to better jobs and dwellings than they. The cooperative efforts that had been cultivated began to break apart.

Under the Bashir government, humanitarian organizations working in Port Sudan and in the whole of the country were watched more closely, and all of them were forced to reregister, some fearing they would be banned from the country. No explanations were forthcoming. In addition UNHCR was in a funding crisis that affected every program for refugees. Developmental projects that had been implemented were in imminent danger of being closed, particularly education projects, for in the world of refugee assistance, education is seen more as a luxury than a basic necessity.

Kashas, such as those executed in Khartoum, did not happen in Port Sudan. But access to the internally displaced became more limited, and those who worked with them were watched more closely by government officials. As goods for Sudanese citizens dwindled, the refugees and internally displaced suffered more because their status in society put them on the lowest rung of the ladder.

About fifteen miles outside of Port Sudan a semiurban settlement like Tawawa was built. Originally it was thought that the refugees who would live there would have access to the city and to jobs while being separated from the Sudanese population. In many respects, the living conditions would be better in Asotoriba than in the town, for the cement structures were far superior to the wooden and burlap shacks the majority lived in within the city. But some of the same problems that plagued the people in Tawawa became acute in Asotoriba.

The failure of the Sudanese economy reached Port Sudan and affected all, nationals and foreigners alike. The Bashir government did not turn things around as the people had hoped. As in Khartoum, shelves in the markets of Port Sudan emptied and were not replenished. Sugar, kerosene, gasoline, flour, vegetables, firewood, and all manner of goods simply disappeared. The lack of gasoline for transportation became critical. Not only were trucks unable to travel from Port Sudan to Kassala, Gedaref, and Khartoum, but buses could not transport adults from Asotoriba to jobs in the city or students to school.

In the late afternoon light, Elias sat at a small wooden table in the small open area attached to the two-room living quarters the family of eight shared in Asotoriba. He was intent on his studies even though he had not been to his classes at the Comboni school for more than a month. He wanted to graduate with his class, but his hopes dimmed as the weeks passed. His father, too, was discouraged, as he was not able to find regular transportation into the area in the city where he could offer himself daily for casual labor. His wife, Elias' mother, was terminally ill — in the final stages of cancer. There was little the family could do for her. She lay on a rope bed near Elias' desk, a thin sheet covering her, more to keep the flies away, for it was hot and muggy in Port Sudan in April. Mibale, Elias' younger sister, who at five did not understand her mother's illness, had retreated inside herself. She stood motionless beside her mother's head, never uttering a word. Flies swarmed across Mibale's face and down her arms. The young girl did not blink an eye or even brush them aside. Inert, Mibale's reaction to the specter of death before her characterized the suspension of life that emerged from government policies whose tactics were to rout and raze all that would detract from a pure and ruthlessly controlled Islamic society. Bashir wanted the refugees to go home, the southern Sudanese to meet defeat, and his total control over a nation to be unquestioned.

The ending of the war in Ethiopia and Eritrea with the 1991 overthrow of Mengistu Haile Mariam in time will take care of the refugee presence. They will return to their homelands. But the government will not relent until the southern Sudanese are vanquished and a fundamentalist Islamic state rules the whole of Sudan.

The real leader behind Bashir is Hassan al-Turabi, who heads the National Islamic Front. In 1989 it purportedly was he who instigated the overthrow of Sadiq al-Mahdi when Mahdi and John Garang were on the verge of settling the civil war. Turabi has encouraged Iranian influence in radicalizing Islamic politics in Sudan, invited Iran's Revolutionary Guards to train a new Sudanese militia, and accepted Iranian military assistance.

Bashir's government took advantage of the split that occurred in the SPLA ranks in August 1991 by waging his most unmerciful offensive against the south. Backed by hard-line Muslims, he turned it into a holy war against southern Christians and animists. Fighting became so intense by April 1992 that the neutral corridors that had enabled Operation Lifeline Sudan to transport food to millions of starving people had to be shut down. Relief convoys moving from Kenya into southern Sudan were being attacked by government militia. Food as a weapon of war reemerged just as Bashir had been a party to an agreement among Horn of Africa nations at a summit held in Ethiopia's capital, Addis Ababa, that prohibited the use of food as a weapon by warring parties.

At the same time in the north, the Sudanese government forced almost half a million southern Sudanese from their Khartoum squatter settlements to areas far beyond the city. The sites to which they were transported and dumped have no facilities for food, shelter, water, medicine, or sanitation. They have no access to jobs, and relief organizations have not been given access to the new camps.

Sudanese hospitality to the downtrodden vanished under a government that could not sustain a viable economy and a government that was not willing to foster a Sudanese society of diverse religious, cultural, and ethnic backgrounds. Bashir's million-dollar-a-day war frustrated dreams of development, even the smallest projects. And because of the dictatorial nature of his government, his alignment with hard-line fundamentalist Muslims, and his decision to side with Iraq in the Persian Gulf War, development aid from many Western nations is no longer forthcoming. Even the continuation of humanitarian aid is in jeopardy. With peace in Eritrea, Eritreans will soon return to their homeland. But the southern Sudanese who remain internally displaced in the north continue to suffer and languish as unwelcomed objects of their government's wrath, whose goal is to crush them in body and spirit. Unless the question of the limits of sovereignty in the face of human rights abuses is addressed, the internally displaced will continue to be brutalized by the government that has a mandate to protect all of its citizens.

Two Eritrean women celebrating "Women's Day" in Asmara, Eritrea's capital. This day of euphoria celebrated the new and enhanced role of women in the future of the country and their hopes of returning home.

9

Eritrea Return

Justice shall roll down like waters
and peace like an ever flowing stream.
—Amos 5:24

Liberation

The former Kagnew Station, a military intelligence-gathering base of the U.S. government in 1953 when it supported Emperor Haile Selassie's claim to Eritrea, is a backdrop for a massive graveyard of war-ravaged tanks, armored vehicles, trucks, and jeeps. "I feel at once proud and powerful as well as sad when I look at this scene," offered thirty-three-year-old Sanaet Lejam. She had joined the Eritrean People's Liberation Front (EPLF) fighters in 1975 when she was sixteen. "I feel proud and powerful because we defeated the army of Mengistu Haile Mariam and won our independence. I feel sad because all the money and effort went into destroying rather than building our land and our people."

The depression of land that holds these instruments of war extends almost farther than one can see. It is a grim and proud reminder to the Eritrean people that after thirty consecutive years of war, from 1961 to 1991, the guerilla band of the EPLF defeated the largest army formed in black Africa. For more than seventeen of those thirty years, the troops of Colonel Mengistu Haile Mariam occupied Asmara, the Eritrean capital, laid waste to the Eritrean countryside, and brutalized its people. Between 1974 and 1991 the Kagnew facilities housed and provided office space for Dergue (the Ethiopian government's Military Central Committee) generals stationed in Asmara. Today, the blue and green flag of the EPLF as well as the multicolored flag of Eritrea fly above the main building that now houses officials of the Provisional Government of Eritrea.

On May 24, 1991, EPLF troops liberated Asmara and Keren, a town about sixty kilometers northwest of Asmara; Mengistu's generals lifted off from the Kagnew Station grounds in helicopters while the defeated troops retreated on foot, some toward Sudan, others toward Ethiopia. It was not easy to enter the city from any direction. Roads were sprayed with bullets and bodies from the last battles and retreating troops. Once the EPLF troops entered the capital and the wide boulevards belonged to the Eritrean people, they raised branches and voices in celebration. They climbed onto the entering troop trucks and danced in the streets. The people raised and waved the flags of the nation and the EPLF all over the city, no longer controlled by occupying forces.

Families and friends embraced, some of whom had been separated for as many as twenty or even thirty years. Mothers and fathers discovered sons and daughters were alive whom they had not heard from for years. Sons and daughters, in turn, found parents who had lived out the war in the occupied city.

Other reunions took longer. There were no commercial flights into Asmara for several months after liberation. Eritreans who had gone into exile in Rome, London, Los Angeles, and in other cities and towns scattered around the world chartered planes and filled them with those who fled and those who were born in exile, never having seen their homeland. Hundreds of Eritreans crowded on the small balcony of the Asmara airport each time a plane pulled to a halt on the tarmac. As the passengers disembarked, many stopping to kiss the Eritrean ground, the welcomers called out in the traditional greeting and waved. Both groups searched for familiar faces. When Ethiopian Airlines instituted flights from Addis Ababa to Asmara, homecoming became more common, but no less emotionally stirring.

As an Ethiopian Airline 767 from Rome neared Asmara, a woman in her fifties looked over to the American passenger seated next to her. She raised ten fingers once, and then twice, and then five fingers indicating the years she had been away. She pointed out the window to a conical structure on the ground, a familiar housing construction in villages throughout Eritrea. Tears welled up in her eyes, and over and over again she repeated, "Asmara. Asmara. Asmara."

Along Asmara's streets there were always surprise reunions. Kisses four times alternately on each cheek became a common sight. Gerie Tekie had not been in Eritrea in fifteen years and had no word whether his parents were alive. He was given the opportunity to drive some passengers from Khartoum. Shortly after he drove into Asmara, he passed a filling station and recognized the attendant to be his father.

Euphoric, the people made each greeting and each reunion a cause for celebration. It was as though they were in the midst of a year of jubilee. Even the simple fact of being able to walk on the streets after dusk became a celebration. Around seven each evening people began to promenade throughout this Italian-inspired town where red, purple, and orange bougainvillea draped the walls. The sidewalks and the coffee shops were filled. People remained outside as long as they wanted. During all the years of occupation, there had been a curfew at dusk. Being caught out after the curfew could mean a person's life, for occupying soldiers shot without warning or exception.

After May 24, guns disappeared from the streets. EPLF fighters checked their guns at the police station when they entered Asmara. Members of the police force walked the streets unarmed. People felt totally secure.

THE FALL OF PRESIDENT MENGISTU HAILE MARIAM

The war had been stalemated until late 1988 when the EPLF began making advances. When the end of the war came in May 1991, it came swiftly. President Haile Mengistu Mariam faced three different ethnic rebel groups, all advancing toward either Asmara or Addis Ababa. Both the Tigrayan People's Liberation Front (TPLF) and the Oromo Liberation Front (OLF) were fighting to oust Mengistu and take over the government in Addis Ababa, while the EPLF fought to become the independent nation of Eritrea. Although the three groups had different goals, they loosely coalesced to rid the country of the Mengistu regime.

The government of the former Soviet Union drastically reduced its assistance to the Mengistu armed forces when attention to the changes in Eastern Europe and the demise of the Soviet Union took precedence for Soviet leaders. From 1977 until 1990, the Soviets poured in at least $12 billion of war materials, 350,000 troops, support for advisors and Cuban troops, and other related goods. Without such assistance, Mengistu Haile Mariam could not contend with the determined forces of the liberation fronts.

The United States realized that the takeover by the fronts could result in blood baths in Addis Ababa and Asmara as well as in social disintegration because of ethnic conflicts, similar to those in Somalia and Liberia. And a death-threatening famine loomed. To facilitate a "soft landing" when the fronts inevitably defeated Mengistu and to stave off famine, the U.S. government initiated peace talks. They were convened in London at the end of May 1991 by U.S. Assistant Secretary of State for African Affairs Herman Cohen.

Before the peace talks began, rebels surrounded both Addis Ababa and Asmara. On May 21 President Mengistu announced that he planned to inspect some operations in southern Ethiopia; however, his plane spirited him first to Kenya and then to Zimbabwe, where he was given asylum by Zimbabwe's President Robert Mugabe. Mengistu relinquished the government to Vice President General Tesfaye Gibre-Kidan, formerly Mengistu's defense minister.

At the London peace talks the U.S. government pressed the leaders of the liberation fronts not to engage in a massacre. Both Meles Zenawi, leader of the newly formed coalition, the Ethiopian People's Revolutionary Democratic Front (EPRDF), and Isaias Afewerki, the EPLF leader, agreed. Not a single shot was heard inside Asmara, and turmoil in Addis Ababa was brief when Acting President Tesfaye ceded control to guerilla forces.

The new provisional heads of state of Ethiopia and Eritrea are relatively young. Mr. Zenawi, thirty-seven, was a medical student at Addis Ababa University from 1973 until he dropped out three years later to help form what became the Tigrayan People's Liberation Front. He is fairly short and moves with unflagging energy. Zenawi is a tough commander who is extremely cultured and speaks flawless English. Significantly, he was born to peasant parents in Adwa in Tigray Province where in 1896 the Ethiopian forces of Emperor Menelik defeated Italian troops swooping from their northern stronghold in Eritrea.[1]

He will head the transitional government of Ethiopia until free, democratic, and internationally monitored elections are held. As a Tigrayan, Mr. Zenawi is an interloper, according to the Amharas who ruled Ethiopia since the late nineteenth century when Emperor Menelik ascended the throne. Mengistu's defeat ended the rule of the Amharas. In mid-1992, even in the midst of growing ethnic conflict, the coalition that comprises the EPRDF is holding together, and this in a nation where more than seventy languages are spoken and at least forty different ethnic groups reside.

Isaias Afewerki, forty-seven, was a student in pharmacy when he joined the struggle for Eritrean independence in the 1960s. After a few years of fighting, he was sent to China for further training in guerilla warfare. Upon his return to the front, both his political talents and his brilliance as a strategist were recognized, and he became one of the youngest leaders of the newly formed EPLF. During the EPLF's first formal convention in 1977, Mr. Afewerki was designated official leader.

Those who know him describe him as a self-effacing person who rarely socializes. Tall and lean, he is consumed with thinking about Eritrea — first in leading it to victory and now working for its development. They see him as a far-sighted person, highly articulate, widely read, abreast of world affairs, and internationally oriented. He can be unbending and authoritarian. But in moving toward democratization as he governs a civilian population, he is discovering other attributes are more appropriate.

The nascent nation he will govern as secretary general of the Provisional Government of Eritrea — until and if independence becomes a reality — is more homogeneous than the rest of Ethiopia. Nevertheless, Mr. Afewerki must not neglect the nine ethnic groups with different languages spread throughout Eritrea's 3.2 million people.

The hope of Ethiopians and the Western world was that Ethiopia would be united, with Eritrea agreeing to join Ethiopia's moderate coalition government. But after fighting for thirty years with little outside support to gain independence, Eritrea declined to attach itself to the government in Addis Ababa. Reluctantly, the EPRDF supported Eritrea's desire to decide its future. Likewise, for the first time the U.S. government gave its blessing to the right of Eritrea to self-determination. Although Eritrean independence is thought to be a foregone conclusion, the Eritreans, in turn, agreed to delay calling a U.N.-sponsored referendum on independence until the middle of 1993, and Eritrea guaranteed Ethiopia free access to the southern Eritrean port of Assab. At the time of the London agreement, Isaias Afewerki felt that a delay would afford Eritreans the time needed to form an independent government. He saw, too, that a stable Ethiopia was important to the welfare of an Eritrean nation. Both Eritrea and Ethiopia hoped that Eritrea's willingness not to declare independence immediately could serve to temper the aspirations of other groups to break away, particularly the Oromos, the largest ethnic group in Ethiopia.

DEMOBILIZED ETHIOPIAN SOLDIERS

While Mengistu, one of Ethiopia's most brutal leaders, fled to comfort and safety in Zimbabwe, those who served him in Eritrea were booted out of Eritrea with little more than a canteen of water and the clothes they wore. As Eritreans saw it, those "colonizers," especially the military, must leave. Some who left early, including civilians, looted banks and businesses, draining reserves to practically zero. Throughout the war Ethiopian troops had dismantled offices and stripped schools and libraries and sent the equipment, supplies, and books south. Officers and their troops who remained and who had lived in relative comfort just days before, albeit with minimal services, left on foot and in military vehicles as quickly as possible when it became clear that the returning Eritreans would control the whole of Eritrea. Citizens watched as Ethiopian soldiers laid down their weapons and fled. These were the cream of the Ethiopian army, for Mengistu had concentrated his efforts on defeating the Eritreans. Many who remained were gathered up by the Eritreans, put on buses, taken to the Eritrean border with Tigray, and left without further assistance. The rest were simply told to walk.

Many, though, did not make it to safety either in Sudan or south into the Ethiopian province of Tigray. Some died of thirst, others who had tried to escape in tanks and armored vehicles were victims of mines placed by advancing Eritrean troops. The bodies of Ethiopian soldiers lying on the road leading to Sudan became food for hyenas and other animals of prey.

It was the rainy season. Left to the elements, a number of soldiers who made it to Tigray became sick and died. Many were young men who had not volunteered to fight, but who had been conscripted, plucked from their herds or passed by a military officer at the wrong moment. During times of drought, Mengistu's soldiers had rounded up young boys who went to food distribution points in government-held areas of Eritrea. Among them there was no great loyalty to Mengistu. The brutality he exercised against the people was abhorrent to most. With the end of the war, the troops simply wanted to return to their homes, farms, parents, or wives. But in a country with few jobs and where government attention to other groups of people took priority over assistance to former soldiers, the soldiers became the most destitute and neglected people in Ethiopia.

Meles Zenawi's government had more than ex-soldiers to consider. Mengistu had worsened the conditions of all Ethiopians. Under his leadership, a country that could have been prosperous had become one of the poorest nations in the world, with a per capita income of $120.00. Urban and rural

Ethiopians lived in desperate poverty. The slums of Addis Ababa were as bad as any in the world. Tens of thousands of street children huddled in clusters at night for warmth and tried to survive by performing myriad jobs during the day—shining shoes, selling cigarettes and gum, washing cars. Farmers and pastoralists from the highlands, who had been forcibly resettled in the south by Mengistu, were now trying to find their way back to their towns and villages, with little promise of economic security. When the Somalian regime also collapsed in 1991, Ethiopians who had taken refuge in Somalia returned home, and Somalis took refuge in Ethiopia from the clan fighting in their country. Ethnic clashes in Somalia made use of powerful weapons left over from the days of superpower involvement. Southern and southeastern Ethiopia near the Somali border were troubled by ethnic clashes, drought, and the commandeering of relief supplies. Everywhere disaster threatened.

Ethiopian soldiers were not the only persons asked to leave Eritrea. Civilians who worked in government jobs, teachers who spoke Amharic not Tigrigna, Ethiopian port workers in Assab, and also Eritrean women who were wives or mistresses of Ethiopian soldiers and their children were no longer welcome. The Eritrean government emphatically denied that it had forced out Eritrean women and their children whose fathers were Ethiopian soldiers. Most of these women left in search of the Ethiopian fathers of their children, but few found them. Their living conditions became more and more precarious, especially if they remained in Addis Ababa.

Fourteen thousand displaced persons found shelter in the Jan Meda camp in Addis Ababa, one of several camps sheltering demobilized soldiers and their dependents, most of whom were Eritrean women and children. For several months they received relief assistance from the government, until the government determined the population of Jan Meda camp was no longer in an emergency situation. Rations were then discontinued.

The new Ethiopian government, like many other governments that have given asylum to refugees and internally displaced, did not want large numbers of demobilized soldiers and their dependents in Addis Ababa. The camp's inhabitants were told to move to other locations, mostly in the south, and that once there they would continue to receive assistance for a brief period until they were settled.

Of the fourteen thousand, approximately five thousand, mainly women and children, refused to move. They believed they would be more likely to find work in the city and also have a better chance to find the men they sought. They were forced to leave Jan Meda, some contend at gunpoint, by bus and were left on the road some distance from the city.

Most returned and sought abandoned residences. One such area had been a housing compound for Soviet advisors, with modest, single-family homes. As many as sixty-five people, mostly Eritrean women and children, crowded into a single house and a dirt-floored garage area. Twelve to fifteen people lived in a bedroom where no more than two had slept before. The bathrooms did not work, and they had no latrines. Safe drinking water and food were difficult to find. Children gathered hard bread discarded by hotel restaurants, and many joined the growing numbers of street children. Malnutrition rose and communicable diseases spread. Infants died because lactating mothers could not provide nutrients for their babies. None of the residents had access to health care. Older children did not attend school. The few men could not find even casual labor.

Eritrean Reconstruction and Returning Refugees

In spite of the euphoria that permeated Eritrean society, enormous problems confronted the people, not the least of which was the conversion of a guerilla movement into a civilian governing body of an unrecognized nation. When the EPLF began to govern the whole of Eritrea, not simply the population behind the war front, and when its members began to live above the ground in the daylight, they realized what a monumental task it would be to rehabilitate the devastated countryside and to give birth to a nation.

Isaias Afewerki, the secretary-general, and the other heads of departments moved into government offices in Asmara previously occupied by Mengistu's people. Mr. Afewerki lamented, "Our country is in ruins, our cities are destroyed, and our population is displaced and dispersed. A gigantic task of national reconstruction awaits us."[2] While they faced the ravages of thirty years of war, drought, and famine, they were thwarted by a continuing, deadly drought and challenged to rehabilitate a devastated infrastructure with little or no money. They had to make the land habitable for the people who had remained throughout the war and for the hundreds of thousands who wanted to return from exile. Those who had fought for so long knew a different struggle was just beginning. One commented, "It is difficult, difficult. We were better off in the mountains where we knew our work and had our routines and discipline."[3]

When journalists, diplomats, and other visitors visited refugee camps in Sudan during the war years, Eritrean refugees pressed them with this question: "Isn't it better that we remain here in Um Gargur [Karkora, Wad el-Hileau, Tawawa] rather than settling in another country, so that when peace does come we will be close to home and can easily return?" They wanted affirmation, for they were living in trying conditions in a foreign land for ten or twelve years—some for as many as twenty-five years.

A spontaneous return of refugees, without international assistance from UNHCR, began almost immediately after peace was declared. The village of Teseney just across the border from the Sudanese town of Kassala became the point of entry for first hundreds and then thousands. In less than a year more than twenty thousand refugees had crossed the border to Teseney. Its population of 2,500 swelled to 10,000, an impossible number of people for Teseney's limited infrastructure. Housing, water supplies, medical facilities, and schools were strained to breaking. Still refugees continued to return—at a rate of one hundred a day. In a year's time, if the rate continued, more than thirty-five thousand would stop in Teseney.

Medina and Medhanie had lived in Karkora camp in eastern Sudan for more than a decade. They fled their small village near Barentu in Eritrea's eastern lowlands in 1975 when bombardments became so frequent that everyone in the area was threatened with destruction. At the time they had two very young sons, Asmoram and Ayoub. In fact, Ayoub had not yet reached his first birthday. They lived first in another camp before moving to Karkora in 1980 where some of their relatives lived. There two daughters, Hewit and Alganish, were born. Another son was born, too, but he died of cholera in 1985.

"We are ready to go home," Medhanie said.

Even though our family has remained intact throughout our years in exile, and even though I have tilled the five feddans of land given to us and Medina has worked with women teaching them how to sew, we no longer want to remain in a camp. Eritrea is home and we are anxious to live there in peace. The boys were too young to remember their homeland, even though now they are almost men. The girls were born in exile and do not know their homeland.

Four evenings before they left, Medina invited some of the women to her grass *tukul* (hut) to perform one final coffee ceremony, an ancient Eritrean custom. Medina greeted her guests warmly at the door of her home. Inside, a small kerosene lantern cast shadows on the grass vaulted ceiling revealing the impeccable cleanliness of the small room. Not a twig lay on the well-swept dirt floor. Two rope beds, four porch chairs, a small table, and a bureau filled the space. Medina's thin veil draped gracefully over her dark hair as she sat on a low stool before the coal fire on the ground.

Medina poured coffee beans onto a small, flat grass tray and tossed them slowly, picking out stray pieces of grass or sand. While she heated water in a thin-necked coffee carafe, she ground by pestle and mortar the beans mixed with anise. Carefully she put the ground mixture into the steaming water. She poured the aromatic brew into delicate demitasse cups and added sugar, a precious commodity. She offered each guest a cup and took one for herself. According to custom, they sat talking long into the evening. Medina repeated the ceremony twice more. By tradition, the hostess serves three cups to each guest. Alganish fell asleep in Medina's arms; Hewit crawled onto one of the beds.

Medina knew that she would face great hardships when she returned to Eritrea. She would not perform the coffee ceremony again for quite some time she felt. But, at least when she did, it would be in Eritrea. Before the women left, Medina reminded them of two sayings they had hung on the wall of the sewing center. She, herself, wanted to remember them as much as she wanted her friends to hold onto what they meant. Women would be very important in the rebuilding of Eritrea, and the sayings conveyed their importance.

"I am called a refugee," the first one read, "but I have made that into a ministry of peace. We are women of courage. We have to swim rivers without perhaps knowing how to swim. Sometimes we take refuge because we want to own our lives."

The second one said, "The world community has only a father and a son when it comes to issues of power. The world community has no mother, and that is why there is chaos. We swallow before we chew. We have to go and hold the lion with its whiskers."

The family of six made their way to Gedaref in the back of a hot, open Toyota truck. They took only a few belongings with them. From Gedaref to Kassala, they rode a crowded bus along the only tarmac road in Sudan. From Kassala, they walked the few kilometers to Teseney and joined thousands of spontaneous returnees. Camp life had been poor and cramped, and five *feddans* of not very fertile ground never produced enough for the family to eat. But they had received supplemental food from the World Food Program, and the older boys had found work with one of the NGOs working in the camp. The children received some education in the camp's EPLF school. The conditions in Teseney were a great shock to them.

"We remembered Teseney as a quiet border village of not more than 2,500 people," Medhanie recalled.

When we arrived there were more than ten thousand. So many of us were so eager to return to our homes, but it was not as simple as we had supposed. We wanted to remain in Teseney only a week or so before traveling on to our village. That was not to be.

After we learned about the dreadful condition of our village, we decided we had better remain in Teseney for a while. Those of us who were refugees went to the edge of the village to build whatever shelter we could. I saw that some who had been there six months or more built round shelters of mud and stone, the sort we lived in before the war. My sons don't know how to build that sort of structure, and I am not sure I remember. It has been so many years.

For the first few days we lived in the open air until we could gather enough straw and branches to construct a small tukul. We had to travel long distances to find enough material because others had stripped the area clean both for housing and fuel for cooking.

Life in Teseney is much more difficult than it was in the camp. At first we had nothing in the camp, but after years of living there, we made a home, small though it was. We had water and sanitation facilities within easy walking distance. From Teseney, we have to walk two or three kilometers for water. Our sanitation facilities are so poor that diarrheal diseases and malaria spread very easily. Alganish almost died because of diarrhea, and I became quite sick with malaria. There is little left of Teseney's hospital. By the time we arrived, we were told that only one physician, four nurses, one midwife, and fifteen health assistants served a population of sixty thousand to seventy thousand people. The staff might see as many as 150 patients a day. When my daughter and I were sick, it was very difficult for us to get the proper medication or even to see a health worker. A real health crisis can develop very easily.

Both the residents of Teseney and those of us who returned from Sudan have to depend on relief food from the Eritrean government. Food in Teseney is as scarce as it is in the rest of the country. Almost the whole country depends on relief assistance. The drought is very bad right now, and with the war just over, we have very few resources to try to feed ourselves. Crops have failed and oxen and goats have died.

Hewit and Alganish were particularly eager to attend school. A number of refugee children were going to classes in tents. Each tent had one teaching tool—a locally made blackboard. There were no pens or pencils, no books or notebooks. By the time the two girls arrived, the Teseney school had been closed to any more returnees. It had no more rooms or teachers. Although Eritrea could not build a nation without educated citizens, education had to be given a lower priority than basic food and shelter. Emergency needs overshadowed aspirations for development, even in something as basic and essential as education.

As the returnees ventured away from Teseney toward their own villages, they found destruction beyond their comprehension. Many villages no longer existed. The road between Teseney and Asmara was so heavily damaged by the weight of tanks and armored vehicles that drivers were forced to navigate more off the road than on it. Those who found their villages intact discovered that destitute relatives could not help them. Normally, the extended family in Eritrea would reach out and provide food and shelter for any family member in need. But in 1991 and 1992 at least three out of every four people in Eritrea required relief food. War, drought, and famine had taken their toll.

"I decided I wanted to see if I could take my family back to our village," Medhanie continued.

I walked and rode part of the way. Sometimes a truck would pick me up, but it was very difficult to remain on the road. I saw the wreckage of many tanks and armored trucks.

When I reached our village, I could not believe the devastation. Much of it had been destroyed. Those who remained could barely exist. Our relatives have no means to accommodate my family. The family lost their goats, oxen, and one camel to the drought and to Ethiopian soldiers who took them as they left Eritrea following liberation. Some of the animals died of thirst. They had to borrow money to buy coffee, sugar, and other foods. They do not know how they are going to repay the shopkeeper.

The village has a grinding mill nearby, but very few can afford to use it. The women must grind the grain by hand. They carefully ration what grain they receive, because they do not know when they will receive another supply.

In addition to grinding the grain, the women have to walk for more than an hour to the nearest water source, which is not that clean. Many fall ill from drinking it.

Medhanie's cousin has two small children who clearly are malnourished. Sadia, herself, is extremely thin and not well. "I am exhausted because I have to continue to breast feed my daughter, even though she is two."

We do not have enough food to feed her. She is so underweight that she does not even look like she is two. I do not know if she will live. I am not sure any of us will live if we do not have rain soon and a crop to harvest. If you bring your family here, they will live as we do. Stay in Teseney for a while longer and see if things get better here.

Refugees from the Port Sudan area entered Eritrea through its northern-most province, Sahel. Although Sahel was behind the front for most of the war, in the mid-1980s Mengistu's troops advanced, and Sahel reaped the army's vengeance. Nacfa, the largest town, was heavily bombed, as were villages and fields. Half of the province's population had fled and readied themselves to return. Those who remained throughout the war did not dare to cultivate more than small plots; larger planted areas would attract the attention of bombers.

Drought also devastated Sahel. In 1992 fully 95 percent of those who remained depended on emergency food relief. Only 5 percent of Sahel's people could feed themselves. Most of its population were pastoralists who had lost their livestock. Those who farmed had no oxen for plowing.

According to a U.N. study early in 1992, less than 10 percent of the population had access to clean drinking water, health care, sanitation, or education. Few children had been immunized, and malnutrition among children was extensive. Indeed, Sahel Province had the highest number of war orphans in Eritrea.[4]

The problem of reintegration for those returning to Sahel proved to be as difficult as in Teseney. The amount of land under cultivation was negligible. Given the proper conditions, the land in Sahel can yield grains, cotton, and vegetables. Without rain or oxen, nothing can be planted or grow.

In Ethiopia, Meles Zenawi made it clear that he did not favor an early return of refugees from Sudan into the provinces of Tigray, Gondar, and Wello. The land and the people were not prepared to absorb them. Isaias Afewerki, on the other hand, seemed anxious to have Eritrean refugees return. He believed that all Eritreans could help rebuild the land and urged all Eritreans, including those who opted for permanent asylum, even citizenship, in other countries, to return, at least temporarily, to participate in Eritrea's reconstruction. None of Eritrea's military was demobilized. They were asked to stay on for an additional two years to begin reconstruction. As soldiers they were provided with shelter, food, and clothing and a monthly allowance of approximately U.S. $3.00.

The United Nations responded quickly to Afewerki's proposal to facilitate a speedy homecoming for the 500,000 Eritrean refugees in Sudan. The UNHCR devised a plan and budget for bringing home 250,000 in the first year. The Provisional Government of Eritrea rejected the proposal, protesting that such limited funds would leave the returnees destitute in an already destitute land. The PGE wanted a fourfold increase. In addition, the PGE asked for immediate funding of a broad-reaching blueprint while the UNHCR wanted to take a step at a time, particularly in funding. The two parties went back to the conference table.

Although tension grew, they remained at the negotiating table. While the UNHCR contended that Eritrea's expectations were too high and were far beyond the UNHCR's mandate or monetary capacity to provide, PGE officials countered that the UNHCR's mandate included resettling refugees in dignity. Why, asked Eritreans, was Cambodia allotted $116 million from the UNHCR for the return of 360,000 refugees plus millions more for a U.N. peace-keeping force when Eritrea, with 500,000 returnees from Sudan alone, was allotted no more than half that amount? Why, they asked, would the UNHCR allot nine hundred dollars per head for Namibians and only two hundred dollars per head for Eritrean returnees?

A member of a U.N. mission to Eritrea in December 1991 commented:

They [Eritreans] are being very unrealistic about what they're going to get out of the donors. They classified their entire reconstruction needs— schools, hospitals, roads and everything else—as emergency needs deriving from the war. It's as if they want foreigners to give them the infrastructure of a middle-income country, all at one fell swoop.[5]

RECOGNITION OF ERITREA

This debate between the UNHCR in Eritrea and the PGE has implications far beyond Eritrea's borders and goes far deeper than a pocketbook. It deals with issues of donor fatigue, Eritrean sovereignty, the actual mandates of relief and development organizations, and the targeting of their funds.

The office of the UNHCR, twice winner of the Nobel Prize for Peace, is struggling for its survival. As the numbers of refugees have risen at an alarming rate around the world, the willingness of donor nations to increase their gifts proportionately has faltered shockingly. "Compassion fatigue" grows within the donor community, as disastrous calamities befall more and more people. In 1991 alone the plight of the Kurds in Iraq, and the victims of Bangladesh's worst cyclone, and the possibility of almost forty million Africans starving seemed to overwhelm the donor community's capacity and will to respond. "Too many, too long,"[6] once the cry of the Sudanese government as hundreds of thousands sought asylum within its borders, is today echoed by many in the international donor community as refugees seek asylum as well as relief from natural disasters and human conflicts. Fewer resources are available and more people are in distress.

Isaias Afewerki knows this and perhaps judges that the time to press donors for larger amounts is now, while people remain conscious of the situation in Eritrea and Ethiopia. All too soon another world event will clamor for attention. But Mr. Afewerki is also new to government and international negotiating. For all of his adult life, he has been in the trenches fighting a war. He and most of his department heads do not fully understand the stringent requirements of bureaucracy. When asked for lengthy reports with precise statistics, he is presumably like a forestry officer in the Pakistani government who, when asked for statistics on the environmental impact of refugees, replied that he had no pages of calculations, but could drive anyone to the affected areas to see the damage.

Officials of the PGE knew that they had to comply with the rules and thus set about gathering pertinent information. Afewerki did not want to compromise Eritrea's new-found independence by having funds flow through Addis Ababa. Eritrean matters and Ethiopian matters were two separate issues.

The question of sovereignty, nonetheless, was important to the United Nations, to institutions like the World Bank and the International Monetary Fund, and to the diplomatic arms of the nations of the world. Until the 1993 referendum takes place and Eritrean nationhood is a reality, the rules, regulations, and mandates of the donor organizations limit their capacity to deal with Eritrea, whose status remains undefined.

Eritrea stands in a state of diplomatic limbo until the U.N.-sponsored referendum on self-determination takes place in mid-1993. Until then, Eritrea is neither nation nor province. It is not a member of the United Nations and it has been recognized only by Sudan. Eritrea's national status is highly unusual, for the world has no experience in dealing with a province that secedes from a country, yet does not declare independence immediately.[7] In the meantime, this ambiguity jeopardizes progress toward reconstruction.

On the other hand, donor nations and relief and development organizations argue that Eritrea is not being flexible. Why, they ask, does Eritrea so stubbornly reject both money and methods of payment channeled through Addis Ababa when doing so adversely affects their people, even causing some to die. They wonder why Eritrea does not bend, at least until time for the referendum.

In late 1991, however, the United Nations bent in its dealings with Eritrea and opened independent offices in Asmara. NGOs that were considering working in Eritrea began to look for ways to deal with the operational and managerial requirements of the NGOs and still give consideration and respect to Eritrean feelings of independence. The U.S. government and USAID planned to set up offices in Eritrea, although money allocations were still earmarked for Ethiopia with portions designated specifically for Eritrea. Out of $115 million in developmental assistance proposed by the United States in 1992, $10 to $12 million is earmarked for Eritrea. A stumbling block to any allocations to Ethiopia or Eritrea, however, is the Brooke Amendment, which bars developmental assistance to any nation in arrears. Ethiopia owed approximately $6 million, apparently for leasing warehouses to store goods the country never received. Waiving the Brooke Amendment sanctions for Ethiopia was problematical for Congress, for fear that a waiver for Ethiopia would set a precedent for other countries. Release of developmental assistance for a nation in desperate straits was held up over that $6 million debt, and many suffered because of the delay. Ultimately Ethiopia agreed to borrow the money to pay the debt.

In 1991 and 1992 the most dramatic shifts in national boundaries of this century occurred. Massive groups of refugees were on the move. In the name of world stability, and according to their changing strategic interests, donor nations prioritized their giving. Addressing the needs of Eastern Europe and the newly independent republics of the former Soviet Union drained resources, some of which might have gone to the Horn of Africa. In March 1992, the United States, Germany, Japan, Canada, Italy, Britain, and France announced a $24 billion package for Russia, protesting that even during the recession, it was imperative for the world to make every effort to assist the reforms taking place in the Commonwealth of Independent States.

In announcing this aid package to the American public, President Bush called the changes in Russia and the other republics "a defining moment in history," and emphasized that the "stakes were high." Warning that a failure of the "democratic revolution" could "plunge" the world into darker years than at any time during the cold war, Mr. Bush asserted that the cost of assistance given was worth the price if lasting reform could be achieved. The infusion of $24 billion, the G-7 leaders[8] maintained, was little compared to the trillions that went into fighting the cold war.[9]

With the end of the cold war and the determination to build up the republics of the former Soviet Union come reassessments of which countries are strategically important. Proxy wars between the cold warriors were fought around the globe. From Afghanistan to the Horn, and from Cambodia to Central America, East-West adversaries supported local wars with advisors, arms, and troops by infusing billions of dollars. In many of these countries, a scorched-earth policy forced millions of people to seek refuge outside their homelands and killed millions more; these battles decimated livestock and ruined crops, blasted bridges, roads, hospitals, and schools, and frequently bolstered the power of brutal leaders who had no genuine interest in the welfare of their people.

Adequate reconstruction assistance has not been forthcoming in many of the countries on whose soil these proxy wars were fought. It is difficult today to persuade donors to provide the millions that are needed to help rebuild these countries even though they poured out billions in military aid to destroy them. Eritrea is one of these casualties. Except during the period of the Persian Gulf crisis, the Horn of Africa, including Eritrea with its long Red Sea coastline, is no longer as strategically important to the United States and the other industrial powers as it once was.

Finally, there is the question of organizational mandates. As Nick Southern of Save the Children Federation/UK remarked recently, "[Rigidly designated] mandates limit the flexibility and pragmatic response we of the world community can bring to people in considerable distress."[10] In the aftermath of war there are different populations whose needs are equally urgent and deserving. This is true in Eritrea and in every war-torn nation at battle's end.

There are returning refugees who have lived in exile for years and have no resources, and usually no home to which they can return. Then there are people who are internally displaced, either because they sought refuge within their homeland when their villages and lands were decimated by war, or because they were forcibly resettled by the Mengistu regime; some internally displaced people also migrated because of extreme drought and famine exacerbated by war. And finally, there is the local destitute population, often the most neglected, who remained in their cities and villages.

The UNHCR's mandate extends to refugees (excluding the internally displaced) and within that mandate is the responsibility for their secure repatriation. Generally, the UNHCR provides transportation for the return and some support for a brief period of time, often, for example, until the first harvest. The UNHCR deals in relief rather than development, in return rather than reintegration.

The internally displaced and the locally destitute populations are the responsibility of the government of a country. A government must struggle to balance assistance to the various groups of needy people. If returnees are given basic provisions and other groups are not, resentment toward the returning refugees quickly builds. To provide assistance for one targeted group and to ignore others is to precipitate problems. In any case, returnees put a burden on a population that has little or nothing itself. What is needed is broader development assistance to reach all groups and to strengthen the national economy.

War-torn nations, such as Eritrea, generally do not have the resources to provide what is necessary to reintegrate refugees, to resettle the internally displaced, and to assist local citizens in dire poverty. Until mines are cleared, land is rehabilitated for planting, roads are reconstructed, water and sewage facilities repaired, medical clinics and schools rebuilt—until a basic infrastructure is in place—the country cannot sustain its population. All of this requires a considerable long-term investment as well as trained and skilled personnel.

Organizations with development mandates, such as United Nations Development Program (UNDP) or USAID, hesitate to undertake long-term development projects because of the risks involved. A major risk lies in the unresolved matter of Eritrean sovereignty. Without greater flexibility and coordination among the various relief and development organizations, Eritrea's needs—or the needs of any nation recovering from war—will not be met. It will be difficult for Eritrea to become a viable nation, and large segments of its population may never escape destitution and dependency.

THE BATTLE FOR MASSAWA: INFRASTRUCTURE AND FOOD RELIEF

Transportation is often a vital but missing part of the infrastructure needed for both relief and development. Key to post-war transportation and to relief and development efforts in Eritrea is the port of Massawa. This spectacular city on the Red Sea was built by the Moors in the fourteenth and fifteenth centuries. Since then it has served as a major port. In addition to light industries and port revenues, it was also a lively tourist center with beaches, hotels, and restaurants.

Between 1977 and 1978, Massawa turned into a battlefield and many civilians fled. The Ethiopians eventually won control of Massawa and used it as a depot for military supplies from the Soviet Union and for relief supplies awaiting distribution to civilians. Consequently, food distribution was uneven. More food went to the Ethiopian military and those civilians living in government-controlled areas. Even though more peasants lived in EPLF-controlled areas, they received less food.

In 1990 the battle for control of Massawa resumed. In February, after a long hiatus, the EPLF began an offensive designed as a final blow to the Ethiopian troops still holding the port, the capital city of Asmara, and the city of Keren. The assault began with the port, which was essential for control of the other cities. EPLF forces sunk ships and captured Soviet tanks and heavy artillery. During a pitched and bloody battle on the short causeway separating the port from the city, hundreds more were killed as the two sides met face to face. The EPLF, who held the city of Massawa, crossed over the causeway to take charge of the port.

The battle for Massawa jeopardized the lives of millions, for Massawa was the pipeline for most of the relief food entering the country. With the port and the highway to the city under siege, transportation of food inland was blocked. The United Nations tried to mediate an agreement between the rebel forces and the government so Massawa could be used freely for relief purposes and the transport of food. The Ethiopians balked, saying that the port was out of commission and that relief supplies should go through the port of Assab and then be airlifted to distribution points. The government of Ethiopia believed any concession on its part would give de facto recognition to Eritrean control. The EPLF insisted it be the exclusive funnel of food throughout Eritrea, both from the port of Massawa and from the cross-border operation from Sudan that had been carried out for a number of years by the Eritrean Relief Association.

For two months following the fall of the port to the EPLF, Ethiopian troops tried to regain Massawa and failed. Without warning, on April 5, 1990, Soviet MiGs bombed consecutively for three days with no let up. Of the seventy-five thousand citizens in Massawa, forty thousand fled. From May until October, bombardments continued from the air by day and the sea by night. Most of the remaining civilian population left, many for Port Sudan. A majority of the casualties were women and children. Men remained behind to continue fighting or to protect what property might be left.

It took days to topple solid structures, kill hundreds, wound hundreds more, and demolish the port of Massawa with Soviet MiGs and other costly, advanced weapons, some holdovers from the days when the United States provided the government of former Emperor Haile Selassie with war materials before alliances shifted in Somalia and Ethiopia. It will take years to restore the port and the town with far less in assistance offered to rebuild than was given for its destruction.

While Massawa remained a ghost town of fewer than ten thousand inhabitants, negotiations continued to reopen the port as a conduit for food. President Bush and President Gorbachev agreed to a joint U.S. and Soviet food supply operation. The port of Massawa was to be declared a neutral zone through which relief supplies could pass, and American food would be distributed within the country by Soviet aircraft. Although President Mengistu agreed, he continued the assault on Massawa. The EPLF, however, was not so agreeable. As late as July 1990, when the U.N. World Food Program tried to persuade the EPLF to relent and let ships loaded with relief supplies dock, EPLF officials allowed supplies to enter only if they were transferred to Eritrean ships. It was not until year's end that the problem of the port was resolved and an agreement was worked out with the World Food Program.

At the beginning only one forklift functioned and ships bearing relief food could not actually dock. All the storage facilities had been destroyed. Without satellite communications, the only means of knowing when a vessel was arriving was to see it appear on the horizon. There was no water, no electricity, no means of communication beyond the port. Yet people were in desperate need of relief food. Many were starving; others were in grave danger. Repair of the port facilities took first priority. Four cranes were repaired and put into operation so that ships could off-load. The World Food Program supplied the port with a tug boat, packing machines, three large-capacity generators, and tractors for pulling relief supplies and consumer goods to waiting trucks or to storage, and for moving export cargo—salt to begin with and then hides and skins.

As the port began to operate, the first convoy of trucks filled with bags of donated grain crossed the causeway from the port into the city of Massawa. Still in May 1992, one year after the fall of Mengistu, the drivers passed rubble on either side; residents were trying to live in rooms that had not been leveled in the bombing. Any habitable space within the crumbled concrete became a home. In the rock-strewn, open doorway of one building, a man sat on a rock shaving his beard with a double-edged blade but without soap, shaving cream, or water. Children played between broken buildings. Among the children of Massawa, 60 percent under the age of five were severely malnourished. Irreparable physical and mental damage was done to children who went without minimal food and water for days at a time. Women walked long distances to fetch their allotments of water, and fuel wood for cooking became an ever more precious commodity. Further on, the trucks passed the remains of a seven-hundred-year-old palace used by Haile Selassie when he visited Massawa. Then came rows and rows of shanties made from corrugated tin, odd-shaped pieces of wood, plastic, or burlap—whatever material was available. These belonged to citizens who were returning to Massawa to rebuild their homes and their lives. The area where the shanties stood had once been graced with sturdy homes where people lived securely. No more than twenty thousand of the seventy-five thousand original inhabitants of Massawa had returned in 1992, the year following the liberation of Eritrea.

As if the demolished city did not bear adequate testimony to the fury of Mengistu's army, there was a more brutal reminder just at the city's edge. Someone had placed a high fence of corrugated tin around a small area to protect its contents from further debasement or dishonor. Inside the fence, stacked in no particular order, were ten or twelve green wooden, coffin-sized boxes. They were filled with dismembered bones of Ethiopian soldiers. Mixed and unidentified—the arm of one person, the leg of another—they were testimony that war mixes up everything. Not all the bones were contained in the boxes. The first human remains to be seen at the gate's opening was a lower leg bone standing upright with the foot still wearing its sock and boot as if ready to march. It was said that these were the remains of Ethiopian soldiers killed by other Ethiopian soldiers because they did not muster quickly enough for those behind them.

As the relief effort got underway, fifty long-haul trucks of the World Food Program traveled over a mountainous road with many switchbacks ascending 10,000 feet above sea level and down to Asmara at 7,500 feet. The road to Asmara was built by the Italians and kept in good repair until the war. But tanks and heavy armored vehicles had broken it apart so that traveling the switchbacks was very hard on the trucks. Some of the heaviest fighting in the war, particularly during the final offensives, took place between Massawa and Asmara.

By 1992 the population was desperate for food. Seventy-five percent of the Eritrean people were totally dependent on food supplied by relief agencies. Five hundred thousand tons of food were needed in 1992 as agricultural production had been nearly decimated by the war. Between 1961 and 1991, the most food that had been produced in one year was 220,000 tons. In 1991 Eritrea had produced only seventy thousand tons and by the middle of 1992, the donor community had made few commitments of aid. As a result, the World Food Program was forced to depend on food originally destined for other countries that could be diverted into the port of Massawa. In recent years, there are usually around one hundred ships at sea at any given time carrying food for relief. In a crisis, some of that food is diverted to more critical areas. Such was the need in 1992 in Eritrea and Ethiopia.

Donors are still wary of the situation in Eritrea. Because of its uncertain status, neither a country nor a province, some donors are not comfortable with promising food relief. Some are not willing to concede that the PGE is stable with no factional uprisings. They do not believe that donated food will actually reach the intended beneficiaries. Without that trust and without a clear pipeline, there will not be enough food for the general population, much less for refugees returning to their villages from Sudan. In addition, inadequate food supplies make it impossible to plan government programs of food for work to assist in restoring Eritrea's infrastructure.

Some barren areas to which people wish to return were once fertile and they could be again, given seed and oxen. Without food for either people or livestock during the period before the first harvest, it will not be possible for people to farm. In some of the hardest-hit famine areas, 50 percent or more of the livestock died. What livestock remains has little flesh and is being sold at half the normal price.

One of the biggest worries of the new Eritrean government is that people will become dependent on relief assistance rather than self-sufficient. Prolonged dependency, they acknowledge, lowers morale and motivation, both vital to revive the country. In addition to emergency assistance, Eritrea needs development funds. Without a large infusion of development assistance, dependency will take a firmer grip on Eritrean citizens, making it more difficult to break the cycle of dependence. No one wants unending handouts, but Eritreans do need a bridge to self-sufficiency.

It is estimated that $2.5 billion will be needed to rebuild Eritrea. The most critical needs have enormous price tags. With money not forthcoming from donors, Eritreans feel let down by the international community. In their desire to develop a viable economy under democratic principles, they are dismayed to find funding slow in coming and outsiders unwilling to invest in the country until the sovereignty issue is settled.

Still, the new government initiated one of the most liberal investment codes on the African continent. Soon after liberation, the Eritrean work force of demobilized soldiers restored power generators, made water-pumping stations operational in the capital, and rehabilitated a few factories. Plans moved ahead to privatize almost fifty nationalized industries, with a view toward a liberally regulated market and export-based economy. Eritrea had developed a good industrial base during the Italian colonial era and it can be revitalized. It was a fruit-exporting area before the Mengistu period and farmers are anxious to produce for export fruits, vegetables, grains, fish, salt, and hides, with an eye on the Middle East as the most promising market. The government also encourages small industries and entrepreneurial enterprises. It plans to continue to control certain key elements of the economy such as health, education, transportation, communication, land, mineral resources, roads, and utilities.

SOCIAL CHANGES: THE ROLE OF WOMEN

While war confuses everything, it facilitates change. Eritrea had never known democratic government or independence. All classes of people, save a few elite large landowners, church leaders, and colonizers, had felt the oppression of colonizers, feudal emperors, and totalitarian rulers. Women were the most oppressed group.

During the war, the EPLF developed a philosophy of social change that encompassed the liberation of the land and the people. Part of that philosophy was to include women in all areas of society and to accord them the rights to which they were entitled. Thirty-three percent of EPLF fighters were women. Their presence in battle proved to many men that women should be involved in all areas of society and in decision-making processes as well. Those who were imprisoned with women testify that more often than not, the women were more determined than the men. They had more grit. One former prisoner said that much of the new Eritrea will be built on top of the bones of women.

Askalu Menkerios, Senaet Lejam, and Azieb Fessamaie were among these fighters. They are now dedicating their lives to ensure that the changes for women that took seed in the EPLF-liberated areas during the war years will come to fruition for all Eritrean women. Apolitical in their youth, events propelled them to take a stand and act upon their newly formed convictions. Each of the women arrived at her decision to join the EPLF from a different vantage point, and each came to understand the crucial role of women in society and the need to press for the rightful equality of women through her own experiences as a female fighter.

Askalu, who today is one of six women on the seventy-one-member central governing committee, recalled that while she was working in Addis Ababa, she became more and more aware of discrimination against Eritreans, herself included.

Even Ethiopian Airlines stopped hiring Eritreans, some of their most skilled employees. In mechanical skills, no one can surpass Eritreans.

I was born and brought up in Asmara. When I returned for a vacation and saw tanks in the streets, the prisons packed, even with youngsters, and all that was happening, I decided to join the liberation movement. I was twenty-three. During the war I became a barefoot doctor and drove an ambulance.

In one week in 1978 more than two thousand women joined the EPLF, the largest number at one time. From that time on, more and more women joined.

Everyone was affected. Every family had members who were imprisoned or killed. The more the liberation struggle grew, the more the persecution grew. And the more the persecution grew, the more the liberation struggle grew. Many young people vowed, "When I grow up, I will kill at least one Amhara," for the Amharas had been the ruling elite from the time of Emperor Menelik, through Haile Selassie and Mengistu Haile Mariam.

Senaet remembers clearly the day she joined the liberation movement.

It was February 7, 1975. I would not see my parents again until August 9, 1991. I was sixteen-and-a-half, a student in secondary school. I was to go on to university because my father said, "My daughters must be educated more than my sons." But I never had the chance to continue my education. Instead I went to the front and fought in the war.

In Asmara students were demonstrating against the brutality of Mengistu's policies and the atrocities his soldiers were committing. The soldiers began killing students. Three of my closest friends were killed in cold blood near our school. It was then that I decided to join the struggle of the EPLF. I was the only girl who left with six boys. Although I did not tell my parents I was leaving, I did manage to send a note to them to let them know I was alive. In those days it was awful. Every day parents went into the streets to look at corpses to see if one might be a son or a daughter. I did not want my parents to go through that agony once I disappeared.

I went to a training center on the border with Sudan where thousands came to learn to fight. Most of us were high school and university students. We came in groups of three or four and made up thousands.

Azieb raised a family behind the front.

I was a student in the Italian school in Asmara. When I graduated, I went to Rome where I studied political science in the university. I returned to Eritrea, married and had two children—one girl and one boy.

I then went to the United States to study nutrition at Johns Hopkins. My husband and children were in France at the time. When I completed my studies in 1977, I joined them there. It was then that we decided to join the liberation movement.

I stayed fifteen years in the field with my husband and our children. We were not always together. Few families were able to remain a unit during the war. The children attended school in the field. Following the eighth grade, they attended the front's technical school where they studied survey and construction. Now at eighteen and sixteen, their skills will be needed as we rebuild our country.

As the war progressed in the liberated areas, the question of equal rights for women was given more and more consideration. In 1979 the three women were involved in founding what was to become the National Union of Eritrean Women (NUEW). Askalu was its chairwoman.

We lived in a very traditional society, like most of the African nations. This was particularly true in the rural areas. Urban women had more opportunities. Women were not allowed to vote. They could not own land or property. Women were obliged to accept arranged marriages. Often they were married at twelve or thirteen years of age. If the man divorced the woman, she had no choice but to leave with nothing. Usually a divorced woman could not return to her parents; they did not want her. If she could not find a job as a domestic servant, she frequently turned to prostitution. There was little else for her to do.

Women did not participate in the political process. They were not allowed to attend village or district council meetings. It was considered scandalous for a woman even to pass near the area where a meeting was taking place. A woman could not ask her husband about the meeting. That was not a woman's affair, only a man's.

In the war effort things began to change. One-third of the fighters were women and others provided different sorts of support to the EPLF. Wherever they were—in Sudan, Italy, the United States—they worked as housemaids or office clerks, or whatever job they could and contributed much of their earnings to the liberation cause. Many had only a half day off each week. Yet they donated that half day to work for EPLF needs.

Early in the struggle, many men were opposed to women involving themselves in the war, assisting the war effort, or allowing them equal rights—ownership of land, education, equal pay for equal work. They would say, "My wife is not going out of the house." Or, "Education is not good for women. They must be wives and mothers." Or, "Women are not experienced in governing. Why elect women when they know nothing?"

In the liberated areas things began to change. Mostly it was a change in attitudes—of men toward women and women toward themselves. Women had always been taught to belittle themselves.

In 1977 a law was passed stating that a girl must be eighteen and a boy twenty-one before they can marry. Other laws changed as well. Women were able to marry by choice, ask for a divorce, own land, and become a part of the political process. Twenty-five percent of the people's assemblies now are women. They have become a part of the decision-making bodies. A woman can elect and be elected.

Now that liberation has been achieved, the work of the National Union of Eritrean Women must reach all women. Even during the war, some village men in the liberated areas were not convinced that women should be accorded equal rights. Now some men are reverting to the old ways. Those who did not live in the liberated areas were never exposed to the new thinking about women. Nor were the refugees who lived in camps in Sudan. They lived the old ways.

We face a new challenge. Our task is one of educating all, male and female, on the grassroots level so that a conversion in thinking can take place. It is a matter of education and real conviction to affirm that women, who make up one-half of the population, are vital to the development of an independent Eritrea. Without them, the country will not fare as well.

As we spread throughout the villages and the districts to seek commitment to change the status of women, our first task is to spread literacy among women. It is also important for women to develop skills, be educated, and learn to manage their own lives. Then men, who have always been the decision makers on the political level, can no longer argue that since there are so many literate, professional men, women, who are illiterate and untrained, have no place in the decision-making arena.

The morale in Eritrea remains high, and hopes for growth and change are undiminished. These hopes are mirrored in groups like the NUEW, in spite of the daunting task of reconstruction, the continued suffering of the vast majority of the people, and the trickle of funds from the international community.

Eritrea's leaders face the dilemma of standing firm on their insistence of recognition and their desire to deal directly with the international community independent of Ethiopia. Numbers and statistics of needs are staggering—the return of 500,000 refugees; possibly 600,000 internally displaced; 50,000 seriously disabled soldiers and citizens; 50,000 war dead; 60,000 orphans; 50 percent of the livestock dead; 75 percent of the population on food relief; and more than 500,000 tons of food needed.

Not only the birth of a nation but the survival of a people is at stake if there is not an adequate humanitarian response from the international donor community. Without assistance, a backslide of devastating proportions will occur in this poor country burdened with a ravaged land and deterred from development. There could be a reverse flow of refugees to Sudan. One hundred thousand demobilized soldiers could be jobless when their two years of post-war service ends. The numbers of street children will increase. Further drought will cause starvation. Children will not be educated or immunized. Young and old, male and female—all will be adversely affected.

The hope remains that the international community will support Eritrea as it moves toward nationhood and begins to reconstitute itself after thirty years of war, drought, and famine. Reconstruction and developmental assistance is far cheaper than the cost of war. Helping people lift themselves up is a far nobler effort than neglecting them.

EPILOGUE

The end of the cold war has brought a new set of problems among and within nation-states. While large-scale conflicts backed by the superpowers are on the wane, internal conflicts between ethnic, linguistic, religious, or tribal groups are on the rise. These could remain contained or spill over borders and bring in other interested parties as belligerents. We see internal battles fragmenting and dispersing people in Yugoslavia, Ethiopia, Somalia, and former republics of the Soviet Union—Georgia, Azerbaijan, Armenia, and Moldova. The new world order now borders on disorder.

The question of national sovereignty and human rights will grow larger as more civilians become internally displaced victims of these wars. In World War I, 5 percent of the casualties of war were civilians while 95 percent were from the military. Today the tables have turned. Ninety percent of the casualties of war are civilians; only 10 percent are combatants. The ability to decide who gets food and who doesn't get food is often the most powerful weapon in these wars. Nowhere was this brought more sharply into focus than in southern Sudan in 1988. More than 250,000 civilians—mostly women, children, and the elderly—starved to death. International law which recognizes nation-states as "specific segments of territory and clusters of population"[1] gives them sacrosanct sovereignty. In many nations the principle of sovereignty overshadows the rights of the people to the protection of their government. But sovereign rulers have responsibilities. Professor Aristide Zolberg cautioned, "States may assert that sovereignty is absolute, but we don't have to believe them."[2] One of the greatest challenges of the newly appointed United Nations Under Secretary General for Humanitarian Assistance, Ambassador Jan Eliasson, will be to ensure that starving and suffering citizens caught in the clash of civil wars receive swiftly and securely the food and medical relief assistance to which they are entitled.

While the nature and complexity of the flow of displaced people is changing radically, more than six million people from Eritrea, Afghanistan, and Cambodia are on the verge of returning to homelands they fled at least a decade ago. The people of these nations never lost hope that one day they would return to their villages, towns, and cities. They focused their hearts and minds on going home, and their dream of return helped them survive the long years of exile.

If the 1970s and 1980s were decades of flight, the 1990s can be the decade of return. No returnee will go home the same, nor will the nation to which he or she returns ever be the same. Every person and every place will have been radically altered by the experience of war, exile, and the decimation of structures and land. Most refugees will return to villages that no longer exist. Many relatives and friends who remained in the homeland will have become casualties of war or estranged by fighting one against the other during the war.

As I journeyed among the refugees and to the nations to which they will return, I became tangibly aware of the centuries it takes to build a culture and a nation and the few years it takes to obliterate the land and the people who gave spirit and life to that particular culture and nation.

Today the beauty is that millions can return home. The pity is that in most cases peace is fragile, lands are destroyed, and coffers are empty. The people of the nations who have reached at least a tenuous peace are eager and willing to build new political, economic, and social orders.

The end of the cold war offers the world the opportunity to create peace. This will take uncommon moral will, indomitable spirit, and substantial, purely humanitarian development assistance. We cannot afford to walk away strategically, economically, or morally—for we *do belong to one another.* After humans walked in outer space, Archibald MacLeish wrote of our altered "conception of ourselves and our images of the earth":

> For the first time in all of time men [and women] have seen the earth with their own eyes—seen the whole earth in the vast void as even Dante never dreamed of seeing it.
>
> To see the earth as we see it, small and blue and beautiful in that eternal silence where it floats, is to see ourselves as riders on the earth together, brothers [and sisters] on that bright loveliness in the unending night—brothers [and sisters] who see now they are truly brothers [and sisters].[3]

NOTES

INTRODUCTION

1. "A Summer Preview—Or So Many People Are Hoping," *The New York Times* (May 24, 1992), A1.

2. Michael Wines, "Switching Policy, U.S. Will Return Refugees to Haiti," *The New York Times* (May 25, 1992), A1.

3. George Steiner, *Language and Silence* (London: Faber and Faber, 1967), as quoted in William Shawcross, *The Quality of Mercy: Cambodia, Holocaust, and Modern Conscience* (New York: Simon and Schuster, 1984), 13.

4. Thomas Friedman, "Baker, on Visit to Kurds, Declares U.S. Alone Cannot Resolve Plight," *The New York Times* (April 9, 1991), A12.

5. *Collection of International Instruments Concerning Refugees* (Geneva: Office of the United Nations High Commissioner for Refugees—UNHCR, 1979), 11.

6. Yefime Zarjevski, *A Future Preserved: International Assistance to Refugees* (New York: Pergamon Press, 1988), 252.

7. W. R. Smyser, "Refugees: A Never-Ending Story," *Foreign Affairs* (Fall 1985), 159.

8. Mu Tombo Mpanya, interview (Maryknoll, NY, August, 1990).

9. Lionel Rosenblatt, executive director of Refugees International, "Statement before the Select Committee on Hunger, U.S. House of Representatives" (May 6, 1992).

10. Ibid.

11. Lionel Rosenblatt, "Refugee Emergency Action Program: A Proposal to Protect Refugees in Life-Threatening Situations," unpublished document (March 2, 1992), 2.

12. Roger P. Winter, "The Year in Review," *U.S. Committee for Refugees: World Refugee Survey 1992* (Washington, D.C.: American Council for Nationalities Service, 1992), 4.

13. Mark Sommer, "Who Will Pay for Peace?" *The Christian Science Monitor* (February 19, 1992), 18.

14. Thomas Keneally, *To Asmara* (New York: Warner Books, 1989).

15. Roger P. Winter, "The Year in Review," *U.S. Committee for Refugees: World Refugee Survey 1988* (Washington, D.C.: American Council for Nationalities Service, 1989), 2.

16. Jane Perlez, "Is Food Going to Orphans or Future Sudan Rebels?" *The New York Times* (August 13, 1991), A4.

1. FLIGHT CAMBODIA

1. H. D. S. Greenway, "Report from Cambodia: The Tiger and the Crocodile," *New Yorker* (July 17, 1989), 82.

2. Kingdom of Cambodia 1954–70; Khmer Republic 1970–75; Democratic

305

Kampuchea 1975–78; People's Republic of Kampuchea 1979–89; State of Cambodia 1989.

3. Elizabeth Becker, *When the War Was Over: Cambodia's Revolution and the Voices of Its People* (New York: Simon and Schuster, Touchstone Books, 1986), 47.

4. Ibid., 65.

5. Ibid., 99.

6. Ibid.

7. Ibid.

8. Nayan Chanda, *Brother Enemy, the War after the War: A History of Indochina Since the Fall of Saigon* (New York: Macmillan, Collier Books, 1986), 126–127. Chanda notes that his account of China's role in the Geneva Conference is drawn mainly from Francois Joyaux, *La Chine et le règlement du premier conflict d'Indochine, Gèneve 1954* (Paris: Publications de la Sorbonne, 1979), 231–323.

9. Kimmo Kiljunen, ed. *Kampuchea: Decade of Genocide, Report of a Finnish Inquiry Commission* (London: Zed Books, 1984), 4. There is a similar situation with Afghanistan. In the 1950s the U.S. government made military aid to Afghanistan contingent on Afghanistan's joining CENTO (Baghdad Pact). Afghan Prime Minister Daoud declined and sought arms from the U.S.S.R.

10. Becker, *When the War Was Over*, 46.

11. Haing Ngor, *A Cambodian Odyssey* (New York: Warner Books, 1987), 30.

12. Ibid., 410.

13. Becker, *When the War Was Over*, 34.

14. Kiljunen, *Kampuchea*, 5–6.

15. Becker, *When the War Was Over*, 77.

16. Ibid., 148.

17. Ibid., 163–164.

18. Ngor, *Cambodian Odyssey*, 71, 112–113.

19. Becker, *When the War Was Over*, 167.

20. Ngor, *Cambodian Odyssey*, 41.

21. Becker, *When the War Was Over*, 156.

22. Ibid., 237.

23. Eva Mysliwiec, *Punishing the Poor: The International Isolation of Kampuchea* (Oxford: Oxfam House, 1988), 1.

24. The KPNLF (Khmer People's National Liberation Front) became one of the noncommunist Khmer factions formed after the defeat of the Khmer Rouge. Many members were former Lon Nol soldiers, some of whom became warlords along the Thai-Cambodian border and engaged in lucrative cross-border smuggling.

25. The war along the Thai-Cambodian border between the warring Vietnamese-backed troops of Heng Samrin and Hun Sen and the three Khmer border factions had to take place during the dry season. During the rainy season, tanks and troops bogged down and were unable to engage effectively in warfare.

26. At this writing Chhuon remains in Site 2. Since repatriation to Cambodia has begun for the Khmer people, Chhuon hopes to return soon to his village in Siem Reap Province.

2. CLOSED IN

1. Richard F. Mollica, M.D., and Russell R. Jalbert, and quoted in *Community of Confinement: The Mental Health Crisis in Site Two (Displaced Persons Camps on the Thai-Kampuchean Border)* (Boston: The Committee on Refugees and Migrants, The World Federation for Mental Health, February 1989), 24.

2. Lindsay French, Barnabas Mam, and Tith Wuthy, eds., *Displaced Lives: Stories of Life and Culture from the Khmer in Site II, Thailand* (Bangkok: International Rescue Committee, 1990), 41.

3. Susan Walker, *Handicap International Thailand Program January–June, 1989 Report* (Bangkok: Operation Handicap International, 1989), 2.

4. Mollica and Jalbert, *Community of Confinement*, 49.

5. Dr. Rene F. W. Diekstra, Division of Mental Health, WHO, *Psychosocial and Mental Health Problems of the Khmer Refugees in Site 2 and Site 8 on the Thai-Kampuchean Border* (Geneva, November 1988), 8.

6. Tony Jackson, *Just Waiting to Die?: Cambodian Refugees in Thailand* (Oxford: Oxfam House, July 1987), 4.

7. Josephine Reynell, *Political Pawns: Refugees on the Thai-Kampuchean Border* (Oxford: Refugees Studies Program, 1989).

8. Elizabeth Becker, *When the War Was Over: Cambodia's Revolution and the Voices of Its People* (New York: Simon and Schuster, Touchstone Books, 1986), 321–322.

9. William Shawcross, *The Quality of Mercy: Cambodia, Holocaust and Modern Conscience* (New York: Simon and Schuster, 1984), 82–83.

10. *Collection of International Instruments Concerning Refugees*, Article 1 (2), (Geneva: Office of the United Nations High Commissioner for Refugees, 1979), 11.

11. Ibid., Article 33 (1), 22–23.

12. Jackson, *Just Waiting*, 4.

13. Tony Banbury, *Kampuchean Displaced Persons in Thailand: Between the Devil and the Deep Blue Sea*, unpublished report (Boston, May 1988), 3; Reynell, *Political Pawns*.

14. Angela M. Berry, "The Early Days of Sakaeo: A Volunteer Worker's Experience," *Years of Horror, Days of Hope: Responding to the Cambodian Refugee Crisis*, edited by Barry S. Levy and Daniel C. Susott (New York: Associated Faculty Press, 1986), 42–43.

15. Ibid., 46.

16. Shawcross, *The Quality of Mercy*, 227.

17. Ibid., 228–230.

18. Ibid., 233.

19. Ibid., 237.

20. ASEAN nations are the Philippines, Malaysia, Singapore, Indonesia, and Thailand.

21. "Declaration of the Formation of the Coalition Government of Democratic Kampuchea," *Documents on the Kampuchean Problem 1979–1985* (Bangkok: Ministry of Foreign Affairs, 1985), 119–120.

22. Ibid., 119.

23. Court Robinson, U.S. Committee for Refugees, interview (Washington, D.C., August 14, 1989).

24. Ibid.

25. Ibid.

26. Jim Anderson, International Rescue Committee, interview (Bangkok, February 25, 1989).

27. Ibid.

28. Definition of UNBRO. UNBRO Headquarters, Bangkok.

29. Reynell, *Politcal Pawns*, 35.

30. Rebecca Parks, "At the Border: Late 1984," *Years of Horror, Days of Hope*, 358–359.

31. Andy Pendleton, UNBRO coordinator, Site 2, interview (Thailand, October 27, 1989).

32. Lawyers Committee for Human Rights, *Refuge Denied: Problems in the Protection of Vietnamese and Cambodians in Thailand and the Admission of Indochinese Refugees into the United States* (New York: Lawyers Committee for Human Rights, 1989), 15.

33. The account of the 1984–85 evacuation is told in an article by Brother Bob Maat, S.J., *"The Major Disruption at Samet, Christmas, 1984"* (Washington, D.C.: Jesuit Refugee Service/U.S.A., 1985), 3–37.

34. Ibid., 22.

35. Vitit Muntarbhorn, "Displaced Persons in Thailand: Legal and National Policy Issues in Perspective," *Chulalongkorn Law Review* (vol. 1, 1982), 10–11. As cited in Banbury, *Kampuchean Displaced Persons*, 19.

36. Lawyers Committee for Human Rights, *Seeking Shelter: Cambodians in Thailand, A Report on Human Rights* (New York: Lawyers Committee for Human Rights, 1987), 37–38.

37. Lawyers Committee for Human Rights, *Refuge Denied*, 56.

38. Lawyers Committee for Human Rights, *Seeking Shelter*, 44–47.

39. Reynell, *Political Pawns*, 135.

40. Dr. David Loveridge, clinical psychologist, ICM Mental Health Program, interview (Phanat Nikhom Camp, Thailand, February 23, 1989).

41. Jim Anderson, International Rescue Committee, interview (Bangkok, February 25, 1989).

42. Susan Walker, *Operation Handicap International Report, July–December 1989* (Bangkok: Operation Handicap International, 1989), 14.

43. Lawyers Committee on Human Rights, *Seeking Shelter*, 74–76.

44. Susan Walker, *1988 Operation Handicap Annual Report* (Bangkok: Operation Handicap International, 1988) 10; *Operation Handicap January–June 1989 Report* (Bangkok: Operation Handicap International, 1989), 11.

45. Susan Walker, *Operation Handicap International Thailand 1988 Annual Report* (Bangkok: Operation Handicap International, 1988), 18.

46. Friedemann Bartu, "The Khmer Rouge Take the Offensive," *Swiss Review of World Affairs* (January 1989), 24.

47. Steven Erlanger, "Khmer Rouge Move Their Refugees," *The New York Times* (September 3, 1990).

48. The Asia Watch Committee, *Khmer Rouge Abuses Along the Thai-Cambodian Border* (Washington, D.C.: The Asia Watch Committee, 1989), 18. Quoted in a press statement issued by the U.S. Department of State (November 14, 1988).

49. Chhoeuth Sarun, Site 2 (Thailand), as spoken to Dr. Louis Braile.

3. CAMBODIA RETURN

1. Peggy Braile, letter to her parents (October 27, 1991) quoting Brother Bob Maat, S.J.

2. Philip Shenon, "The Prince of Survivors: Norodom Sihanouk," *The New York Times* (October 25, 1991).

3. Sheila Teft, "Cambodia's Sihanouk Pushes Peace," *Christian Science Monitor* (August 8, 1991), 3.

4. Shenon, "Prince of Survivors."

5. Hun Sen lost one eye in the war. Sihanouk referred to him as a lackey of the Vietnamese.

6. Rodney Tasker and Murray Hiebert, "Back to the Unknown: Cambodia Before and After," *Far Eastern Economic Review* (November 7, 1991), 28.

7. If Sihanouk is to be the symbol of a peaceful Cambodia and the security against the Khmer Rouge, the prince will have to attend to more than the urban dwellers, which is his tendency. It is in the countryside that the Khmer Rouge maintain their greatest strength and support.

8. Philip Shenon, "Cambodians Clash on Memorials," *The New York Times* (November 16, 1991).

9. A.F.P., "K. Rouge Papers Show Direct Reports to Pol Pot," *Bangkok Post* (December 3, 1991), 6.

10. Ibid.

11. Urs Boegli, head of delegation, International Committee of the Red Cross, Thailand, "Talk for CCSDPT Annual Conference: Repatriation" (Bangkok, October 20, 1989), 1.

12. Susan Walker, "Threat of Forced Repatriation, Site 8, Thai-Cambodian Border," Operation Handicap International Press Release (October 10, 1991), 2.

13. Some of the sentences in the text have been altered for structure, not content.

14. S.A.M.S. Kibria, Press Statement (Bangkok: United Nations, October 12, 1991).

15. The above excerpts from letters from Site 8, October 3–17, 1991, are taken from Operation Handicap International Press Release (October 21, 1991).

16. Roger A. Fordham, "The Khmer Border: The Never-Ending Story" (Bangkok: CCSDPT, July 1991), 4.

17. Operation Handicap International Press Release (October 21, 1991).

18. The diarist was among the first Khmers to repatriate to Cambodia in May, 1992. He was reunited with his mother after thirteen years of separation.

19. Peggy Braile, physician for American Refugee Committee, letters to her parents (August 31, 1991, and October 12, 1991).

20. "UNHCR Information Bulletin No. 2 on Cambodia Repatriation Plan" (November 21, 1991), 3.

21. Daniel Conway, UNHCR representative in Thailand, interview (Bangkok, December 3, 1991).

22. Asia Watch and Physicians for Human Rights, *Land Mines in Cambodia: The Coward's War* (Washington, D.C.: Human Rights Watch and Physicians for Human Rights, 1991), 1.

23. Ibid., 4.

24. Ibid., 23.

25. Ibid., 36. According to this report "one out of every 236 Cambodians has lost one or more limbs after stepping on a land mine." By comparison in Vietnam with 60,000 amputees from the Vietnam War out of a population of 75 million, one out of every 1,250 Vietnamese are handicapped from the war (p. 36). And, "In 1989 surgeons in the United States, with a population of 220 million, performed no more than 10,000 amputations on patients who had suffered traumatic injuries" (p. 1).

26. Ibid., 22–23.

27. Ibid., 57–58, 60.

28. Women's Commission for Refugee Women and Children Delegation Report, "Cambodia — On the Brink" (January 1991), 5–6.

29. Roger A. Fordham, *Cambodian Report: CCSDPT* (Bangkok, August 1991), 22, 18.

30. Bret Ballard, Phnom Penh director, American Friends Service Committee, interview dealing with the current agricultural situation in Cambodia (Phnom Penh, October 20, 1991).

31. UNICEF, *Cambodia: The Situation of Women and Children* (Phnom Penh: UNICEF Office of the Special Representative, 1990), 115.

32. Eva Mysliwiec, *Punishing the Poor: The International Isolation of Kampuchea* (Oxford: Oxfam House, 1988), 28–30; Women's Commission for Refugee Women and Children, "Cambodia—On the Brink," 14–15.

33. Women's Commission for Refugee Women and Children, "Cambodia—On the Brink," 17.

34. Asia Watch and Physicians for Human Rights, *Land Mines in Cambodia*, 42, 39.

35. UNICEF, *Cambodia*, xv.

36. Fordham, "Cambodian Report," 34.

37. UNICEF, *Cambodia*, xiv.

38. J. R. Rogge, "Return to Cambodia: The Significance and Implications of Past, Present, and Future Spontaneous Repatriations" (Manitoba: Disaster Research Unit, University of Manitoba, March 1990), 123, as quoted in Asia Watch and Physicians, *Land Mines*, 49.

39. Women's Commission for Refugee Women and Children, "Cambodia—On the Brink," 7.

40. Henry Kamm, "Return of Refugees to Cambodia to Take Longer Than Planned," *The New York Times* (April 12, 1992), 22.

41. Peggy Braile, letter to her parents (April 12, 1992).

42. Kamm, "Return of Refugees," 22.

43. Maha Ghosananda, *Step By Step* (Berkeley: Parallax Press, 1992), 69 and 33.

44. Peggy Braile, letter to her parents (April 12, 1992).

4. FLIGHT AFGHANISTAN

1. Louis Dupree, *Afghanistan* (Princeton, N.J.: Princeton University Press, 1980), 5.

2. Ibid., 272–283.

3. Ibid., 316.

4. Raja Anwar, *The Tragedy of Afghanistan: A First-Hand Account* (New York: Verso, 1988), 19.

5. Dupree, *Afghanistan*, 483.

6. Ibid., 516, 523.

7. Thomas J. Abercrombie, "Afghanistan, Crossroad of Conquerors," *National Geographic*, vol. 134, no. 3 (September 1968), 302.

8. Anwar, *The Tragedy*, 71.

9. Dupree, *Afghanistan*, 523.

10. Anwar, *The Tragedy*, 92-93.

11. Ibid., 151.

12. Arthur Bonner, *Among the Afghans* (Durham, N.C.: Duke University Press, 1987), 45.

5. REFUGEE WOMEN

1. Suzy Comerford, "To Be a Refugee Woman," *Maryknoll Women's Coordinating Group Issue Paper #5: Refugee Women* (Maryknoll, N.Y., June 1989).

2. Margaret Segal, "The Lycee Malalai: A Hopeful Place for Afghan Girls," unpublished report (Peshawar, Pakistan, 1989), 1.

3. Lindsay French, project coordinator, Barnabas Mam and Tith Wuthy, editors,

Displaced Lives: Stories of Life and Culture from the Khmer in Site II, Thailand (Bangkok: International Rescue Committee, 1990), 114–115.

4. Nancy Hatch Dupree, "A Sociocultural Dimension: Afghan Women Refugees in Pakistan," unpublished paper (1989), 5–6.

5. The *chader* used in Afghanistan can be a simple veil that covers a woman's head only, or, in its more extreme form, can cover the entire body, leaving only a woman's face exposed. Over a period of extended exile and because of a growing conservatism among some Afghan leaders, it became more and more common for Afghan women to wear the more extreme form, usually of heavy black cloth. The *chaderi* is the most radical mode of veiling. Not even the face shows. The woman sees through a cloth grill that covers the face.

6. Even though Najibullah, who led Afghanistan from May 1986 until April 1992, is Afghan, he is not acceptable to the majority of Afghans because he was installed by the Soviets. Fiercely independent, Afghans will not accept an imposed leader, particularly one who is communist. Hence Afghans, even after the departure of Soviet troops, still saw the war as *jihad* against the infidel. Leaders of other governments, however, called the continuation of fighting a civil war.

7. Barbara Crosette, "As Accord on Afghan Future Nears, Refugees Live in Fear and Hardship," *The New York Times* (August 19, 1990), A14.

8. Margaret Segal, International Rescue Committee, and Anne Hurd, Mercy Fund, interviews (Peshawar, Pakistan, April 15 and 16, 1989).

9. Pushtun proverb as cited in the Abstract of Sima Wali's thesis, "Revolutionary Trends in Afghanistan," 3.

10. Margaret Segal, interview (April 15, 1989).

11. This loose coalition of seven parties, fundamentalist and liberal, based in Peshawar, was formed in May 1985. From 1989, under pressure from the governments of Pakistan and Saudi Arabia, it served as the Afghan government in exile. The fundamentalist groups and their leaders are: Hezb-i-Islami of Gulbuddin Hekmatyar; Hezb-i-Islami Afghanistan (Khales Group) of Mohammad Yunus Khales; Ittehad-e-Islami of Abd Al-Rasool Sayaf; and Jamiat-e-Islami Afghanistan of Professor Burhanuddin Rabbani (moderately conservative). The liberal groups and their leaders are: Mahaz-e-Melli-e-Islami or National Islamic Front of Afghanistan (NIFA) of Sayuyed Ahmad Gailani; Jabha-e-Melli Nejat or Afghan National Liberation Front (ANLF) of Sebghatullah Mojaddidi; and Harakat-e-Enquelab-e-Islami of Mohammad Nabi Mohammadi. For a brief synopsis of the alliance cf. Sabahuddin Kushkaki, "An Assessment of the New *Mujaheddeen* Alliance," *The Tragedy of Afghanistan*, edited by Bo Huldt and Erland Jansson (New York: Croom Helm, 1988), 164–172.

12. Anne Hurd, interview (April 15, 1989).

13. Margaret Segal of the International Rescue Committee in Peshawar, Pakistan, contributed to the material in this interview with Latifa (not her real name).

14. The two major languages of Afghanistan, one Persian, the other of the largest Afghan tribal group.

15. Margaret Segal, "The Lycee Malalai," 2. Information on the Lycee Malalai is drawn from interviews with Tajwar Kakar and Margaret Segal and International Rescue Committee reports on Lycee Malalai written by Margaret Segal.

16. Doris Lessing, *The Wind Blows Away Our Words* (London: Picador, 1987), 145–154.

17. Ibid., 151–153.

18. Margaret Segal, International Rescue Committee report on the progress of creating the school (August 1986).

19. Margaret Segal, "Monthly Report on Secondary Female Education" (September and October 1986), 1–2.

20. Margaret Segal, "Monthly Report on Secondary Female Education" (November-December 1986), 1-2.

21. Margaret Segal, Unpublished "Monthly Report on Secondary Female Education" (January, 1987), 1.

22. Richard MacKenzie, "A Brutal Force Batters a Country," *Insight* (December 5, 1988), 8.

23. Some of the above material is cited in Elizabeth Neuenschwander's "1988 Annual Report" on her programs for women and is interspersed with my interview.

24. Nancy Dupree, "Women in Afghanistan: Preliminary Needs Assessment," speech prepared for the United Nations Development Fund for Women (August 1988), 10.

25. Ninette Kelley, "Working with Refugee Women: A Practical Guide" Summary Report (Geneva, 1989).

26. "Afghan OBS/GYN Hospital Annual Report" (Peshawar, Pakistan, 1987), 2.

27. Veronica Doubleday, *Three Women from Herat* (London: Jonathan Cape, 1988), 62–63.

28. Nancy Dupree, "Women in Afghanistan," 7; Dupree, "A Sociocultural Dimension," 14.

29. Kelley, Summary Report, 2.

30. A person who "owing to a well-founded fear of being persecuted for reasons of race, religion, nationality, membership of a particular social group or political opinion, is outside the country of *his* nationality and is unable or, owing to such fear, is unwilling to avail *himself* of the protection of that country . . ." (emphasis added). Article 1A (2) 1951 Convention Relating to the Status of Refugees, as quoted by Anders B. Johnsson, senior legal advisor, Office of the United Nations High Commissioner for Refugees, "The International Protection of Women Refugees—A Summary of Principal Problems and Issues," a paper submitted to the International Consultation on Refugee Women (November 14–18, 1988), 2.

31. Ibid.

32. Nancy Hatch Dupree, "The Afghan Refugee Family Abroad: A Focus on Pakistan," *WUFA (Writers Union of Free Afghanistan)*, vol. 2, no. 4 (1987), 21.

33. Ninette Kelley, Summary Report.

34. "UNHCR Policy on Refugee Women" (May 21, 1990).

35. Major sources for this section: "Working with Refugee Women, Draft Report of the Expert Group Meeting on Refugee and Displaced Women and Children" (Vienna, July 2–6, 1990); "UNHCR Policy on Refugee Women" (May 21, 1990); and Mary Anderson, "Gender Analysis Framework for Refugee Work" (February 1990).

6. AFGHAN RETURN

1. "Text of the Geneva Accord," *Central Asia, Journal of Area Study Centre* (University of Peshawar, no. 23, Winter 1988), 99–103.

2. Najibullah replaced Babrak Karmal in May 1986 because Karmal could not get the Afghans to support a Soviet-controlled government.

3. John Burns, "Afghans, Now They Blame America," *The New York Times Magazine* (February 4, 1990), 27.

4. After the Soviet invasion, Khad intelligence agents grew to 25,000 from only 120 agents under former King Zahir Shah.

5. Sima Wali, unpublished notes (February 1992).

6. Rob Schultheis, "In Afghanistan, Peace Must Wait," *The New York Times Magazine* (December 29, 1991), 16.

7. Ibid., 23. Many *mujahideen* would not call Najibullah by his full name. They shortened it to Najib, indicating a lack of deference.

8. "Moscow Warms Up to the Rebels," *Asiaweek* (December 6, 1991), 28.

9. Justin Burke, "Afghan Rebels Aim for Concessions in Moscow," *The Christian Science Monitor* (November 15, 1991), 5.

10. Anwar-ul-Haq Ahady, "Looming Afghan Terror," *The Christian Science Monitor* (January 13, 1992), 18.

11. Salamat Ali, "The Royal Card," *Far Eastern Economic Review* (January 23, 1992), 22.

12. Edward A. Gargan, "Afghan President Agrees to Step Down," *The New York Times* (March 18, 1992), A3.

13. Donatella Lorch, "At Kabul's Gates, Tough Rebel Chief," *The New York Times* (April 21, 1992), A8.

14. Ahmed Rashid, "Warriors of the North: Ethnic Minorities Hold Military Advantage," *Far Eastern Economic Review* (May 7, 1992), 12.

15. "Distinct Identities: Afghanistan's Ethnic Groups," A Table. *The New York Times* (April 23, 1992), A6. Sources cited: the *CIA Yearbook*; Louis Dupree, *Afghanistan* (Princeton, N.J.: Princeton University Press, 1980).

16. "Distinct Identities," A6.

17. Donatella Lorch, "Afghan Guerrillas Differ on Makeup of Interim Regime," *The New York Times* (April 20, 1992), A1.

18. Edward A. Gargan, "U.N. Envoy Tells the Rebels They Must Be Afghans First," *The New York Times* (April 22, 1992), A1.

19. Edward A. Gargan, "Rebels' Leader Arrives in Kabul and Forms an Islamic Republic," *The New York Times* (April 29, 1992), A1.

20. Thomas L. Friedman, "U.S. Urges Afghan Factions to Avoid Violent Anarchy," *The New York Times* (April 17, 1992), A10.

21. Burns, "Afghans, Now They Blame America," 27.

22. "International Rescue Committee Program for Afghans," *Quarterly Report April–June 1989* (Peshawar, Pakistan: The International Rescue Committee, 1989), 18.

23. Ibid., 4.

24. Ibid., 6

25. Nancy Dupree, "Women in Afghanistan, Preliminary Needs Assessment," speech prepared for the United Nations Development Fund for Women (August 1988), 15.

26. Operation Salam, *Second Consolidated Report* (Geneva, Office of the United Nations Co-ordinator for Humanitarian and Economic Assistance Programmes Relating to Afghanistan, October 1989), 56.

27. Dupree, "Women in Afghanistan," 12.

28. Ibid., 14.

29. Thomas Hammarberg, "A Convention for the Future," *Making Reality of Children's Rights* (Stockholm: Radda Barnen, 1989), 11. This is from the final report of the International Conference on the Rights of the Child, Stockholm, Sweden, June 11–12, 1989.

30. *Making Reality of Children's Rights* (1989), 111.

31. Dr. Azam Dadfar, interview (Peshawar, Pakistan, April 29, 1989).

32. Dr. Azam Dadfar, *The Impaired Mind* (Peshawar, Pakistan: Psychiatry Centre for Afghans, 1988), 39–41.

33. *To Win the Children: Afghanistan's Other War* (New York: Helsinki Watch/Asia Watch, 1986), 2.

34. Convention on the Rights of the Child (New York: United Nations, 1991), 2.

35. Ibid., 4–8.

36. *The Children of Afghanistan in War and Refugee Camps* (Goteborg, Sweden: Novum Grafiska AB, 1988), 64. This is a document of the International Hearing in Stockholm (April 4–5, 1987).

37. "Children of War," *Cloud of Witnesses*, Vicki Kemper and Michael Verchat, interviewers, edited by Jim Wallis and Joyce Hollyday. (Maryknoll, NY: Orbis Books, 1991), 38.

7. FLIGHT ERITREA

1. Bereket Habte Selassie, *Eritrea and the United Nations and Other Essays* (Trenton, N.J.: The Red Sea Press, 1989), 31, quoting U.S. Secretary of Defense James Forrestal.

2. Ibid., 31–35.

3. James Firebrace with Stuart Holland, M.P., *Never Kneel Down: Drought, Development and Liberation in Eritrea* (Trenton, N.J.: The Red Sea Press, 1986), 19, as quoted in Permanent Peoples Tribunal 1980; Selassie, *Eritrea and the United Nations*, 37, as quoted in Linda Heiden, "The Eritrean Struggle for Independence," *Monthly Review*, vol. 30, no. 2 (June 1978), 15.

4. Firebrace, *Never Kneel Down*, 20; Robert Machida, *Eritrea: The Struggle for Independence* (Trenton, N.J.: The Red Sea Press, 1987), 23.

5. Selassie, *Eritrea and the United Nations*, 36–42; Firebrace, *Never Kneel Down*, 149–150.

6. Selassie, *Eritrea and the United Nations*, 42.

7. Firebrace, *Never Kneel Down*, "The 1950 UN Resolution on Eritrea," 149–152.

8. Machida, *Eritrea*, 52.

9. Selassie, *Eritrea and the United Nations*, 43; John Markakis, *National and Class Conflict in the Horn of Africa* (New York: Cambridge University Press, 1987), 94.

10. Firebrace, *Never Kneel Down*, 60 (from the Introduction by Dan Connell).

11. Selassie, *Eritrea and the United Nations*, 52.

12. Markakis, *National and Class Confict*, 94–95. There are conflicting accounts as to exactly how the federation was terminated. Some say a vote was taken. Others argue that by 1962 those who wanted either to retain the federation or to separate completely from Ethiopia had been forced from the assembly, leaving an unrepresentative majority in favor of complete union.

13. Selassie, *Eritrea and the United Nations*, 38; (*Final Report to the United Nations Commissioner to Eritrea*, chapter II, para. 201); Firebrace, *Never Kneel Down*, 21.

14. Markakis, *National and Class Conflict*, 106.

15. Ibid., 143; Firebrace, *Never Kneel Down*, 30–31.

16. Markakis, *National and Class Conflict*, 137–138.

17. Al Santoli, *New Americans, an Oral History: Immigrants and Refugees in the U.S. Today* (New York: Viking, 1988), 91.

18. Firebrace, *Never Kneel Down*, 77–78.

19. Ibid., 81.

20. Thomas Keneally, *To Asmara* (New York: Warner Books, 1989), 204ff; "In Eritrea," *The New York Times Magazine* (September 27, 1987), 42ff.

8. URBAN REFUGEES

1. U.S. Committee for Refugees, *World Refugee Survey, 1991* (Washington, D.C.: American Council for Nationalities Service, 1991), 54.

2. John R. Rogge, *Too Many, Too Long: Sudan's Twenty-Year Refugee Dilemma* (Totowa, N.J.: Rowman & Allanheld Publishers, 1985).

3. Aristide R. Zolberg, Astri Suhrke, and Sergio Aguayo, *Escape from Violence: Conflict and the Refugee Crisis in the Developing World* (New York: Oxford University Press, 1989), 50.

4. Africa Watch Report, *Denying "The Honor of Living": Sudan, a Human Rights Disaster* (New York: The Africa Watch Committee, 1990), 13.

5. Kathleen Hunt, "Sudan's Leaders Split on Ending Civil War," *The Christian Science Monitor* (January 9, 1989).

6. Robert Press, "In Sudan, Protesters Hope to Force End to Civil War," *The Christian Science Monitor International* (December 20, 1988), 7.

7. Africa Watch Report, *Denying "The Honor of Living,"* 19–20.

8. Neil Henry, "After Coup, Unsettled Sudan Faces Yet Another Fresh Start," *The Washington Post* (June 17, 1989), A1.

9. Lance Clark, "Internal Refugees—The Hidden Half," *U.S. Committee for Refugees: World Refugee Survey 1988 in Review* (Washington, D.C.: American Council for Nationalities Service, 1989), 18.

10. Ibid.

11. Africa Watch Report, *Denying "The Honor of Living,"* 92–93.

12. Roger P. Winter, "In Sudan Both Sides Use Food as a Weapon," *The Washington Post* (November 29, 1988), A25.

13. Africa Watch Report, *Denying "The Honor of Living,"* 119–120.

14. Margaret A. Novicki, "Bishop Paride Taban: Standing Up for the South," *Africa Report* (March–April 1991), 59.

15. Mary Battiata, "Sudan's Hungry: Let Them Eat Bullets," *The Washington Post National Weekly Edition* (November 21–27, 1988), 10.

16. Jane Perlez, "Hundreds Said to Starve Each Day in War Areas of Southern Sudan," *The New York Times* (September 10, 1988), A1.

17. Battiata, "Sudan's Hungry," 10. Ms. Battiata was quoting a radio message of Juba relief officials begging for relief. "Once more the citizens are left to eating only leaves and waiting to be buried."

18. Novicki, "Bishop Paride Taban," 59.

19. Robert Press, "Historic Food-Relief Effort," *The Christian Science Monitor* (June 7, 1989), 6.

20. Ibid.

21. Neil Henry, "Lifesaving Food Barge Stuck in Sudan Quagmire," *The Washington Post* (December 6, 1990), A1.

22. Roberta Cohen, *Human Rights Protection for Internally Displaced Persons* (Washington, D.C.: The Refugee Policy Group, 1991), 17, 19.

23. Ibid., 18.

24. Millard Burr, "Khartoum's Displaced Persons: A Decade of Despair," U.S. Committee for Refugees Issue Brief (Washington, D.C.: U.S. Committee for Refugees, 1990), 3.

25. Ibid., 1.

26. Ibid., 28, 36–37. From "The Final Report and Recommendations," the National Conference on the Displaced People (Khartoum, February 3–10, 1990).

27. Ibid., 39.

9. Eritrea Return

1. Jane Perlez, "A Hard-Line Marxist Who Mellowed: Meles Zenawi," *The New York Times* (May 30, 1991), A10.

2. Dan Connell, "Eritrean Rebels Prepare for Life After War—And After Marxism," *The Christian Science Monitor* (November, 15, 1990), 10.

3. "Eritrea, Freedom at Last," *New African* (November 1991), 21.

4. United Nations, Eritrea. "Inter-Agency Mission to Sahel Province: Findings with Recommendations" (Asmara, Eritrea, February 1992), 4, 17.

5. Michael A. Hilzik, "Eritrea: Vote an Issue," *Los Angeles Times* (December 28, 1991).

6. John R. Rogge, *Too Many, Too Long: Sudan's Twenty-Year Refugee Dilemma* (Totowa, N.J.: Rowman and Allenheld Publishers, 1985).

7. Trevor Page, personal representative of United Nations undersecretary-general for special political questions and special representative of the World Food Program in Eritrea, interview (Massawa, Eritrea, March 23, 1992).

8. Group of Seven industrialized democracies—United States, France, Germany, Canada, Japan, Britain, and Italy.

9. "Excerpts from Bush's Remarks on Aid Plan: 'Today We Must Win in the Peace,' " *The New York Times* (April 2, 1992), A11.

10. Nick Southern, remarks at a reception hosted by the Women's Commission for Refugee Women and Children (Addis Ababa, Ethiopia, March 10, 1992).

EPILOGUE

1. Aristide R. Zolberg, Astri Suhrke, and Sergio Aguayo, *Escape from Violence: Conflict and the Refugee Crisis in the Developing World* (New York: Oxford University Press, 1989), 12.

2. Quoted in Roger P. Winter, "The Year in Review," *U.S. Committee for Refugees World Refugee Survey 1992* (Washington, D.C.: American Council for Nationalities Service, 1992), 4.

3. Archibald MacLeish, *Riders on the Earth* (Boston: Houghton Mifflin, 1978), xiii-xiv.

BIBLIOGRAPHY

GENERAL

Books and Reports

Anderson, Mary B., and Peter J. Woodrow. *Rising From the Ashes: Development Strategies in Times of Disaster*. San Francisco: Westview Press, 1989.

Ashabranner, Brent, and Ashabranner, Melissa. *Into a Strange Land: Unaccompanied Refugee Youth in America*. New York: Dodd, Mead & Company, 1987.

Baedjaoui, Mohammed. *Modern Wars: The Humanitarian Challenge*. A Report for the Independent Commission on International Humanitarian Issues. New Jersey: Zed Books, Ltd., 1986.

Bennett, Jon, with Susan George. *The Hunger Machine: The Politics of Food*. New York: Polity Press with Basil Blackwell, 1987.

Capa, Robert. *Children of War, Children of Peace*. Edited by Cornell Capa and Richard Whelan. Boston: A Bulfinch Press Book, Little, Brown and Company, 1991.

Clark, John. *For Richer For Poorer: An Oxford Report on Western Connections With World Hunger*. Oxford: Belmont Press, 1986.

Clark, Lance. *Country Reports on Five Key Asylum Countries in Eastern and Southern Africa*. Washington, DC: Refugee Policy Group, April 1987.

———. *Post-Emergency Assistance For Refugees in Eastern and Southern Africa: An Overview*. Washington, DC: Refugee Policy Group, April 1987.

Cohen, Roberta. *Introducing Refugee Issues Into the United Nations Human Rights Agenda*. Washington, DC: Refugee Policy Group, 1990.

Collection of International Instruments Concerning Refugees. Geneva: Office of the United Nations High Commissioner for Refugees, 1979.

Convention On the Rights of the Child. New York: United Nations, 1991.

Crittenden, Ann. *Sanctuary: A Story of American Conscience and Law in Collision*. New York: Weidenfeld & Nicolson, 1988.

Davidson, Miriam. *Convictions of the Heart: Jim Corbett and the Sanctuary Movement*. Tucson: The University of Arizona Press, 1988.

Fenton, Thomas P. and Mary J. Heffron, editors. *Third World Resource Directory: A Guide To Organizations and Publications*. Maryknoll, NY: Orbis Books, 1984.

Forbes, Susan S. *Adaptation and Integration of Refugees to the United States*. Washington, DC: Refugee Policy Group, August 1985.

———, Timothy Eckels, and Deborah Kogan. *Future Directions in the U.S. Refugee Settlement Program*. Washington, DC: Refugee Policy Group, n.d.

Fry, Varian. *Surrender on Demand*. New York: Random House, 1945.

Gallagher, Dennis, Guest Editor. *Refugees, Issues and Directions: Special Issue, International Migration Review*. Staten Island, NY: Center For Migration Studies, Vol. 20 (Summer, 1986).

———, Susan Forbes, and Patricia Weiss Fagen. *Safe Haven: Policy Responses to*

Refugee-Like Situations. Washington, DC: Refugee Policy Group, June 1987.

————, Susan Forbes, and Patricia Weiss Fagen. *Of Special Humanitarian Concern: U.S. Refugee Admissions Since Passage of the Refugee Act.* Washington, DC: Refugee Policy Group, September 1985.

Gioseffi, Daniela, editor. *Women on War: Essential Voices for the Nuclear Age From a Brilliant International Assembly.* New York: Simon and Schuster, Inc. A Touchstone Book, 1988.

Goodwin-Gill, Guy S. *The Refugee in International Law.* Oxford: Clarendon Press, 1983.

Gozdziak, Elzbieta. *Older Refugees in the United States: From Dignity to Despair.* Washington, DC: Refugee Policy Group, 1988.

Hancock, Graham. *Lords of Poverty: The Power, Prestige, and Corruption of the International Aid Business.* New York: The Atlantic Monthly Press, 1989.

Harrell-Bond, Barbara E. *Imposing Aid: Emergency Assistance to Refugees.* New York: Oxford University Press, 1986.

Helsinki Watch. *Detained, Denied, Deported: Asylum Seekers in the United States.* New York: Helsinki Watch, June 1989.

International Bibliography of Refugee Literature. Geneva: International Refugee Integration Resource Centre, 1985.

International Symposium on the Protection of Children. Independent Commission on International Humanitarian Issues and Radda Barnen. Amman, Jordan (November 1984).

Keely, Charles B., with Patricia J. Elwell. *Global Refugee Policy: The Case for a Development-Oriented Strategy.* A Public Issues paper of the Population Council. New York: The Population Council, 1981.

Kelley, Ninette. *Working With Refugee Women: A Practical Guide.* Presentations and Discussion at the International Consultation on Refugee Women. Geneva (September 1989).

Kent, Randolph C. *Anatomy of Disaster Relief: The International Network in Action.* New York: Pinter Publishers, 1987.

Kismaric, Carole. *Forced Out: The Agony of the Refugee in Our Time.* New York: Random House, 1989.

Lawyers Committee for Human Rights. *The UNHCR at 40: Refugee Protection at the Crossroads.* New York: Lawyers Committee for Human Rights, February 1991.

Levenstein, Aaron. *Escape To Freedom: The Story of the International Rescue Committee.* Westport, CT: Greenwood Press, 1983.

Lockman, Zachary and Joel Beinin. *Intifada: The Palestinian Uprising Against Israeli Occupation.* Boston: South End Press, 1989.

Loescher, Gil and John A. Scanlan. *Calculated Kindness: Refugees and America's Half-Open Door 1945—Present.* New York: The Free Press, A Division of Macmillan, Inc., 1986.

Loescher, Gil, and Laila Monahan, editors. *Refugees and International Relations.* New York: Oxford University Press, 1989.

MacEoin, Gary, editor. *Sanctuary: A Resource Guide For Understanding and Participating in the Central American Refugees' Struggle.* New York: Harper and Row, 1985.

Making Reality of Children's Rights. Final Report. Stockholm Conference on the Rights of the Child. Stockholm: Radda Barnen, 1989.

Martin, Susan Forbes, and Emily Copeland. *Making Ends Meet?: Refugee Women and Income Generation.* Washington, DC: Refugee Policy Group, May 1988.

————. *Refugee Women.* Atlantic Highlands, NJ: Zed Books Ltd., 1991.

Nichols, Bruce, and Gil Loescher, editors. *The Moral Nation: Humanitarianism and U.S. Foreign Policy Today.* Notre Dame, IN: University of Notre Dame Press, 1989.

————. *Uneasy Alliance: Religion, Refugee Work, and U.S. Foreign Policy.* New York: Oxford University Press, 1988.

Overholt, Catherine, Mary B. Anderson, Kathleen Cloud, and James E. Austin, editors. *Gender Roles in Development Projects.* West Hartford, CT: Kumarian Press, 1985.

Refugee Service and Mission Today. Rome: Centrum Ignatianum Spiritualitatis, 1983.

Refugees, Victims of Xenophobia. A Round Table Organized by the United Nations High Commissioner for Refugees. Geneva: UNHCR, 1984.

Refugees: The Dynamics of Displacement. A Report for the Independent Commission of International Humanitarian Issues. New Jersey: Zed Books, Ltd., 1986.

Ressler, Everett M., Neil Boothby, Daniel J. Steinbock. *Unaccompanied Children: Care and Protection in Wars, Natural Disasters, and Refugee Movements.* New York: Oxford University Press, 1988.

Rogge, John R., editor. *Refugees: A Third World Dilemma.* Totowa, NJ: Rowman & Littlefield, 1987.

Rose, Peter I. *Working With Refugees.* New York: Center for Migration Studies, 1986.

Said, Edward W. *After the Last Sky: Palestinian Lives.* New York: Pantheon Books, 1986.

————, and Christopher Hitchens, editors. *Blaming the Victims: Spurious Scholarship and the Palestinian Question.* New York: Verso, 1988.

Santoli, Al. *New Americans, An Oral History: Immigrants & Refugees in the U.S. Today.* New York: Viking, 1988.

Schiff, Ze'ev and Ehud Ya'ari. *Intifada: The Palestinian Uprisings: Israel's Third Front.* New York: Simon and Schuster, 1990.

Schultheis, Michael J., S.J. *Refugees: The Structures of a Global Justice Issue.* Washington, DC: The Center of Concern, July 1983.

Smyser, W.R. *Refugees: Extended Exile.* New York: Praeger, 1987.

Taft, Julia Vadala. *Issues and Options for Refugee Women in Developing Countries.* Washington, DC: Refugee Policy Group, 1987.

World Refugee Report. Washington, DC: United States Department of State: Bureau for Refugee Programs, Consolidated 1986-1991.

Zarjevski, Yefime. *A Future Preserved: International Assistance to Refugees.* New York: Pergamon Press, 1988.

Zolberg, Aristide R., Astri Suhrke, Sergio Aguayo. *Escape From Violence: Conflict and the Refugee Crisis in the Developing World.* New York: Oxford University Press, 1989.

GENERAL

Articles

Anderson, Mary B. "Gender Analysis Framework for Refugee Work." Draft (February 1990).

Barringer, Felicity. " 'Repatriation' Is the Trend for Refugees World Wide." *The New York Times* (November 17, 1991).

Bhagwati, Jagdish. "A Champion for Migrating People." *The Christian Science Monitor* (February 28, 1992), 1.

Boothby, Neil, Abubacar Sultan, and Peter Upton. "Children of Mozambique: The Cost of Survival." U.S. Committee for Refugees Issue Brief, Washington, DC: American Council for Nationalities Service (November 1991).

————, and John Humphrey. "Under the Gun—Children in Exile." *U.S. Committee for Refugees: World Refugee Survey 1987 in Review,* Washington, DC: American Council for Nationalities Service (1988), 11-12.

Clark, Lance. "Internal Refugees—The Hidden Half." *U.S. Committee for Refugees: World Refugee Survey 1988 in Review,* Washington, DC: American Council for Nationalities Service (1989), 18-24.

————. "Promoting Refugee Participation in Assistance Projects." Refugee Policy Group Report, Washington, DC (December 1987).

————. "The Refugee Dependency Syndrome." *UNICEF News,* 124 (1986), 21-23.

Cohen, Roberta. "Human Rights Protection for Internally Displaced Persons," Refugee Policy Group Report (June 1991).

"Conclusions and Recommendations." Draft for U.N. Commission on Status of Women (June 7, 1990), 41-53.

Cushman, John H., Jr. "The Babies That Won't Blossom: New Anguish in a Kuwaiti Refugee Camp." *The New York Times International* (July 16, 1991), A3.

Dietrich, Laura Jordan. "Two Perspectives on Asylum in the United States, U.S. Asylum Policy." *U.S. Committee for Refugees Survey 1985 in Review,* Washington, DC: American Council for Nationalities Service (1986), 5.

Feldmann, Linda. "Disaster Relief: From Bangladesh to Costa Rica, Demand for Aid Floods Agencies." *The Christian Science Monitor* (May 24, 1991), 1-2.

Frelick, Bill. "Refugees: A Barometer of Genocide." *U.S. Committee for Refugees: World Refugee Survey 1988 in Review,* Washington, DC: American Council for Nationalities Service (1989), 13-17.

Friedman, Thomas L. "Today's Threat to Peace Is the Guy Down the Street." *The New York Times* (June 2, 1991), E3.

Goodwillie, Susan. "Refugees in the Developing World: A Challenge to the International Community." Unpublished Paper for Meeting of Experts on Refugee Aid and Development, Geneva (August 5, 1983).

Greenhouse, Steven. "Bush and Kohl Unveil Plan for Seven Nations to Contribute $24 Billion in Aid For Russia." *The New York Times* (April 2, 1992), 1ff.

Grier, Peter. "Massive Tide of Refugees Defies Worldwide Effort to Relieve Plight." *The Christian Science Monitor* (May 24, 1990), 1-2.

Hartling, Paul. "To Make the Reasons of the Heart Prevail." *U.S. Committee for Refugees: World Refugee Survey 1985 in Review,* Washington, DC: American Council for Nationalities Service (1986), 4.

Henkel, Joachim, Dr. "The International Protection of Refugees and Displaced Persons: A Global Problem of Growing Complexity." United States Committee for Refugees Issue Brief, Washington, DC: American Council for Nationalities Service (December 1985).

Holtan, Neal R., M.D., M.P.H. "When Refugees Are Victims of Torture." *U.S. Committee for Refugees: World Refugee Survey 1986 in Review,* Washington, DC: American Council for Nationalities Service (1987), 24-26.

Hottelet, Richard C. "The UN Labyrinth." *The Christian Science Monitor* (September 16, 1991), 18.

Hunt, Kathleen. "Daring to Heal." *The New York Times Magazine* (July 28, 1991), 31ff.

Ingram, James. "Sustaining Refugees' Human Dignity: International Responsibility and Practical Reality." Third Joyce Pearce Memorial Lecture, Oxford University (November 30, 1988).

Iris, Nancy. "Refugee Women: In 1985, No Longer 'The Forgotten Majority'." *U.S. Committee for Refugees World Refugee Survey 1985 in Review,* Washington, DC:

American Council for Nationalities Service (1986), 32-34.

Jones, Clayton. "UN Official Seeks Help for 17 Million Exiles." *The Christian Science Monitor* (February 5, 1992), 6.

Keely, Charles P. "Filling a Critical Gap in the Refugee Protection Regime: The Internally Displaced." *U.S. Committee for Refugees: World Refugee Survey 1991,* Washington, DC: American Council for Nationalities Service (1991), 22-27.

Kemper, Vickie and Michael Verchot. "Children of War: Sharing the Dream of Peace." *Cloud of Witnesses,* edited by Jim Wallis and Joyce Hollyday. Maryknoll, NY: Orbis Books, 1991, 35-43.

Kissinger, Meg and Richard Kenyon. "Empty Cradles." *The Milwaukee Journal* (November 29 through December 6, 1987).

Lewis, Paul. "U.N. to Centralize Its Relief Efforts." *The New York Times* (January 26, 1992).

Loescher, Gil. "Mass Migration as a Global Security Problem." *U.S. Committee for Refugees: World Refugee Survey 1991,* Washington, DC: American Council for Nationalities Service (1991), 7-14.

McClory, Robert J. "The Century of Refugees, Refugees, Refugees. . ." *National Catholic Reporter* (January 11, 1991), 11-18.

Minear, Larry. "Civil Strife and Humanitarian Aid: A Bruising Decade." *U.S. Committee for Refugees: World Refugee Survey 1989 in Review,* Washington, DC: American Council for Nationalities Service (1990), 13-19.

Mouat, Lucia. "UN Peace Keepers Face Tough, New Challenges." *The Christian Science Monitor* (March 25, 1992), 10-11.

———. "UN Summit to Assess Role, Funding Crisis." *The Christian Science Monitor* (January 30, 1992), 1.

Mullen, William. "Refugees: Caught In the Middle." *The Chicago Tribune Magazine,* Section 10 (October 9, 1988), 12ff.

———. "Nowhere to Hide." *The Chicago Tribune,* Section 5 (October 12, 1988), 1ff.

———. "Pawns of Politics." *The Chicago Tribune,* Section 5 (October 10, 1988), 1ff.

———. "The Manipulators." *The Chicago Tribune,* Section 5 (October 14, 1988), 1ff.

———. "The Unprotected." *The Chicago Tribune,* Section 5 (October 13, 1988), 1ff.

———. "Trapped for Life." *The Chicago Tribune,* Section 5 (October 11, 1988), 1ff.

Post, Tom, Ron Moreau, Jeffrey Bartholet, and Jane Whitmore. "Disaster Fatigue." *Newsweek* (May 13, 1991), 38-40.

"Public Attitudes on Refugees." United States Committee for Refugees Issue Brief, Washington, DC: American Council for Nationalities Service (June 8, 1984).

"Report on Refugee Women." Submitted by the High Commissioner, United Nations General Assembly, Executive Committee of the High Commissioner's Programme, Fortieth Session, A/AC. 96/727 (July 19, 1989).

Robinson, Court. "Sins of Omission: The New Vietnamese Refugee Crisis." *U.S. Committee for Refugees: World Refugee Survey 1988 in Review,* Washington, DC: American Council for Nationalities Service (1989), 5-12.

Rose, Peter I. "On the Jubilee of the International Rescue Committee." *U.S. Committee for Refugees World Refugee Survey 1984,* Washington, DC: American Council for Nationalities Service (1984), 23.

Rosenblatt, Lionel. "US Loses Its Bearings on Refugees." *The Christian Science Monitor* (December 17, 1991), 18.

Rubin, Gary E. "The Asylum Challenge to Western Nations." U.S. Committee for

Refugees Issue Brief, Washington, DC: American Council for Nationalities Service (December 1984).

Scholz, Dieter B., S.J. "The World Refugee Problem: Our Responsibility and Role." Address Given at the Third International Symposium of the Institute for the Study of Social Justice at Sophia University, Tokyo (December 9-11, 1983).

Sexton, Robert C. "Political Refugees, *Nonrefoulement* and State Practice: A Comparative Study." *Vanderbilt Journal of Transnational Law,* Vol. 18, No. 4 (Fall 1985), 731-806.

Silk, James. "Despite a Generous Spirit: Denying Asylum in the United States." U.S. Committee for Refugees Issue Brief, Washington, DC: American Council for Nationalities Service (December 1986).

Smyser, W.R. "Refugees: A Never-Ending Story." *Foreign Affairs* (Fall 1985), 154-168.

Sommer, Mark. "Who Will Pay for Peace?" *The Christian Science Monitor* (February 19, 1992), 18.

Stanley, Allessandra. "Child Warriors." *Time Magazine,* Vol. 135, No. 25 (June 18, 1990), 30-52.

Stein, Barry N., and Fred C. Cuny. "Repatriation Under Conflict." *U.S. Committee for Refugees: World Refugee Survey 1991,* Washington, DC: American Council for Nationalities Service (1991), 15-21.

Stephenson, Robin, Dr. "Access to Food Assistance: Strategies for Improvement," Refugee Policy Group Report, Washington, DC (March 1992).

Tanton, John H. "End of the Migration Era." *The Christian Science Monitor* (April 17, 1992), 18.

"The Year of the Refugee." *The Economist,* (December 23, 1989), 17-27.

"UNHCR Policy on Refugee Women." (May 21, 1990).

UNHCR. "Guidelines on Refugee Children." Geneva (August, 1988).

Wali, Sima. "Refugee Women and Development." Expert Group Meeting on Refugee and Displaced Women and Children, Vienna (July 2, 1990).

Winter, Roger. "The Year in Review." *U.S. Committee for Refugees: World Refugee Survey 1991,* Washington, DC: American Council for Nationalities Services (1991), 2-6.

————. "The Year in Review." *U.S. Committee for Refugees: World Refugee Survey 1992,* Washington, DC: American Council for Nationalities Services (1992), 2-5.

CAMBODIA

Books and Reports

Asia Watch and Physicians for Human Rights. *Land Mines in Cambodia: The Coward's War.* New York: Human Rights Watch and Physicians for Human Rights, September 1991.

Asia Watch Report. *Khmer Rouge Abuses Along the Thai-Cambodian Border.* New York: Asia Watch, February 1989.

Banbury, Tony. *Kampuchean Displaced Persons in Thailand: Between the Devil and the Deep Blue Sea.* Boston, May 1988.

Becker, Elizabeth. *When the War Was Over: Cambodia's Revolution and the Voices of Its People.* New York: Simon and Schuster, A Touchstone Book, 1986.

Buddhism and the Future of Cambodia. Khmer Buddhist Research Center Rithisen Camp, 1986.

Cambodia: The Situation of Children and Women. Phnom Penh: United Nations International Children's Emergency Fund, Office of the Special Representative, 1990.

Carney, Timothy. *Kampuchea: Balance of Survival*. Bangkok: D.D. Books, 1983.

Chanda, Nayan. *Brother Enemy: The War After the War. A History of Indochina Since the Fall of Saigon*. New York: Collier Books, Macmillan Publishing Company, 1986.

Chantavanich, Supang and E. Bruce Reynolds, editors. *Indochinese Refugees: Asylum and Resettlement*. Bangkok: Institute of Asian Studies, Chulalongkorn University, 1988.

Chantavanich, Supang. *Thailand: A First Asylum Country for Indochinese Refugees*. Bangkok: Institute of Asian Studies, Chulalongkorn University, 1988.

Del Vecchio, John M. *For the Sake of All Living Things*. New York: Bantam Books, 1990.

Diller, Janelle M. *In Search of Asylum: Vietnamese Boat People in Hong Kong*. Washington, DC: Indochinese Resource Action Center, November 1988.

Freeman, James. *Hearts of Sorrow: Vietnamese-American Lives*. Stanford, CA: Stanford University Press, 1989.

Hasson, Virginia M. *Organization of Education Programs For Displaced Khmers On the Thai-Kampuchean Border*. Unpublished Dissertation, New York: Fordham University, 1989.

Hayslip, Le Ly with Jay Wurts. *When Heaven and Earth Changed Places: A Vietnamese Woman's Journey From War to Peace*. New York: Doubleday, 1989.

International Rescue Committee, and Barnabas Mam, Tith Wuthy (Khmer Editors). *Displaced Lives: Stories of Life and Culture From the Khmer in Site II, Thailand*. Bangkok: The International Rescue Committee, November 1990.

Kiljunen, Kimmo, editor. *Kampuchea: Decade of the Genocide*. London: Zed Books, 1984.

Lawyers Committee for Human Rights. *Kampuchea: After the Worst*. New York: Lawyers Committee for Human Rights, 1990.

————. *Refuge Denied: Problems in the Protection of Vietnamese and Cambodians in Thailand and the Admission of Indochinese Refugees Into the United States*. New York: Lawyers Committee for Human Rights, 1989.

————. *Seeking Shelter: Cambodians in Thailand*. New York: Lawyers Committee for Human Rights, 1987.

Levy, Barry S. and Daniel C. Susott, editors. *Years of Horror, Days of Hope: Responding to the Cambodian Refugee Crisis*. New York: Associated Faculty Press, Inc., 1986.

Marking Time: The Human Cost of Confinement. CCSDPT Annual Conference Proceedings. Bangkok (July 15, 1988).

May, Someth. *Cambodian Witness: The Autobiography of Someth May*. New York: Random House, 1986.

Ministry of Foreign Affairs, Government of Thailand. *Documents on the Kampuchean Problem 1979-1985*. Bangkok: Department of Political Affairs, 1985.

Mollica, Richard F., M.D. and Russell R. Jalbert. *Community of Confinement: The Mental Health Crisis in Site Two: Displaced Persons Camps on the Thai-Kampuchean Border*. Brighton, MA: Committee on Refugees and Migrants, the World Federation for Mental Health, February 1989.

Muskie, Edmund S. *Exploring Cambodia: Issues and Reality In a Time of Transition*. Washington, DC: Center for National Policy, October 1990.

Mysliwiec, Eva. *Punishing the Poor: The International Isolation of Kampuchea*. Oxford: Oxfam House, 1988.

Ngor, Haing. *A Cambodian Odyssey*. New York: Warner Books, 1987.

Pack, Mary E. *The Human Dimension of Long-Term Encampment: Vietnamese Boat Refugees in First Asylum Camps*. Bangkok (1988).

Phurong, Ann Cusak. *Poems*. Unpublished. 1989.

Reynell, Josephine. *Political Pawns: Refugees on the Thai-Kampuchean Border.* Oxford: Refugee Studies Program, 1989.

Saipiroon, Pranee. *ASEAN Governments' Attitudes Towards Regional Security.* Bangkok: Institute of Asian Studies, Chulalongkorn University, January 1982.

Shawcross, William. *The Quality of Mercy: Cambodia, Holocaust and Modern Conscience.* New York: Simon and Schuster, 1984.

Simmons, Stephanie, Patrick Vaughan, and S. William Gunn. *Refugee Community Health Care.* New York: Oxford University Press, 1983.

Szymusiak, Molyda. *The Stones Cry Out: A Cambodian Childhood 1975-80.* London: Sphere Books, 1988.

Theeravit, Khien and MacAlister Brown, editors. *Indochina and Problems of Security and Stability in Southeast Asia.* Bangkok: Chulalongkorn University Press, 1981.

Walker, Susan B. *Handicap International Thailand Program 1988 Annual Report.* Bangkok: Operation Handicap International, March 1989.

————. *Handicap International Thailand Program January-June 1989 Report.* Bangkok: Operation Handicap International, September 1989.

————. *Handicap International Thailand Program July-December 1989 Report.* Bangkok: Operation Handicap International, April 1990.

————. *Handicap International Thailand Program January-June 1990 Report.* Bangkok: Operation Handicap International, September 1990.

————. *Handicap International Thailand Program July-December 1990 Report.* Bangkok: Operation Handicap International, June 1991.

CAMBODIA

Articles

Abramowitz, Morton. "The Next Refugee Deluge." *The Washington Post* (October 13, 1991).

Bartu, Friedemann. "The Khmer Rouge Take the Offensive." *Swiss Review of World Affairs* (January 1989), 24-25.

Beiser, Morton. "Changing Time Perspective and Mental Health Among Southeast Asian Refugees." *Culture, Medicine and Psychiatry* 11 (1987), 437-464.

Bekaert, Jacques. "The Turning-Point." *Bangkok Post* (October 19, 1991), 1.

Boegli, Urs. "Statement by Mr. Urs Boegli, Head of Delegation, International Committee of the Red Cross Delegation in Thailand." CCSDPT Conference on Repatriation. Bangkok (July 22, 1989).

Burutphat, Khachatphai. "Indochinese Refugees." Unpublished Paper, n.d.

"Cambodia on the Brink of Peace." *Report and Recommendations of the Women's Commission for Refugee Women and Children* (January 1991).

"Cambodia: A Time for Return, Reconciliation and Reconstruction." Washington, DC: Refugee Policy Group, October 1991.

"Cambodians in Thailand: People on the Edge." U.S. Committee for Refugees Issue Paper, edited by Virginia Hamilton. Washington, DC: American Council for Nationalities Service, 1985.

Cerquone, Joseph. "Southeast Asian Refugees: Back to the Future." *U.S. Committee for Refugees Survey 1986 in Review,* Washington, DC: American Council for Nationalities Service (1987), 34-35.

Chorn, Arn. "The World Seemed Strange, Silent, and Slow to Move." *U.S. Committee for Refugees: World Refugee Survey 1987 in Review,* Washington, DC: American Council For Nationalities Service (1988), 13.

Conway, Daniel E. "Seminar on the First Phase of the Peace Settlement in Cambodia and UNHCR's Repatriation Plan." Bangkok: Chulalongkorn University, October 3, 1991.

Crossette, Barbara. "Cambodians in Pol Pot's Camp Await a Liberator." *The New York Times* (January 17, 1988), A3.

Diekstra, Rene F.W., Dr. "Psychosocial and Mental Health Problems of the Khmer Refugees in Site 2 and Site 8 on the Thai-Kampuchean Border." Geneva: World Health Organization, November 1988.

Elias, Christopher, M.D. "Beyond Apology: A Practical Response to the Mental Health Crisis in Site 2." Unpublished Paper Prepared for the Task Force on Mental Health in Site 2. (August 1989).

Erlanger, Steven. "Cambodian Refugees Think of Home With Hope and Dread." *The New York Times* (October 22, 1991).

———. "No Haven From Agony for Cambodians." *The New York Times* (May 2, 1991), A5.

Fordham, Roger A. "The Khmer Border: The Never-Ending Story." Bangkok: CCSDPT, July 1991.

Fox, Thomas C. "Refugees Languish While the World Loses Interest." *National Catholic Reporter* (July 31, 1987), 9-11.

Gallagher, Dennis. "Cambodia: The UN Needs the Means to Do Its Job." *International Herald Tribune* (October 23, 1991).

"Ghosts From the Past." *Asiaweek* (July 29, 1988), 16-20.

Goldfeld, Anne E., M.D. "Cambodia: An Humanitarian Agenda." Testimony Before the Asia Pacific Sub-Committee of the House Foreign Affairs Committee (April 10, 1991).

Golub, Stephen. "Looking for Phantoms: Flaws in the Khmer Rouge Screening Process." U.S. Committee for Refugees Issue Brief, Washington, DC: American Council for Nationalities Service, April 1986.

Goodwillie, Susan. "The Dilemma of Khmer in Thailand: An Opportunity for Action, A Comprehensive Strategy." Washington, DC: Refugees International, September 1986.

Greenway, H.D.S. "Report From Cambodia: The Tiger and the Crocodile." *The New Yorker* (July 17, 1989), 72-83.

Hawk, David. "Human Rights Aspects of a Comprehensive Solution to the Conflict in Cambodia." New York: Cambodia Documentation Commission, n.d.

Hiebert, Murray. "A Basket Case." *Far Eastern Economic Review* (November 7, 1991).

———. "A Lick of Paint." *Far Eastern Economic Review* (November 7, 1991).

———. "Exit Heng Samrin." *Far Eastern Economic Review* (October 31, 1991), 11.

Houtart, Myriam. "Perceptions of the Cambodian Medical System and Possibilities for the Re-integration of Khmer Medical Personnel From the Border Camps." Bangkok: Operation Handicap International, February 1989.

Jackson, Tony. "How Pol Pot Dominates the Coalition Government of Democratic Kampuchea." Oxford: Oxfam House, September 1988.

Jennar, Raoul M. "The Cambodian Gamble: Three Months of Negotiations Towards a Peace Fraught With Dangers." *European Far East Research,* NGO Forum on Cambodia, London and Phnom Penh (September 13, 1991).

Jones, Sidney. "War and Human Rights in Cambodia." *The New York Review of Books,* Vol. XXXVII, No. 12 (July 19, 1990), 1-7.

Kanwerayotin, Supapohn, and Nusara Thaitawat. "A Nation in for Shock." *Bangkok Post* (November 17, 1991), 1.

Koch, Elinor. "Cambodia: Famine and Flight." Washington, DC: Cambodia Crisis Center, n.d.

Lansner, Tom. "Phnom Penh, Cambodia." Unpublished paper (June, 1990).

Lertcharoenchok, Yindee. "Bloodied Khieu Flees Cambodia." *The Nation* (Bangkok) (November 28, 1991), 1.

Maat, Robert, Brother, S.J. "The Major Disruption at Samet, Christmas, 1984." Washington, DC: Jesuit Refugee Service/USA, 1985.

MacKinlay, John. "UN Monitors in Cambodia Have a Big Task Ahead." *The Christian Science Monitor* (October 28, 1991), 19.

MacSwan, Angus. "Years of Turmoil Ending in Cambodia." *Bangkok Post* (October 19, 1991), 1.

Mastro, Timothy, M.D. "Khmer Self-Management of Health Care in Thai-Kampuchean Border Encampments" (May 31, 1988).

McAuliff, John, and Mary Byrne McDonnell. "The Cambodian Stalemate." *World Policy Journal,* Vol VII, No. 1 (Winter 1989-90), 71-105.

Neou, Kassie, and Al Santoli. "Peace and Human Rights in Cambodia: Exploring From Within." New York: Freedom House, 1990.

O'Brien, Heather M. "Jump-Start for Cambodia." *The Christian Science Monitor* (May 21, 1991), 18.

Pesavento, Barbara. "Psychotherapy of Diversity: Cross-Cultural Treatment Issues." Paper Presented for the Harvard Medical School Department of Continuing Education. Boston (May 19-20, 1989).

Porter, Gareth. "Cambodia: Sihanouk's Initiative." *Foreign Affairs,* Vol. 66, No. 4 (Spring 1988), 809-826.

"Press Statement of H.E. Mr. Khieu Samphan and H.E. Mr. Son Sen, Members of the Supreme National Council of Cambodia, on the Situation of Site 8 Camp." (October 17, 1991).

"Pressure Mounts to Revoke Backing for Khmer Rouge." *Bangkok Post* (November 4, 1989), 4.

Robinson, Court, and Arthur Wallenstein. "Unfilled Hopes: The Humanitarian Parole/Immigrant Visa Program for Border Cambodians." Washington, DC: U.S. Committee for Refugees, September 1988.

———. " 'The War Is Growing Worse': Refugees and Displaced Persons on the Thai-Burmese Border." Washington, DC: U.S. Committee for Refugees, April 1990.

———. "Refugee Protection in Thailand and the Closing of Khao I Dang." *U.S. Committee for Refugees Survey 1986 in Review,* Washington, DC: American Council for Nationalities Service (1987), 54.

———. "Refugees in Thailand." *U.S. Committee for Refugees Survey 1987 in Review,* Washington, DC: American Council for Nationalities Service (1988), 52-53.

Shaplen, Robert. "The Captivity of Cambodia." *The New Yorker* (May 5, 1986), 66-105.

Shenon, Philip. "Cambodian Refugees Face Minefields on Their Return." *The New York Times* (November 10, 1991).

———. "Khmer Rouge's Plan to Move Refugees Back Into Cambodia Creates Panic." *The New York Times* (December 31, 1991), 2.

Solarz, Stephen J. "Cambodia and the International Community." *Foreign Affairs,* Vol. 69, No. 2 (Spring 1990), 99-115.

Spicer, Andi. "An End to the Killing Fields?" *South* (June/July 1991), 30.

"Statement by HRH Samdech Norodom Sihanouk, President of the Supreme National Council of Cambodia." Paris (October 17, 1991).

Swain, Jon. "Refugees Hospital Burnt by Jittery Khmer Rouge." *The Sunday Times* (London) (January 15, 1989), B8.

Tasker, Rodney and Murray Hiebert. "Back to the Unknown." *Far Eastern Economic Review* (November 7, 1991), 27-35.

————. "Old Foes, New Friends." *Far Eastern Economic Review* (December 5, 1991), 25-26.

————. "The Odd Couple." *Far Eastern Economic Review* (November 28, 1991).

Tefft, Sheila. "Cambodia's Long Tough Road Home." *The Christian Science Monitor* (May 20, 1992), 9-12.

————. "Cambodian Families Reconnect." *The Christian Science Monitor* (August 27, 1991), 8.

————. "Cambodian Refugees Wait—and Hope." *The Christian Science Monitor* (July 12, 1991), 10-11.

————. "Cambodians Return to Tough Land Disputes." *The Christian Science Monitor* (November 21, 1991), 5.

————. "Rebuilding Lives on Killing Fields." *The Christian Science Monitor* (June 12, 1991), 10-11.

"The Repatriation of Khmer Living in Encampments on the Thai-Cambodian Border." Results of a Workshop Held on the Khmer, Aranyaprathet. Bangkok: CCSDPT, July 22, 1989.

"The Second International Conference on Indo-Chinese Refugees: A New Humanitarian Consensus?" Washington, DC: The Refugee Policy Group, May 1989.

U.S. Committee for Refugees. "Cambodians in Thailand: People on the Edge." Issue Paper (December, 1985).

Vickery, Michael. "Cambodia (Kampuchea): History, Tragedy, and Uncertain Future." *Bulletin of Concerned Asian Scientists* (1989), 35-58.

"What the Peace Accord Means." *Bangkok Post* (October 23, 1991).

Ytzen, Flemming. "Cambodia's Long Road Home." *Choices* (April, 1992), 5-8.

AFGHANISTAN

Books and Reports

Anwar, Raja. *The Tragedy of Afghanistan: A First-Hand Account.* New York: Verso, 1988.

Bonner, Arthur. *Among the Afghans.* Durham, NC: Duke University Press, 1987.

Borovik, Artyom. *The Hidden War: A Russian Journalist's Account of the Soviet War in Afghanistan.* New York: Atlantic Monthly Press, 1990.

Brailsford, Guy. *Opium Crop Substitution Programme Achin District, Nangarhar: Evaluation Report 1989.* Afghanaid, January 1990.

Caroe, Sib Olaf. *The Pathans: With an Epilogue on Russia.* Karachi, Pakistan: Oxford University Press, 1958.

Carter, Lynn, Dr., and Dr. Kerry Connor. *A Preliminary Investigation of Contemporary Afghan Councils.* Peshawar, Pakistan: Agency Coordinating Body for Afghan Relief (ACBAR), 1989.

Chaffetz, David. *A Journey Through Afghanistan: A Memorial.* Chicago: University of Chicago Press, 1984.

Christensen, Hanne, and Wolf Scott. *Survey of the Social and Economic Conditions of Afghan Refugees in Pakistan.* Geneva: United Nations Research Institute for Social Development (UNRISD), 1988.

Christensen, Hanne. *Afghan Refugees in Pakistan: From Emergency Towards Self-Reliance.* Geneva: UNRISD, 1984.

————. *Sustaining Afghan Refugees in Pakistan: Report on the Food Situation and Related Social Aspects. UNRISD Refugee Settlement Series.* Geneva: UNRISD, 1983.

————. *The Reconstruction of Afghanistan: A Chance for Rural Afghan Women.* Geneva: UNRISD, 1990.

Dadfar, M.A. *The Impaired Mind.* Peshawar, Pakistan: Psychiatry Centre for Afghans, March 1988.

Doubleday, Veronica. *Three Women of Herat.* London: Jonathan Cape, 1988.

Dupree, Louis. *Afghanistan.* Princeton, NJ: Princeton University Press, 1980.

English, Richard, Ph.D. *Preliminary Report On Conditions Affecting the Repatriation of Afghan Refugees.* Geneva: United Nations High Commissioner for Refugees, June 20, 1988.

Fange, Anders, Coordinator. *The Agricultural Survey of Afghanistan.* First Report on the Agricultural Survey of Afghanistan. National Trends and Averages. First Draft, May 1988.

Farr, Grant M., and John G. Merriam, editors. *Afghan Resistance: The Politics of Survival.* Karachi, Pakistan: Vanguard Books, 1988.

Goodwin, Jan. *Caught in the Crossfire.* New York: E.P. Dutton, 1987.

Helsinki Watch. *Tears, Blood and Cries: Human Rights in Afghanistan Since the Invasion 1979-1984.* New York: Helsinki Watch, December 1986.

Helsinki Watch/Asia Watch. *By All Parties to the Conflict: Violations of the Laws of War in Afghanistan.* New York: U.S. Helsinki Watch Committee and Asia Watch Committee, 1988.

———. *To Die in Afghanistan.* New York: U.S. Helsinki Watch Committee and Asia Watch Committee, 1985.

———. *To Win the Children: Afghanistan's Other War.* New York: Helsinki Watch, December 1986.

Hodson, Peregrine. *Under a Sickle Moon: A Journey Through Afghanistan.* New York: Abacus, Penguin, 1989.

Huldt, Bo, and Erland Jansson, editors. *The Tragedy of Afghanistan: The Social, Cultural and Political Impact of the Soviet Invasion.* New York: Croom Helm, 1988.

International Rescue Committee Annual and Quarterly Reports: Program for Afghans 1987-1990 (inclusive). Peshawar, Pakistan: I.R.C. Printing Press, 1987-1990.

Khan, Shah Zaman, editor. *Voluntary Agencies' Role in Provision of Humanitarian Assistance to Afghan Refugees in North West Frontier Province Pakistan.* Peshawar, Pakistan: Afghan Refugee Commissionerate, N.W.F.P., November 1987.

———. *Humanitarian Assistance Programme for Afghan Refugees in North West Frontier Province Pakistan.* Peshawar, Pakistan: Afghan Refugee Commissionerate N.W.F.P., December 1985.

Kiernan, Victor, Translator. *Poems by Faiz.* London: Vanguard Books, 1971.

Laber, Jeri, and Barnett R. Rubin. *"A Nation Is Dying": Afghanistan Under the Soviets 1979-87.* Evanston, IL: Northwestern University Press, 1988.

Lessing, Doris. *The Wind Blows Away Our Words.* New York: Vintage Books, 1987.

Lindholm, Charles. *Generosity and Jealousy: The SWAT Pukhtun of Northern Pakistan.* New York: Columbia University Press, 1982.

Lofstedt, Vivi, and Mike Powers, editors. *The Children of Afghanistan in War and Refugee Camps.* A Documentation of the International Hearing Held in Stockholm April 4-5, 1987. The Swedish Committee for Afghanistan (SCA), 1987.

Malik, Abdul Hamid. *Socio-Economic and Political Factors Related to the Impelled Afghan Migration to Pakistan: 1978-84.* A Dissertation Submitted to Area Study Centre (C.A.) University of Peshawar in Candidacy for the Degree of Doctor of Philosophy, 1985.

Moorhouse, Geoffrey. *To the Frontier.* London: Sceptre, 1984.

O'Connor, Ronald W. *Managing Health Systems in Developing Areas: Experiences from Afghanistan.* Lexington, MA: Lexington Books, 1980.

Rasul, A., editor. *Life in Refugee Camps.* N.W.F.P., Pakistan: Writer's Union of Free Afghanistan, n.d.

Roy, Olivier. *Islam and Resistance in Afghanistan*. New York: Cambridge University Press, 1986.

Siddiqi, Dr. Mohammad Shamsuddin, editor. *Afghanistan Today*. Peshawar, Pakistan: University of Peshawar, 1987.

Spain, James W. *The Way of the Pathans*. Karachi, Pakistan: Oxford University Press, 1987.

UNHCR Background Reports: Nangarhar Province; Kandahar Province; Kunar Province; Paktia Province; Paktika Province. Prepared by the Data Collection for Afghan Repatriation Project, September 1, 1989.

United Nations Plan of Action 1990. Humanitarian and Economic Assistance Programmes Relating to Afghanistan. Islamabad, Pakistan, November 23, 1989.

Ward, William A., Richard English, Vernon Robertson, and Barry J. Doren. *Impact Evaluation Report: Pakistan—Income Generating Project for Refugees Areas (Phase I)*. McLean, Virginia: The Institute for Development Programs, April 15, 1988.

AFGHANISTAN

Articles

Abercrombie, Thomas J. "Afghanistan: Crossroad of Conquerors." *National Geographic Society*, Vol. 134, No. 3 (September 1968), 297-345.

"Afghan Refugees: A Global Concern." Webster University Study Trip to Pakistan. Third Annual San Remo Seminar, Geneva (November 11-15, 1987).

Ahmad, Akbar S., Dr. "Pathan Society." *Central Asia, Journal of Area Study Centre*, No. 13 (Winter 1983), 17-30.

Anwar, Raja. "A Political Report on Afghanistan." Frankfurt (April 10, 1989).

Azam, Farouq, Dr. "Unity Among the Afghan Mujahideen." *Central Asia, Journal of Area Study Centre*, No. 20 (Summer, 1987), 91-97.

Boeson, Inger W. "Ten Years of War and Civil War in Afghanistan—An Educational Catastrophe for an Entire Generation." *WUFA (Writers Union of Free Afghanistan)*, Vol. 3, No 3 (July-September 1988), 32-44.

Burns, John F. "Afghans, Now They Blame America." *The New York Times Magazine* (February 4, 1990), 23ff.

Carter, Lynn, Dr. "Assessment of Current Activities and Priorities in Primary Education and Teacher Training for Afghans." Peshawar, Pakistan (December 1988).

Chamberlain, Caral. "Prospects of Training Programme for Women During Repatriation." *WUFA (Writers Union of Free Afghanistan)*, Vol. 4, No. 1 (January-March 1989), 59-63.

Citizens Commission on Afghan Refugees. "The Challenge of the Coming Afghan Refugee Repatriation: Fulfilling Our Commitments in the Final Chapter of the Afghanistan War." On Behalf of The International Rescue Committee, New York (June 1988).

"Constitution of Republic of Afghanistan." *Central Asia, Journal of Area Study Centre*, No. 23 (Winter, 1988), 115-150.

Dadfar, M. Azam, Dr. "From Mental Peace to Impaired Minds." Presentation at the Third International Seminar on Afghanistan, Olso (September 28-October 1, 1989).

———. "Refugee Camps and Torture Victims." *Central Asia, Journal of Area Study Centre*, No. 23 (Winter, 1988), 53-66.

Desmond, Edward W. "We Really Must Go." *Time Magazine* (February 22, 1988), 36-38.

Douglas, H. Eugene, Ambassador. "Pakistan: Country of First Asylum." *U.S. Com-*

mittee for Refugees World Refugee Survey 1984, Washington, DC: American Council for Nationalities Service (1984), 5-6.

Dupree, Louis, and Nancy Hatch Dupree. "Afghan Refugees in Pakistan." *U.S. Committee for Refugees: World Refugee Survey 1987 in Review.* Washington, DC: American Council for Nationalities Service (1988), 17-21.

Dupree, Louis. "Afghanistan's Future Government: Regional Federation, Islamic State or Both?" *WUFA (Writers Union of Free Afghanistan),* Vol. 3, No. 3 (July-September 1988), 15-31.

Dupree, Nancy Hatch. "A Few Comments on Afghan Women." Unpublished Paper, n.d.

————. "Observations on Afghan Women Refugees in Pakistan: 1990." *U.S. Committee for Refugees: World Refugee Survey 1991.* Washington, DC: American Council for Nationalities Service (1991), 28-31.

————. "Repatriation of Afghan Refugees." Unpublished Paper. Duke University (May 26, 1988).

————. "The Afghan Refugee Family Abroad: A Focus on Pakistan." *WUFA (Writers Union of Free Afghanistan),* Vol. 2, No. 4 (1987), 15-29.

————. "The Role of Afghan Women After Repatriation." *WUFA (Writers Union of Free Afghanistan),* Vol. 3, No. 4 (October-December 1988), 16-38.

Eliot, Theodore L., Jr. "The Afghans' Next Ordeal." *World Monitor,* Vol. 31, No. 3 (December 1988), 41-47.

Fournot, Juliette, Dr. "Conflict, Devastation and Displacement Inside Afghanistan." Conference On War In Afghanistan and the Plight of the Afghan Family. Center for Strategic and International Studies, Georgetown University, Washington, DC (April 21, 1986).

Galster, Steven R. "Rivalry and Reconciliation in Afghanistan: What Prospects for the Accord?" *Third World Quarterly,* Vol. 10, No. 2 (April 1988), 499-518.

Haddad, Yvonne. "Islamic Fundamentalism: Muslim Mandate or Western Invention?" n.d.

Holtzman, Steve, Olwen Herbison, and Abdul Qayum Adil. The GTZ/ACBAR Afghan Management Program Study Team. "A Discussion of Afghan Involvement in Reconstruction and Relief Programmes." Peshawar, Pakistan (1990).

Hunte, Pamela. "The Physical and Mental Health Status of Afghans With Special Emphasis on Women and Children." Conference On War in Afghanistan and the Plight of the Afghan Family (Panel II: Family Welfare in Afghanistan at War). Center for Strategic and International Studies, Georgetown University, Washington, DC (April 21, 1986).

Jawad, Nassim. "The Social Aspects of Recovery in a Fragmented Society." A Paper Presented at the Seminar on the Potential for Recovery in Afghanistan and the Role of International Assistance. Geneva (May 5-7, 1989).

Jones, Allen K. "Afghan Refugees: Five Years Later." U.S. Committee for Refugees Issue Paper. Washington, DC: American Council for Nationalities Service, January 1985.

Kaldor, Kathryn. "Assisting Skilled Women: Personal Observations and Considerations Regarding Implementation of Income-Generating Projects for Female Afghan Refugees." Unpublished Paper for the Austrian Relief Committee, Peshawar, Pakistan (May 1988).

Khan, Azmat Hayat. "Afghan Refugees in N.W.F.P.—Campwise Data." *Central Asia, Journal of Area Study Centre,* No. 13 (Winter 1983), 155-169.

————. "Afghanistan After the Soviet Withdrawal: An Appraisal." *Central Asia, Journal of Area Study Centre,* No. 23 (Winter, 1988), 7-18.

Khan, Mohammad Anwar, Dr. "Peace Chances in Afghanistan." *Central Asia, Journal of Area Study Centre,* No. 23 (Winter, 1988), 85-97.

Klass, Rosanne. "Afghanistan: The Accords." *Foreign Affairs,* Vol. 66, No. 5 (Summer 1988), 922-945.

Luijcky-Westerop, Jamilla. "The Afghan Refugee Repatriation Problem." *Central Asia, Journal of Area Study Centre,* No. 20 (Summer, 1987), 99-102.

MacKenzie, Richard. "A Brutal Force Batters a Country." *Insight* (December 5, 1988).

Majrooh, Sayd Bahaouddin. "Afghan Intellectuals in Exile: Philosophical and Psychological Dimensions." Unpublished Paper, n.d.

Molyneux, Therese H., and Bryce A. Isham. "Mother-Child Centre Programme Work Plan: October 1988-December 1989" and "Mother-Child Centre Programme Work Plan: January-December 1990." Peshawar, Pakistan: International Rescue Committee, 1989 and 1990.

Moussard, Isabelle. "Afghan Women Culture and Life: Survey and a Resource Compilation of Information." On Behalf of the Austrian Relief Committee for Afghan Refugees, Peshawar, Pakistan (November/December 1987).

Naby, Eden. "Islam Within the Afghan Resistance." *Third World Quarterly,* Vol. 10, No. 2 (April 1988), 787-805.

Noorzoy, M. Siddieq. "Issues on and Problems of Social and Economic Reconstruction in Afghanistan." *WUFA (Writers Union of Free Afghanistan),* Vol. 4, No. 2 (April-June 1989), 34-61.

"Pakistan: Follow-up Mission: Development of Refugee Human Resources and Training/Education Systems." UNHCR Technical Support Service Mission Report. Geneva (July 1990).

"Pakistan: The Economic Impact of Afghan Refugee Settlement on the Tribal Areas of Northwest Pakistan." *UNHCR Technical Support (TSS) Report.* Geneva (May 31, 1989).

Pedersen, Gorm. "Afghan Nomads in Exile—Patterns of Organization and Reorganization in Pakistan." *Afghanistan Studies Journal,* n.d.

———. "Is There a Future for the Nomads of Afghanistan?" *WUFA (Writers Union of Free Afghanistan),* Vol. 3, No. 4 (October-December 1988), 72-85.

Rubin, Barnett R. "The Fragmentation of Afghanistan." *Foreign Affairs,* Vol. 68, No. 5 (Winter 1989/90), 150-168.

———. "The Situation in Afghanistan." Testimony Before the Commission on Security and Cooperation in Europe, U.S. Congress (May 3, 1990).

———. "Redistribution and the State in Afghanistan: The Red Revolution Turns Green." Paper Presented at the Seminar on the State and Social Transformation in Afghanistan, Iran, and Pakistan. Center for International Studies, Massachusetts Institute of Technology (December 12, 1988).

———. "Afghan Repatriation." *U.S. Committee for Refugees: World Refugee Survey 1988 in Review.* Washington, DC: American Council for Nationalities Service (1989), 70-71.

———. "Lineages of the State in Afghanistan." *Asian Survey.* University of California Press, Vol. XXVIII, No. 11 (November 1988) 1188-1209.

Segal, Steve, and Bobbi Thami. "A Multiple Food Distribution Approach in Afghanistan: Coping with the Problems." On Behalf of the Agency Coordinating Body for Afghan Relief (ACBAR), Peshawar, Pakistan (March 21, 1989).

Shepard, William. "Fundamentalism: Christian and Islamic." *Religion* (1987) 355-378.

Sidni, Lamb. "Afghans in Pakistan: The Target of Blame, the Beneficiaries of Hospitality." *Refugees* (May 1987), 19-28.

Sliwinski, Marek. "Afghanistan: The Decimation of a People." *Orbis: Journal of the Foreign Policy Institute.* (Winter 1989), 39-56.

"Text of the Geneva Accord." *Central Asia, Journal of Area Study Centre,* No. 23 (Winter, 1988), 99-114.

Thami, Bobbi. "Assessment of Secondary Education and Its Alternatives in Afghanistan and Among Afghan Refugees in North West Frontier Province." Report on Behalf of The International Rescue Committee, Peshawar, Pakistan (May 1990).

————. "Monitoring." Unpublished Paper. On Behalf of the Agency Coordinating Body for Afghan Relief (ACBAR), Peshawar, Pakistan (November 1989).

UNHCR. "Refugee Origins Survey." Islamabad, Pakistan (September 1989).

Wingo, Gunilla. "Social Service Unit's Survey on Females." A Report for UNHCR, Quetta, Pakistan (1990).

Yaqub, Mian Mohammad. "Afghanistan and the Soviet Union." *Central Asia, Journal of Area Study Centre,* No. 20 (Summer, 1987), 45-53.

ERITREA AND SUDAN

Books and Reports

Abdelmageed, Dr. Fawzi, and Ramaga, Philip. *Refugee Law With Particular Reference to the Sudan.* Khartoum: Office of the Commissioner of Refugees, 1988.

Al-Rahim, Muddathir Abd, Raphael Badal, Adlan Hardallo, and Peter Woodward, editors. *Sudan Since Independence: Studies of the Political Development Since 1956.* Redding, England: Gower, n.d.

Amate, C.O.C. *Inside the OAU: Pan-Africanism in Practice.* London: MacMillan Publishers, Ltd., 1986.

Cater, Nick. *Sudan: The Roots of Famine.* Oxford: Oxfam House, 1986.

Children and Women in Ethiopia: A Situation Analysis. Prepared by Children, Family and Youth Service Organization and UNICEF, 1989.

Clapham, Christopher. *Transformation and Continuity in Revolutionary Ethiopia.* New York: Cambridge University Press, 1988.

Clay, Jason W., and Bonnie K. Holcomb. *Politics and the Ethiopian Famine 1984-1985.* Cambridge, MA: Cultural Survival, Inc., 1986.

Denying "The Honor of Living": Sudan, A Human Rights Disaster. An African Watch Report. New York: The African Watch Committee, 1990.

Famine: A Man-Made Disaster? A Report for the Independent Commission on International Humanitarian Issues. New York: Vintage Books, 1985.

Firebrace, James with Holland Stuart, MP. *Never Knell Down: Drought, Development and Liberation in Eritrea.* Trenton, NJ: The Red Sea Press, 1986.

Gill, Peter. *A Year in the Death of Africa: Politics, Bureaucracy and the Famine.* London: Paladin Grafton Books, 1986.

Giorgis, Dawit. *Red Tears: War, Famine and Revolution in Ethiopia.* Trenton, NJ: The Red Sea Press, 1989.

Harden, Blaine. *Africa: Dispatches From a Fragile Continent.* Boston: Houghton Mifflin Company, 1990.

Harrison, Paul. *The Greening of Africa: Breaking Through in the Battle for Land and Food.* An International Institute for Environment and Development—Earth Scan Study. New York: Viking Penguin Inc., 1987.

Iliffe, John. *The African Poor: A History.* New York: Cambridge University Press, 1987.

Keneally, Thomas. *To Asmara: A Novel of Africa.* New York: Warner Books, 1989.

Kibreab, Gaim. *Refugees and Development in Africa: The Case of Eritrea.* Trenton, NJ: The Red Sea Press, 1987.

Korn, David A. *Ethiopia, The United States and the Soviet Union.* Carbondale, IL: Southern Illinois University Press, 1986.

Machida, Robert. *Eritrea: The Struggle for Independence.* Trenton, NJ: The Red Sea Press, 1987.

Markakis, John. *National and Class Conflict in the Horn of Africa.* New York: Cambridge University Press, 1987.

Mazrui, Ali A. *The African Condition.* New York: Cambridge University Press, 1980.

Mottern, Nicholas. *Suffering Strong: The Journal of a Westerner in Ethiopia, The Sudan, Eritrea and Chad.* Trenton, NJ: The Red Sea Press, 1988.

Okri, Ben. *Stars of the New Curfew.* New York: Viking, 1988.

Rogge, John R. *Too Many, Too Long: Sudan's Twenty-Year Refugee Dilemma.* Totowa, NJ: Rowman and Allanheld, 1985.

Rosenblum, Mort, and Doug Williamson. *Squandering Eden: Africa At the Edge.* New York: Harcourt Brace Jovanovich, 1987.

Selassie, Bereket Habte. *Eritrea and the United Nations and Other Essays.* Trenton, NJ: The Red Sea Press, 1989.

Socio-Economic Survey of the Spontaneously Settled Refugees in Kassala. Development Studies and Research Center, Faculty of Economic and Social Studies, University of Khartoum, 1986.

Solberg, Richard W. *Miracle in Ethiopia: A Partnership Response to Famine.* New York: Friendship Press, 1991.

Special Emergency Programme for the Horn of Africa (SEPHA), Consolidated Inter-Agency Appeal. New York: Special Emergency Programme for the Horn of Africa (October 1, 1991, January 15, 1992 and February 1, 1992).

Ungar, Sanford J. *Africa: The People and Politics of An Emerging Continent.* New York: Simon and Schuster, A Touchstone Book, 1986.

Whitaker, Jennifer Seymour. *How Can Africa Survive?* New York: Harper and Row, 1988.

ERITREA AND SUDAN

Articles

Almedom, Astier M., Dr. "Evaluation of Relief and Rehabilitation Programmes in Eritrea, From a Gender Perspective." United Kingdom: Oxfam House (April 1992).

"Basic Information on Education in Eritrea." Provisional Government of Eritrea Department of Education. Asmara, Eritrea (1992).

Belland, Lynn, Hiram A. Ruiz, and Michael Gildner, editors. "Report of PVO Fact-Finding Mission to Eritrea." Inter-Action. New York (January 16-February 4, 1990).

Burr, Millard. "Khartoum's Displaced Persons: A Decade of Despair." U.S. Committee for Refugees Issue Brief, Washington, DC: American Council for Nationalities Service (August 1990).

Cater, Nick. "The Forgotten Famine." *Africa Report* (May-June 1991), 60-62.

———. "The Nightmare Scenario." *Africa Report* (September-October 1991), 57-58.

Clark, Lance, and Sandy Lewis. "Refugee Participation Case Study: Karkora Settlement in Eastern Sudan." Refugee Policy Group. Washington, DC (November 1987).

Connell, Dan. "A New Country Emerges." *Links,* Vol. 9, No. 2 (Spring 1992), 8-10.

Constable, Pamela. "Sudanese Are Said To Hamper Aid." *The Boston Globe* (October 26, 1990).

Cook, P., T. Ekvall, T. Lee, A. Lwegaba, and A. Scott-Villiers. "Eritrea Inter-Agency Mission to Sahel Province. Findings With Recommendations." Asmara: United Nations (February 1992).

Crossette, Barbara. "Sudan Is Said to Force 400,000 People Into Desert." *The New York Times* (February 21, 1992).

" 'Facing' The Enemy: Conflict Resolution Rooted in the Horn of Africa." Public Education Document Based On: "A Review of Conflict Resolution in the Horn of Africa." Horn of Africa Project Consultation (April 22-24, 1988).

Harrell-Bond, Barbara, Karim Hussein, and Patrick Matlou. "Contemporary Refugees in Africa: A Problem of the State." n.d.

Hedges, Chris. "Sudan: Famine As a Weapon." *The Dallas Morning News* (August 6, 1989), 15M-17M.

Hubbell, Stephen. "Color Sudan 'Islamic' Green." *The Nation* (July 9, 1990).

Jacobs, Scott H., and Kathy Paar. "An Assessment of the Economic Integration and Impact of Urban Refugees in Port Sudan, Gedaref and Kassala." Khartoum: Office of Refugee Affairs, Embassy of the United States (August 1983).

Kebede, Yonas, Tekie Fessenhatzion, Rogleh Gabriel, Abdulqawi A. Yusuf, Mohamed Jibrell, Amanuel Negasa, Markos Teklu, editors. "Eritrea: War and Drought." *Horn of Africa: An Independent Journal.* Summit, NJ: Horn of Africa Journal, Vol. 4, No. 1 (1981), 20-28.

―――. "Sudan: The Business of Relief." *Horn of Africa: An Independent Journal.* Summit, NJ: Horn of Africa Journal, Vol. 4, No. 1 (1981), 68-77.

Lesch, Ann Mosely. "A View From Khartoum." *Foreign Affairs,* Vol. 65, No. 4 (Spring 1987) 807-826.

Lewis, Herbert. "Beginning Again." *Africa Report* (September-October 1991), 59-62.

Mann, Jonathan. "No Sovereignty for Suffering." *The New York Times* (May 12, 1991).

Mazrui, Ali A. "African Islam and Competitive Religion: Between Revivalism and Expansion." *Third World Quarterly,* Vol. 10, No. 2 (April 1988) 499-518.

Meldrum, Andrew. "Mengistu's Golden Parachute." *Africa Report* (July-August 1991), 42-44.

Morrison, Stephen, and Jeffery Clark. "Ethiopia, Eritrea and Democracy: Significant Opportunities Amidst A Fragile Transition." A Report to the National Endowment for Democracy (October 1991).

Onyango, Joe Oloka. "Plugging the Gaps: Refugees, OAU Policy and the Practices of Member States in Africa." U.S. Committee for Refugees Issue Brief, Washington, DC: American Council for Nationalities Service (October 1986).

Perlez, Jane. "A Fundamentalist Finds a Fulcrum in Sudan." *The New York Times International* (January 29, 1992).

―――. "A New Chance for a Fractured Land." *The New York Times Magazine* (September 22, 1991), 49ff.

―――. "Is Food Going to Orphans Or Future Sudan Rebels?" *The New York Times* (August 13, 1991).

―――. "Peace Is Bursting Out; Will the Crops Do As Well?" *The New York Times International* (July 16, 1991), A4.

―――. "Sudan Forces Refugees Back to Barren Lands." *The New York Times* (July 13, 1990), A2.

―――. "Sudanese Troops Push Into South." *The New York Times* (March 18, 1992).

Peters, Alain. "The Relationship Between Local NGOs and Multilateral Agencies." Presented to the Conference on the Role of Indigenous NGOs in African Recovery and Development. Khartoum (January 10-15, 1988).

Peterson, Scott. "Khartoum Squatters Forcibly Displaced." *The Christian Science Monitor* (March 31, 1992), 4.

―――. "Sudan's Islamic Regime Cultivates Ties With Iran" and "Bashir Forges Harsh 'New Democracy'." *The Christian Science Monitor* (March 31, 1992), 5.

————. "Sudanese Rebel Faction Wages War on Two Fronts" and "Dry Season Offers Refugees Chance to Return Home." *The Christian Science Monitor* (February 7, 1992), 7.

Press, Robert M. "30 Million Africans Need Food, UN Says." *The Christian Science Monitor* (October 15, 1991), 5.

————. "Displaced by War, Drought, Refugees Spill Into Kenya." *Christian Science Monitor* (April 7, 1992), 1-2.

————. "Plight of Millions of Migrants Begins to Stir Global Response." *The Christian Science Monitor* (April 29, 1990), 10-11.

————. "Shadowy Ruling Council Guides Sudan to Fundamentalist Goals." *The Christian Science Monitor* (November 20, 1990), 1.

————. "Sudanese Rebel Claims Children Used in Combat." *The Christian Science Monitor* (October 22, 1991).

"Refugees in Sudan's Urban Centers." Office of Refugee Affairs, Embassy of the United States. Khartoum (April 1984).

Ruiz, Hiram A. "Beyond the Headlines: Refugees in the Horn of Africa." U.S. Committee for Refugees Issue Brief, Washington, DC: American Council for Nationalities Service (January 1988).

————. "Detained in Exile: Ethiopians in Somalia's Shelembod Camp." U.S. Committee for Refugees Issue Brief, Washington, DC: American Council for Nationalities Service (October 1987).

Shields, Todd. "A Tragedy In the Making." *Africa Report* (March-April 1991), 54-57.

Simon, Arthur. "Move Past 'Donor Fatigue' on Africa Famine." *The Christian Science Monitor* (April 7, 1992), 1.

Suau, Anthony. "Region in Rebellion: Eritrea." *National Geographic,* Washington, DC: National Geographic Society, Vol. 168, No. 3 (September 1985), 384-405.

"The Eritrean Refugee Problems: Issues and Challenges." The Commission for Eritrean Refugee Affairs. London (April 24, 1989).

Vallely, Paul. "A Chance for Ethiopia." *The Tablet* (June 15, 1991), 730-731.

van Praag, Nicholas. "Sudan Emergency—A Personal Account." *U.S. Committee for Refugees: World Refugee Survey 1985 in Review.* Washington, DC: American Council for Nationalities Service (1986), 21-25.

Winter, Roger P. "Ending Exile: Promoting Successful Reintegration of African Refugees and Displaced Peoples." U.S. Committee for Refugees Issue Brief, Washington, DC: American Council for Nationalities Service (November 30, 1990).

————. "War and Famine in Sudan." Testimony Before a Hearing of the U.S. House of Representatives Committee on Foreign Affairs, Subcommittee on Africa. U.S. Committee for Refugees, Washington, DC: American Council for Nationalities Service (October 25, 1990).

————. "War and Famine, Peace and Relief in the Horn of Africa." Statement before the Subcommittee on Africa, Committee on Foreign Affairs. U.S. Committee for Refugees, Washington, DC: American Council for Nationalities Service (May 30, 1991).

————, and John Pendergast. "An Embargo For the People of Sudan." *The Washington Post* (October 31, 1990).

————. "Refugee Protection in Africa: Current Trends." U.S. Committee for Refugees Issue Brief, Washington, DC: American Council for Nationalities Service (September 19, 1984).

Wodajo, Kifle. "The Eritrean Conflict: Beyond Partisanship." Transcript of a Talk At a Symposium Organized by Eritreans For Peace and Democracy. Alexandria, VA (March 12, 1990).

INDEX

Acheson, U.S. Secretary of State Dean, 225

Afewerki, Isaias: compassion fatigue and, 291; Eritrean destruction, rehabilitation and, 285; as head of state, 281-82; refugees return, 289

Affected Thai Village program, 85

Afghan Interim Government (AIG): conflict within, 197; evolution of, 156; leaders of, 202; Peshawar, as base of, 195; replacement of, 196; *shura* in Islambad, 194

Afghan refugees: Catholic Relief Services and, 172; children, 213-14; civil war and, 193-202; employment for men, 179; Islamic faith among, 155; Mohammad Kheil camps, 176, 179; population statistics, 148, 203; Quetta, 172-73; radicalized religion among, 155; rations and, 176; refugee family in flight, account of, 140-45; return of, 202. *See also* Afghan women

Afghan women: anemia in, 185; basic health unit, importance to, 183-84; confinement and culture and, 152-58; *dai*, role and training of, 180-83; diet of, 184-85; education of, 162-64, 169, 207-8; Elizabeth, employment projects, 174-79; equality for, 139; family and, 209; illiteracy of, 183; International Rescue Committee and, 168; Islam tenets and, 158-61, 181; invaders' treatment of, 167; *Koran*, equality of women in, 208; lady health workers (LHW), treatment by, 185; literacy in, 128, 139, 161, 169; Lycee Malalai, 171-72; mine-awareness training, 207-08; Nashrin, account of life of, 209-11; Nuria, account of life of, 172-89, 187; postwar, 207-11; pregnancy, statistics of, 180-81; secondary school for, establishment of, 165-66; self-sufficiency of, 209; sewing and quilting projects, 173-79; social reforms and, 133, 159-60; symbolism of, 155-56; widowhood, 161-62, 209. *See also Purdah*; Refugee women

Afghan Women's Center: creation of, 154, 158; Islam tenets and, 158-61; Latifa and Sohaila, creators/directors of, 154, 158-65, 187

Afghanistan: Baghdad (CENTO) Pact and, 133; bazaars, described, 142-43; *buz kashi*, 129; children, 211-16; civil war in, 193-202; death and destruction in, statistics of, 193; Durand Line of 1893, 131-32; Durrani Pushtuns in, 131, 136; ethnic groups, population statistics, 200; family in flight from, account of, 140-45; free elections in, 199; Gardez, 197; Geneva Accord, 192-93; geography of, 130; Great Britain, relationship with, 131; Great Saur Revolution, 135-36; health care in, 186; Herat, destruction in, 202; historical background, 130-32; Islamic religion in, 129, 155; Jalalabad, 195, 197; *jihad*, defined, 129; Khan, Mohammad Daoud, 132-36; King Zahir Shah, 132-36; land mines, 141, 145, 206; Mazar-i-Sharif, 201; military support for, 156; modernization of, attempts at, 131; Mohammadzai clan, 137; *mujahideen*, 8, 141, 192-96, 198-202; national unity, problem of, 201; Pakistan and, 132-33, 141; peace, political deterrents to, 191-202; *Pushtunwali*, 155; reconstruction needs, 202-7; refugee family, account of, 140-45; refugee women, *see* Refugee women; repatriation plan, 110; as a republic, 135; Saur Revolution, 136-40; Saleng Pass, 129;